Andrew Grossman
Editor

Queer Asian Cinema:
Shadows in the Shade

Queer Asian Cinema: Shadows in the Shade has been co-published simultaneously as *Journal of Homosexuality*, Volume 39, Numbers 3/4 2000.

Pre-publication
REVIEWS,
COMMENTARIES,
EVALUATIONS . . .

"**W**estern interest in Asian queer cinema, both native and diasporic, is at an all-time high, but there's been little in the way of really useful writing in English on the subject outside zines and film festival catalogs. Andrew Grossman's superb anthology *Queer Asian Cinema: Shadows in the Shade*, goes a long way toward remedying the situation. This strong collection covers a happily wide range of styles from hard academic analysis to straightforward history, and so should appeal to both students and educated fans. Among the standouts are Jonathan Hall's brilliant analysis of Japan's "gay boom cinema," Timothy Liu's fascinating study of the first official Taiwanese gay film, and See-Kam Tan's appealing discussion of the cross-gender performances of legendary Hong Kong actress Yam Kim-Fei. While the book is heavily weighted toward Japan and Hong Kong, there are also welcome forays into more obscure realms, including the fragmented Korean queer cinema and the mysterious queer presence in Bollywood."

Gary Morris, Editor/Publisher
Bright Lights Film Journal

Queer Asian Cinema: Shadows in the Shade

Queer Asian Cinema: Shadows in the Shade has been co-published simultaneously as *Journal of Homosexuality,* Volume 39, Numbers 3/4 2000.

The *Journal of Homosexuality* Monographic "Separates"

Below is a list of "separates," which in serials librarianship means a special issue simultaneously published as a special journal issue or double-issue *and* as a "separate" hardbound monograph. (This is a format which we also call a "DocuSerial.")

"Separates" are published because specialized libraries or professionals may wish to purchase a specific thematic issue by itself in a format which can be separately cataloged and shelved, as opposed to purchasing the journal on an on-going basis. Faculty members may also more easily consider a "separate" for classroom adoption.

"Separates" are carefully classified separately with the major book jobbers so that the journal tie-in can be noted on new book order slips to avoid duplicate purchasing.

You may wish to visit Haworth's website at . . .

http://www.HaworthPress.com

. . . to search our online catalog for complete tables of contents of these separates and related publications.

You may also call 1-800-HAWORTH (outside US/Canada: 607-722-5857), or Fax 1-800-895-0582 (outside US/Canada: 607-771-0012), or e-mail at:

getinfo@haworthpressinc.com

Queer Asian Cinema: Shadows in the Shade, edited by Andrew Grossman, MA (Vol. 39, 3/4, 2000). *"The range of films covered is impressive: it includes Japanese, Hong Kong, Taiwanese, Chinese, Indian, Korean, and Filipino cinema. Of value to students in film studies, Asian studies, and queer studies . . . enables us to appreciate the diversity as well as the commonality of queer Asian cinema."* (Laurence Wai-Teng Leong, PhD, Senior Lecturer, Sociology Department, National University of Singapore)

Gay Community Survival in the New Millennium, edited by Michael R. Botnick, PhD (cand.) (Vol. 38, No. 4, 2000). *Examines the notion of community from several different perspectives focusing on the imagined, the structural, and the emotive. You will explore a theoretical overview and you will peek into the moral discourses that frame "gay community," the rift between HIV-positive and HIV-negative gay men, and how Israeli gays seek their place in the public sphere.*

The Ideal Gay Man: The Story of Der Kreis, by Hubert Kennedy, PhD (Vol. 38, No. 1/2, 1999). *"Very Profound . . . . Excellent insight into the problems of the early fight for homosexual emancipation in Europe and in the USA. . . . The ideal gay man (high-mindedness, purity, cleanness), as he was imagined by the editor of 'Der Kreis,' is delineated by the fascinating quotations out of the published erotic stories."* (Wolfgang Breidert, PhD, Academic Director, Institute of Philosophy, University Karlsruhe, Germany)

Multicultural Queer: Australian Narratives, edited by Peter A. Jackson, PhD and Gerard Sullivan, PhD (Vol. 36, No. 3/4, 1999). *Shares the way that people from ethnic minorities in Australia (those who are not of Anglo-Celtic background) view homosexuality, their experiences as homosexual men and women, and their feelings about the lesbian and gay community.*

Scandinavian Homosexualities: Essays on Gay and Lesbian Studies, edited by Jan Löfström, PhD (Vol. 35, No. 3/4, 1998). *"Everybody interested in the formation of lesbian and gay identities and their interaction with the sociopolitical can find something to suit their taste in this volume."* (Judith Schuyf, PhD, Assistant Professor of Lesbian and Gay Studies, Center for Gay and Lesbian Studies, Utrecht University, The Netherlands)

Gay and Lesbian Literature Since World War II: History and Memory, edited by Sonya L. Jones, PhD (Vol. 34, No. 3/4, 1998). *"The authors of these essays manage to gracefully incorporate the latest insights of feminist, postmodernist, and queer theory into solidly grounded readings . . . challenging and moving, informed by the passion that prompts both readers and critics into deeper inquiry."* (Diane Griffin Growder, PhD, Professor of French and Women's Studies, Cornell College, Mt. Vernon, Iowa)

Reclaiming the Sacred: The Bible in Gay and Lesbian Culture, edited by Raymond-Jean Frontain, PhD (Vol. 33, No. 3/4, 1997). *"Finely wrought, sharply focused, daring, and always dignified . . . In chapter after chapter, the Bible is shown to be a more sympathetic and humane book in its attitudes toward homosexuality than usually thought and a challenge equally to the straight and gay moral imagination." (Joseph Wittreich, PhD, Distinguished Professor of English, The Graduate School, The City University of New York)*

Activism and Marginalization in the AIDS Crisis, edited by Michael A. Hallett, PhD (Vol. 32, No. 3/4, 1997). *Shows readers how the advent of HIV-disease has brought into question the utility of certain forms of "activism" as they relate to understanding and fighting the social impacts of disease.*

Gays, Lesbians, and Consumer Behavior: Theory, Practice, and Research Issues in Marketing, edited by Daniel L. Wardlow, PhD (Vol. 31, No. 1/2, 1996). *"For those scholars, market researchers, and marketing managers who are considering marketing to the gay and lesbian community, this book should be on required reading list." (Mississippi Voice)*

Gay Men and the Sexual History of the Political Left, edited by Gert Hekma, PhD, Harry Oosterhuis, PhD, and James Steakley, PhD (Vol. 29, No. 2/3/4, 1995). *"Contributors delve into the contours of a long-forgotten history, bringing to light new historical data and fresh insight . . . An excellent account of the tense historical relationship between the political left and gay liberation." (People's Voice)*

Sex, Cells, and Same-Sex Desire: The Biology of Sexual Preference, edited by John P. De Cecco, PhD, and David Allen Parker, MA (Vol. 28, No. 1/2/3/4, 1995). *"A stellar compilation of chapters examining the most important evidence underlying theories on the biological basis of human sexual orientation." (MGW)*

Gay Ethics: Controversies in Outing, Civil Rights, and Sexual Science, edited by Timothy F. Murphy, PhD (Vol. 27, No. 3/4, 1994). *"The contributors bring the traditional tools of ethics and political philosophy to bear in a clear and forceful way on issues surrounding the rights of homosexuals." (David L. Hull, Dressler Professor in the Humanities, Department of Philosophy, Northwestern University)*

Gay and Lesbian Studies in Art History, edited by Whitney Davis, PhD (Vol. 27, No. 1/2, 1994). *"Informed, challenging . . . never dull. . . . Contributors take risks and, within the restrictions of scholarly publishing, find new ways to use materials already available or examine topics never previously explored." (Lambda Book Report)*

Critical Essays: Gay and Lesbian Writers of Color, edited by Emmanuel S. Nelson, PhD (Vol. 26, No. 2/3, 1993). *"A much-needed book, sparkling with stirring perceptions and resonating with depth . . . The anthology not only breaks new ground, it also attempts to heal wounds inflicted by our oppressed pasts." (Lambda)*

Gay Studies from the French Cultures: Voices from France, Belgium, Brazil, Canada, and The Netherlands, edited by Rommel Mendès-Leite, PhD, and Pierre-Olivier de Busscher, PhD (Vol. 25, No. 1/2/3, 1993). *"The first book that allows an English-speaking world to have a comprehensive look at the principal trends in gay studies in France and French-speaking countries." (André Bèjin, PhD, Directeur, de Recherche au Centre National de la Recherche Scientifique (CNRS), Paris)*

If You Seduce a Straight Person, Can You Make Them Gay? Issues in Biological Essentialism versus Social Constructionism in Gay and Lesbian Identities, edited by John P. De Cecco, PhD and John P. Elia, PhD (cand.) (Vol. 24, No. 3/4, 1993). *"You'll find this alternative view of the age old question to be one that will become the subject of many conversations to come. Thought-provoking to say the least!" (Prime Timers)*

Gay and Lesbian Studies: The Emergence of a Discipline, edited by Henry L. Minton, PhD (Vol. 24, No. 1/2, 1993). *"The volume's essays provide insight into the field's remarkable accomplishments and future goals." (Lambda Book Report)*

Homosexuality in Renaissance and Enlightenment England: Literary Representations in Historical Context, edited by Claude J. Summers, PhD (Vol. 23, No. 1/2, 1992). *"It is remarkable among studies in this field in its depth of scholarship and variety of approaches and is accessible." (Chronique)*

Coming Out of the Classroom Closet: Gay and Lesbian Students, Teachers, and Curricula, edited by Karen M. Harbeck, PhD, JD, Recipient of Lesbian and Gay Educators Award by the American Educational Research Association's Lesbian and Gay Studies Special Interest Group (AREA) (Vol. 22, No. 3/4, 1992). *"Presents recent research about gay and lesbian students and teachers and the school system in which they function." (Contemporary Psychology)*

Homosexuality and Male Bonding in Pre-Nazi Germany: The Youth Movement, the Gay Movement, and Male Bonding Before Hitler's Rise: Original Transcripts from* Der Eigene, *the First Gay Journal in the World, edited by Harry Oosterhuis, PhD, and Hubert Kennedy, PhD (Vol. 22, No. 1/2, 1992). *"Provide[s] insight into the early gay movement, particularly in its relation to the various political currents in pre-World War II Germany." (Lambda Book Report)*

Gay People, Sex, and the Media, edited by Michelle A. Wolf, PhD, and Alfred P. Kielwasser, MA (Vol. 21, No. 1/2, 1991). *"Altogether, the kind of research anthology which is useful to many disciplines in gay studies. Good stuff!" (Communique)*

Gay Midlife and Maturity: Crises, Opportunities, and Fulfillment, edited by John Alan Lee, PhD (Vol. 20, No. 3/4, 1991). *"The insight into gay aging is amazing, accurate, and much-needed. . . . A real contribution to the older gay community." (Prime Timers)*

Male Intergenerational Intimacy: Historical, Socio-Psychological, and Legal Perspectives, edited by Theo G. M. Sandfort, PhD, Edward Brongersma, JD, and A. X. van Naerssen, PhD (Vol. 20, No. 1/2, 1991). *"The most important book on the subject since Tom O'Carroll's 1980 Paedophilia: The Radical Case." (The North America Man/Boy Love Association Bulletin, May 1991)*

Love Letters Between a Certain Late Nobleman and the Famous Mr. Wilson, edited by Michael S. Kimmel, PhD (Vol. 19, No. 2, 1990). *"An intriguing book about homosexuality in 18th Century England. Many details of the period, such as meeting places, coded language, and 'camping' are all covered in the book. If you're a history buff, you'll enjoy this one." (Prime Timers)*

Homosexuality and Religion, edited by Richard Hasbany, PhD (Vol. 18, No. 3/4, 1990). *"A welcome resource that provides historical and contemporary views on many issues involving religious life and homosexuality." (Journal of Sex education and Therapy)*

Homosexuality and the Family, edited by Frederick W. Bozett, PhD (Vol. 18, No. 1/2, 1989). *"Enlightening and answers a host of questions about the effects of homosexuality upon family members and the family as a unit." (Ambush Magazine)*

Gay and Lesbian Youth, edited by Gilbert Herdt, PhD (Vol. 17, No. 1/2/3/4, 1989). *"Provides a much-needed compilation of research dealing with homosexuality and adolescents." (GLTF Newsletter)*

Lesbians Over 60 Speak for Themselves, edited by Monika Kehoe, PhD (Vol. 16, No. 3/4, 1989). *"A pioneering book examining the social, economical, physical, sexual, and emotional lives of aging lesbians." (Feminist Bookstore News)*

The Pursuit of Sodomy: Male Homosexuality in Renaissance and Enlightenment Europe, edited by Kent Gerard, PhD and Gert Hekma, PhD (Vol. 16, No. 1/2, 1989). *"Presenting a wealth of information in a compact form, this book should be welcomed by anyone with an interest in this period in European history or in the precursors to modern concepts of homosexuality." (The Canadian Journal of Human Sexuality)*

Monographs "Separates" list continued at the back

Queer Asian Cinema:
Shadows in the Shade

Queer Asian Cinema: Shadows in the Shade has been co-published simultaneously as *Journal of Homosexuality,* Volume 39, Numbers 3/4 2000.

Andrew Grossman
Editor

Harrington Park Press
An Imprint of
The Haworth Press, Inc.
New York • London • Oxford

Published by

Harrington Park Press, 10 Alice Street, Binghamton, NY 13904-1580 USA

Harrington Park Press is an imprint of The Haworth Press, Inc., 10 Alice Street, Binghamton, NY 13904-1580 USA.

Queer Asian Cinema: Shadows in the Shade has been co-published simultaneously as *Journal of Homosexuality,* Volume 39, Numbers 3/4 2000.

The development, preparation, and publication of this work has been undertaken with great care. However, the publisher, employees, editors, and agents of The Haworth Press and all imprints of The Haworth Press, Inc., including The Haworth Medical Press® and Pharmaceutical Products Press®, are not responsible for any errors contained herein or for consequences that may ensue from use of materials or information contained in this work. Opinions expressed by the author(s) are not necessarily those of The Haworth Press, Inc.

The Haworth Press, Inc., 10 Alice Street, Binghamton, NY 13904-1580, USA

Cover design by Monica Seifert

Cover photo by Shimomura Kazuyoshi

Library of Congress Cataloging-in-Publication Data

Queer Asian cinema : shadows in the shade / Andrew Grossman, editor.
    p. cm.
    "Co-published simultaneously as Journal of homosexuality, volume 39, numbers 3/4, 2000."
    Includes bibliographical references and index.
    ISBN 1-56023-139-4 (alk. paper)–ISBN 1-56023-140-8 (alk. paper)
    1. Homosexuality in motion pictures. 2. Motion pictures–Asia. I. Grossman, Andrew.
PN1995.9.H55 Q39 2000
791.43'653–dc21
                                                                                        00-063369

Indexing, Abstracting & Website/Internet Coverage

This section provides you with a list of major indexing & abstracting services. That is to say, each service began covering this periodical during the year noted in the right column. Most Websites which are listed below have indicated that they will either post, disseminate, compile, archive, cite or alert their own Website users with research-based content from this work. (This list is as current as the copyright date of this publication.)

Abstracting, Website/Indexing Coverage .... Year When Coverage Began

- *Abstracts in Anthropology* **1982**
- *Abstracts of Research in Pastoral Care & Counseling* **1982**
- *Academic Abstracts/CD-ROM* **1993**
- *Academic Search: database of 2,000 selected academic serials, updated monthly* **1995**
- *Alternative Press Index <www.nisc.com>* **1996**
- *Applied Social Sciences Index & Abstracts (ASSIA) (Online: ASSI via Data-Star) (CD-Rom: ASSIA Plus)* ... **1987**
- *BUBL Information Service, an Internet-based Information Service for the UK higher education community* **1995**
- *Cambridge Scientific Abstracts (Health & Safety Sciences Abstracts/Risk Abstracts) <www.csa.com>* **1993**
- *CNPIEC Reference Guide: Chinese National Directory of Foreign Periodicals* **1995**
- *Contemporary Women's Issues* **1995**
- *Criminal Justice Abstracts* **1982**

(continued)

(continued)

- *PASCAL, c/o Institute de L'Information Scientifique et Technique. Cross-disciplinary electronic database covering the fields of science, technology & medicine. Also available on CD-ROM, and can generate customized retrospective searches. For more information: INIST, Customer Desk, 2, allee du Parc de Brabois, F-54514 Vandoeuvre Cedex, France <www.inist.fr>* 1986

- *Periodical Abstracts, Research I (general and basic reference indexing and abstracting data-base from University Micro-films International (UMI))* 1993

- *Periodical Abstracts, Research II (broad coverage indexing and abstracting data-base from University Microfilms International (UMI)* 1993

- *PlanetOut "Internet site for key Gay/Lesbian Information <www.planetout.com>* 1999

- *Psychology Today* 1999

- *Religion Index One: Periodicals, the Index to Book Reviews in Religion, Religion Indexes: Ten Year Subset on CD/ROM <www.atla.com>* 1986

- *RESEARCH ALERT/ISI Alerting Services <www.isinet.com>* 1985

- *Sage Family Studies Abstracts (SFSA)* 1986

- *Social Sciences Citation Index <www.isinet.com>* 1985

- *Social Scisearch <www.isinet.com>* 1985

- *Social Services Abstracts <www.csa.com>* 1982

- *Social Sciences Index (from Volume 1 & continuing)* 1991

- *Social Science Source: coverage of 400 journals in the social sciences area; updated monthly* 1995

- *Social Sciences Index (from Volume 1 & continuing)* 1991

- *Social Work Abstracts* 1994

- *Sociological Abstracts (SA) <www.csa.com>* 1982

- *Studies on Women Abstracts* 1987

- *Violence and Abuse Abstracts: A Review of Current Literature on Interpersonal Violence (VAA)* 1995

Special Bibliographic Notes related to special journal issues
(separates) and indexing/abstracting:

- indexing/abstracting services in this list will also cover material in any "separate" that is co-published simultaneously with Haworth's special thematic journal issue or DocuSerial. Indexing/abstracting usually covers material at the article/chapter level.
- monographic co-editions are intended for either non-subscribers or libraries which intend to purchase a second copy for their circulating collections.
- monographic co-editions are reported to all jobbers/wholesalers/approval plans. The source journal is listed as the "series" to assist the prevention of duplicate purchasing in the same manner utilized for books-in-series.
- to facilitate user/access services all indexing/abstracting services are encouraged to utilize the co-indexing entry note indicated at the bottom of the first page of each article/chapter/contribution.
- this is intended to assist a library user of any reference tool (whether print, electronic, online, or CD-ROM) to locate the monographic version if the library has purchased this version but not a subscription to the source journal.
- individual articles/chapters in any Haworth publication are also available through the Haworth Document Delivery Service (HDDS).

Queer Asian Cinema: Shadows in the Shade

CONTENTS

ABOUT THE EDITOR

Andrew Grossman, MA, studied film and philosophy at Sarah Law-rence College, followed by a Master's Degree in English and Creative Writing from Rutgers University. His obsession with cinema began at a young age, a passion that presently focuses on an interest in Hong Kong and other East Asian cinemas. He is currently working on writing proj-ects that attempt to cross and synthesize the genres of avant-garde the-ater, the screenplay, and cultural criticism. His writing has appeared in *American Book Review.*

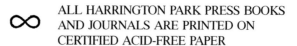

Preface

This anthology, which began as a single essay written in 1998 for my mentor Louie Crew, without whose intervention this volume would not have been possible, offered me a fortuitous convergence of my lifelong passions for both writing and film. Ever since I was about twelve, when my first viewing of Werner Herzog's *Aguirre, Wrath of God* forced my jaw to drop ajar in a state of awe, I knew there was nothing I would rather do than write about films. This volume coincidentally rides the cusp of a recent and unprecedented wave of popular books in the West on Hong Kong cinema, and particularly the rise and fall of its new-wave movement. It is a recognition of a continentally Asian film culture that might have been more groundbreaking, and encouraging, if it had not come ten years too late, and if top Hong Kong talent were not now quickly, and indeed voluntarily, being all-too-efficiently homogenized into Hollywood normativity. Never before has there been such a focused interest in Asian films in the English language, even if the focus of that interest is indeed narrower than we might like, and even if it is generally uninterested, unwilling, or perhaps even still embarrassed to speak of Asian "queerness." Even now, despite the increased visibility of Asian action films (which have in fact always been popular in the West since their importation in the early 1970s), a minuscule fraction of Asian–and especially South Asian–films are granted a journey to Western shores. With the international press surrounding Deepa Mehta's Indian-Canadian *Fire* (1996) or Hong Kong director Wong Kar-wai's *Happy Together* (1997), we might at first be heartened that a meeting and synthesis of alternative cinemas and queer cinemas is happily turning this tide. But in light of both directors subsequently distancing themselves from the idea that their films are about homosexuality *per se*, that "turning" is perhaps more tenuous than the more politically active among us would like to conclude. Indeed, in Asian countries as in all others, a great many of the most commercial/visible queer films are made by heterosexual directors whose intentions are often at odds with their queer audiences.

[Haworth co-indexing entry note]: "Preface." Grossman, Andrew. Co-published simultaneously in *Journal of Homosexuality* (The Haworth Press, Inc.) Vol. 39, No. 3/4, 2000, pp. xxi-xxvi; and: *Queer Asian Cinema: Shadows in the Shade* (ed: Andrew Grossman) Harrington Park Press, an imprint of The Haworth Press, Inc., 2000, pp. xv-xx. Single or multiple copies of this article are available for a fee from The Haworth Document Delivery Service [1-800-342-9678, 9:00 a.m. - 5:00 p.m. (EST). E-mail address: getinfo@haworthpressinc.com].

xv

If there is a single thematic thread or point of departure that is commonly shared amongst the diverse offerings here, it is the recognition of the pulling and pushing between the mutually inclusive and mutually informing cultures of the East and West. Sexual minorities are universal, but their interpretations, and more so their politicizations, are not. So if this recognition of "pulling and pushing" is not always explicit, it is implicit, if only by dint of the common English language we use here, that language in which queer politics and theory have been most encoded and disseminated worldwide. Thus, the title *Queer Asian Cinema: Shadows in the Shade* has a double significance. The image it conjures is of a Eurocentric or Western queer-theory umbrella intervening between the alternately sexual Asian films themselves and their reception, distribution, and interpretation. Not necessarily originating from Western concepts of sexual identity as a political phenomenon, these films' meanings should also not be freighted with chimerical notions of a truth found in indigenousness. Indeed, the "shadows," the films themselves, would not be objects of "local" truth even without such an umbrella: They are not only representations projected in the Platonic sense, but also the products of their own locally artistic, social, economic, and (of course) sexual relativisms. So we must navigate through two systems of compounded imagery and interpretation–the one internal to the films themselves, and the external, imported shade under which they, in the darkness, are often sightlessly scrutinized.

The artistic qualities of many queer films–or at least the mainstream ones, Asian or otherwise–may coexist with their political aspirations in a state of tension greater than that negotiated by heteronormative films–many of which, remember, have been ironically written, directed, and otherwise constructed by gays and lesbians since the very beginning. Likewise, a queer film may have political ambitions that outstrip its real capabilities, and because we are no longer cinematic beggars scrounging for precious morsels of queer representation, we needn't applaud the naively liberal intentions of bad films, or overlook homophobias that may be the unintentional yield of artists well-intentioned but ill-advised. Although much of the material here tends toward scholarly interests, also included are pieces by poets, activists, and filmmakers, in a modest attempt to broach the myriad issues and audiences our necessarily broad subject will attract. A diversity of styles, aesthetic and political concerns, and even page lengths will, I hope, reflect the heterogeneity and polymorphous fascination that movies, in their universality, continue to exude.

With essays on Japan, the "three Chinas," India, Korea, and the Philippines, the organization of the essays is perhaps as arbitrary as the category "Asian film" itself. My introduction focuses on two gay male Japanese films whose sadomasochism removes them from "progressive" or Westernized homosexual discourses. They belong instead to the Japanese genre of the "pink film," a veritable industry of usually heterosexist erotica sometimes tinged with political undertones. By choosing these two films to explicate possible differences between Eastern and Western criticism, the introduction stands outside the bulk of this volume's body, which tends to focus on either semiotic sociology or the "new" homosexuality in Asian cinemas, part of a trend towards sexual democracy (or pseudo-democracy). Pink films, rarely democratic and more abstractly symbolic than socially semiotic in terms of their content, are more often concerned with the politics of sadomasochism, if political at all. Yet it is through this more radical lens that we can first posit a problematized homosexuality that is apart from easily defined social movements, one which represents an alternative approach to non-Western filmic sexuality. My introductory essay's "East versus West" transnational binary, while obviously limited and admittedly oversimplified, may nevertheless be a concern whose form, if not particular content, can be distributed to the other essays collected here, essays whose own transnational concerns may intersect with the introduction's on political, theoretical, and/or post-colonial axes.

The following four essays continue the focus on Japan, the first two of which investigate Japan's "gay boom" in the early 1990s—a period of new openness regarding the presentation of homosexuality in Japan's media. In his ambitious essay, Jonathan Hall is reluctant to see the proliferation of the Japanese gay films that followed the popular *Okoge* (1992) to be part of a politically progressive or liberal trend. Rather, he argues that many of Japan's gay boom films are staked on systems of both sexism and misogyny which not only marginalize women but wind up narrowly defining gay men as well. Dr. Stephen Miller discusses one of the gay boom's most remarkable and visible achievements, the television miniseries *Dôsôkai* (1993), which, though conforming to the conventions of a serial melodrama, goes far beyond anything we have witnessed on North American television. Yet *Dôsôkai*'s success, both popular and critical, has significantly yet to be duplicated. Julian Stringer's *Two Japanese Variants of the Absolute Transvestite Film* steps back from Japan's "out" trend of the 1990s to look back at the older tradition of transvestism, long a staple of Japan's classical theater. Whereas most transvestite plots in the West unmask gender and restore heterosexuality at their climaxes, the transvestisms of the beguiling *Black Lizard* (1968) and *Summer Vacation 1999* (1988) occur before the films' diegeses begin. *Summer Vacation 1999*'s gay male teenager characters are all played by disguised female actresses, creating a content that is both gay *and* lesbian—and also strictly neither—in the same instance. This "permanent" cross-dressing, which does not exist for the purpose of its own unmasking, then becomes a question of aesthetic performance, and is not a diegetic contrivance brought about by mere plots. Thus, we might be totally unaware that the actor we are watching in these films is cross-dressed if we weren't informed beforehand, a ruse that calls into question our (self-) consciousness of gender performance conventions and, more importantly, the differences constructed among appearance, polymorphous desire, and sexual object choice. The last essay on Japanese film, by Udo Helms, documents the atmosphere of film censorship in which these films were made, and in which their creators have labored. With some of the most puzzling film censorship rules in the world, including its legendary ban on the pubis, Japanese censorship has constructed perverse problems which only Japanese filmmakers' equally perverse–and often necessarily creative–solutions can resolve.

We then move on to China, Hong Kong, and Taiwan. Hong Kong, enjoying the decriminalization of homosexuality under British law in the early 1990s, had become possibly the number one film industry in Asia for the production of gay and lesbian films, and, as gay Hong Kong director Stanley Kwan has argued, possibly number one in the world. Hong Kong, like Japan, also experienced a "gay boom" in the early 1990s, one that straddled Chinese history and Western gay-liberation politics. In the mid-1990s, seemingly every other film was obliged to have queer characters–at first supporting players but eventually the leads–yet ones frequently awash with lagging stereotypes. In my introductory essay on Hong Kong film of this period, I discuss a wide range of lesbian, gay, bisexual, and transgender films that all seem to have one thing in common: all can be read as allegories for Hong Kong's 1997 handover syndrome. While it had been common for almost everything in HK to be framed in terms of 1997, it is notable that what became HK filmmakers' ultimate metaphor for political freedom was sexual freedom, as represented by homosexuality–an official taboo in China only in the modernized, communistic 20th century. Chris Berry's essay draws on a particular variation of this political dilemma. Choosing some of the most visible gay films from Taiwan (*Vive L'Amour*), Mainland China (*East Palace, West Palace*–the Mainland's first gay commercial feature), and Hong Kong (*Happy Together*), he analyzes the interrelations amongst political freedom, the politics of sexual representation, and the deconstruction of a "Chinese" national identity. These interrelations converge on the image of "the sad young man," whose homosexual alienation and disempowerment are elevated to an existential condition.

Professor See-Kam Tan's essay on Hong Kong's legendary female cross-dressing star Yam Kim-Fei goes back decades before Hong Kong's new-wave films, asserting definitively the queerness of her art, if not her person. Like the Japanese permanent transvestism described by Julian Stringer, Yam Kim-Fei's Cantonese tradition mandates that the audience authentically disbelieves biological gender categories. Although we would see the legacy of this institutionalized transvestism's queerness reborn in the Hong Kong films of the 1990s, it first came to the attention of many Western film-goers via the Peking Opera world that Mainland Chinese director Chen Kaige depicted in his *Farewell My Concubine*, a co-production between the Mainland and Hong Kong. Sean Metzger's detailed, sustained analysis of *Concubine* is a brilliant close-reading that draws upon both Freudian theory and local Chinese perspective. The poet Timothy Liu gives us a lovely, pithy miniature on *The Outcasts*, Taiwan's first gay male feature. Made in 1986, the film is in some respects more sophisticated than many of the later queer films that were to come from Hong Kong, Taiwan's democratic cousin. Our last entry on Chinese film brings us beyond the queer politics of the new-wave movement and its aftermath into the traditionally homosocial *cum* homosexual waters of the gangster (triad) film, a genre both venerable and cutting-edge. Drawing implicitly on themes made popular by Robert Warshow's seminal essay on the "outlaw hero," I present an intersection of three "post-new-wave" gangster films from 1998 that redefine the image of the outlaw, often explicitly, in terms of a homosexuality that entertains both Western and Eastern constructions. With such films as *Cheap Killers* and *Portland Street Blues*, HK's film industry may be the first to populate a mainstream/commercial violent-action film universe with openly queer protagonists. The final essay on East Asian films offers some rare insight into Korea's queer film world, on the surface still a fledgling with 1995's landmark *Broken Branches*. Yet writer Jooran Lee cites Korea's first real homosexual film as *Ascetic: Woman and Woman*, a lesbian film made about 20 years earlier, and one virtually unknown in the West.

The films of India have proved less accessible to Westerners than their East-Asian counterparts. Despite its vast riches, popular Indian film's stylized song sequences, unapologetic populism, and undivergent moralism are seen as insurmountable obstacles in reaching non-Indian audiences unaccustomed to such conventions. Indeed, I can think of only one popular Indian film, the splendid *Kudah Gawah* (English title: *God Is My Witness*, 1992) to receive even a token theatrical release in North America. To introduce the subject, Gayatri Gopinath's *Queering Bollywood* offers a broad overview of how queer representations figure in four different subgenres of popular Indian film. She pays especial attention to the extra-narrative spaces of song-and-dance sequences which, because of their fantasy, may permit greater sexual transgressions than the heteronormative narratives of which they are an appendage. Dr. Raj Rao, India's foremost gay poet, goes on to investigate one of the four genres Gayatri Gopinath has identified: the action-buddy film, codified and popularized by films the legendarily macho actor Amitabh Bachchan made in the 1970s. Written from personal experience and with a disarming wit, Raj Rao includes translations of famous cinematic song sequences that demonstrate a gay subtext in Amitabh Bachchan's films that always threatens to poke through the surface. He tells us, in fact, that this subtext is duly recognized and even acted upon in the homosocial public space of the Indian movie-theater. Ashok Row Kavi, India's most recognized gay activist and historiographer, spins his own variations on the theme of the homoeroticized male hero. He suggests the implicit homoeroticization of the male hero is manifested covertly as a hybrid of his narcissism and the ongoing marginalization of his heroine. With film director Riyad Wadia's *Long Life of a Short Film*, we have what is more or less our only piece of first-person narrative. Yet it is an invaluable document from the director of India's first openly gay film, *BomGay*, a short video-film that, like Oshima's *In the Realm of the Senses*, became notorious in its native land precisely because it could not be seen. Nevertheless, *BomGay*'s media buzz arguably paved the way for Deepa Mehta's lesbian-feminist *Fire*, a film which, ironically, *was* passed by India's censor board. But the distribution of *Fire*, though predictably acclaimed in the West, was met with acts of arson and terrorism in many of the theaters in India which dared to show it. Finally, Rolando Tolentino critically analyzes cross-dressing and cross-gendering in Philippino cinema, using as primary text one of Lino Brocka's pre-*Macho Dancer* films from the 1970s. Locating the sexual discourse of cross-gender representation within images reinforced by the Marcos regime, we see that even seemingly transgressive sexualities can be the inevitably controlled product of political hegemony, a fact played out not only in Asian countries, of course, but everywhere in the world.

Our volume here is indeed perhaps too modest for such an ambitiously "geographical" subject, yet it threatened at numerous times to be anything but over the course of its gestation. For every fulfilled opportunity, I feel there is also a missed one, as the interests and perseverance of so many in this project are not represented in its final product. Thus, I would like to thank Jenni Olson, Ahmed Afzal, Ariel Herrera, Corey Tong, Ian Iqbal Rashid, Guo-Juin Hong, Jo Smith, Kenneth Lee, Lori Hitchcock, Ming Yuen S. Ma, Paul Lee, Rob Schwartz, Quentin Lee, Richard Fung, Nick Deocampo, Michelle Mohabeer, and Yeung King-to, whose work may not be imprinted here but whose assistance and kindness over the past year were invaluable. Perhaps if this volume warrants a sequel, we might have a chance to work together again.

Andrew Grossman
January 2000

"Beautiful Publicity":
An Introduction to Queer Asian Film

Andrew Grossman

SUMMARY. With a few seemingly apolitical exceptions, openly queer cinemas have generally charted two opposing courses–a propagandistic search for bourgeois acceptance or a radical challenge to sexual hegemony. Yet even the most politically challenging of queer films, for example those of Pasolini, are nevertheless distributed and disseminated through the heteronormative and hegemonically capitalist means they philosophically oppose. This essay thus takes as its texts two low-budget gay male Japanese films of the 1980s, which have been made available on international home video, as opposing examples of politico-economic allegories enacted within the self-reflexive contexts of queer cinema and gay male political history. Taken together, the two films present an interlocking example of how Asian queer films both engage and refute "Eastern" and "Western" conceptions of homosexuality and sexual politics in general. *[Article copies available for a fee from The Haworth Document Delivery Service: 1-800-342-9678. E-mail address: <getinfo@haworthpressinc.com> Website: <http://www.HaworthPress.com>]*

Why is there a need for a volume on queer Asian films? Firstly and simply, there is an ever-present need for more writing about Asian cinemas in English in general. Volumes devoted specifically to Asian films in general have been too few and far between, let alone volumes about queer Asian film. Although

Andrew Grossman, MA, studied film and philosophy at Sarah Lawrence College, followed by a Master's Degree in English and Creative Writing from Rutgers University. He is currently working on writing projects that attempt to cross and synthesize the genres of avant-garde theater, the screenplay, and cultural criticism. His writing has appeared in *American Book Review.* (E-mail: morgold@webtv.net)

[Haworth co-indexing entry note]: "'Beautiful Publicity': An Introduction to Queer Asian Film." Grossman, Andrew. Co-published simultaneously in *Journal of Homosexuality* (The Haworth Press, Inc.) Vol. 39, No. 3/4, 2000, pp. 1-29; and: *Queer Asian Cinema: Shadows in the Shade* (ed: Andrew Grossman) Harrington Park Press, an imprint of The Haworth Press, Inc., 2000, pp. 1-29. Single or multiple copies of this article are available for a fee from The Haworth Document Delivery Service [1-800-342-9678, 9:00 a.m. - 5:00 p.m. (EST). E-mail address: getinfo@haworthpressinc.com].

1

in the past five years that trend has slowly been changing, the subject of
Asian film is still largely the domain of only a few. Secondly, the visibility of
queer subjects in recent Asian films in particular has been relatively more
radical and less apologetic than in their mainstream Western counterparts.
The very suddenness of Asian film-making's about-face when it comes to
homosexual positivity has been arguably more startling than elsewhere in the
world. But perhaps most significantly, when it comes to furthering the art of
movies overall, the 1980s and 1990s have been disproportionately the realm
of Asian film-makers. This fact, combined with the fortuity of a new liberality in gay and lesbian representations in film-making during the same decades, has logically resulted in many of the best recent gay and lesbian films
having been produced in Asia.

With the exception of a Westernizing Japan, the cinematic new wave
movements of the 1960s failed to intersect with the still-insular political
economies of South and East Asia. But even then, the United States, Great
Britain, Italy, France, and so forth saw their new-waves peter out in the late
'60s and early '70s, just as the gay liberation movement got underway. Other
leftist new waves, such as those of Brazil and Czechoslovakia, were more
concerned with agit-prop politicizing than homosexuality. Perhaps because
Germany experienced its film renaissance somewhat belatedly, in the late
1960s through the 1970s, were the works of gay directors such as R. W.
Fassbinder, Werner Schroeter, and Rosa von Praunheim able to coincide with
socio-sexual progressiveness. Elsewhere in the West, homosexual films were
most visible from iconoclastic philosopher-film-makers–Pasolini, Warhol,
and later Jarman–whose ideological individualisms were able to withstand
and/or transcend the short-lived politics and economies of a "new wave."
Some other directors, say a Chantal Akerman, made films but for intentionally small and sympathetic audiences. The Japanese new-wave, from the late
1950s through its death in the early 1970s, occasionally did address questions
of "aberrant" sexuality, though mostly as a leftist tactic of political shock.
Thus, the homosexualities of Matsumoto Toshio's *Funeral Procession of
Roses* (1969) or Terayama Shuji's *Throw Away Your Books* (1971) were not
homosexual *per se*, but were intended to symbolize positions of radical
leftism; thus, they may be not so different from, say, the anarchic sadomasochism of Wakamatsu Koji, insofar as all portrayals of unconventional sexuality amounted to outspoken liberalism, be they anti-feudal or anti-bourgeois.

Recent gay and lesbian films from Asia have differed from this model in
that they are more often intended to be popular yet still unapologetically
political films about queerness *per se*. This also makes them different from
recent 1990's American treatments of homosexuality, which are demographi-
cally designed as either hip "independent" films for urban areas or conservative national social propaganda films (such as Demme's *Philadelphia* [1994]

or writer Paul Rudnick's *In and Out* [1997]) which attempt to both homogenize and beatify homosexuality to defuse any potential controversy. Also, while contemporary Asian film-makers such as Stanley Kwan Kam-pang, Tsai Ming-liang, Hashiguchi Ryosuke, and the late Lino Brocka have become identified with gay films, none of them has (or had) developed any gay or lesbian philosophical or artistic credo beyond realist humanism. (Indeed, the films of Kwan's recent tenure as an "out" director/producer, which include two documentaries, have marked a return to realism.) Thus, their collective project differs also from the homosexual film-making of 1960's/1970's Western leftism, whose homosexuality had often engendered a political manifesto or an aesthetic elitism. There are some exceptions, of course, such as the less commercial films of Oki Hiroyuki, but even his aesthetic is often predicated on hyper-realism. So to a certain degree, instead of an iconic planetary figure such as Fassbinder (or Warhol in the U.S.) playing host to a group of disciples (or artistic "satellites"), a generally humanistic homosexual imperative has itself been the planet around which these Asian film-makers revolve. Indeed, this may be because 30 years after Stonewall there is less of a need for individual charismatic figures to spearhead the movement's politics, which have since been mainstreamed; on the other hand, Eurocentric/Stonewall politics can obviously not be the main criterion with which to judge Asian homosexualities. It is also perhaps true that the leftist movements whence sprung the new-waves are now nonexistent, and what has replaced political ideology is mere factionalized, issue-oriented politics, of whose issues homosexuality, like abortion, is one of the most knee-jerk.

We must next qualify and, if you prefer, even discard the oft-maligned term "Asian cinema," whose overly broad and indeed arbitrary boundaries include countries that may indeed have less in common with each other than any one of them with the West. We must deal with the paradoxical notion of a cinematic orientalism that, as the direct result of distribution practices which ensure that only the most "importable" films (i.e., those palatable to Westerners) receive theatrical release, necessitates a *de facto* geographical solidarity (the collective term "Asian films") to combat the prejudices of its own creation. The capitalism of commercial film distribution mandates that products must be sellable and visible–a visibility that at present can only be marshalled by less-than-utopian means. In the marketplace, one cannot sell "a Japanese film," or "an Indian film." It must instead be "an Asian film"–not only to simplify the film's content but to demonstrate there is a large enough market to warrant its international distribution. The function of North America's own history of nationalist isolationism, coupled with its geographic removal from other major film-producing nations, ensures that so-called foreign films remain just that: "foreign."

We could perhaps attempt to group together the shared East Asian histories of China and Japan, for example, but when we try to introduce a Southern country such as India, whose conventionally-inclined and religiously-attended film culture requires no need for export and whose generic "masala" films are rarely shown at international festivals, all-encompassing definitions fall to pieces. For now, "Asian film" is a perhaps despicable and hopefully temporary term of convenience, a monologic evil necessary to unite film cultures that have been ignored, devalued, and/or trivialized in Western readerships by dint of their merely common geography (and its linguized designation). Such a volume on "homosexual Asian films" could ideally also cover films from Israel, Turkey, Thailand, and so forth, and although may be indeed desirable, schedule constraints and other practicalities conspired against this. Indeed, the inclusion of a queer Israeli film, for example, would not merely serve to introduce some interesting films to a new audience but would more blatantly call into question the preconceived constructions of "Asian-ness." Regardless, no book short of a (much-welcome) encyclopedia would be able to address the totality of our subject, and this book cannot nor will not be everything to everyone; if anything, its shortcomings will hopefully inspire others to superior work.

As geographical contingencies can do as much to divide cultures as to unite them, there is no overriding, monothematic ideological program here. The greatest purpose here is also the simplest: to disseminate ideas about films whose common geographical origins *themselves* have delegitimized those films in the eyes of Western criticism. The recently exploded Euro-American interest in sex-and-violence Asian cinemas, largely buttressed by a recognition of the Hong Kong new-wave so belated the industry had already begun to desiccate by the time Western fans took notice, has added fuel to the fire. It is not that sex-and-violence films are not worth taking seriously, but precisely *because they are.* Too often cult audiences and fan magazines, the latter breeding grounds of homophobia, view such spectacles as a faddish Eurocentric thrill, rather than investigating them as being important in themselves, aesthetically or semeiotically–unfortunate, since in North America cult audiences usually beat tardy mainstream critics to the punch. But cult audiences and fan magazines, indeed, can wear their homophobias and heterosexisms on their sleeves, not only as crude evidence of their common-sense populism but to signify the distance between themselves and an academy that is perceived as phony, elitist, and/or politically correct. But this unwillingness or fear, even if unintentional, to take even the most popular Asian imports at anything more than face value only reinforces the image of callous Western imperialism.

To avoid perpetuating this image, care, I hope, has been taken to distinguish between Eurocentric criticism and traditionalist or Eastern interpretations. By now it is fairly (hopefully?) common knowledge that famous premodern writings such as the Chinese *Records of the Cut Sleeve* or Saikaku Ihara's popular *Great Mirror of Male Love* reveal that not only was there a homosexual tradition in Asia entirely counter to the neurotic prejudice of Western Christendom, but that by the sexually primitive standards of the West such works of Asian premodernity could seem "modern," if not exactly "progressive." It should be emphasized, however, that absolute delineations are naive at best, and that even film-makers from the most insular countries– i.e., ones which do not regularly participate in the commodification of inter-national film festivals–do not live in a vacuum. Furthermore, it is equally foolish and narrow-minded to insist upon myopic "traditionalist" criticism of an Asian film, such as Hong Kong director Shu Kei's *A Queer Story*, which may explicitly situate itself within Western gay-liberation politics. Still, there probably should be some self-critical approach between interpret-ing, say, Chen Kaige's *Farewell My Concubine*, a film rooted in traditional culture, and Hashiguchi's *Like Grains of Sand* (1995), whose immaculately and lyrically minimalist directorial style may be "Japanese" but whose teen-age coming-out theme is typically "Western."

To give an example of some of the difficulties in cleanly sorting out Eastern versus Western interpretations, I would like to discuss two Japanese gay male "pink films" (*pinku eiga*), the apparently "Western" *Muscle* and the apparently "Eastern" *Beautiful Mystery*. The pink film, that particularly Japanese genre of usually heterosexual film eroticism which rose to such prominence in the early-to-mid-1960s that it would later almost eclipse main-stream films, has often been one of Japanese film's preferred vehicles in which to envision politico-sexual neurosis. Pink films are low-budget and hence low-risk, a fact which has allowed film-makers (most famously Waka-matsu Koji) to perversely politicize their films to extremes less allowable in mainstream films. *Beautiful Mystery* and *Muscle*, two rare gay examples of the genre, are films sadomasochistically obsessed with the male body, and how the S/M impulses of those bodies unwittingly engage and perpetuate sociopolitical structures–in groups, in the former, and without them, in the latter. Furthermore, they are both films obsessed with famous homosexual ghosts–of Mishima Yukio in *Mystery* and of Pier Paolo Pasolini in *Muscle*. As these ghostly specters cast their shadows (or lack of same) across these films, we are given a vision of a sad past (*Mystery*) and a sad future (*Muscle*). In both, the body attempts–and fails–to break free of the political system in which it is inscribed. *Beautiful Mystery* is a film which presents a Western solution to an Eastern problem–in this case, an individual *cum* Freudian overcoming of Japanese conformist-masochistic politics. *Muscle*, on the oth-er hand, presents a Japanese solution to a Western problem–in this case, a masochist/conformist overcoming of a sadistically modern Western capital-ism. I admit this is a bipolar reading of the films; however, this bipolarity serves not only the example of this essay but is, I would argue, the most fruitful way to come to terms with these two particular films.[1] The predications, plots, and influences of each film may be superficially and obviously Western or Eastern, but that their resolutions invite the opposite suggests neither cultural world is mutually exclusive. Indeed, modern internationality/ intertextuality may be a built-in condition of the inherently modern medium of film, as well as a condition of international cinema "literacy."

Director Nakamura Genji's *Beautiful Mystery* (1983) satirizes both particularly Japanese militaristic nationalism and its implicitly homosexual pretexts (not just *sub*texts). "Mitani Makio" is the Mishima Yukio-like leader of a cult of contemporary body-worshipping nationalists, the homosocial atmosphere of whose living arrangement and militaristic training facilities seek to embody pre-Western ideals of loyalist feudalism. Attracted to their anachronistic samurai spirit while they exercise scantily-clad in a gym, university freshman "Takizawa Itsuro" asks to be admitted to the group. He quickly becomes indoctrinated into the group via their militaristic propaganda, which draws him into a world that equates gay ritualism with a philosophy of nationalism. "I don't understand things like philosophy yet, but I want to become a true patriot." The group's rightist militarism is, like Mishima's, nationalistic but not fascistic in the modern sense because its premodernity entertains no notions of Western socialism. It is, rather, the equally sadomasochistic nationalism of the feudal era[2] (Mishima sought to recentralize the emperor's power), whose hierarchical male code of *bushido* joined warriors in a misogynistically homosexual bond.

The naive and uncorrupted Takizawa is accepted immediately into the group: in these desperate and sadly liberal times, the elitist criterion of acceptance is not the feudal birthright of yore, but the individual purity of a pseudo-Nietzschean will. This is *not* because, as we will soon see, they paradoxically attempt to adopt democratic mobility into their brand of feudalism. Rather, feudalism's "pure" homosexual content is their real interest, and the pseudo-political form which happens to contain it is merely a pretext.[3] Even when determined and defined by the group, sexual desire can only manifest itself though individuals and cannot exist in the abstract. Yet the individual's willful consciousness must be first surrendered to the group–hence its "pseudo" character of that will. (I am assuming "personal honor" and other individual, and individuating, notions of the samurai are unexamined, received ideas, and thus impersonal.) If that individual can manifest his will unconsciously–his conscious self having already been surrendered–perhaps he can resist full assimilation.

The leader Mitani then delivers a lecture to Takizawa and his other followers: "Just like our classical poetry does not exist only of love between man and woman, [patriotism] is also made up of love for our country, love for our brethren. . . . In the West, love suicide does not exist." The history of Japanese homosexuality (in poetry) is also the homosexual history of its (premodern) political system. The abstract aesthetic of love for one's country is in fact the aesthetic of the literal sexual love for that country's citizens, or "brothers." A Mishima figure, Mitani too plans on staging a suicidal coup–for which he and his disciples even hold dress rehearsals. His own plans for *seppuku* will be a sort of male love suicide, a gesture of loyal devotion to an ideal superficially of politics but substantially of a "pure" and loyal samurai-homosexuality that modern, Westernized Japan no longer recognizes.

For his next step as a novitiate, Takizawa is assigned a mentor, yet only slightly older. Still, this model approximates the feudal *wakashu*-type relationship of older man/younger apprentice, a homosexual code of brotherhood engendering a system of nurturing mediated by S/M power hierarchies. The goal of the group–to reinstate the emperor's power–is ironic in its implications. Mitani Makio, of course, is himself not an emperor figure, only a hyper-masculinized soldier. The emperor, and the feudal system of lords he represents, commands masculinity but does not embody it himself; he is a figurehead, an abstract ideal. As Barrett says[4] of the feudal relationship between retainer and lord, the retainer's social role is masculine but masochistically passive in his servility, while the lord's persona is effeminate but sadistically powerful. Going a step further, he suggests the homosexual loyalty mandated by *bushido* is furthermore incestuous, since the lord (or, by my extension, the emperor) is the retainer's "father." The minor age discrepancies and internal hierarchy of Mitani's group–which allow for *wakashu*-style role-playing–do not make him or his right-hand man effeminate–they are "higher" samurai, not lords. The fact that the hegemonic figures for whom they fight and by whom they are represented–hierarchical figures above themselves–are effeminate discloses the basic homosexual imperative of their enterprise. The narcissism of their masculinity, like Mishima's bodybuilding, protests too much against a certain–and accurate–interpretation of their feudalism as being a mere pretext for a desired homosexual society. Yet the actors cast to play Mitani's followers are boyish, fit without being muscular; they are all too effeminate despite the paramilitary training their characters undergo, and therein lies the beginning of the film's satire. Indeed, after a hard day's training, the group's true *raison d'etre* is revealed when at night bed-hopping ensues, as the young "samurai" are barely able to contain themselves when the lights–and the politics–go down. Because homosexuality had been a standardized product of the Japanese right, it does not fear, as does the Western militaristic right, that its homosexuality will be disclosed. It only fears that it will disclosed as *effeminate* and individualistic *cum* bourgeois.

Takizawa's mentor, Shinohara, rapes him on his first night at the group's compound, as part of his initiation: "Do you see? The left wing is all about philosophy, but the right is about feeling." On the one hand, this seems like only a joke: the "right," pretending to righteousness, is devoted only to self-interest, in this case the enticement of sex. On the other hand, irrational and indefinable "feeling" for rightists *is* their philosophy, and their only philosophy, and therein lies the danger of their nationalism. Nevertheless, Takizawa falls in love with his mentor, because rape, though a form of violence, is a *correct* form of feudalistic violence and thus produces the desired effect. "Sex is not the desire of the flesh, but the etiquette of the body," one group member says. Or, sex is not natural or biological, but a homosocial component necessary to nationalism or feudalism–or at least this is what those who have been indoctrinated would believe. But in fact, as their groaning night-time activities (and later on, the final scene) attest, it is just the opposite: the homosocial "etiquette" of the feudal structure is just a pretext to fetishize and codify an already present homosexual desire. Although retainers pretend to serve lords and emperors, the feudal system those lords and emperors represent in turn "serves" and feeds the latent homosexual desires of its adherents. Mitani's group is *a priori* homosexual, but not *a priori* sadomasochistic; the S/M of the rightist political form shapes and codifies the homosexual content of individuals such that their conformism thereupon will perpetuate the hegemonic system that controls them. Textually, the jingoism of their speeches is an incongruous joke, but subtextually (and pretextually) it is, in fact, logical.

Mitani Makio finally decides to implement his coup, after biding his time with some bare-chested paramilitary training and a number of soft-core sex scenes (which occupy much of the film's brief, one-hour running time). Like Mishima's coup attempt, Mitani's will end with predestined *seppuku*, an act of nihilism because the object of its ostensible loyal devotion is merely an abstraction of the unrecoverable empire obviously no longer extant in post-War Japan. In a previous lecture, Mitani compared himself to the leaders of the short-lived Tokyo rebellion of 1936–known as the "February 26 Incident"–in which militaristic junior officers led their troops in assassinating prominent members of the civilian government.[5] "The young officers of the 1936 coup d'etat had no desires, no proclamations, and died without accomplishing anything. In return, they became a beautiful mystery. Eternal." Again, politics is in service of sex, and not their sex for politics. Politics–such as desires and proclamations–are transient; Mishima, too, knew he was going to accomplish nothing, and died as an eternal symbol and not a man of transient accomplishment. Indeed, Mishima did read a "proclamation" before his death, but Mishima surely knew his speech would be unanimously ridiculed; if anything, the speech was directed towards an abstract, nonexistent (dead) audience. The politics of reality are ugly. Only abstract or godlike (or anachronistic) ideals like the emperor or classical poetry are beautiful– and yet sex, the vehicle through which their devotion is manifested, cannot be abstract. Within this incongruity lies the film's critique. To *live* (as opposed to merely think) abstractly, and therefore beautifully, one must "feel" like the right and not philosophize (i.e., be rational) like the left. Philosophy, because it self-criticizingly acknowledges its own limitations, is ugly. The imagination of irrational feeling is beautiful because it refuses the idea of impossibility, such that the absurd notion of not only reviving the emperor but transubstantiating his abstraction through the reality of gay sex seems feasible. In order to be beautiful, homosexuality must be abstracted, hidden, and sadomasochistically irrationalized. Its causal relationship with politics must be inverted: sex pretends to be the result of politics when in fact it is the cause. The beautiful mystery of Mitani's planned love-suicide/*seppuku* transforms the Buddhism of a traditional double suicide into a metaphysical masochism–miming the social expectation of devotion to a superior, only in a masochistically willed suicide will that devotion to homosexuality be beautifully eternal. They preform mock-*seppuku*s and then immediately indulge in a *fundoshi*-clad orgy: there can be no question that the masochism of their suicidal desire is a sex artificially sublimated into politics, and not a politics sublimated into sex. After a practice *seppuku*, Mitani says, "Isn't it beautiful? Isn't it handsome?" His own philosophy reduces politics to a subjective sensibility, the "feeling" of the right, a feeling that is here comically reducible to homosexual lust.

Then we get the real joke. After mutual exchanges of brotherly devotion, Takizawa and his mentor make love on the night before the coup, perhaps their final night together. However, they forget to set the alarm clock for the next morning. They oversleep and miss the entire military operation. Panicked, they attempt to commit *seppuku* but utterly and farcically fail; their commitment was their love for each other, not a love for the cause. We then cut to two years later. Takizawa and his mentor are now "Scarlet" and "Maria," transvestite bar "hostesses" entertaining male clientele at the "Days of Wine and Roses" bar. Earlier, Mitani had given a speech about the noble traditions of battle make-up for men, to which a student had protested, "But we're not queer." Now, in full drag, we see the "battle" these soldiers were truly preparing for–overt homosexuality, not covert homosexuality. The masculine devotion of *bushido* is revealed as a farce, for what lies underneath the soldier is a drag queen trying to get out. Over an image of the rising sun of the Japanese flag flapping in the wind, a final on-screen title reads: "Mitani Makio shines brilliantly in history while Takizawa and Shinohara faded like seaweed to the bottom of a neon sea." The joke here is obvious enough, but the title ironically suggests precisely the opposite of what Mitani wanted. He saw the greatest beauty in mystery, but to "shine brilliantly" is to not really be a mystery; paradoxically, to become a well-known mystery one cannot be a closed secret (like the secret of their homosexuality) but a public, solvable mystery. Although floating at the bottom of a neon sea, it is Takizawa and Shinohara, while climactically disclosing the "mystery" of *bushido*'s homosexuality, who are the ones with "no proclamation" and who, after metaphorically drowning, "died without accomplishing anything."

Sexual desire, though group-directed here, can only manifest itself individually–sexuality cannot exist in the abstract, without any human subject and/or object identification. Yet this is precisely Mitani's ideal of beauty, the surrender of individual sexuality to an abstracted group sexuality. But such a thing cannot realistically exist; its fallacious reasoning forces one to escape, either through death (suicide) or via a "willed accident"–forgetting the alarm clock. For the ending to have any meaning beyond a one-note joke, forgetting the alarm must represent an unconscious exercise of will. After all, it can be no coincidence that the one day they forget to set the alarm is the very day of their suicidal coup! Their conscious selves having already been surrendered to the group and immobilized, only the secretly preserved mobility of their unconscious selves can save them. Because the predication of their political involvement was a sublimated sex (and not a sublimated politics), they can recover that origin to break through the political facade. Their unconsciousnesses are preserved because the equality and mutuality of their love overcomes the sadomasochistic "love" of a sexual nationalism.

Mishima Yukio's own homosexuality is the proof of the film's jokey thesis, but, if you accept the film's satire, this thesis would theoretically exist even if he had been straight–Mishima's extremism just makes the idea more blatant. Oshima Nagisa, in his essay "Mishima Yukio: The Road to Defeat of One Lacking in Political Sense," comments on Mishima's suicide and his second's failure to cleanly decapitate him:

> Our cameraman . . . who as a military aviator . . . was made to practice slitting the necks of soldiers everyday, believes that Mishima–who had put all of his strength into committing *seppuku*–had muscles that he had trained over and over, which were extremely solid between his elbows and neck. People will probably say that he hardened those muscles for his death that day; those muscles, however, opposed his death.[6]

The narcissism of body-building/worship is contained within and shaped by the masochism of the feudal mandate for conformity; ostensibly, the strength of one's body must symbolize not individual vanity by the muscular *uniformity* of authoritarian group will. Bodily uniformity is authoritarian insofar as the desired "uniform" is invested with (sadistic) power, either in rightist capitalism or rightist feudalism, as sexual power overarches particular political forms. In the West, conformist body-worship is a stereotypical staple of often fallaciously leftist mainstream gay culture, which by attempting to subvert heterosexist definitions of muscularity too often winds up only rein-forcing muscular authoritarianism in gay culture as well. The form of muscu-larity can subsume and homogenize its social manifestations–muscularity's biological sexual imperative is very good at resisting attempts to subvert or reconstruct it. Muscles are the biological extension of a dress military uni-form–what must be beneath the uniform should be as strong as what it represents, lest we encounter a "Wizard-of-Oz" formula. Japan's history, though sexist, had not been heterosexist, as was Europe's; furthermore, Japan attempted to codify and nationalize its homosexuality through its political conformism.

Beautiful Mystery, in its satire of both Mishima's rightism and historical Japanese militaristic nationalism, suggests just such an Oz-like ruse (if their politics is really sex, what is really their politics?). Oshima's metaphor above, however, suggests that individual narcissism can actually resist the social imperative for masochistic conformity. The narcissism of Mishima's muscles resisted his own death blow, even though those muscles were supposed to be "group muscles," and as such should be masochistically willing to receive such a blow. The feudal paradox is that males are supposed to be both potently muscular and *servile* to authoritarianism. Generally, militaristic muscle-building pretends to be for the good of the individual body, when it is in fact only for the good of the group body, a formula Mishima's vain muscles try to resist. Political hegemonies conspire to create the illusion that a self-preserving narcissism is indistinguishable from a self-sacrificing mas-ochism. This indistinguishability conflates the self-preserving will of the individual with the mask of social servility under which he labors, a will whose muscularity is in fact the very homosexual vanity it attempts to deny, a homosexual vanity which, when its mask is discarded, is reducible to Takiza-wa and Shiboharu dressed as whoring drag queens.

But *how*, exactly, is this discarding possible? By forgetting to set one's alarm clock–that is, when the conscious will has already been surrendered, only an unconscious "accident" can resist the oppressive contingencies of one's environment (here, feudalism). The idea of intentionally forgetting something is archetypally Freudian–not that, obviously, its existence doesn't predate Freud, but that its common identification is as a "Freudian," and therefore Western, idea. This is also not scholarly Freudianism: it is a com-monplace Freudianism everyone knows, and such is the commonplace extent to which "bourgeois" Freud has invaded proud Japan. The commodification of sexual nationalism in the form of whoring drag queens, the selling of nobility to the merchant classes (or Freud's bourgeoisie), would be Mitani Makio's nightmare. The unconscious here allows the individual will feudal-ism has repressed to defiantly–if comically–resurface. The unthinkingness of the unconscious can only rescue individuals, however, and not whole societies. Thus, they are as whores still masochists–Japan is always socially masochistic whether in feudalism or capitalism–but they're *happy* ones. Indeed, the paradox of Mishima's own muscles narcissistically resisting his suicide has this sort of unconscious, or "unthinking," accidental quality, even though the result of Mishima's resistance was a tragic death instead of a comic life. Because muscles are both biological and sociological, their unstable duality can represent both narcissism and masochist conformity to a sociopolitical ideal. The battle between these two poles is analogous to the overlapping struggle between the unconscious (individualism) and the conscious (conformity).

The thesis of *Beautiful Mystery* seems to be that feudal surrender of the individual will to the group is, cyclically, in the service of personal sexual desire–a cycle in feudalism's own self-interest. Although the film's orgy sequences are seemingly ones of group desire, privilege is still given to individual pairs of devoted lovers and lovemaking only occurs in pairs. Sex may appear to be a service to a group, but it is manifested individually and also begins as an individual desire to join the group in the first place. Just as the individual in Japan must mask his desires for the sake of the group, here personal desire masquerades as group desire. The group attempts to homogenize these desires, but they can, if strong enough, remain unconscious and latent. The strength of Takizawa's and Shinohara's homosexual *individualism* is unconscious; they transcend the group only against their own consciousnesses, which have already been surrendered. But because they love in pairs, as individuals, their wills can unconsciously remain intact. It is, the film tells us, impossible to sanely love a group; only a rightist lunatic like Mitani can irrationally love in the abstract.

While *Mystery* is a satire of the right about the survival of individual desire beyond the group, Sato Hisayasu's *Muscle* (1988; North American release, 1994) is a fascinating, if confused, satire of the left about the madness of desire without social groups. In *Mystery*, the sadomasochism of sexual relationships was transmuted to the power hierarchies of the group; the love relationships in the film are extremely tender and committed, once all aggressions and neuroses are channeled through and tamed by the feudal power structure. *Muscle*, however, posits a hopelessly alienated and loveless world whose sadomasochism is explicitly sexual, not social. Its nihilist world is a product of the rising right, and the failure of the vanishing left.

The film's hero is a writer and photographer for the magazine "Muscle." Visiting a body-building contest, he becomes entranced with "Kitami Yukahiro," a narcissist who enjoys pitting his beautiful but thin frame against the much beefier bodies next to him on stage. Unlike the bodily uniformity of *Mystery*, in which bodily sameness unites and conforms individuals to mass identity, here calibrations of competitive muscularity capitalistically individuate people into degrees of sadomasochism–as bodies are individuated on the bodybuilding stage–while the dominant sadist can also be a narcissist. They soon become sadomasochistic lovers, with our hero seemingly more obsessed with Kitami than Kitami with him. Kitami is by far the more sadistic, and slices our hero's nipple with a razor blade while they have sex. Their "love" is hardly that of a conventional bourgeois romance. Their sex is only pain, and when they dance together in our hero's apartment, it is an act blatantly mechanical and awkward, a parody of the blissfully romantic love that cannot exist in their painful world.

Although our hero is himself sadomasochistic, he can neither fulfill nor withstand the extremes of Kitami's sadistic demands. Our hero chops off Kitami's arm with a Japanese sword during a photo shoot, a single defiant act of castrating sadism that far outstrips any of Kitami's perversions. His use of a samurai sword attempts to reclaim pre-Western Japan, directing intrinsically Japanese (samurai) power against sadistically Westernized Kitami. We see the severed arm framed though the lens of the camera used in the photo shoot; the arm, and by extension Kitami, has become no longer human but "framed art," a beautiful abstraction. But unlike the beautiful abstraction of *Mystery*'s group-identity, this abstraction is without any controlling system and embraces its irrationalism rather than attempting to hide it. Our hero will later attempt to explain his action: "Something inside crumbled and exploded at the same time." That is, if we accept "crumbling" as an *inward* masochistic impulse, and "exploding" as an *outward* sadistic impulse, the rise of a sadistic movement will fight with his masochism for control of his identity. This struggle will decide whether he is on the "giving" (sadistic-exploiter) or "receiving" (masochistic-exploited) end of a sexual capitalism. Yet it is not capitalism's exploitive power *per se* that makes it sadistic. *Muscle*'s critique inverts capitalism such that it prevents mobility rather than facilitating it; as it will force its hero to ultimately choose between *only* a sadistic role or *only* a masochistic one, sexual capitalism creates immobile self-identities as repressive as those of feudalism.

Cut to a year later, and our hero is released from jail with two missions: track down Kitami, with whom he is still obsessed, and track down a copy of Pasolini's final film, *Salo* (1975), which was released while the hero was still in prison. "He [Pasolini] was killed the same time I cut off the arm"–which now places the action of the film in 1976. Although this line is cryptic, from later passages in the film we will be able to equate the death of Pasolini–and the humanist Marxism he represents–with the deathly transformation of the hero's masochism into sadism. Yet the only real connection the hero has to this ideal of Marxism is the very tenuous one he grasps through Pasolini's films. When asked by someone whether or not Pasolini was "important," he even responds, "I don't know," a perplexing response considering he will soon hold a retrospective of Pasolini's films. We can assume our hero would not care about Marxist doctrine if it were handed to him in a pamphlet, but since the idea is contained within an artistic image–and one created by a famous *Marxist-homosexual*–it becomes important. As a still photographer, moving towards the "living" erotic image is for him one step towards replacing his displaced and unfulfilled living (real) desires, embodied by his search for Kitami.

To compensate for his lacking Kitami, our hero seeks out encounters with men on the street. Filling Kitami's shoes, he is now sadistic aggressor, and the anonymous men he has sex with are objectifications of himself. But our hero still holds a masochistic torch for Kitami, and, try as he might, his new sadism cannot replace his old masochism. Sadism here is willfulness, and masochism is non-willfulness, and the internal struggle between these poles is analogous to that between unconscious willfulness and conscious un-willfulness in *Mystery*. In feudal-obsessed *Mystery*, willful drives were in service not to individual humans, but to a masochistically immobile ideal whose abstraction beautifies their sexual discourse while denying its freedom. In *Muscle*, the only ideals are defeatist ones, and the only value is quasi-capitalist *mobility itself*. In a world with no ends, the mobility that is otherwise capitalism's means *becomes* the end; this world's nihilism, furthermore, ensures any and all mobility/freedom is read as sadistic. Capitalism is not personal freedom because it is only a mechanism in service to a S/M order designed to keep people in line with deterministic roles. In *Muscle*, the personal force that attempts (and fails) to resist group ideals is, as we will see, artistic imagining: a stage performance, the films of Pasolini, or the role-playing "art" of S/M sex.

The unconscious here is not the resistant force it was in *Mystery*, because in *Muscle*'s world the unconscious has already been surrendered, the consequence of which is the nullification of desire. *Mystery*'s unconscious further succeeds where *Muscle*'s conscious will fail because the particular love between the former's heroes is not sadomasochistic, even though they are trapped in an overarching masochist power structure. The issue of artistic imagining that will arise in *Muscle* is not a freedom, mobility, or will to power that constructs positive reality. On the contrary, the authoritarian conformity to capitalism in which the hero is trapped will characterize his imagination's attempts at freedom as irrational, and order him to surrender his active imagination to inactive, masochist passivity. The art through which the hero looks to escape S/M structures is only a displacement of those structures. People are sadists and masochists in response to each other, not to external ideals (which are themselves only displacements), because the film's nihilism demands that even the illusory ideals of art must be ultimately discarded. In Kitami's absence, the hero's sexual desires and encounters increase and grow more frenetic. His increasing appetites seem to symbolize what Oshima Nagisa refers to as the postwar "sexual abundance" of "sexual GNPism" or "sexual careerism":

> The issue of sex has been narrowed down exclusively to a matter of sexual organs and sexual pleasure . . . the popular weeklies and middle-brow novel magazines . . . all concentrate on totally fragmented issues, such as the size of the sexual organs, the intensity of sexual feeling, and frequency of sex. Praise is given to those who can accumulate the greatest number of sexual encounters . . . This is exactly the same phenomenon manifested by postwar Japan when it turned unquestioningly and single-mindedly toward economic prosperity, proceeding blindly toward a prosperity based exclusively on numbers. This sexual GNPism . . . is the flip side of what should be called the sexual militarism of the prewar era . . . [which] consisted of imposing the morals of the warrior class on the people at large.[7]

This sexual militarism quashed the communal folk sexuality of the Edo period (1600 until the 1868 Meiji Restoration), Oshima continues (243). Insofar as they are both anti-authoritarian and decentralized, this folk sexuality is analogous to Pasolini's,[8] though both are not without their own prostitutional economies. Yet this prostitution is not overarchingly sadistic because it is opposed to centralized authoritarianism. Although economically exploitive and more or less immobile in its categories, its decentralization is opposed to nationalism, the same sexually militaristic nationalism that Mitani Makio, troubled by the capitalization of sex's nobility, attempts to recentralize through governmental agency. The masochism of the warrior class–Mitani's anachronistic samurai in *Mystery*–is transmuted to the middle class via Takizawa and his Shinohara in drag (indeed, even in feudal times the homosexuality of the merchant classes was centered around the cross-dressed theater and not the military). The "neon sea" into whose bottom they float is a happily masochistic version of the neon limbo populated by the sadly sado-masochistic hero of *Muscle*, who wants not a hopeless feudal return but a quixotic Marxist advance–quixotic because it is held within the artistic illusion of Pasolini's films. Takizawa and Shinohara literally sell themselves at the transvestite bar; the hero of *Muscle*, however, sells not his body but his will (or, if you prefer, sanity) in a world of nihilistic sexual capitalism. Escaping sexual militarism, Japan's post-war/post-MacArthur era has instead adopted too quickly the capitalist alienation the West takes for granted. Japan's traditionally communal and non-individualistic values cannot withstand the suddenness of the culture shock this alienation imparts, and as *Muscle* and so many other *pinku eiga*, straight and gay, would have it, Japanese society turns imported capitalism into a neurotically neon mass of individualized and unchecked sadomasochism, as opposed to the controlled group S/M of feudalism. Because the thesis of *Mystery* pulls the rug from under sexual militarism, its heroes are individualistically and subversively mobile enough to graduate from feudal masochism to modern capitalist masochism (some victory!–but unlike *Muscle*'s hero, at least they are mobile). They are sexual careerists trapped in the bodies of sexual militarists.

Our eccentric (lunatic?) hero has meanwhile kept in his apartment Kitami's severed arm, preserved in a formaldehyde-filled jar–a fetish that is literally the bodily "fragmentation" Oshima recognizes. After being told that "there's a one-armed man walking the streets," he is given new hope that he can reunite with Kitami, senselessly thinking to return his phallic arm to him. He searches the city at night carrying the jar while, in the film's most sublime absurdity, handing out pictures of the severed arm to passersby who might recognize to whom the arm belongs. The sadomasochism of the arm-severing-by-sword scene recalls the masochism[9] of martial arts films such as Chang Cheh's *One-Arm Swordsman* (1967; followed by several pseudo-sequels) or Lee Yan-kong's *What Price Survival* (1994, *aka One-Arm Swordsman '94*) which, although Chinese, generically share the bloody sadomasochism and rightist homosocial codes (and homosexual codings) of Japanese samurai films, whose *bushido Beautiful Mystery* mocks. In Chang's films, the hero's arm is severed in combat, yet he is able to overcome this masochist disability through force of will, and becomes a better swordsman (and a better man) than normal swordsmen. His allegiance is still to a militaristic form, even though his own style (content) has been personalized and individuated: he overcomes the masochism of his person but not the militarism of his society. But by becoming a better (i.e., more masculine) swordsman despite his lack, his agency is rendered sadistic–he is a winner instead of a loser.

In Lee's (more leftist) 1994 update, the martial hero, ashamed by the bloodshed his martial codes have wrought, voluntarily dismembers himself, literally severing the social ties that bind him to a violent way of life. He is literally "disarming" himself, and even though he wins battles he is still a loser because he is a pawn in militaristic society. The self-severing of his phallically potent, sword-wielding arm excommunicates him from the world of masculine violence; unlike the apologetic emasculation of a *yakuza*'s finger-severing, the arm-severing is a total renunciation of the group by the individual. But because individual will is subsumed by masochist group will, the greatest statement of will is also the greatest display of self-emasculation. The overcoming of masochism in Chang's *One-Arm Swordsman* can be seen as a naive gesture, since its hero will in reality always be a loser if he never challenges the rightist hegemony to which he is ultimately subservient. He may at times pay lip service to nonviolence, but we know he can only flourish and gain respect when he is violent. *Muscle*, of course, is not a martial arts film nor any other genre that is predicated on sexual militarism; thus its GNP-istic limb-severing is an extroverted *cum* capitalistic act of sadism, not masochism, and the one whose arm is severed is the object, not the subject-protagonist. As long as our hero actively asserts his (sadistic) will, he can slide between sadism and masochism as a result of GNPism's mobility, whose sadism, though emasculating, is not the Freudian infantile pathology of, say, Wakamatsu Koji's *Violated Angels* (1966)–it is sociological, not individually psychological. However, this mobility only increases the hero's appetitiveness, and thus his unhappiness. As our identification with the subject (hero) grows deeper, we fear that happiness (read as sadism) is only for the privileged, upwardly mobile few who can succeed as *single-minded* sadists. Because we know he still masochistically pines for Kitami, he cannot be one of these select few; and his archaic samurai sword, an emblem whose powers are as futile as would be the emperor's today, is no match for capitalist "advance."

The masochistic rejection of right-wing society in Lee's *What Price Survival* is inverted in *Muscle*: here, the death of leftist Pasolini (mystically, aesthetically) transforms a masochist into a sadist who will remove the phallic potency (arm) of the very sadism of the society responsible for Pasolini's death. For now, the hero's subsequent sexual encounters–including a bisexual encounter with a sadistic female friend and her masochist boyfriend–increase in their sadism as the film continues. He continually gazes and caresses the preserved severed arm, as if it were a magic totem passing along its sadistic powers to him. He cruises for anonymous sex, brandishing his arm-severing sword in one encounter, or being dominant with male hookers in others. He accumulates more and more sexual partners, a la "sexual GNPism," as a substitute for his true love. His desire for Kitami appropriates the latter's sadism within the schema of his own masochism. Meanwhile, his sadistic female friend becomes obsessed and starts stalking him; he is, of course, uninterested in her heterosexual sadism. As a woman, she has little currency in the capitalist scale of sexual GNPism; he is only "worthy" of being abused by a man. By the film's end, however, he will "snap out" of his sadism and return to the masochist role, as if resisting masochism were an experience necessary in ultimately and fully subscribing to it. His female friend even asks him, "Are you 'S' or 'M'?" as if one cannot be both and must eventually choose between them.

At night, our hero cruises for sex. However, he also has a day job, managing the "Lunatic Cinema," where *Pigsty* (1969), Pasolini's most radically Marxist film, is the first offering in their retrospective of the director. During the day, his "lunatic" life is lived through films (perhaps also this one we watch, *Muscle*), and indeed the helplessness (if not passivity) of film spectatorship is a sort of masochism. The hero's gaze here is both sadistic and masochistic. It is normatively sadistic in its objectifications, but also masochistic because its object is a narcissistic–either the narcissistic self-containment of a film or the self-containment of Kitami's self-love. Our hero says to a customer at the cinema, "If you don't like what you see, you don't have to pay . . . that is the principle of the Lunatic Cinema." This idea extends the Marxism in *Pigsty* to a Marxism *of Pigsty* as a commercial commodity, as are practically all films, including *Muscle* itself.[10] Even Pasolini could not control the commodification of his art, just as he can also not control our hero and other members of sadistic societies from misinterpreting the humanism of *Salo* as mere sadism. Our hero pretends to be Marxist, but *Muscle* presents no images of community (with the peculiar exception of a gang of sadists at the end); rather, it is filled only with skewed, avant-garde images of empty, desolate streets and crazy loners.

Muscle also seems to invite a quasi-Platonic (and thus Western) interpretation along the lines of Book X of the *Republic*. As an iconic figure, Pasolini only represents a point of identification with Marxism, not the thing itself. *Pigsty*, in turn, is only a representation of that representation. The film *Muscle*, itself, is a representation yet another level removed–thus, when we interpret *Muscle* we must take its citations of Marxism as that much more false. By living through and in worlds of art, our hero retreats further into irrationalism and away from (rational) politics. Hence, the "Lunacy" of his "Lunatic Cinema." *Muscle*, however, is a world of physics, not of Plato's transcendental metaphysics: what replaces the metaphysics of Platonism's formal world is the spiritualization of S/M through art/imaging. The sadistic component of *Muscle*'s S/M fails to positivize the mobility which the authoritarian religiosity of *Beautiful Mystery* tries to deny. *Muscle*'s sadism is nihilistic because its capitalism has no liberating ends, only conformist means, insofar as the film's S/M is conventionally performed and role-played (as art). It presents the possibility of mobility but not its reality; the structural denial of mobility is as authoritarian as feudalism. Because the film will ultimately deny art, creative imaging denies reality instead of creating it. Here, reality is not created by the individual, but is achieved by one's assimilation into sociological patterns. In the individualistic world of *Muscle*, our camera-toting hero is a voyeuristic outsider to the bodybuilding contest where he first meets Kitami, while the muscularity Kitami represents is the utmost reality of the physical world. Kitami is sadistic to the hero as an outsider; the power hierarchies of *Muscle* are without any checks and balances. It is sadomasochistic Darwinism,[11] as opposed to sadomasochistic nationalism. Thus our hero uses sadism (severing Kitami's arm) against sadism, since sadism is all that is left. Without any social structure, worshipping art is no different from worshipping the body, insofar as both are aesthetically received objects or performances. The only difference is that the body exists (or exists *more*) in the natural world. It is to this natural world that our hero will eventually return, but his masochism will return with it. By the time of his return, however, life and art will be hard to tell apart. If S/M performance is a form of art–if life itself is art–then the difference will be between personally-identified life and group-identified life, between an art chosen and an art received.

The hero's desire to see *Salo*, as opposed to any of Pasolini's other films, is significant. *Salo*, an updating of de Sade's *The 120 Days of Sodom* to fascist Italy, was censored in Japan (whose laws disallow frontal nudity in film) as it had been elsewhere in the world. Having the film take place in 1976 brings to mind the most famous Japanese film censorship case of that year, the banning in Japan of Oshima's *In the Realm of the Senses*. *Senses*, about 1930's castrating folk heroine Sada Abe, expressly locates its sadomasochism within the militaristic nationalism of '30s Japan. In *The Waves at Genji's Door*, Joan Mellen says, "Japan was never a fascist country. Never having had a French Revolution to dismantle or even interrupt its feudal institutions, the freedoms against which fascism moves never existed in Japan"[12] (137). The French Revolution begged by de Sade's *120 Days of Sodom* ironically made way for the bourgeoisie whose own eventual rightist, capitalist oligarchy Pasolini's *Salo*, in turn, begged to be destroyed. If we accept Mellen's statement, what the hero of *Muscle* sees in *Salo*, then, is a reflection of his own Westernized society's collapse. The sadistic *Salo* is a perfectly interlocking match for his masochistic desires. He would not, in a spirit of social progressiveness, join Pasolini in decrying *Salo*'s horrors, but enjoy them; the function of masochism is that it is self-perpetuating and circular. The most controversial anti-rightist films of their day, *Senses* and *Salo* are in some ways similar, both set more or less around WWII: the Eastern *Senses* is a shout of individual power, castrating a society of "sexual militarism," and the Western *Salo* is a vision of that sexual militarism's victory. The idea of sexual militarism may exist apart from country-specific notions of rightism. In *Beautiful Mystery*, feudalism uses masochism to incorporate individuals; in *Salo*, fascism uses sadism to destroy them. *Muscle*'s hero is obsessed with the Pasolini, not the Oshima, because he knows the lone protest of the former seems moot compared to the more realistic pessimism of the latter. Pasolini is our hero's "beautiful mystery," who "died without accomplishing anything"–his Marxism, indeed, has not helped humanize modern sexuality. It is the Western film's model that is more relevant to today's Japan. Although *Senses* initially shares with *Muscle* the common theme of the sadistic appropriation and control of the phallus, *Muscle*, through its hero, will climactically–and *mindlessly*–attempt to *return* the phallus to its owner. (The heroes of *Mystery*, of course, control their own phalluses in the end–but only to sell them.)

Pasolini had renounced his "trilogy of life" films (1970-74) because he thought the naive optimism of their communal folk sexuality had become anachronistic; with *Salo*, the charm of earthily pure sexuality would be washed away in a statement as antifascist as de Sade's *120 Days of Sodom* was anti-monarchical and anticlerical. Although he seemingly subscribes to quasi-Marxist or anarcho-Marxist views, *Muscle*'s hero masochistically situates himself within the psychic world of both the rightists of *Mystery* and the victims of *Salo*. We know too little about *Muscle*'s hero to know if he thought Pasolini had more in common with de Sade than the director himself would admit, whether or not he secretly enjoyed the sadisms he simultaneously condemned in his films. We must assume the hero's grasping at a dead, unrecoverable Marxism is a pretext for his sexual masochism, in the way that Mitani Makio's grasping at a ghostly feudalism in *Beautiful Mystery* was a pretext for his masochism.

The antifascism of *Salo*, allegedly, attempts to reveal the dangers of predicating politics on sexuality. As Schwartz notes, Pasolini himself did not want to directly link his gay identity with his politics:

> Many in the [leftist "Radical Party"] knew that Pasolini himself did not think sexuality the basis for either political philosophy or a political movement . . . He was not interested in voluntary organizations to promote individual liberation; he once said, "Civil rights have nothing to do with class struggle." And the least attractive world he could imagine was one where homosexuals were like everyone else.[13] (70)

But should we accept this idea merely because it comes from Pasolini? Would we accept it if it came from a lesser artist?–yet it would be still the same idea. The idea that the least attractive world would be one in which homosexuals were like everyone else is in itself a connection between sexuality and politics. Presumably, Pasolini is against assimilationism because it is tantamount to adopting the bourgeois ideals of the host society. Yet this would mean that homosexuals (and other minorities) would be the carriers of the Marxist torch–a *de facto* equation of Marxism and homosexuality. This idea also makes the distinction between civil rights and class struggle, as if the egalitarianism of each enterprise were two different *types* of egalitarianism, and not in fact one and the same (which they are). Pasolini's distinction here is an aesthetic or artistic one. His attempt to irrationalize politics into unstable aesthetics is naive because no two aesthetic subjectivities can be exactly alike, and therefore political consensus would be impossible. But unlike the Platonic denouncement of irrationality, Pasolini embraced it:

> He wrote that Marxism's "great mistake" was in confusing all irrationality with that which came out of late nineteenth-century European decadence. In arguing for "rationality above all," he contended the Left

had fallen into prudery, wrongly rejecting all fantasy and imagination as "reactionary." (370)[14]

Granted–not all types of irrationalism have the foolish stamp of the irrational political "feeling" of *Mystery*. One could theoretically have a rational irrationalism, an irrationalism governed by rational checks and balances (as in Plato's *Republic* or *Beautiful Mystery*). But how could one have an irrational rationalism? If the structure, and its checks and balances, are themselves irrational–if rationality is not *above all*–the result is anarchy, not Marxism. When *Muscle* compounds this irrational rationalism (there is a S/M system, but it is *un*checked) with sexual GNPism, the result is nihilism, what Pasolini probably did *not* have in mind.

The seeming empowerment of *Beautiful Mystery*'s devilish subversion of feudal structure only seems optimistic by dint of its jovial satire. It is a subversion of the dangerously causal connection between (homo)sexuality and politics, a connection Pasolini wanted to resist or simply not recognize. Yet it is an empty subversion, in which the heroes overcome their political form without overcoming its–and their own–masochistic substance. Takizawa and Shinohara are free only to consciously sell themselves to individuals, not to a group. *Salo* seeks to subvert nothing, because no subversion is necessary; the hegemonies it attacks are constructions which must be destroyed wholesale from without, not "innately" sexual instincts that must be undone and remolded from within. Before *Salo*, sex in Pasolini is generally humanist–sex is love. But the loveless S/M world of *Muscle* is the ritualization of desire in de Sade and *Salo*, the destruction of love through its dehumanization. In *Muscle*, sex is art, but only predetermined art: figuratively, by the ritual of its performance, and literally, in that the hero's seeking of the film fetishizes and eroticizes the existence of the film *itself* (as opposed to its contents) as a work of irrational art, and in the process fetishizes its Marxism. The missing-ness of *Salo*'s sadism in Japan substitutes for the missing-ness of Kitami's sadism in the hero's life. This may, indeed, be a pessimistic or one-dimensional interpretation of *Salo*: as artistic sadism and not politics. This also may be a misinterpretation of Pasolini's insistence on separating homosexuality and politics, as the hero's insistence on sadism at the expense of politics fails to recognize Pasolini's humanism. By viewing *Salo* as irrational art, the hero reduces it to an irrational sadism, rather than the rational (goal-oriented) sadism it was intended to be. Pasolini's own insistence on irrationalism, however, invites such misinterpretations.

In his insanity, our hero still loves Kitami. It is an irrational love, not the positive, mythical, apolitical love of the "Trilogy of Life" but the pathological lusts of *Salo*. Not finding him, he indeed searches for a copy of *Salo* instead, a political work of art substituting for the performance of their relationship. It may be true that Pasolini himself thought the separation of homosexuality from politics was progressive; here, in a nihilist, regressive world, one substitutes for the other all too easily. The "Eastern" *Mystery*'s critique of prefascism and the "Western" *Muscle*'s critique of post-fascism may be tantamount to similar theses. Would the hero of *Muscle* in fact desire the communal nationalism of *Mystery*'s milieu, which conforms his masochistic desires to a safe and controlled environment? His sexual GNPism has turned him into a sad masochist, instead of a happy one. He thinks he is a leftist, but the masochism of his twentieth-century version of leftism, including his misinterpretation of Pasolini (as a sadist instead of a humanist), has more in common with premodern feudalism. Is it, then, that living in postwar Japan is *inescapably* a state of desperately sad masochism, since most people are on the receiving end of capitalist sexual exploitation, while still laboring under the feudal structure of patriarchal servility held over from centuries past?

Our hero finally obtains a copy of *Salo*, but, amusingly, he cannot convert the NTSC tape to PAL because the Japanese censors will not allow conversion of uncensored films. (A slightly disorienting plot point, since the availability of home video was not widespread in 1976; we wonder if the characters are living in 1976 or the year of the film's release). Although he has the tape, the current conditions of Japan disallow its–and thus his–sexual freedom, while metaphorically disallowing the leftist values it represents. The sexual freedoms repressed in *Muscle* are allegorized through their homosexualization–because homosexuality is a more visible target for repression, it becomes the film's example. Yet the heterosexual S/M relationship of the hero's female friend shows that all sexualities are at the mercy of capitalism, if less obviously. Modern liberalism, the kind which fosters bourgeois acceptance of homosexuals, is actually less homosexual than sexual militarism; although we easily associate "queerness" with leftist Western theory, in Japan homosexuality had also been the province of the feudal right. But because *Muscle*'s homosexuality ignores the controlled homosexuality of pre-Western Japan to focus instead on capitalism's commodification of human life, what is at stake here is not gay freedom, but freedom itself.

In searching for Kitami, our hero finds a friend of Kitami's, whose life story sounds much like the plot to Pasolini's 1968 *Teorema*. Unable to find a work of Pasolini's, he instead meets a man who seems to have *lived* Pasolini's work–as our hero himself attempts to displacedly live the sadism he sees in *Salo*. Assuming the man's life-story is a seeming fabrication, our hero says, "Don't steal stories from movies." The hero had sublimated his sexual desire to art, or in Platonic terms had irrationalized it as art. Now his films have seemingly come to life, as if he and his film-world were being dragged into life-reality. Seeing the hero's prized tape of *Salo*, the man destroys the tape, saying, "A video? You can't even fuck yourself?" The sadistic destruction *of*

the film *Salo* is the catalyst for sadistic destruction *in* the film *Muscle*, whose sadism seems inspired by Pasolini and yet whose masochism rejects him. The destruction of the hero's tape forces him back into the world of the living, not the ghost-world of a dead artist, for he will in the next scenes be reunited with living Kitami. But first the hero beats the *"Teorema*-man*"* to death, as if he will no longer pay lip service to a dead Pasolinian Marxism, insofar as this man represents Pasolini's life-films (there is no distinction anymore). It is an act of both physical sadism and yet also psychic masochism, for that Marxism is what he wants but denies himself–or the world has denied it to him. He is still both sadistic and masochistic.

One day, he finds an anonymous note in his apartment, inviting him back to the theater where Kitami's bodybuilding show originally entranced him. Kitami is there waiting for him, with a gang of followers identically disguised in stockings; it is a conformity of sadists, not a *Mystery*-like conformity of masochists. He joins Kitami and his gang on the stage where Kitami once posed; now it is our hero who will "perform," and he is now placed in a blinding spotlight. The spotlight now frames him, as he had framed Kitami in his camera; he is now an artistic performer. From standing outside art to witnessing art is "live" in the person of "Teorema-man," he now is spotlit art, and life and art overlap. Life does not imitate art, it is art. In order for the hero to climb step by step back to reality, he will at the final step stand in both places and choose between the two. Our hero offers back to Kitami his severed arm (still in the jar), but he refuses it, smashing it to the ground. Our hero kept the arm in Kitami's stead; in the latter's absence, he used the arm's power to be sadistic to both others and himself, embodying Kitami's masochism and his own sadism within the same body. Now that he has found Kitami, the "rightful" alignment of S/M can be redistributed. But Kitami refuses the arm because the permanence of its unattachability is a sign of weakness; rather than accepting sadism, our hero will need to demonstrate his own masochism again to win Kitami back.

Our hero tells Kitami about his homicidal run-in with his friend, the "Teorema-man": "He told me about his family, like it was from some screenplay." One of Kitami's cohorts answers, "It's true–but it's *Kitami's* family story." Kitami says, "Everything is an illusion, just like in the movies." Of course, the "Teorema"-story *should be* Kitami's, since it is he who represents the sadomasochistic link among the hero, his photographic art, and his cinematic obsession, represented by Pasolini. This cinematic obsession, to the extra-diegetic degree *Muscle's* film-versus-life formula invites, is also his attempt to realize his own life, insofar as he is a life trapped in a movie (as are we all?). Their reunion occurs on the stage where they first met–a venue of art, it is still illusory, but that the hero now participates in the action it is one step closer to reality, whatever that might be.

Yet Kitami, even if his life is *Teorema*'s, in no way represents any form of Marxism; Pasolini's death in 1975 also marked the end of his Marxist ideals, and only his superficial sadism remained for mass audiences. Just as our hero had been fascinated with the sadism of *Salo* at the expense of its politics, which had been rendered moot by capitalism's commodification of the film, so too has Kitami appropriated the Marxism of *Teorema* under his sadistic umbrella. The gang, which had also kidnapped the hero's sadistic female friend so that she could finally torture him too, beats and humiliates him. Our hero apologizes, "Back then, I couldn't stand the pain. I love you." In other words, he still resisted the painfully competitive sadomasochism of a rightist post-War Japan, but now he has given in; his "love" is obviously not Pasolinian, but simply "lunatic," as would be all love in the corrupted society known as the "Lunatic Cinema." Kitami asks, "What did you love about me?" "Your hard body," our hero replies. This would be the only answer he could give that would make sense, since in this nihilistic world, in which Pasolini's Communism had made little headway, it is the concrete and quantifiable commodities that have value, not abstract and/or unstable ideals like Marxism, or the Emperor in *Beautiful Mystery*. As our hero discards the abstract ideals of film/art, he gradually re-admits himself into reality. The liberating will of the artistic imagination is a romantic ideal obviously dead in the era of GNPism, which destroys or subsumes the unconscious and everything else that is not apparent.

Kitami answers back, "You only love yourself. I couldn't sleep for four months . . . my severed arm was trying to find me." Although the accusation of the hero's narcissism may be accurate, it obscures Kitami's even greater narcissism, who thinks not only can he not live without his arm (i.e., penis) but that it can't live without him! To compensate for his "lack," Kitami now has accrued a gang of sadists who remold the social standards of their group around the idea of his severed arm. To have a masculine leader without a phallus, their sadistic "philosophy," and his, must refocus around this lack, and increase its sadism to compensate for it. Kitami motions to chop off our hero's arm to even matters out, but our hero asks to masochistically do the honors himself. In a continuation of the film's inventory of Pasolini, he decides not to disarm himself, but uses the sword to slice out his eyes, *a la* the blinding of Oedipus (and Pasolini's own 1967 *Oedipus Rex*). "Now I'll see your body the way it was when we met," he explains. By blinding himself, by removing the visual gratification of the sadistically objectifying gaze, our hero surrenders his sado-masochism to *pure* masochism. As the Japanese sword now turns against his body, it is as if Japan itself, in its weakness, were betraying him for the sexual capitalism Kitami symbolizes; but since the hero does this "turning" onto himself, we assume he (and Japan) is powerless to do otherwise. This becomes a symbol of the renewed masochist "love" of our hero, who, surrendering to the lunatic world, sacrifices himself for the perpetuation of social systems, in the way that *Mystery*'s "samurai" unwittingly sacrifice themselves to hegemony. He will see Kitami's body the way it was when they met not because he will see it as he remembers, but because he will see it though the masochism of his eyes' absence. The masochistic shame that causes Oedipus to tear out his eyes–the shame of transgressing conventional parent-child relationships (to put it mildly)–is here the "shame" of even trying to resist Japan's *modern* sadism, which forces one to infantilize oneself as a masochist. He resisted that sadism by chopping off Kitami's arm, an act of emasculation–a foolish act, because it was not a destructive act of social protest like the castration in *In the Realm of the Senses*, but merely an exaggerated denial of what he already was–a masochist, as most of us who are not "rare specimens" like Kitami are. Our hero's eye-tearing satisfies Kitami, and the two leave together and dance by the pier, "happy" again in the role-playing conformity of their relationship. Both Kitami and our hero are satisfied only when the latter is totalized and immobilized in his masochism. He is no longer an active participant and perpetuator of sexual GNPism, but only one of its victims. Being a sadist–like being a "winner" in the capitalist/GNPism system–is only for the privileged few. This ending further suggests that this sadism, and the aggressiveness with which it is systematized, is to compensate for the sadist's own personal lack (arm/penis).

Our hero has seemingly realized reality, a realization which has returned him to masochism. This time, however, he has voluntarily and permanently removed the sadism of his gaze–and for that matter, the gaze's masochism, too, since he no longer even has a gaze. He is, in effect, being masochistic to his masochism, by destroying it altogether–*the* ultimately debilitating masochism. All ostensible art–the stages, the films, the photos–has been discarded, such that the hero can slowly, Platonically climb back to the level of reality. But he can only do this by surrendering his sadistic side, the choice he makes when he as spotlit "living art" sees the *reality* of his obsession–Kitami–and not an artistic substitute. Yet this reality, robbed of imagination, makes him little more than a mindless zombie. So what has he chosen? Has he, in fact, *consciously* chosen the opposite of what *Beautiful Mystery*'s heroes *unconsciously* choose? If so, then happiness is mindlessness. Or, if we know his unconscious (desire) has been nullified because its attempts to escape through art have been self-sabotaged, is his consciousness nonexistent as well? By eliminating the mobile power of the unconscious, the distinction between desire and behavior is obviated in the way that *Mystery* made narcissism and masochism, respectively, indistinguishable.

The political hegemonies of *Mystery* attempt to portray sexual militarism as the natural state of affairs, a structure which sociologically homogenizes individual wills into its explicitly conformist mass will (read: anti-will). To combat this archaic Japanese feudalism, we are given a modern Western solution–Freud's unconscious will. The political hegemonies of *Muscle* attempt to portray sexual GNPism as the natural state of affairs, an implicit structure which sociologically controls individuals to abide by its S/M rules of sexual Darwinism. To combat this form of modern Western capitalism, we are given an archaic Japanese solution–to masochistically surrender one's consciousness to the masochistic rules of traditional Japanese conformism. The hero of *Muscle* is fascinated with Pasolini, who, as a Marxist, sought to return to a communal folk (homo)sexuality. But that failure of that Marxism also means the failure of that return to folk sexuality. In light of that failure, he has no options but to surrender fully to the "group," which in this case are only the implicit social laws of S/M, since there are no physical groups in the film. *Mystery*'s heroes could fight back against the group with their unconsciousnesses. But *Muscle*'s hero has no unconscious to fight back with–here, unconsciousness is surrendered to a group unconsciousness, whereas in *Mystery* it is only the conscious self that is surrendered to the group. A masochist without an unconscious would be an example of that impossible idea of "irrational rationalism"–the masochism may seem to be in the control of the masochist, but the desires whence that masochism originated have been stolen by the sadist. The hero of *Muscle* has chosen to safely conform to a controlling masochism, while *Mystery*'s heroes seek to escape it. *Mystery*'s heroes escape masochism's old form (feudalism) but not its content (prostitution/classism). Likewise, *Muscle*'s hero escapes its new form (capitalism) but not its content (more than mere prostitution, he is a soulless pawn). Thus, sexuality is the basis for social structures, and not the result of them, for it is sexuality's content that is consistent.

Our hero may "Platonically" reachieve life, but what exactly is this life? It is a life still unreal on two counts. Firstly, as it is constructed by a S/M hegemony in which he has no say, it is a false consciousness, an allegiance to a structure not in one's own best interests. More importantly, however, he will still live within the prescribed and performed role of a masochist, such that the S/M relationship that he will continue with Kitami is itself a kind of performance art. In the previous scene, the hero had synthesized life and art when he stood in the spotlight–yet he is unable to move beyond the stasis of that synthesis and posit himself as a free subject beyond its circumscribed performance. This synthesis of life and reality is in fact even *less* mobile than the hero's previous masochism. The sadism of GNPism has commodified sexuality into a game of conspicuous accumulation. Because in *Muscle* both reality and art are also predicated on sex, sexual GNPism can colonize all aspects of life. Sadistic GNPism has not only commodified art, but *reality* as well, and has synthesized the two into a commodified performance that sadistically (and nihilistically) negates their distinction.

The Eastern-obsessed *Beautiful Mystery* spoofs the right, although this does not necessarily make the film politically leftist; it is leftist because it parodies Mishima, not because it revels in homosexuality. On the other hand, the Western-obsessed *Muscle* satirizes the capitalization of sex and the too-easy death of Marxism, but its reduction of Pasolini to a malleable symbol renders its political association foggy. If anything, it criticizes most clearly the dead-end of (homo)sexual capitalism's masochism, a criticism that the film's experimental style should not obscure. The film's thesis is that leftists have played directly into the hands of the right, having turned the leftism of their homosexuality into a content that is self-defeating and a form that is hypocritically capitalist, what Oshima calls "sexual GNPism," a form which creates only sexual pawns. *Muscle*'s hero is only happy when he has been immobilized; *Mystery*'s are only happy (they laugh for the first time) when they have been mobilized–yet only by prostitution, an unflattering vision of the options GNPism has to offer. The satire and comic (happy) endings of each film deny our pathetic engagement with the characters–their happiness is something to laugh at, not laugh with. *Mystery*'s comedy critiques rightist Mishima and the modern capitalism he opposed. *Muscle*'s comedy critiques leftist Pasolini and the modern capitalism he opposed. By investigating politico-sexual sadomasochism through the shortcomings of either the far right or the far left, we see that the real tragedy was not Mishima's or Pasolini's, but our own. We, often under the wicked guise of centrism, have ourselves constructed this sadistic world, an unreal world which we actually perceive, perhaps in our own masochism as passive spectators, to be a victory.

We have playfully tried to convolute an easy attempt at "Westernizing" *Muscle* and "Easternizing" *Beautiful Mystery*. Indeed, such an easy attempt would be very tempting, since as their points of departure they use the Western Pasolini and the Eastern Mishima, respectively. Yet to the degree that *Mystery* attempts to subvert conformism with individualism, and to the degree *Muscle* attempts to subvert individualism with conformism (because under capitalism individualism is too difficult), such assessments are short-sighted. When a film is not as inarguably grounded in geographic historicity (i.e., a *Farewell My Concubine*), theoretical approaches should not resist debatability but instead invite it. By the same token, one should have no qualms with a Buddhistic or Taoistic interpretation of a Western film, as long as the author is self-aware of his or her methods. Asian films will undoubtedly continue to rise in popularity, and as a result they will be more and more written-about, eventually escaping their relegation to specialized or exotic categories to rightfully enter the domain of general film studies from which they are still often excluded. Indeed, as the world itself gradually becomes smaller, this issue hopefully will be rendered moot entirely.

NOTES

1. Indeed, I think especially *Muscle*, a film which exhibits some of the avant-garde tendencies often indulged in the low-budget, artistically permissive world of *pinku-eiga*, is almost impossible to understand without imposing some strict critical framework upon it.

2. Depictions of sexual sadomasochism in *pinku eiga* actually set in feudal times–1960's films such as Wakamatsu Koji's *The Concubines* or Ishii Teruo's *Joys of Torture* series–are generally more sadistic than masochistic and almost exclusively heterosexual (I am also considering lesbian images aimed at the ego fantasies of a straight male audience to be "heterosexual"). Legitimate homosexuality in "pink films" tends towards contemporary settings, as if to masochistically feed from modern, Western-derived taboos. For example, see *All Night Long 2* (1995), a brief film of extraordinary sadism which details a gay teenage bully's torture of a nerdy student. Nevertheless, this male homosexuality is masochistically displaced as misogyny and murder when the two, together, wind up torturing women and killing the bully's cohorts. Although on the surface one of the most sadistic narrative films ever made, it reveals an internal masochism by really not being able to deal with its textual homosexuality in any terms other than violent displacements.

3. Suzuki Seijun's anti-military farce *Fighting Elegy* (1966) comes to more or less the same conclusion, only from a heterosexual point of view. The would-be soldiers, locked into the stifling homosocial environment of para-military groups, become violent as a result of their heterosexual frustration, and sublimate their unfulfilled (hetero)sexual desires in the brutal yet infantile war games in which they ridiculously engage. Set in the 1930s, the film will ultimately have its hero journey to meet the rightist leader of the 1936 coup attempt, the same historical figure to whom the characters in *Beautiful Mystery* pay homage.

4. Barrett, Gregory. *Archetypes in Japanese Film*. Selinsgrove: Susquehanna University Press, 1989. See Chapter 1.

5. The highest-ranking victim of the 1936 coup attempt, one of many in Japan in the 1930s, was anti-imperialist Minister of Finance Takahashi Korekyo, who had opposed Japan's military annexation of Manchuria in 1931.

6. Oshima, Nagisa. "Mishima Yukio: The Road to defeat of one Lacking in Political Sense." *Cinema, Censorship and State: The Writings of Nagisa Oshima*, ed. Annette Michelson. Trans. Dawn Lawson. Cambridge: MIT Press, 1992. Pp. 223-229.

8. Most famously in the "Trilogy of Life" films: *The Decameron* (1970), *Canterbury Tales* (1971), *Arabian Nights* (1974). However, Pasolini's interest in folk sexuality is most obvious in his documentary *Love Meetings* (1964), which literally interrogates the sexuality of the masses via person-on-the-street interviews.

9. I cannot help but also think of Kawabata Yusinari's short story *One Arm*, whose equation of dismemberment-fetish and Kafkaesque social alienation *Muscle* echoes.

10. In some territories, *Muscle* (original Japanese title *Kurutta Butokai*) is actually known under the alternate title *Lunatic Cinema*. Self-identifying one's film as "lunatic" may try to self-defensively defuse any attempt to unpack its admittedly convoluted themes–any attempt to write about "Lunatic Cinema" would have to be a "Lunatic Essay." It also, however, reminds us that the capitalist venues in which this film are shown do not share the policies of the Marxist "Lunatic Cinema" of the film's

diegesis. Indeed, that *pinku eiga* themselves are low-budget, and thus profitable, may invite their easy capitalist commodification.

11. The "Darwinistic" aspect of sexual GNPism's normative *heterosexuality* has been most directly and outrageously satirized in Kitano Takeshi's *Getting Any?* (*Minna Yatteruka*, 1994), a film which brings to the fore the absurdist comedy latent in the director's earlier films. In *Getting Any?*, a young loser's only goal is to experience the archetypally masculine pleasure of "car sex." To achieve this goal, he engages in a variety of manly pursuits–a bank robbery, skydiving, portraying a *Zatoichi*-like swordsman in a film, and becoming a *yakuza*–and fails pathetically at all of them. He finally is turned into a Godzilla-esque monster by mad scientists, and is destroyed muttering the words "car sex," as if his original purpose had been forgotten during this wild journey. That his pursuits draw upon cinematic archetypes suggests that (hetero)sexual GNPism is the product of both projected fantasies and a media-constructed reality. As GNPism divides people into winners (sadists) and losers (masochists), the masochistic failure of *Getting Any*'s loser hero is comparable to the masochistic surrender of *Muscle*'s loser hero.

12. Mellen, Joan. *The Waves at Genji's Door.* New York: Pantheon Books, 1976.

13. Schwartz, Barth David. *Pasolini Requiem.* New York: Pantheon Books, 1992.

14. Ibid. Schwartz, Barth David. Pasolini Requiem. NY: Pantheon, 1992.

Japan's Progressive Sex:
Male Homosexuality, National Competition, and the Cinema

Jonathan M. Hall

University of California, Santa Cruz

SUMMARY. This essay serves as a broad investigation of the origins of what came to be called the "gay boom" in 1990's Japanese cinema: a culmination of print media, television, and especially films which made the gay male not merely a visible (political) subject but also the site of displaced contestations of gendered (female) desire. The most visible transnational signifier of the "gay boom" was the 1992 film *Okoge*, a film which, in keeping with a Japanese trend which relocates the gay male as a safe displacement of female desire, posits the heterosexual female as the audience's point of identification in a film about the lives of gay Japanese men. Using this as a starting point, this essay seeks to explore how male homosexuality

Jonathan M. Hall is a doctoral candidate in History of Consciousness at the University of California, Santa Cruz. His dissertation in progress examines psychoanalysis and sexuality in twentieth-century Japan at the interstices of filmic, literary, and historical texts. Currently a visiting student at the University of Tokyo's Department of Interdisciplinary Cultural Studies, he has written articles in Japanese on sexuality, cinema, and economy for both popular and academic publications.

An earlier version of the argument can be found in Japanese. See Mimura Chieko, trans., "Itsuwari no tomo: Dansei dôseiai no hyôshô to josei no kankyaku, kyûsai no wana" in Kazama Takashi, Keith Vincent, and Kawaguchi Kazuya, eds., *Jissen suru sekushuariti: Dôseiai/iseiai no seijigaku* [Practicing sexualities: the politics of homosexuality/ heterosexuality], (Tokyo: Ugoku gei to rezubian no kai [OCCUR]), 1998) 80-92.

Address correspondence to the author at: Department of History of Consciousness, University of California, Santa Cruz, CA 95064.

[Haworth co-indexing entry note]: "Japan's Progressive Sex: Male Homosexuality, National Competition, and the Cinema." Hall, Jonathan M. Co-published simultaneously in *Journal of Homosexuality* (The Haworth Press, Inc.) Vol. 39, No. 3/4, 2000, pp. 31-82; and: *Queer Asian Cinema: Shadows in the Shade* (ed: Andrew Grossman) Harrington Park Press, an imprint of The Haworth Press, Inc., 2000, pp. 31-82. Single or multiple copies of this article are available for a fee from The Haworth Document Delivery Service [1-800-342-9678, 9:00 a.m. - 5:00 p.m. (EST). E-mail address: getinfo@haworthpressinc.com].

and gender construction operate within both Japanese nationalism and the transnational discourse of Japanese cinema's dissemination. *[Article copies available for a fee from The Haworth Document Delivery Service: 1-800-342-9678. E-mail address: <getinfo@haworthpressinc.com> Website: <http://www.HaworthPress.com>]*

COMMANDING TURNS

The current collection is tied up in a paradox and in a conundrum of sorts, as if each of this volume's signatures had offered persuasive testimony denouncing the binding the very moment the bookbinder's string, glue, and staples appeared. When it comes time for the radically heterogeneous contexts comprising both Asia's cinemas and Asia's sexualities to be sewn together, it is little surprise that the United States academic market now provides that final stitching. The late nineties have seen what Elizabeth Povinelli and George Chauncey call a "'transnational' turn in lesbian and gay studies and queer theory" which takes as its object "the effect of the increasingly transnational mobility of people, media, commodities, discourses, and capital on local, regional, and national modes of sexual desire, embodiment, and subjectivity."[1] Concurrent to this turn, which signifies practices running the gamut from newfound theoretical colonialism to profoundly subversive destabilizings of Euro-American assumptions concerning sexuality and identity, is the divergent context of Asian national film studies traditions, which for the most part have resisted what at one point seemed to be an inevitably *Queer Planet*–to borrow selectively from the title of Michael Warner's 1993 anthology (a book, as is often suggested, where the non-West seems to have little place at all.)[2] Instead, the perennial inclusion of sexuality as a suitable topic on the rosters of calls-for-papers on Chinese, Japanese, and other Asian cinemas continues to go largely unheeded, with sexuality frequently folded into gender as mainly a woman's concern. In such national film studies traditions, sexuality thus figures as the exhortatory turn–less a "turn" of events, and much more something that one might "turn to," but rarely does. Located tenuously between these two kinds of "turns," a volume such as this is long overdue.

If its paradox is its placement between these two, mutually disinterested academic domains, then this volume's conundrum is how to resist at once the neocolonial or homophobic readings that writing from one position might potentially allow the other. Precisely because of this positioning and because it is written for an English-language readership so frequently weighted toward North American ideologies, my essay like the other projects found here confronts the daunting task of discussing not just sexuality and visual culture in specific Asian locales but also the organization of knowledge that solicits this volume *in toto*. Required of us here is an examination of cinema and of sexuality that keeps never far from view the post-colonial relations that structure interaction between sites in Asia and the West.[3] Our work cannot stop merely at an understanding of cinema as a moving commodity within global late capitalism, yet another tired example of the new globalism; instead, it must interrogate sexualities and their representations as the very effects of these relations. Here, I refer less to the mushrooming global exchange of sex and pornography than to the traffic in imaginations and conceptualizations of sexuality and nationhood, or what Lisa Rofel, in an effort to resist "the rush toward a discourse of globalization" and to "invert the premises of sex and globalization that have so quickly colonized our imaginations," usefully labels sexualities' "discrepant transnationalisms."[4]

I direct this essay especially to two readerships that overlap, at best, infrequently. In laying out the cinematic contours of male homosexuality in mainstream cinema of early nineties Japan, I intend this essay in part as a contribution to Japan film studies. Despite the important critical position that sexuality has played both for Japanese film since the war (especially surrounding the New Wave) and, in mirror-fashion, for the film studies that has taken up that cinema as its object, Japan film studies still has not seen a productive intersection with the queer theoretical intervention that has marked cinema studies in other terrains. At the same time as dislodging this constipation, I also hope to join Rofel's cautioning project, directed to a queer studies readership, to weigh in against the overenthusiastic discourse of queer globalization and to focus rather on the discrepant cross-meanings of nation and sexuality. How do "two of the most powerful global discourses shaping contemporary notions of identity"–the nation and sexuality–"interact with, constitute, or otherwise illuminate each other?"[5] Any answer to this question posed nearly a decade ago can be only provisional, and my goal here will be one of drawing out implicit meanings. Heeding Arjun Appadurai's call to "follow the things themselves, for their meanings are inscribed in their forms, their uses, their trajectories," I will link in this paper a structuralist reading of Japan's gay boom cinema to the national and global contexts in which it is situated. If *Okoge* and the other Japanese films of the early-to-mid-nineties comprised a cinematic commodification of male homosexuality, then I bring to that site a formal cinematic and narrative analysis based in feminist, lesbian, and gay theories at the same time as following *Okoge*'s own global trajectory as a film commodity, projected through what Appadurai calls "different *regimes of value*."[6] My examination of Japan's gay boom cinema and its context will require three movements: first, an examination of the metaphor of the closet within a global context of competitive nationalisms; second, a close reading of *Okoge*, the central text of the gay

boom cinema, to foreground a feminist critique; third, a re-situating of the
texts within a global economy of representations of sexuality and gender.

Looking primarily at *Okoge* (*Okoge*, 1992), but also at *Kirakira hikaru*
(*Twinkle*, 1992), and *800 tsū rappu rannâzu* (*800 Two Lap Runners*, 1994), I
will demonstrate how a seemingly novel attention to male homosexuality was
set into motion (pictures), possibly forestalling more effective interrogations
in Japan of the gender/sexuality nexus. Yet, just as this volume's interest in
Asian sexualities and Asian cinemas hints at the phantom presence of that
looming Euro-American other, I consider it essential to reflect on how these
early 1990s mainstream Japanese films operated within a global system of
film circulation and reception. This consideration of the dubious advance of
male homosexuality in Japanese cinema from a pejorative bit part to lauded
central role will thus mean wrestling with what appear to be only corollary
concerns: a nationally structured teleology of sexual capital, a desire to shore
up the hold of patriarchy in the wake of feminist critiques, and an (in)differ-
ence to cultural particularity on the part of would-be progressive proponents
of gay and lesbian visibility.

NATIONAL CLOSETS AND SEXUAL ECONOMIES

The first evil we see among them is indulgence in sins of the flesh . . .
The gravest of their sins is the most depraved of carnal desires, so that
we may not name it. The young men and their partners, not thinking it
serious, do not hide it.

–Alessandro Valegnani, Jesuit Visitor to Japan, c. 1582[7]

We can understand cinema as a visual language metaphorizing unconscious fantasies that are based in difference, which then take form not simply
in sexed, but also in national, racial, and gendered constructions.[8] With plural
sights of difference, how shall we, other Jesuits, contend with the vision of
Japanese male homosexuality when it is so suddenly and so copiously shown
in 35mm? How do we maintain the belief that, as one prominent *New York
Times* reviewer catholically asserted, the gay boom cinema "comes from a
country that remains puritanical in all matters relating to sex"?[9] With the
tides turned and the sin of Sodom now evangelized from Western shores to
the purportedly puritan Orient, are we to find the figure of Japanese homosexuality again a symbol of backwardness? Is it this time in the closet, or
perhaps–more satisfying to the dual American desires for a sense of superiority and voyeuristic pleasure–perpetually just stepping out, like worn footage
motored by quarters, looping back for an endless revelation? Violence in
cross-cultural readings of sexuality is frequently achieved by the compari-

son's own projection of difference (and, desire) *onto* the other, with the result that the act of suggesting difference is effaced or naturalized at the point of its enunciation; when severed off from its point of origin, the projection then figures the difference *of* the other. Refuting the absurd claim of a purportedly puritanical or closeted Japan, then, is not a question of detailing how 'sexually progressive' Japan may be, nor one even of rummaging the historical attic for a fertile homosexual past before the arrival of European morals.[10] Rather, it means identifying and isolating the particular logic of difference in operation, in this case a predominantly national difference whereby a mainstream U.S. critic gets to speak for Japan's homosexual poverty.

Summoning Gayatri Spivak's assertion that "the so-called non-West's turn toward the West is a *command*," Brett de Bary's compelling reading of Shinoda Masahiro's 1969 *Double Suicide* provides an example of an analytic practice that can at once destabilize Euro-American assumptions of a mythical Japanese identity at the same time as undoing the director's own reductive mappings of gendered hierarchies. Likewise, Mitsuhiro Yoshimoto's pathbreaking 1991 article "Melodrama, Postmodernism, and Japanese Cinema" provides an astute "socio-critical" model for the inclusion of colonial and neo-colonial ideologies in a discussion of Japanese film in his implicit foregrounding of the West as the absent figure of the modern in postwar Japanese melodrama. While de Bary and Yoshimoto focus on what are considered canonical films within the field, de Bary's insistence on bringing gender into a discussion of the national and Yoshimoto's emphasis on a trans-national consciousness in relation to genre together provide a critical impetus for my discussion of contemporary Japanese film, nationhood, and sexuality in a concatenation that might have otherwise remained short-circuited.[11]

Outside Japan film studies, a similarly useful language linking film, transnationality, and sexuality can be found in the writings of Asian American queer scholars, particularly in a short exchange between David Eng and Mark Chiang over the Taiwanese-U.S. co-production *The Wedding Banquet.* Chiang suggests the problematic of nation and sexuality in a post-modern, globalized economy in his analysis of that critically and financially successful 1993 family melodrama. Director Ang Lee portrays a Taiwanese slumlord (and American citizen) living in New York City with his Caucasian male lover. Wai-Tung, in his attempts to remain in the closet and satisfy his Taipei parents' desire that he marry and father children, weds and beds his impoverished PRC tenant, who will go onto provide the labor that patriarchal reproduction demands. Analyzing this text as it operates within the 'representationally laundered' space of global capital, Chiang calls for "an investigation of sexuality as a component of various transnational practices."[12] Chiang's linking of the sexual and the transnational is complemented by his later discussion of sexuality and nationalism, where certain homophobic, nationalist logics would identify homosexuality as a Western pathology and accordingly understand homosexuality in Asian communities as deviating from normative, nominally anti-colonial constructions of identity.[13] Heteronormative homophobia is a component summoned into the service of national and ethnic identities while, as Chiang argues in the case of *The Wedding Banquet*, male homosexuality can be patriarchically recuperated into the service of post-modern, transnational identities. Chiang's critique is a salient one, but it operates from an assumption of sexuality as a discursively stable site, an extant place that is subsequently appropriated by an ethnic, national, or transnational agency. If we allow that both sexual and ethnic or national identities are discursive constructs of public and private fantasy, we can rhetorically reverse the direction of Chiang's logic while still maintaining his point. By claiming that sexualities can themselves be constituted by internal, global logics of race, nation, and ethnicity, we can assert that geopolitics also comprise sexuality. One could then complement the present commonplace that nations and colonies are written over with the sexual ideologies with a corollary logic that the sexual is itself constituted by national, colonial, or transnational imaginations–to understand nation and sexuality as *mutually constitutive* within the realm of fantasy.[14]

Critiquing a reading by Eng that collapses *The Wedding Banquet* too narrowly into identarian binaries of a queer and Asian-American experience, Chiang turns to a discussion of the closet. "What is occluded in a national reading is the way in which the closet itself is reconstructed, in the course of the narrative, under the pressure of globalization."[15] Chiang's foregrounding of the potential effects of globalization and late capitalist movement in reformulating the closet in the service of the transnational capitalist class is a critical move that decenters the closet from a singularly sexual discourse. But like the "'transnational' turn" described above, Chiang's focus on the effect of globalization risks too rigid an "ideological antinomy between modernity and post-modernity–or to put it in more concrete terms–the nation-state and the global system."[16] In the more conservative interest of explicating his particular text, Chiang's understanding here reneges on the more radical aspect of his claim about the closet, its ability to be reconstructed according not simply to a regime of sexual knowledge but to an economic, global one in an international context. Content to conclude that "the trope of the closet signifies the deviation from ethnic identity that must be covered up" by the transnational class, Chiang proposes a bifurcated closet that enters the service of either a homophobic national project or a whitewashing, concealing trans-capitalist class. Chiang's move here dispenses with the more intriguing possibility that, given the power of colonial and neo-colonial ideologies of sexuality, the closet in a post-colonial Asian context might be the product from its inception of a discrepantly transnational figuring of center and periphery.

Might we rather push the model of mutual constitution even further to suggest that sexuality be understood, in part, as the function of a closet imagined along national, economic lines?[17] Indeed, what more fitting parallel for modernization theory than the closet with its dichotomies of ignorance and enlightenment, darkness and light, bondage and liberation, underdevelopment and progress, as well as its faceless beneficiaries and its permanent, unceasing movement? If the closet is "a never ending process of constrained avowal, a perpetually deferred state of achievement, and uninhabitable domain," then its coordinates are part of a globalizing, universalist vector marked by "'pre-political' homosexual practice" on one end and by a "politicized, 'modern,' gay subjectivity" on the other.[18]

ENVISIONING JAPANESE HOMOSEXUALITY– "THE GAY BOOM"

Chiang's attention to homosexuality and its closet within transnational economies allows us to think not simply narratively but also at a broadly socio-critical level about the Japanese closet supposedly flung open by the gay boom films. Might that closet be inseparable from its placement within a global context? The question is an apt one for early nineties Japan. Anyone familiar with Japan's lesbian or gay scenes during the gay boom years knows the ubiquity of the Anglo-American discourse of 'coming out' and 'visibility,' a language that was taken up with vigor not only in gay or lesbian publications but also in the mainstream media and such widely circulating journals as *Imago*, *Gendai shisô*, and *Yurīka*. She may also sense the more cautiously expressed reservations about this rhetoric: might the politics of lesbian or gay visibility be an inherently Euro-American concern? Or, as Yukiko Hanawa asks, what are "the ways in which our political language and vision are confined by our impulse to correct the conditions of invisibility"?[19] Eve Kosofsky Sedgwick has described the metaphor of the closet as one whose "origins in European culture are . . . so ramified that the vesting of some alternative metaphor has never, either, been a true possibility."[20] What of Japan? The lingo of visibility appears to derive from a cultural metaphor borrowed out of hand. Almost untranslatable terms, 'coming out' and 'visibility' are kept more often in transliterated English as *kamingu auto* and *bijibiriti*, than rendered as in one awkward case into the clumsy Japanese "becoming an existence visible to the eye" (*me ni mieru sonzai to naru*).[21] We will need to examine the nature of the relation between Japanese male homosexuality and this attenuated rhetoric of visibility. In the context of the gay boom films, how did the language of visibility hasten their narrative attention to homosexuality and constitute a cinematic attraction for their spectators ?

The discourse of gay visibility with its attendant notion of the closet brings to mind its compelling analyses in recent North American criticism. Judith Butler notes the opposition that any notion of an "out" sexuality intends, its ultimate reliance on the notion of a concealed sexuality. Being "out" insists then upon a reproduction of the closet, which in turn "produces the promise of a disclosure that can, by definition, never come."[22] Diana Fuss links the parlance of "out" more directly to the concept of visibility where "the preposition 'out' always supports this double sense of invisibility (to put out) and visibility (to bring out) . . ."[23] Most notably, it is Sedgwick who explicates the polarity of the invisible and the visible that are the optic corollaries to the closet's logic of "in" and "out." In Sedgwick's analysis, the closet itself is a spectacle that is manufactured by a phallic, heterosexist system, a spectacle that is retroactively endowed with a purported truth value vis-à-vis the male homosexual. In arguing that "*the spectacle of the closet* [is presented as] *the truth of the homosexual*," Sedgwick performs a standard deconstructive move that first inverts the conventionally sacrosanct dichotomy of the closet's 'in' and 'out' and secondly displaces its meaning.[24] First, Sedgwick redefines the closet and its favored metaphors of concealment, masquerade, and dishonesty as themselves the site of the apparent, remarking the closet as a space of fabricated visibility. Second, Sedgwick shifts the axis of debate from the homosexual's own visibility or invisibility–an axis of sight–to the social production of knowledge about the homosexual–an axis of knowledge or, in Sedgwick's choice of words, an "epistemology of the closet."[25] In the shift from the former axis to the latter, from sight to knowledge, Sedgwick suggests that the discourse of (in)visibility is part and parcel of the desire to know and, in a Foucauldian sense, control homosexuality.

Sedgwick's closet is useful here as impetus to speculate on the ideologies of visibility and progress that this construct serves within a U.S.-Japan context. Inseparable from the two rhetorical nets of the closet and the orientalizing rhetoric of modernization, contemporary male homosexuality in Japan can never be severed from the globally circulating images of homosexuality of which the United States has been a primary exporter. Both the Japanese and U.S. mass medias frequently associate the West, in particular the United States, with the visible, purportedly advanced, or 'out'-side of the closet and Japan with the invisible, retarded 'in' of the closet.[26] If "being 'out' always depends to some extent on being 'in'" as Butler has categorized the polarity of (in)visibility, then the early nineties' newly 'out' images of Japanese male homosexuality underwrote a discursively unremitting pubescence, understood as always emergent but never mature. On the North American release of *Okoge*, the U.S. press instantiated this logic by describing the film as a "once-taboo topic" "erupting on the Japanese screen," reinforcing the stereotype of repression at the same time as it announced the closet's opening.[27]

Of course, in Japan the trope of (in)visibility often occurred at the denotative level given the gay boom phenomenon's predictable attention to 'coming out' narratives. But, more importantly the representations of the gay boom operated *in toto* as a staging of the (in)visible homosexual in a nationalized trajectory towards the fantasy of liberal equality.

This orientalized dichotomy of the closet is characterized by its intensely incongruous and contradictory valence, what in economic terms we could call its uneven development. Locating a similar gap at the fissure of U.S. discourses on ethnicity, sexuality, and generation, Dana Takagi wittily conjures up an image of this unevenness: "Imagining your parents, clutching bento box lunches, thrust into the smoky haze of a South of Market leather bar in San Francisco is no less strange a vision than the idea of Lowie taking Ishi, the last of his tribe, for a cruise on Lucas' Star Tours at Disneyland."[28] At the very moment it insists on the modernizing trajectory of development and progress, it also refuses the possibility of evening the score.

This linking of an economic metaphor to sexuality finds further consideration in film-maker and critic Ôshima Nagisa's 1971 critique of Japan's "sexual poverty," a poverty manufactured by the unequal relations of American cultural imperialism and commodity fetishism and the legacy of Japan's pre-war militarism. Sarcastically distorting the language of the commodity as developed by marketing strategists, phrases with foreign pretensions such as *mai kā* (my car) and *mai hômu* (my home), Ôshima criticizes the popular hold of a *mai-sekkusu-izumu* (my-sex-ism) established to assuage Japan's postwar ideological crisis, an "ism" where discourses of sex were deployed like houses and cars in the garage as self-affirming commodities to ground the individual in "the truth of sex."[29] Pursuant to the imitation of "Western, particularly American, sexual culture," and to the quantification of sexual pleasure that emerged, Ôshima identifies a discursive osmosis between sexual discourse and Japan's postwar policies of high-growth:

I am now thinking about sexual abundance, because I usually think about sexual poverty. . . . The majority of stories in the popular weeklies and middle-brow novel magazines and the supposed "sex education pages" that fill the women's magazines all concentrate on totally fragmented issues, such as the size of the sexual organs, the intensity of sexual feeling, and the frequency of sex. Praise is given to those who can accumulate the greatest number of sexual encounters, increase their sexual sensitivity, and have the largest sexual organs; efforts to achieve these goals are applauded. This is exactly the same phenomenon manifested by postwar Japan when it turned unquestioningly and single-mindedly toward economic prosperity, proceeding blindly toward a prosperity based exclusively on numbers.[30]

Ôshima goes onto to label this sexual prosperity in numbers alone a 'sexual GNPism,' an economic model of sexual accumulation organized through a neo-colonial comparison with the West. Sexual GNPism would signal an ideology of real 'sexual poverty' characterized by its plethora of "fake" (*nise*) images of sexual abundance.

Ôshima's model is complicated by his wistful nostalgia for rural folk traditions of free sex and his similarly utopian curiosity about the sexual mores of the radical student culture of a few years earlier. Despite–or perhaps because of–his frequent misogyny and the ambivalence towards male homo-sexuality that crosses his oeuvre, Ôshima's critique of "sexual GNPism" provides a good characterization of the gay boom of the early 1990s that underwrote the gay boom cinema.[31] A quick look at a 1993 gay boom television slot will point out the relevance of Oshima's politico-economic model in relation to the homosexual closet. Kamioka Ryūtarô's popular ga-meshow, *Kamioka Ryūtarô ga zubari* (*Kamioka Cuts to the Heart*), was a weekly 1993 show that quizzed media personalities on their ability to predict the collective response of a group of fifty visitors to the show. Riding the crest of the gay boom by offering a fortnightly special, *Gei gojûnin* (*Fifty Gay Men*), Kamioka began the mini-series by gesturing at the guest audience of fifty gay men, approximately half of them masked. One of the four media personalities, Ôtake Makoto, remarked, "Well, it looks like we're almost at a New York level here," a comment to which Kamioka ironically retorted, "I get the feeling that Japan has finally joined the ranks of the developed world."[32] Although displaced to a level of humor ironically suggesting that such development was hardly progress, Kamioka's joke could resonate be-cause of the viewing audience's familiarity with a nationalized and economic teleology of (homo)sexual "modernization."

On the following week of Kamioka's *Fifty Gay Men*, in an effort to better entertain the viewing audience, the mother of one of the fifty gay men was brought to the studio for a discussion as tear-jerking as her computer-altered voice and concealed body could allow. But when the secreted gay man, subject to the simultaneous scrutiny of family and nation, made the political gesture of removing his mask, the 'coming out' that the liberationist ideology demanded, the camera refused to show his face. In a fascinating inversion of the international joke with which he began the fortnight, Kamioka now relied on the domestic metaphor of family, reminding the man of his "responsibility to his father" and of the awful burden that a public assertion of sexual identity would place upon his family. Taking no heed of Kamioka's solicita-tion, the man finished his self-revelation. And though the camera caught the action in medium close-up, his identity was now concealed by mosaic which covered his face for the few remaining minutes of the program. The young man was refused, at an individual level, the staging of a 'coming out,' an ideology that the program, at the level of nation, ambivalently reenacted.

Suggestive already of a bust to surely follow, the 'gay boom' is a term used by advocates and detractors alike to refer to the 1990-1995 massive commodification and marketing of male homosexuality in Japanese popular culture, not just programs like *Fifty Gay Men*–but also films, magazines, sensationalized books, upmarket photo collections, television melodramas, and *anime*. Akin to the women's weeklies that made up the target of Ôshima's 1971 critique, again it was the Japanese women's fashion magazines, *Crea* in particular, that were prominent forces in developing its mass appeal. In fact, although *Crea* is regularly credited with inaugurating the boom with its February 1991 issue entitled *Gei runessansu* (Gay renaissance), Hirano Hiroaki points out that the boom was already in the making by the end of 1990; *Crea*'s special 46-page special section on the "gay renaissance" was simply the most notable example of an increased interest that included attention to male homosexuality in SM sex magazines as well as a special issue of the popular journal of psychology and psychoanalysis, *Imago*, on *Gei no shinrigaku (The Psychology of Gays)*.[33] Following such leads, other magazines with major circulation, such as the fashion glossies *More* and *Peach*, the men's culture magazine *Da Vinci*, and the weekly entertainment guide *Pia* each produced special features on male homosexuality. On television too, the ten-week social melodrama, *Dôsôkai (The Alumni Club)*, its title close to a phonetic play on the Japanese term for homosexuality– (*dôseiai*), featured homosexual intrigue and passion regularly among its intertwining tales of graduates.[34] Even the staid literary newspaper, the *Readers' Weekly*, gave "The Direction of the Gay Boom" as a front-page article in 1994.[35]

While almost all commentators describing the boom begin with the *Crea* issue, definitions of the boom vary. Wim Lunsing first locates it as a media-manufactured phenomenon, but goes on to include even the work of activists who criticized it, describing Tokyo-based OCCUR as having "contributed to the boom by producing books and articles" and the above-cited Hirano as "not hesitat[ing] to publish his ideas in a book, including a critique of the very boom that more likely than not made its publication possible."[36] Lunsing accurately recognizes what is necessarily a complex interconnection between political movements and the larger social role of media, the impossibility of taking any position free from the effects of media. But his satisfaction with a broad definition specifying only its term and content–homosexual subject matter widely available between 1991 and 1996–elides pivotal distinctions in the political and social stance of the materials he cites and overlooks what could be a more productive means of assessing the gay boom through a generic or formal analysis. While this paper is not intended as a review of the gay boom *per se*, it will be necessary to understand its coordinates before moving on to a discussion of the gay boom films. Hence, I propose a rough set of elements through which the gay boom texts can be recognized: (1) a presumption that the reader or spectator is neither gay nor lesbian, nor has much understanding of these positionalities or communities, (2) an emphasis on male homosexuality, (3) a focus on coming-out experiences, (4) frequent representation of gay/lesbian scenes in Europe and North America, with special attention to the United States, and (5) a suggestion of the potential threat that heterosexual masculinity poses to women. One can also notice the patterned absence of other elements: (1) the frequent absence of any discussion of female desire, (2) the absence of any discussion of chronic imbalances in sexual or gender constructs, (3) the absence of representations of lesbian sexuality. While these criteria are rough ones, I suspect that four of the five elements can be identified in most gay boom texts, and that the three negative conditions are regularly satisfied.

The effect of these elements on the cinema is best captured in film critic Yodogawa Nagaharu's comparison of *The Wedding Banquet* and two of the Japanese gay boom films. The recently deceased Yodogawa, whose homosexuality was long a public secret, noted what he called *The Wedding Banquet*'s absence of *kage*, alternately translated as "shadows" or "secrets," but in either case a term highly suggestive of the closet. "Unlike the Japanese *Okoge* and *Kirakira hikaru*, this film is without shadows." In closing his short, enthusiastic review with a description of Winston Chao and Michael Liechentstein, the two male leads, Yodogawa continues, exuding "the two are both dapper and masculine. Not a trace of shadow on them. We've reached a time where homos and gays can kiss with little worry."[37] Yodogawa's reference to "shadows" here echoes in part Mark Chiang's argument cited above: while the Taiwanese-U.S. production sustains the closet, it does so only to dissipate/recuperate it at film's end in the service of a transnational patriarchy. By contrast, the gay boom films reside under the national marker of Japaneseness, and equally critically, a kind of femininity that is 'avoided' by the manly Chao and Liechtenstein. The irony of Yodogawa's public secret aside, it is uncanny that among the three films, the "shadow"-less *Wedding Banquet* is in fact the only one of the three where the closet survives intact until the narrative closure—the film's narrative suspense in fact is whether Wai Tung's parents will find out. In contrast, the proverbial cat is out of the bag quite soon in the two Japanese films.

We could hunt for narrative reasons to support Yodogawa's observation at the diegetic level, but I would argue its real import lies not so much in differences between the film's stories, but in the films' own positionings vis-à-vis their national and gendered markets and their assumed spectatorships. Chiang argues that the success of *The Wedding Banquet* was tied to its "proximity to the culture and values of the transnational capitalist class," a fact underscored by the film's bland apartments and generic Chinese restaurants which rejected any particular sense of place."[38] Contrary to this generic quality, the Japanese films were unable to circulate in the same deracinated global market that was *The Wedding Banquet's* turf, nor were they assimilable to the post-modern globalism that Chiang details. Yodogawa's domestic review figures the closet as a structure comparable at a national level. Still, the *kage* the Japanese gay boom films cast, the closets they summon, equally participated in international comparisons of sexuality and the closet. Yet, as I will go on to argue, the very fact that gay-themed films from Japan were received in the international market uncritically as Japanese representations of male homosexuality would mean that the film's internal shadows, the heavily gendered shadows that Yodogawa might have sensed, even misogynously, would go unnoticed.

NAKAJIMA TAKEHIRO: REMEMBRANCE

Through an analysis of the 1992 film *Okoge*, now codified as one of the major texts of the "gay boom," I want now to highlight how the epistemological production of male homosexual (in)visibility is amalgamated to what I consider a virulently regressive politics of gender that is frequently overlooked by progressive critics. Male homosexuality is offered, as spectacle, lure, and displacement to the film's spectators–who tended to be young women. But before a detailed reading of the film, let us pause to consider the director's own history. Known in the Japanese film and television world more as screenwriter than as director, Nakajima Takehiro began his career with the Nikkatsu Studio in 1961. After producing a few screenplays for youth dramas that saw general release, Nakajima then went to work in Nikkatsu's *roman-porno* division in 1972. A genre almost synonymous with its studio, the Nikkatsu *roman-porno* films are characterized by their highly erotic storylines and their emphasis on female stars, and can be described as soft pornography with the notation that, due to Japanese obscenity laws, male and female genitalia are not shown. The films relied on inventive editing and camera-work to eliminate the need for the blur, and the industry provided a training ground for new directors as well as considerable room for experimentation by its masters, such as Tanaka Noboru and Kumashiro Tatsumi. The genre emerged in the early seventies, peaking in the middle of the decade, only to disappear by 1982. Beginning with his screenplay for *Mahiru no jôji* (*A Midafternoon Affair*, 1972), twelve of Nakajima's screenplays saw final production, and now he is recognized as one of the major screenwriters of the genre. Particularly noted is his screenplay for Tanaka Noboru's 1977 *Onna kyôshi* (*Female Teacher*).[39] Without severing his ties to Nikkatsu, Nakajima also wrote for two ATG (Art Theater Guild) productions in the seventies, Saitô Kôichi's 1973 *Tsugaru jongarabushi* (*Tsugaru Folksong*) and Kuroki Kazuo's 1975 *Matsuri no junbi* (*Preparations for the Festival*). The latter film is currently understood as a key ATG production. In the late seventies and in the eighties, Nakajima also wrote for television. Now, he has over forty film credits, including the screenplay for the recent *Aa, haru* (*Aa, Spring*, 1998).

Nakajima began his directorial career in 1986 at the age of 51 and made his debut a year later with *Kyôshū* (*Remembrance*), a film reminiscent in story and setting of the screenplay for the 1975 Kuroki film, which Nakajima had based on an autobiographical account. One of the last few films to be understood as an ATG product (receiving distribution and awards) but lacking the political punch of *Kazoku gêmu* (*Family Game*, 1983, dir. Morita Yoshimitsu) or even *Gyakufunsha kazoku* (*Crazy Family*, 1984, dir. Ishii Sôgô), *Remembrance*'s overwhelmingly nostalgic tone befits the twilight years of a system which had in its heyday supplied independents such as Ôshima Nagisa, Matsumoto Toshio, and Yoshida Yoshishige with production funds and avenues for distribution, and was substrate to Japan's most significant postwar discourse on sex, politics, and film.[40]

Vaguely autobiographical, *Remembrance*'s coming-of-age story is set in postwar, rural Shikoku, and focuses on the tongue-tied teen-ager Sumio, whose family's poverty has forced him, mother, and sister to stay on in the remote town to which the family had evacuated during the war.[41] Distant from his mother who constantly criticizes Sumio's artist father and estranged from this father who has abandoned the family to move in with his patroness elsewhere in the small community, Sumio (Nishikawa Hiroshi) is slow witness to the failure of paternal figures. These figures include not simply the negligent father, but also Sumio's initially upright high school teacher who had hailed from the city mouthing the postwar jingoisms of democracy. Pinioned between Sumio's teacher, whose lust makes for a laughable descent into the local rough-hewn fishing culture, the possessive bus driver whom she takes as a lover, and her own father who has suggested she take up prostitution, is Sumio's sister Yasuko (Komaki Sairi), around whom much of the film's action is focused. Sumio occupies the observer role that Sayoko would fill in Nakajima's subsequent film, *Okoge*, and as the film's protagonist, he functions effectively as the taciturn witness to the constraints of village life and familial responsibility that Yasuko suffers (Photo 1).

A more subtle and more probing film than *Okoge*, *Remembrance* sets in motion the same questions that Nakajima would less successfully try to bring together in 1992. Precursor perhaps to *Okoge*'s famous, much more explicit gay kiss and its male-male sex scenes, *Remembrance* is steeped in a homoeroticism (certainly more cinephilic than *Okoge*) suggestive of Yanagimachi Mitsuo's *Himatsuri* (*Fire Festival*, 1985; the problematic adaptation of the Nakagami Kenji story), an apt comparison given both films' location of a

PHOTO 1. Sumio as taciturn witness to the failures of masculinity in *Remembrance* (1987).

cinematic and narrative homoeroticism precisely within the diegetic destruction of the masculine order. As if to somehow forestall the increasing failure of the male figures of authority that encircle Sumio, *Remembrance* compensates for this loss of a phallic order with a visual, fetishistic dedication to its young star, Nishikawa, who makes a handsome fix for Nakajima's devoted camera (cinematography by Hayashi Jun'ichirô).[42] Shots are frequently balanced around Sumio's buttocks and the occasional close-ups of his posterior anticipate the buttock fetishism of *Okoge*'s opening sequence, what one well-established film critic would overexcitedly go on to call "one of the most delightful credit sequences in the cinema."[43]

But if the film's nostalgic browns and golds and its fascination with Sumio's body can keep the spectator, it is largely in contradistinction to the film's major subplot surrounding Sumio's sister, which is raised only to be disbanded (the French "débander" captures best the concomitant sense of detumescence): how is the Gide-reading, fast-talking Yasuko to maintain her independence from male control? While Sumio is like *Okoge*'s female protagonist in his role as witness or observer of his sister's social struggles (Photo 2), the similarity ends there, for Sumio finds no transformative potential in Yasuko, as Sayoko does in her gay friends. Instead, Sumio secures the spectatorial gaze and centrifugally spins away the narrative question of female subjectivity. A key example of the camera's and narrative's refusal to entertain female subjectivity substantially can be seen in a riverside sex sequence near the end of the film, where Sumio loses his virginity to the arranged wife of an older buddy, a woman who, more than even Sumio, seems perpetually at a loss for words. A series of shots and reverse shots establishes the circuit of desire, put into action when the wife reaches forward to unbutton Sumio's trousers and lets them drop to the ground centrally revealing (once again) his buttocks. Almost obscured by Sumio's body in this long shot, the friend's wife begins to undress, and in a reverse shot, the film offers a medium close-up of Sumio's intently watching face. Given the intensity of Sumio's stare, the spectator expects a point-of-view shot of the wife's face or even upper torso, which had been partially revealed two shots earlier. Partly mirrorng the earlier shot filmed from behind Sumio, Nakajima, however, pulls his camera back to capture the two prospective lovers in an extraordinary retreat. The subsequent long take is an extreme long-shot from well across the river; in the far distance, not unlike figurines, the wife continues to undress and the two begin sex.

Nakajima's deliberate avoidance of the female body marks the manner through which female desire is cited, is thematized, and is detailed–only to be quickly displaced from the film. The extreme long-shot and long take of Sumio's 'deflowering,' his 'man-making' is resolved by the camera turning away from the riverside to a shot deep into the dark woods, where something

PHOTO 2. Sumio observes his sister's battles in Nakajima's *Remembrance*

rustles on the forest floor. As if this inchoate image were grounds enough (this spying by the husband, a rabbit, the wind–we are never certain what), the following sequence is of the wife with her belongings packed high on a cart being driven out of town in shame, observed by a wistful Sumio. Nakajima's story and camera raise the question of female desire and action, but through an intimate, yet distant observer who is complicit with their banishment from the space of activity. Yasuko, too, is the target of the film's observation and, more immediately, of Sumio's own spying as he masturbates in the outhouse–the camera once again plays at his buttocks. And in similar fashion to the earlier sex scene, the film gives both its narrative conclusion and its displacement of the question of Yasuko's independence in the final image of an out-of-breath Sumio failing to catch up with the bus, his sister's secret escape from town.

THE LOOK OF RESISTANCE

Having accepted the claim that interiorities and core gender identities are effects of normalizing, disciplinary mechanisms, many queer theorists seem to think that gender identities are therefore only constraining, and can be overridden by the greater mobility of queer desires. Predictably enough, gender of the constraining sort gets coded implicitly, when not explicitly, as female while sexuality takes on the universality of man.

–Biddy Martin, U.S. lesbian feminist, 1994[44]

If there is no place for female desire and female action within the rural past, Nakajima's 1992 film *Okoge*–literally, faghag–provides an excellent site for the kind of independence that Nakajima can imagine in contemporary, urban Japan. As the emblematic text of the gay boom cinema and of the gay boom itself, it is also a key forum to analyze the boom's gendered contours. During its U.S. circuit, where the film was understood foremost as a portrayal of Japanese homosexuality, one mainstream critic called it a film where "a homosexual subculture unknown to mainstream audiences erupts on the Japanese screen."[45] But given the particular citation of gender that characterizes Nakajima's work, we can more productively consider it as a representation of both a gendered and sexualized economy.

A key sequence near the beginning of the film solders the triangular relation between two gay lovers, Gô (Murata Takehiro) and Tochi (Nakahara Takeo), and the film's central character, Sayoko (Shimizu Misa). In an earlier sequence, Gô's mother has not only intruded into the son's bachelor pad, causing a *coitus interruptus*, but in deciding to remain permanently, has forced the gay couple to find a new trysting spot beyond the sight of either Gô's mother or the older Tochi's wife. Now in a Tokyo gay bar, Tochi rejoins Gô at the counter unable to secure a hotel room at a reasonable rate. Much as sex was perturbed by the mother's intrusion, here too they are disturbed, but now through the arrival of drinks sent, the camera then reveals, from the naive young woman. Her red evening gown obtrusive in the dark bar, Sayoko waves unabashedly from the bar's far side and invites herself into their surprised company. So begins Sayoko's relation with the two men, and her gradual education in her role as *okoge* or, put crudely, fag hag.

Contrary to Gô's and Tochi's poor recall, this bar is not the first place the three have met. Let us turn back to the film's opening sequence: an effort to find a quieter place on the shore in the city's southern suburbs has landed Sayoko and a friend's family in the midst of a gay enclave. While her companions react alternately with denial and disgust, Sayoko finds herself instead drawn to this exotic space. As the opening credits roll, the camera slowly pans the top of a concrete embankment revealing, one after another, figures from a lexicon of gay stereotypes: the daddy, the dandy, the bodybuilder, the queen. This panning movement, cross-cut with close-ups of Sayoko's face, effects an extended point-of-view shot that rejects the familial injunction just given the younger children by their mother: *Itcha dame; miete mo mienakatta no (Don't say a thing; pretend you've seen nothing)*. Sayoko does not shun the spectacle of homosexuality; quite the contrary, through her insistence on looking and her distant, pensive expression, she appears emotionally moved by this vision of another world.[46] When the mother leads her brood to the ocean, for "at least the ocean is the same," Sayoko refuses the water's normalizing force. Instead, in a long shot, she stands brazenly on land the better able to take in the scene around her. At the scene's end, the camera pulls in close on her stare. Cut now to an uncommon scene for Japanese cinema–the slow kiss of the two gay lovers, revealed in a subsequent pseudo-point-of-view close-up as the object of Sayoko's deliberate regard (Photo 3).

The beach sequence's doubled visual structure, namely Sayoko's diegetic ability to see what other women must not and the extra-diegetic attention of camera and narrative on Sayoko's seeing, underlines a parallel drawn throughout the film between Sayoko and these gay men. As the camera looks at Sayoko's resistant looking, the social dispossession of her new gay friends goes beyond allusion to become a refiguring of her own social marginalization. Thus, the opening scene disrupts one conventional assumption about the fag hag, namely that the gay male and straight woman are drawn together by a common object of desire–man. But, if the film disrupts the one phallic hubris, it proposes another. Indeed, the film goes far beyond the logic of metaphor or replacement, far beyond substituting her marginalization with theirs, for the story of *Okoge* is that of Sayoko's embracing the gay male

PHOTO 3. Sayoko's vision of the gay world in the opening beach sequence of *Okoge* (1992)

world *as* alternative to the confines of a patriarchal ideology. Ôshima opened the essay on sexual poverty we examined earlier with a query about the peak of the student revolts that had just passed into history. He begins with the fantastic imagination of record-keeping and orgies:

> There are a number of records left from the 1968-69 campus struggles, but there aren't, as far as I have observed, any that deal with relations behind the barricades between the sexes . . . records really ought to have been written about relations between the sexes, and about their sexual lifestyle . . . I really want to believe that something happened behind those barricades.[47]

The importance of Ôshima's question and in reposing it now lies in the necessary interrogation of the sexual politics of utopia, or rather the politics of sexual utopia. If the gay world provides an option for Sayoko, what is the nature of this 'alternative' to patriarchy? What sex was had that Tokyo summer?

One of what is only a handful of recent Japanese films getting extensive film and video distribution overseas, *Okoge* and the Japanese films of the *gay boom* differ from other homosexually themed Asian films of the early nineties in their structuring of gender. The question of gender is central, yet at the same time ultimately dispensable. Where the female roles in Ang Lee's 1993 *The Wedding Banquet* or in Chen Kaige's 1993 *Farewell, My Concubine* are complications or elaborations of a central homosexual relationship, in *Okoge* and the other gay boom films it is the so-to-speak female adjunct about whom the film revolves. *Okoge* is about Sayoko's increasing participation in and acceptance by the gay world. After assisting Gô and Tochi with their trysting troubles, Sayoko plays matchmaker for Gô when the relation with Tochi falls victim to the homophobic pressures of Tochi's company life. Sayoko's efforts fail when the interests of Kurihara, the intended beau, are directed instead towards herself and culminate in his rape of her. The narrative resumes a year later when, burdened with the child she has had by Kurihara and harassed by mafia figures after the deadbeat dad, Sayoko returns to the gay district to find respite and ultimately protection. Gô and a band of drag queens fend off the mobsters, and Sayoko is ultimately forgiven her "stealing of Gô's man." The film concludes when Gô welcomes Sayoko and baby into his home, and now united, the new family strolls among the neon night life of Tokyo's gay bars and brothels.

(IN)DIFFERENT REPRESENTATION

As if the figure of homosexuality could not quite suffice, *Okoge*'s assumption of the mantle of discrimination is overdetermined by the suggestion of other discourses of discrimination and suffering. Gô's occupation as a leather craftsman suggests a person from a Discriminated Village (*hisabetsu buraku*) community, an amalgamated 'race/class' largely composed by the Meiji (1868-1912) government's "Emancipation Edict" of 1871. This amalgamation of "former outcasts" including butchers, leather-workers, and undertakers, all of whom had occupied liminal but vital positions in Edo (1600-1868) society, has led to struggles against the new forms of discrimination it has engendered. The struggles of the Discriminated Villagers have come in various forms of activism across the late nineteenth and twentieth centuries, including most prominently the Suiheisha (Levellers Association) of the early century and, in the post-war era, Buraku Liberation League. In contemporary Japan, leather-work, especially of the high-fashion sort that Gô pursues, is no longer a occupation of the Discriminated Villagers, nor does Gô depiction suggest other of the conventional, discriminatory tropes that are their representational indices in literature and film. This granted, the historical association with the leather trade still is well known and encourages a metonymical linking. More to the point, in a manner akin to current understandings of homosexuality, Discriminated Villager status is understood as something that resides invisibly on the body–hence its metaphors of secrecy and revelation and the related logic of the closet, which further overdetermine the reference.

An otherwise unintelligible jump-cut reinforces the language of 'race' and filth, suggested as we will shortly see by Sayoko's "filthy blood" and the later suggestion of Sayoko's American otherness.[48] In a scene that lacks immediate diegetic motivation and that might cursorily appear as simply filler, merely reinforcing our belief in the film's diegetic world, we see a shot of Sayoko at work, where she earns her living as a voice actress, in this case dubbing Japanese lines for a fantasy *anime* already subtitled in Chinese. Like the scene itself, the point of the lines that Sayoko and her female co-workers read aloud are initially unclear. "Give us your filthy blood and rotten flesh. Give them to us. Make yourself into a sacrifice." That this command is made to Sayoko's character becomes clear only when she responds in return with the quizzical line, "If you turn me into a tree, who will make the sacrifice?" But, Sayoko's performance is not heartfelt, and off-screen male voices demand she do her lines over again. The lights come up in the recording studio, where the swaggering male chief and the male technicians are lined up in a row, managing the production. This time putting more of herself into her performance, she repeats and continues, "If you turn me into a tree, who will make the sacrifice? You are the spirit of the outcast."[49] The extent to which Sayoko's body is abjected within the economy of the film and the degree to which its men metaphorically run the show is something the film will never admit. Uncannily here, as we will see later, the film has revealed its own critique, but safely and too early in the film for it to bear much meaning. Likewise, the extent of Sayoko's sacrifice and the degree to which she will need to give her very all in that performance are turning points that the film will not make clear until much further into the narrative. But, the immediate referent of who is outcast, but not sacrificed, becomes obvious with a scene change and abrupt cut to Gô who, in the next scene, is tricked into meeting a prospective bride, in an *omiai* setup, a situation that will prompt his coming out as gay to his family and provide one of the film's points of high drama.

While the 'racial' question is certainly an operative one within its economy, the film's predominant metonymy is that between gender and sexuality, where Sayoko figures the constraints faced by women, and Gô figures those faced by gay men. In this squeaky-clean division of labor (he does sexuality, she does gender), *Okoge* like the gay boom of which it is a microcosm, addresses its spectators by suggesting a female inability to achieve independence from a male system. Even the most careless viewer would be hard pressed not to understand *Okoge* as a commentary on the status of women. Sayoko is an unusual young woman, but unusual in the very categories that mark women's conventional social role as matron of the domestic space. Delighted to have the gay men cook for her, it is obvious that she hates to cook, and she announces to Gô that she is afraid even to turn on the gas stove. When Sayoko brings the couple back to her apartment the very first night, she hurriedly tries to cover up the clutter of empty milk cartons and fast-food wrappers that cover the table. After Sayoko rushes upstairs to lead the way, Gô and Tochi look at each other as much aghast at the mess they see as at the prospect of making love in someone else's domain. Urban, employed, and independently living alone, Sayoko represents already the dream of freedom from the traditional binds of money, family, marriage, or men. Moreover, Sayoko's autonomy is figured as modern and, through the common Japanese metaphor, as Western. Even her diet, influenced by modernity's personification–her American stepfather–presents a corresponding break with tradition: she drinks milk and does not eat rice.

Despite this "achievement," Sayoko is haunted by the past. Sayoko's freedom is encroached by history, where male violence is signaled through the figure of black-and-white flashbacks There, in front of a Christian church, Sayoko's American step-father entrusts her to a second foster family after his Japanese wife dies and he returns to the States. Sayoko's third home with its traditional decor, its working-class feel, and its in-house shop is suggestive of the old quarters of Tokyo's traditional *shitamachi*, and it is here that Sayoko is molested (possibly raped) by her new Japanese step-father, in a second over-determination, this time of memory, tradition, and male sexual privilege. Sayoko's memories come notably when her new gay friends are next door in the bedroom she has lent them, and the space of gay intimacy is offered by the film as antidote to conventional male privilege and aggression. Awakened by the terror of sexual abuse represented in her dream/memory, Sayoko gets up to peer in on the sleeping men. Her knotted brow softens (actress Shimizu Misa is known for her Frida-esque thick eyebrows), finally giving way to a peaceful visage that evidences the gay men's innate ability to disrupt the anxieties that emerge from the past, from poverty, and from heterosexual desire. Sleeping as they are, Sayoko's gay men need do nothing, save provide a fixed visibility that contests and dispels the anxieties symbolized filmically by the use of black-and-white film, in contrast to the rich, voluptuous colors of the bedroom scene.

The suggestion of gay male sexuality as an alternative to the demands of heterosexual *hommo-sexuality*, a term I shall explain shortly, is made more explicitly in an earlier scene. After meeting the two men again in the bar, Sayoko offers the closeted couple her cramped apartment. That night, Sayoko prepares for bed as the two begin their love-making. As she looks into a mirror applying cream to her face, each small noise from the men distracts her, bringing a knowing smile to her face. Sayoko is represented as deriving vicarious pleasure, and it is she who gets to "come" into the scene. Much as Sayoko was interpolated in the opening beach sequence into that littoral world of gay men through a technique of alternating shots of her pleasured face with the gay male bodies on display, in this five-minute sex scene, graphic matches and similar, but more extensive, crosscutting from Sayoko to the men make their sex her sex, their pleasure, narratively speaking, hers. Indeed when the sex culminates in a long-shot filmed from the ceiling, it is Sayoko's face that registers the jouissance. The money-shot is hers. Sayoko's leafing through a collection of Frida Kahlo self-portraits during this scene and the numerous bedroom portraits of Kahlo that oversee both Sayoko and the men's lovemaking make the point less than subtle. *Okoge* establishes a relation of corresponding persecution between the two men and the woman, only to break the parallel by highlighting the emancipatory potential of male-male erotics for the heterosexual protagonist (Photo 4).

Margaret Lindaeur has recently characterized the 1990's "fetishizing" of Frida Kahlo as an obsession whereby interpretation of Kahlo "crops political relevance" producing "a floating signifier . . . employed at the service of patriarchal prescription."[50] Transformed into a mere index of female suffering, Frida Kahlo's self-portrait, "as commodity serving a post-modern global economy, reinforces a 'mythic' time outside history and symbolizes a 'mythic' place outside politics."[51] In the following argument, I will reinscribe Sayoko within history and deconstruct the mythic place of male homosexuality that at once figures oppression and resistance, but that removes both Sayoko and gender to its own "'mythic' time." To do this, I will rely on the phantom character who has been present with us all along, present in the

PHOTO 4. Sayoko as corollary to the homosexual pair in *Okoge*

opening beach sequence, present in the critical bar scene, and present too in the dubbing studio: Okei, the lesbian. Writing not on male-male erotics, but instead on the prerequisites for lesbian representation, Teresa de Lauretis provides a theory of representation that can explain the confusion *Okoge* instantiates. In bringing de Lauretis' work to bear on *Okoge*, we can see how homophobia and misogyny are mutually reinforcing structures, and also how an anti-homophobic politics will fail unless it is equally able to engage questions of gender. "Lesbian representation, or rather its condition of possibility," writes de Lauretis, "depends on separating out the two contrary undertows that constitute the paradox of sexual (in)difference, on isolating but maintaining the two senses of homosexuality and hommo-sexuality." The theory of a difference that is ultimately indifferent, de Lauretis' articulation of sexual (in)difference describes *Okoge*'s mapping of sexuality and gender. While Sayoko's role within the film is precisely as woman, the articulation of gender is useful for the film only because it can be consistently recuperated by the indifferent male subject position that is offered to the film's spectators.

To understand this process, let us consider de Lauretis' theory of (in)difference. De Lauretis' notion of sexual (in)difference derives from Luce Irigaray's observation that "the feminine occurs only within models and laws devised by male subjects." Thus, *homosexuality*, the marker for lesbian and gay eroticisms, must at once be predicated upon and kept in tension against *hommo-sexuality*, where *hommo-* refers to the French word for man, namely *hommo*, a marker for the differentiating but indifferent male-based system of sexuality and gender.[52] Simple separation of gender and sexuality, or the privileging of the latter domain over the former, cannot offer lesbian representation an adequate alternative to *hommo-sexuality*, since the space of erotics is already written over with gendered categories. Conversely, lesbian representation cannot be understood as a further, teleological distinction within the category *woman*, whereby a politics of gender alone constitutes the sufficient break with *hommo-sexuality*. In other words, the erotic or sexual politics of homosexuality–cannot be separated from their inscription by the dominant male discourse–*hommo-sexuality*.[53] Lesbian representations appear in *Okoge* only under the mark of erasure–an issue to which I shall return later; nonetheless, de Lauretis' observations can inform a reading of the film that marks its privileging of the erotic politics of male homosexuality at the expense of a gendered politics. Certainly, *Okoge*'s model of female resistance, through an appropriation of gay politics and an assumption that these erotic politics have incorporated and superseded gender politics, fails to remember that the categories must always be kept in tension for fear of the return to *hommo-sexuality*.

THE HOMMO-SEXUAL WOMAN

Much as *Okoge*'s opening sequence directs the spectator's attention to Sayoko's uncanny ability to see the gay male world, so in converse, the film obscures a more likely alternative to the dilemmas of a young Japanese woman. Alluded to in the dialogue following the opening credits, Okei is Sayoko's co-worker at the animation dubbing agency. Important to the film's first scenarios but simultaneously concealed, Okei's presence is both necessitated by the film's sequential structure and threatening to its narrative coherence. Chance directs the initial, seaside meeting of Gô, Tochi, and Sayoko–a misguided family outing and an ensuing fallen can of beer to be returned across a tall embankment. Yet, their later Tokyo reunion is diegetically motivated only by Okei, a phantom character who helps Sayoko recoup the alien, but attractive possibilities witnessed at the littoral edge. Directly following the opening credits and title, Sayoko's AIDS-phobic, homophobic companion announces that she was invited to a 'homo bar' by Okei. If male homosexuality's position within the film is the subversion of patriarchy, its prerequisite is a fantastic distance from the social order. Sayoko cannot meet her gay friends at work or as neighbors; to do so would implicate homosexuality within the already domestic regimen and remove the pleasant perversion from its utopia.

My observation here is not a faulting of the film for the absence of a character, a project that relies on an essentialist concept of identity and representation. Rather, within the logic of *Okoge*'s narrative construction of gay (in)visibility and given the significance of the lesbian character in linking the space of the normal–the family and the workplace–with the utopic space of the gay bar, Okei's own absence is striking. In the context of the bar sequence, her inevitable occlusion is essential for the success of the narrative. Vexed over their inability to find a room for the night, Gô and Tochi discuss their misfortune until the waiter surprises them with two drinks sent from an off-screen "lady." When the camera imitates Gô's and Tochi's surprise and offers a shot now from the counter towards the rear of the bar, Sayoko and Okei are framed in a standard two-shot. However, this two-shot is marked by an uncanny dichotomy of light. Sayoko, to the left, is frontally lit, while in the frame's right Okei, darkly clothed, seated behind a flowery plant, and further hidden behind a large pair of sunglasses, is obscured by shadows diegetically motivated by the bar's tall pillars. Inviting herself to the counter, Sayoko abandons her lesbian scout whose disapproving mumbles are her first and nearly last dialogue. A subsequent three-shot from behind the counter frames Sayoko between the two men. Indeed, as Sayoko sits down on the stool the men have opened up between them, Sayoko's bright red dress eclipses from the camera's view the darkly clothed lesbian who remains in the background shadows. The shot continues for more than a minute with little glimpse of

Okei. Only when she finally leaves do we see Okei again, but now in a reverse shot that shows her back as she pays the bartender her bill, "I'm leaving." But, Sayoko is so absorbed by the men's stories of cruising that she ignores the exasperated Okei who intones Sayoko's name in irritation. In response to the lesbian's bad humor, the gay men suggest Okei leave Sayoko with them, a formula which Sayoko's nonchalant *bai-bai* confirms.

Okei suggests the rhetorical trope of ellipsis, the structured "suppression of [an] element necessary for a complete syntactic construction."[54] Okei's short presence on the screen–less than twenty seconds for the two scenes where she appears–is an important structural requirement of the film's logic. To ask, within *Okoge*'s double articulation of male homosexuality as both diegetic and extra-diegetic spectacle, of the other homosexuality–lesbianism–risks the very politics of visibility I critiqued in the previous section. Faulting the film for the absence of a character participates in the ultimately reductive politics of accumulation; an addition of missing figures cannot correct politi-co-social imbalances. More than a simple critique of the lesbian's absence, it is imperative to ask what the absent rendering of Okei enables. The lesbian figure must be obscured, for, within the film's transferal of gendered politics to sexual politics, there can be no place for the figure of a woman's woman. Performing what Biddy Martin has called "a tendency . . . to construct 'queer-ness' as a vanguard position that announces its newness and advance over an apparently superseded and now anachronistic feminism with its emphasis on gender," *Okoge* ascribes the constraints of gender onto the female, lesbian body. Martin criticizes precisely the emergence of a discourse that deploys the rhetoric of queer identities if that rhetoric conscripts feminism and the female body to the abject. In the context of Japan's gay boom, it is less "queerness" than male homosexuality itself which functions as avant-garde fashion. Still, Martin's observations are apt:

> I am worried about the occasions when anti-foundationalist celebra-tions of queerness rely on their own projections of fixity, constraint, or subjection onto a fixed ground, often on to feminism or the female body, in relation to which queer sexualities become figural, performa-tive, playful and fun. In the process, the female body becomes its own trap, and the operations of misogyny disappear from view.[55]

The female body functions most frequently in the film as the site of the repulsive. Gô's mother, for example, is troubled with a persistent bed-sore. Kojima Miyoko, a potential wife through a planned arranged marriage that Gô's coming out precludes, later returns in the film to torment Gô for his failed masculinity. Slowly removing her clothes in a medium close-up, Miyo-ko is unable to arouse Gô's interest except through shame. Back at the gay bar in the next scene, Gô agrees that he "couldn't do it, because she opened her legs too wide."

Given Sayoko's central role in the film, it remains surprising that both mainstream and gay/lesbian critics have paid so little attention to the element required for the film's narrative closure: the violent transformation of a heterosexual woman into a gay man. After Gô and Tochi part romantic ways, Gô hosts a party for Sayoko and his gay friends. In an amusing scene where Gô's mother realizes that Sayoko is not a man-in-drag but a 'real' woman, the mother drags Sayoko to another room where she recounts her own peculiar etiology for her son's homosexuality–a rusty knife during pregnancy. Meanwhile, the boys in the next room are themselves heatedly arguing the nature/ nurture debate. But the palpable animosity among the boys melts into a resounding chorus of laughter when Sayoko and the mother peer from the door to suggest a logical conclusion in a society of compulsory marriage of the *okoge*-gay male relation: the marriage of Gô and Sayoko. The party scene ends with a tight close-up of Sayoko's face, hurt and humiliated by the cackling men about her. This placement of Sayoko and the mother in one room and the gay men in another effects a movement contrary to the metonymic architecture of the sex scenes. The latter scenes which occur in Sayoko's apartment highlight the possibility of Sayoko's interpellation as woman into the adjacent, elysian space of gay male intimacy. Instead, the party scene in Gô's apartment underlines the difference that must separate Sayoko as woman from the freedom and play that gay men signify.

A cut from Sayoko's hurt face to the subsequent scene in the gay bar suggests a diegetic resolution of the problem. Sayoko is waiting for Gô at the bar where they were first reacquainted, her face tight as if still angry from the humiliation of the party episode. Although the cut from the previous scene suggests that a narrative resolution of Sayoko's anger will ensue and the return to the bar suggests a dissolution of the terms of their initial meeting, spectatorial attention is diverted by the now single Gô's desire for a man at the back of the bar. In an bizarre scene lacking narrative motivation, Sayoko takes it upon herself to arrange this new affair, and invites the man for a drink. In subsequent scenes, Sayoko maneuvers for a resolution of Gô's desire, but when the possible boyfriend turns out to be not simply straight but a rapist, Sayoko is victim.

In this rape scene, memories of her childhood molestation are carried to a violent outcome. She resists the attack, only to be slapped into submission. There, supine on the bed, Sayoko becomes unresponsive, falling into a trance-like state where she invites the rapist, Kurihara. "Yes, you are, aren't you. You're the man Gô is pining for. Imagine I'm a man, imagine I'm Gô." Then, Sayoko proclaims a love whose subject does not become apparent until halfway through its profession: "Love you . . . really wanting you . . . Gô is

. . . so it's okay . . . it's okay." Operating through a metonymic shift of attention from the tension between Sayoko and the gay men to Sayoko's usefulness as agent for their desire, *Okoge*, some may argue, avoids the crucial antagonism between the concerns of women and those of gay men. But, this critique misses the regressive function of gay (in)visibility reproduced in *Okoge* and, by synecdoche here, characteristic of the gay boom's manufacture of a falsely progressive, utopian trajectory.

The impossibility of the *okoge*'s position as panacea to the confines of *hommo-sexuality*, the dilemma demonstrated in the party scene and source of Sayoko's anger, is not avoided or dispensed with. Rather, it is resolved by the diegetic identification of the *okoge* with the homosexual male, Sayoko's transformation into Gô, into a gay man.[56] While pain first marks Sayoko's acquiescence to the rape, her face later suggests a peaceful gratification reinforced by the flute-like music that has accompanied the previous gay sex scenes. Represented now as deriving pleasure from the rape, Sayoko is shown in tightly framed close-up of head with her eyes directed dreamily off-screen. Two diegetic inserts, suggestive of Sayoko's imagination, follow the close-up, the first a gauzy, filtered image of Gô emerging from the water at the gay beach from the film's opening. His arm extended, Gô's figure breaks the cinematic fourth wall as he gazes towards the camera, towards Sayoko, and towards the spectator. Gô beckons with the slow movement of his hand, further confirming the link between his body and the spectator this side of the silver screen. The second insert is of the fast-turning pages from the Frida Kahlo book that Sayoko had perused during the gay sex scenes: the mutilated, pierced, and disfigured body of Frida Kahlo. While the first insert beckons, the second refuses: the pages turn so quickly that the spectator cannot absorb the rapidly changing images. If Kahlo articulates the bind that constrains and that rapes, its false resolution lies in a displaced identification with the gay man; during the rape scene, Sayoko becomes little more than his proxy. Of course, a further implication of this discovery is that of the homophobia that underwrites much of the film. If Gô and Sayoko have been amalgamated into one position, then the rape scene can equally be read as a male rape scene, where it is Kurihara who is violating Gô. In fact, the film goes so far as to suggest this possibility in the racetrack scene directly before the rape. Sayoko, knowing that Kurihara was formerly in the Self-Defense Forces and hopeful that Kurihara will respond to Gô's desire, naively asks the vendor where they are having a snack whether there are homosexuals in the force. Kurihara overhearing her question responds affirmatively, telling her that he and his friends had raped an over-achiever in the force. Here the film plays directly into the audience's homophobic desire to see the male rape, an image that has a ready made precedent in the 1977 Nikkatsu *roman porno*, *Monzetsu!! Dondengaeshi* (*Swooning in Agony!! Tables Turned*, dir. Kuma-

shiro Tatsumi), the story of a young businessman, a Tokyo University graduate, who is trapped and raped by a pimp, eventually competing with the
pimp's girlfriend for sexual attention.

GENDER SUPERSEDED?

In 1970, Ôshima commented on the power of the weeklies and the
women's-oriented women's press:

> One might say that the women's magazines and the popular weeklies
> have been a powerful force when it comes to bringing out new demands
> by revealing and publicizing those of the weak. Of course, this is not to
> overlook the achievements of the many artists and scholars who have
> written about sex, but it is still the editors of the women's magazines
> and the popular weeklies who have made the most significant contribu-
> tion. To put it jokingly, you might say that they have tried so hard to see
> sexual issues from the point of view of the powerless that you almost
> think that they themselves have become sexually powerless.[57]

Ôshima identifies the tabloid-like fascination with the anti-conventional that
weekly and women's magazines held in the 1960s and still hold today. Ôshima's remarks, however, cannot be considered outside his comments on sexual poverty discussed earlier. In foregrounding the positions of women, the
women's weeklies direct attention to issues of social, sexual oppression, but
offer only "technical escape routes . . . that have no essential power." As long
as they do not directly question what Ôshima calls "the myth of sexual
exclusiveness and possessiveness" or what we might call *hommo-sexuality*,
they offer no real alternative.

As I have indicated earlier, the gay boom in its explicit imaging of male
homosexuality within the socio-political rubric of public (in)visibility
emerges in February 1991 with publication of a special edition of the
women's fashion magazine, *Crea*. Many *Crea* readers would recognize in the
special issue's title *Gei runêsansu* [*Gay Renaissance*] reference to an earlier
tradition of representing male homosexuality. From a context the readers
would recognize from their youth, '*runêsansu*' is a term commonly used to
signal the apogee of *shojo manga*, young girls' comics, that began in the
1970s with the genre's revitalization by the introduction of male homosexual
themes regularly shown in highly aestheticized, effeminate images, and portrayed in exclusively homosexual worlds.[58] That *shojo manga*, a form of
women's writing since the early twentieth-century, would reach its flowering
with the introduction of male homosexuality in the 1970s has not received
sufficient critical analysis in English, but the recent work by Matsui Midori

and Aoyama Tomoko has begun that investigation. Matsui astutely observes that these earlier representations of male homosexuality are part of young girls' "rejection of their sexuality as a commodity in the patriarchal structure" and a linking to a fictitious character that "embodying the principle of pure play (fantasy), contests the socially determined definitions and parameters of sexuality." (179) Likewise, Aoyama finds the *shojo manga*'s male homosexual characters "critics of patriarchy."[59]

In the late 1980s and early 1990s, *shojo manga* increasingly deployed the trope of male homosexuality in forms of pastiche, parody and dystopia, a movement that is commonly interpreted in terms of the trope's overuse and slow demise. Precisely at this juncture, women's magazines began marketing the gay boom to a slightly older generation, indeed a generation that had grown up reading the same *manga* authors who began the introduction of male homosexuality into the genre, writers such as Moto Hagio, Ôshima Yumiko, and Takemiya Keiko. In the recent analyses of Japanese popular culture, both *shojo manga* and girls' and women's magazines are discussed specifically in terms their gendered and sexual scope. Frequently however, *manga* are assigned to the realm of "fantasy" and "escape" while the magazines are considered in sociological terms, providing "reinforcement and direction in the area of sexuality."[60] This disjunction between fantasy and reality which rests upon the realist conventions of representation that inform the different representational values of comics and glossy magazines supports the gay boom's own rhetoric of social novelty. Indeed, few will consider the gay boom films within the same discursive field as the women's magazines, let alone the caricatured *manga*, for such a consideration would unsettle the truth value of the gay boom as authentic representation of gay men.

Just as the 1988 film *Summer Vacation 1999* (dir. Kaneko Shusuke), a tale of love and jealousy among four schoolboys each played by a girl, is conspicuous in its cinematic realization of Moto Hagio's 1974 *manga*, *Tôma no shinzô* (*The Heart of Tôma*), so too a film like *Okoge* must be considered in its genealogical relation to the women's weeklies that have foregrounded male homosexuality during the gay boom. In the movement from phantasmatic identifications of *manga* to the realist conventions that govern both magazines and film, the relation of women to male homosexuality has been literalized. The position of the *okoge* has emerged within the last three years as a focal point for much recent Japanese attention to sexuality and pseudofeminist consciousness. While the term *okoge* has long existed in Japanese gay slang, it is only recently that the word has seen a precipitous rise in its fortunes.[61] In the same period, as the *shojo manga* faces "the exhaustion of the boy-boy comic as a signifier for the girl's imaginary subjectivity" and the "literalization characterizing the works of major writers," the potentially

subversive phantasmatic relation between the girl reader and her homosexu-
ally-inclined boy protagonists is repressively literalized into a utopian social
and political identification between the fag-hag and her gay male friends, an
identification that is transcribed within realist conventions.

In the last five years, Japanese female consumers have been offered Tsuka
Kōuhei's *The Story of a Father and Youth's Love Affair (Seishun tousan koi
monogatari)* (1988), Hiruma Hisao's novel *Yes ●Yes ●Yes* (1989), Fushimi
Noriaki's *Private Gay Life* (1990) and Yoshimoto Banana's *Kitchen (Kitchen,*
1988). More than in any single text, however, representations of homosexuality have made their most frequent showing in the more lowbrow, glossy
pages of the women's press. Enthusiastic and curious, women's magazines
such as *Crea, More,* and *Peach* establish gay male sexuality, its vocabularies,
its customs, and its problems, as a vogue of import, and embrace homosexuality in a manner that makes North American equivalents like *Seventeen,
Glamour,* or *Vogue* seem sexually staid. *Crea's* 1991 declaration of a 'Gay
Renaissance' included forty-eight pages of text in a women's magazine that
devotes the rest of its pages largely to women's beauty concerns.

The women's magazines capitalize upon the specific social configurations
that relations between gay men and presumed heterosexual women may
suggest. These representations stress a female desire for male intimacy without the social conditions on which that intimacy is offered–as wife or as
whore. In *Crea, More,* and *Peach,* a common element is the emphasis on
bedtime pleasure; illustrations in the magazines show gay men and women in
bed together, and commonly highlight the physical relationship. A *Crea*
article noted the reactions of one woman:

> When the two of us snuggle up together, there is no disgusting feeling.
> It feels just like petting my cat.[62]

Exemplary for the genre as a whole, this comment underlines sexual contact
with heterosexual men as potentially 'disgusting.' Male advances, the threat
of sexual violence, and potential loss of virginity each disappear when a gay
man replaces the heterosexual in bed. Furthermore, sexuality in the form of
the gay man itself loses its frightening potentials, becoming as domesticated
as a family pet.

The magazines stress the social and political implications of the *okoge*'s
relation to gay men. The opening passage in *Crea's* special feature cited the
unique relationship between gay men and women and notes compelling
potentials:

> Those so-called 'gays' are good at the arts, as well as delicate and
> somewhat malicious. Why then, when we talk to them, is it so very
> reassuring? . . . A free spirit that just cannot be had talking to boring,

straight men. We really want to learn more from this fuzzy sex. The message from "these men who have surpassed women" is both radical and deep.[63]

In this nexus of the specifically female genre of women's magazines and male homosexuality, we encounter the *okoge*, the young woman for whom an interest in and relations with gay men are paramount.

We are now paying attention to that curious relation between "men" and women that can never develop into romance. What kind of relationship can exist between us and these "men" but not men, the gays?[64]

And, as if answering the question that this opening phrase introduces, the article's caption reads, "There can be a deep relation with women where 'sex' drops out." Notably, the word for sex [*sei*] here is the kanji for gender and sexuality, but through the use of *furigana* or reading marks, the reader is instructed to read the term as the English 'sekkusu.' Much as the female reader can create intimate male-female relations where sex is not demanded, so too can she by extension create male-female relations where 'gender' can drop out as well. In this end, the genre continually stresses a didactic goal. Each of the magazines features pages in encyclopedic format that list essential books, films, fashions, and trends. Another common element is the instructive use of footnotes used to explicate, this time in dictionary format, various important slang terms from the Japanese gay community. While elements do function as part of a reality effect, they are such a persistent element that a pedagogic purpose must be assumed. In sum, the magazines instruct young women in the ways of the *okoge*.

Okoge, the film, repeats a similar development in the logic of the women's magazines: that the relation between gay men and straight women offers a possibility of superseding gender categories. A *More* writer comments, "[T]he borderline between man and woman is disappearing."[65] An interview with Fushimi Noriaki, gay author of the recently popular *Private Gay Life*, locates the gay movement and its relationship to women within a pseudo-feminist agenda. Fushimi is quoted:

Fundamentally what I'm trying to say is that we don't need that border between men and women. Women will well understand when I say that the traditional framework in which men were considered stronger and smarter is beginning recently to break down. Now that women are competing directly with men's abilities and winning, the meaning of that frame has disappeared.[66]

That Fushimi directs his comments and even his book at a female audience is significant. *Private Gay Life*, his compendium of notes concerning gay male lifestyles, sexuality, and sex practices, elicits this comment from the interviewer, "In fact, it seems that this book was written with the female reader consciously in mind." Fushimi replies:

> That's right, and what's more, it seems that it's nearly only women who will buy my book. Well sure, it's also selling among the gay people of Shinjuku 2-chome, but . . . (laugh) . . . The publisher that is putting my book out deals right from the beginning with a lot of books in the feminist lineage, as they were talking about viewing male/female sexuality and relationships from a new flank, in other words from the gay position . . .

Fushimi's statement highlights the conflation of consumer forces, feminism, and a gay subject position. As Fushimi's *Private Gay Life* and the plethora of articles in the women's press evidence, a gay subject position is metaphorically up for sale.

This commodification of a gay male subject position appeals to young female consumers for its offering of a free sexual play. Yet, it is offered under the conditions that they dispose of gendered distinctions, or of sexual difference, in embrace of the *hommo-sexual* utopia. As Martin notes, "Queer or perverse desires do not seem very transformative if the claims made in their name rely on conceptions of gender and psychic life as either so fluid as to be irrelevant or so fixed and punitive that they have to be escaped."[67] In the February 1991 "Gay Renaissance" issue of *Crea* introduced earlier, popular writer, Hashimoto Osamu proposes an equivalence of women and gay men. "The truth of women today is the same as that of gay men . . . and though it would perhaps be a jump to say that's why they are discriminated against, it would be right on target to describe their attraction to gay men this way. More than anything, gay men are just like them . . ."[68] Such reasoning underscores the film's falsely utopian agenda, and highlights the folk etymology used to explain the *okoge*. *Koge*, from *kogeru* (to burn), refers to the blackened (often delicious) rice left at the bottom of a pot or *kama*, the latter colloquialism referring to transvestite male homosexuals in particular, but which functions derogatorily for all male homosexuals. *Kama*, a term which can be used alternately to refer to a pot for rice cooking or to the crater of a volcano, derives its pejorative usage of *okama* for the homosexual from the obvious attachments to opening or receptivity that both dictionary meanings suggest. The term emphasizes the male homosexual's anal receptivity and thus the vernacularly assumed feminity that transvestitism supposes. *Okoge* exists solely as a function of the semiotically privileged male term, for without the *kama* there can be no *koge*. In the *okama/okoge* pair, the biologically male *okama* conflates vagina and anus to represent concurrently both femininity and male anality. What position, in this schema, is left the *okoge* save that blackened matter to be discarded, namely shit? And what value is there in this "casting of sexuality against gender" as that realm "which exceeds, transgresses, or supersedes gender"?[69] Only the liberationist teleology that is, in the final analysis, that which traps, which limits, and which conceals.

In my argument, I have detailed the counterfeit transcendence of gendered discrimination through the violent nullification of that originally sexual difference in the marketing of male homosexuality as a form of resistance for young, assumedly heterosexual Japanese women. As Judith Butler writes, "If sexual relations cannot be reduced to gender positions . . . it does not follow that an analysis of sexual relations apart from an analysis of gender relations is possible."[70] I have attempted to bridge feminist concerns and the emergent discourse of Japanese male homosexuality that has followed in the wake of the gay boom. As my argument suggests, the disciplinary division of gender and sexuality further supports the patriarchal structuring of knowledge, and repeats, in effect, the gay boom's own spectacular demands of its transparent representation.

From Stuart Hall and from Antonio Gramsci, we know that hegemony works best through the manufacture of its own critiques. Far less than an alternative for the young woman, these "escapes out" are farcical; styling itself as radical, the (in)visibility of the gay boom, its insistence on its own envisioning, instead removes positions for resistance by substituting a commoditized form of opposition that in function underwrites the binds of virginity, male pleasure, and male dominance that tie the female consumer to *hommo-sexuality*. Male homosexuality, in this schema, serves neither gay male nor feminist revisionings of social systems, but the proprietary standards of female virginity. The films of the gay boom cinema at once insist upon a homosexuality that is impotent and upon the repeated penetration of their female consumers. In the closing scene of *Okoge*, Sayoko, Gô, and the child that is the offspring of her rape walk the neon-lit streets of Shinjuku's Ni-chome. Film scholar and critic Satô Tadao writes of the gay boom cinema, "In Japan, where the performance of the *onnagata* has been praised in kabuki and in new *shimpa* drama and where male *enka* singers can imitate female coquetry without anyone batting an eye, homosexuality has not been made into the target of persecution as it has in the United States. This fact lends a light-hearted touch to films of this kind in Japan, and they stand in striking contrast to this sort of film in America which all to quickly becomes heavy and serious."[71] As an Anglo-American, I have yet to learn this mobile, light sense of Japanese humor. Still, I suspect that the ticket to Ni-chome and its sexual utopia that this kind of new family must buy, namely a sexuality that obscures women and that makes gender play a bit part, comes with a price that is too high to pay.

GENERIC REVERBERATIONS

More than a phenomenon limited to *Okoge*, the misogynous construction of a *hommo-sexual* woman is refigured across other Japanese films of the early nineties, two notable examples being *Twinkle* and *800 Two-Lap Runners*. In the 1992 *Twinkle* (dir. Matsuoka Jôji), the triangular ordering of female lead and gay male couple is repeated in protagonist Shôko's placement in a liaison between her newly betrothed husband, Mutsuki, and his university student lover, Kon. Unlike *Okoge* where the homosexual characters publicly defy the traditional familial system, *Twinkle* suggests a mutual complicity at both the familial and interpersonal levels. The arranged marriage between Mutsuki and Shôko is suggested as a duplicitous exchange of damaged goods, where one family tries to pass off a homosexual son, the other a mentally unstable, alcoholic daughter, as befitting spousal material. By revealing their anomalies at their first private meeting, Shôko and Mutsuki find in each other mutually unobtrusive possibilities. This motif of exchange underlines the film's narrative logic which relates homosexuality and heterosexuality metonymically rather than metaphorically. Where *Okoge* substitutes Sayoko's problems as a woman with a solution of homosexuality and substitutes redemptively Tokyo's gay world for Sayoko's straight one. *Twinkle* resolves Shôko's dilemmas as woman by metonymically shifting them from a woman's problems in a patriarchal society to the more readily resolved, narratively at least, problem of homosexual progeny.

Like *Okoge*'s Sayoko, *Twinkle*'s central figure, Shôko, is presented as a modern, independent and free-spirited woman, successful in her career as a freelance Italian translator. Yet, again like Sayoko, Shôko operates under the mark of male encroachment: while Sayoko's fortunes required a resolution of her history at the hands of men, Shôko's battles are more solitary. Later understood as her release from hospital care, the film's opening sequence is set in a doctor's office, where Shôko's condition of *jōchō fuantei*, or "emotional instability" is declared no longer chronic and easily remediable by a good man and marriage. The succeeding scenarios portray the death of Shôko's childhood dog and Shôko's entry into *omiai*, the system of arranged dating and marriage, and are cross-cut with images, 'curious' for Japanese film, of the two men cooking and cleaning; this cross-cutting suggests a relation between her apparent regret at the loss of youth and its freedoms and the odd space of male homosexual domesticity. Indeed, the film's publicity as a "bizarre, queer *menage-à-trois*" ("fushigi kimyo na sankaku ren-ai") does not quite capture the film's explicit preference for the domestic than the romantic or emotional.

Typical of the characterization of Japan's youth as a *dorai* lot, "dry" in the clinical, calculated and mechanical emotions they maintain for each other, the characters center the film's question as specifically a social, structural one, not one of passion. Indeed, it is her alcoholism that marks at once her resistance to sociality itself and her desire to maintain her independence from familial demands. Her propensity for drunken stupor seems greatest at "family" restaurants or after fulfilling her new chores as dutiful wife; she collapses at one point with the iron she uses to warm her husband's bed in hand. Her anti-social maladies of alcoholism and melancholy, a disease where "something's wrong with my heart," lay the ground for the film's central question of Shôko's happiness. Unlike Sayoko, who derived all emotional and sexual satisfaction vicariously from Tochi and Goh's relation, Shôko is recognizably unfulfilled. Dissatisfaction is figured, though, not as an absence of a meaningful relationship or of female pleasure, but through a desire for children that cannot be consummated. Towards the film's resolution, Shôko approaches a doctor to ask whether she could be inseminated simultaneously with Mutsuki's and Kon's sperm in order to have "everyone's child." While the possibility of Shôko's sexuality is displaced onto a question of reproduction, the film replaces Shôko's dilemmas as a woman within a society oppressive of women with the standard burden for women, reproduction. But, here, of course, reproduction is in the service of the male homosexual's demand for familial, social convention.

In the 1994 release, *800 Two Lap Runners* (dir. Hiroki Ryûichi), teen idol Matsuoka Shunsuke plays Hirose Kenji, a dedicated short-distance runner who comes to terms with the death of his teammate and lover Aihara (Hakamada Yoshihiko). While the former films suggest themselves as social-conscience films, however banally, *Runners* makes no such pretensions. Irrecoverable for a lineage of 'gay film,' *800 Two Lap Runners* differs from *Okoge* and *Twinkle* in its relegation of homosexuality to the status of emotional trauma and pathology. Nonetheless, the film relies considerably upon the same conflation of homosexual male and straight female that mark the former films. Unlike *Okoge* and *Twinkle* where the gay sex is visually explicit, the homosexual relation between Hirose and Aihara is distanced through its position as memory. Aihara appears in the film consistently as ghost on the track field or mirage in the shower room, or is figured through such icons as photographs, binoculars, and clothes. Specifically, in *Runners'* shower scene, Aihara approaches the naked Hirose from behind, and as the boys begin to touch, the scene loses its realistic shower-setting. Through use of steam effects and close-up framing, the shot approximates a limbo effect, a cinematic device where the background extends limitlessly and the set loses defining characteristics. Limbo, too, is precisely the status of homosexuality here: a dream-like state that confines the principal character. A jump-cut guarantees Hirose is wakened from his homosexual reverie; the narrative's unfolding ensures his return to the heterosexual norm.

For the most part, however, *Runners* examines Hirose's attempt to resume his relation to the dead Aihara through Aihara's former girlfriend, Yamaguchi Kyôko (Kawai Miwako). Kyôko appears on the track field as Hirose contemplates his friend, and later surprises Hirose as he trains at a beach where he and Aihara had regularly practiced. Kyôko replaces Aihara, the lost sexual object, at the specific moments of mourning, and instead of helping Hirose accept the loss of Aihara, Kyôko comes to figure Aihara himself. Like the sexually molested Sayoko of *Okoge* or the alcoholic Shôko in *Twinkle*, Kyôko, too, is under the mark of infirmity; within the economy of sports that drives this film, she is a cripple. Living alone in a seaside home, her interactions are limited to those who will come visit her remote, asocial locale. Thus not a complete woman physically or socially, Hirose is able to consummate the affair but, even then, only through a determined glance at Aihara's portrait which Kyôko places on a bedside table.

In a complication of the genre, Hirose's relation to the dead Aihara through the latter's female stand-in is narratively paired with a heterosexual relation between Hirose's track competitors Nakazawa Ryūji (Nomura Yūjin) and Ida Shôko (Arimura Tsugumi). Ryūji from industrial Kawasaki and Shôko from American base-town Yokosuka are figured as working class youth for whom running is an opportunity to exceed the limits of their origins. In the film's opening scenes, as Ryūji is caught having sex with a high-school girl in the school's gymnasium and subsequently reprimanded, homosexuality is marked as incompatible with his rough, working class style. Brought before the school's principal, who remarks on Ryūji's "good body," Ryūji retorts, "I'm not that kind of guy." The value of the evolving romance between Ryūji and Shôko becomes apparent when, at the film's climax, Shôko's working-class heterosexuality is deployed to 'cure' the bourgeois Hirose's homosexuality. By sleeping with Shôko, Hirose is able to assume heterosexual desire, and return to his class. Aihara now a distant memory to him, Hirose is able to visit Kyôko within conventional heterosexual confines. Amidst scenes of a seaside town, the *hommo-sexual* woman is returned to her proper femininity. When Hirose announces to Kyôko, "I've come to visit you," she skeptically retorts "You mean Aihara." The film closes as Hirose confirms his heterosexuality and restores to her conventional value of woman, "No, you."

"QUEER WIND FROM ASIA"

The July 5th cover of *The Nation* dubbed 1993 the year of "A Queer Nation." In a tidy metonymy, critic Lawrence Chua's article within that special issue designated the same year the arrival of a "Queer Wind from Asia."[72] We can mark the year not by the arrival of Asian queer film *per se*, but rather for the advent of Asian queer film within the North American cinematic lexicon. Asian films on homosexual themes are certainly not new; nor are they new to North American audiences. In previous years and decades, *Khush, Summer Vacation 1999, Funeral Parade of Roses, Macho Dancer,* and *Merry Christmas, Mr. Lawrence* among others have shown in extensive albeit metropolitan screenings. What marks the early nineties from former years is the very number of films and videos now available and the attention given them. Three feature-length films–*Okoge* (Japan), *The Wedding Banquet* (Taiwan), and *Farewell, My Concubine* (Hong Kong)–appeared with much success in the U.S. market in 1993 alone; film festivals, both gay/lesbian and otherwise, featured numerous smaller productions. Popular and critical reviews began considering these films in relation to each other, with particular concern for common, generic characteristics.[73] Put otherwise, the early nineties conspicuously instituted Asian film as a new *genre* within the North American taxonomy of queer cinema. At least in the case of the recent Japanese 'queer' cinema, this movement of genre within a logic of a queer cinema and that cinema's regrettably frequent privileging of sexuality *tout court* have occluded other critical axes necessary for an understanding of these texts. Eager to embrace the feature-length gay male films that emerged from the gay boom, this *genrification* ignores the *gendered* complexities that explain their commercial success in Japan. By understanding these films predominantly as representations of Japanese gay men, the inclusion of the gay boom films within North American genre of Asian queer film effectively conceals the reactionary politics of gender which motivated their appearance in late-century Japan.

Given the success of the gay boom of films like *Okoge,* the emergence of the vocal OCCUR activism in Tokyo, and the current cachet, tied to economic ascendancy, for things Japanese, Japan has emerged in a North American imagination as the leader of a new Asian queer sensibility. It is little surprise, then, that this image is carried into film criticism. With the arrival of Asian queer film en masse in 1993 and the obvious insufficiency of a term like 'Asian queer film,' the convenient, uncritical tropes of nationhood and modernization began to dominate generic discussions. While the lines of cinematic production and capital are commonly oblivious to state borders, this film criticism has insisted on the nation as a main organizing trope.[74]

At 1993's San Francisco International Lesbian and Gay Film Festival, for example, where Asian film was one of three film categories that necessitated their own introductory essays, guest curator Paul Lee repeated traditional, national distinctions by contrasting the festival's Chinese-language films with their Japanese counterparts. In his introductory essay for the festival's Asian programs, Lee opposes the Japanese *Okoge, Twinkle,* and *Slight Fever of a Twenty-Year Old* (dir. Hashiguchi Ryōsuke, 1993), to the Chinese *The East is Red, The Silent Thrush,* and *Farewell, My Concubine.* For Lee, the former are 'brash and modern' films for which "Japan was heralded on the international film festival circuit as the leader of a new wave of Asian queer cinema." The Japanese films, set in the present day and concerning themselves overtly with the problems of sexuality and discrimination, are understood as progressive and political. In contrast, the Chinese films, historically and artistically circumscribed and without the "aggressive imagery of queer politics" that the Japanese films purportedly offer, are able "to penetrate the narrow minds of the easily offended" through a subversive subtlety. The danger of an uncritical borrowing of a national analogy becomes apparent when we consider the metaphor's own historical insistence in Lee's usage. Lee's construction of filmic difference along national axes of modernity/ tradition and aggressivity/subtlety, where Japan occupies the former, masculine half of each pair, and China the feminine latter, is disturbing in its identity with an early twentieth-century logic that led Japanese combat boots to the Chinese mainland. Moreover, the logic repeats the tropes of modernization examined in the previous section, but this time within the scope of Asia where Japan mobilizes in its role as proxy for the West.[75]

This modernizing paradigm of national dominance coupled with the closeting, orientalist celebration of Asian male homosexuality's (in)visibility encourages the blinding effect that deracinates the recent Japanese gay cinema from its context of the gay boom. Even within Lee's unpalatable construction of a masculine Japan and a feminine China, there are hints of the metaphor's untenability. Lee can trace a common theme in the Chinese productions, "playful genderbending amidst romantic entanglements in single gender troupes of traditional opera companies," but omits to note the thematic unity of the eminently more popular Japanese films: the gendered relations between heterosexual women and gay men. Instead, Lee avoids any substantial discussion of the recent Japanese films to cite an older Japanese gay cinema–*With Beauty and Sorrow* and *The Funeral Parade of Roses*–as "poignant and powerful today." With the cinematic and political complexity that marks, for example, the latter 1969 film, many of us will concur with Lee's preference for Japanese gay films of decades past. Still, Lee's rush to embrace an older Japanese gay cinema belies his own discomfort with the recent productions of the gay boom that he perhaps was burdened with championing.

That the gay boom might exist more at the level of commercial and media representations than at the level of individual gay subjects has caused one scholar to note the incommensurate relation between an efflorescence of popular images of male homosexuality and the stark absence of a broad, specifically visible homosexual community. In an essay on the "New World of 'Gay Asia,'" Dennis Altman notes the emergence in Asia of gay male identities based on urban, regularly Westernized notions of a male homosexual subject. Focusing on the industrialized and industrializing nations of Southeast and Northeast Asia, Altman finds in three nations, Japan included, exceptions to the broad cultural brush strokes he paints. Altman contrasts an 'open' media and a 'closed' community when he compares Japan to the rest of Asia:

> It is worth noting the slow development of a Western style gay world in Japan, Taiwan, and Korea–in Japan despite both extensive American influence and a considerable commercial world, it does not appear that a large open community is developing despite recent media interest in gay issues.[76]

The problem Altman identifies, however, is less what we are led to suspect–some psycho-social retardation on the part of Japanese gay men–than the discursive construction of the 'open media' against which Altman measures Japanese gay men. Altman's disjunctive proposition naturalizes two relations, first between media and its subject and second between (in)visibility and identity. Ultimately, Altman's statement intends that Japan's more-than-considerable commercial world, its American influence, and its media attention to gay issues ought to mirror, if not produce, an open community. Some cultural anomaly, the reasoning suggests, disturbs what would be an otherwise transparent relation between gay representations and gay identity.

Instead of paradox, the gay boom's success in the commercial market points to its easy amalgamation within the socially constrictive paradigms of social relations that commercialized representations necessarily recoup. Altman's assumption of visibility's transparent relation to its subject operates within the same dialectic that motivates the truth value of the closet's invisibility. As Sedgwick's analysis maintains, it ". . . is *the spectacle of the homosexual closet* as a presiding guarantor of rhetorical community, of authority–someone else's authority–over world-making discursive terrain that extends vastly beyond the ostensible question of the homosexual."[77] Leaving aside Sedgwick's implicit and aggrandizing claims to the "world-making terrain" of the logic she identifies, we can pursue her suspicion that homosexual visibility is more the production of a patriarchal system than any purportedly transparent expression of Japanese gay men themselves. One is left to surmise that the visibility at stake is certainly not that of gay men, but rather the (in)visibility of the closet that demands an incessant and ultimately obscuring restaging.

Unusual in one aspect, Altman's argument avoids the frequent placement of Japan at the vanguard of Asia's 'queer liberation.' Yet, the modernization trope still regulates his logic. Altman rewrites the oriental closet as a parallel movement from tradition to modernity and from gender to sexuality. He characterizes the "new world of gay Asia" by the development of identities based in sexual configurations that simultaneously historicizes 'traditional' gender identities. "In general the new 'gay' groups reject a common identity with more traditional identities, and define themselves as contesting sexual rather than gender norms."[78] While Altman is careful to remark that gender is not insignificant, his essay sunders gender from sexuality in a move that relegates gendered concerns to a significance that is solely historical in light of the globalism he advances. Altman may be correct in labeling the construction of social identities around sexuality as "a distinctly modern invention." Yet the logic, perhaps unwittingly, redeploys the tropes he identifies. His celebration of the movement from gender-based identities to sexually-defined identities warrants skepticism for its *a priori* acceptance of their partition. For Altman, the "sexual identity politics" that characterize the 'new gay Asia'

> grow out of modernity but also show the way to post-modernity, because they both strengthen and interrogate identity as a fixed point and a central reference. The claiming of lesbian/gay identities in Asia or in Latin America is as much about being Western as about sexuality . . . [79]

If an Asian gay identity lies in the oscillation between sexuality and the West, one is left to wonder about the status of gender that Altman is too quick to ascribe to the traditional Asia that purportedly has not embraced the West's modernity. Altman's logic locates under the one sign of "gay Asia's New World" the terms of Westernization, modernization, and sexuality. By implication, the logic places gender within the scope of a pre-or non-industrialized Asia, something that must be shed, embellished, or surpassed in order to attain the sexual liberation that the West steadfastly promises.

Clearly, what needs iteration in this troubled topography is the danger evident in any erasure of gender, whether under the rubric of history or geography. Following her work in *Alice Doesn't,* Teresa de Lauretis highlights the importance of gender in the counter-hegemonic analyses of the social production of sexualities.

> [T]o deny gender, first of all, is to deny the social relations of gender that constitute and validate the sexual oppression of women; and second, to deny gender is to remain "in ideology," an ideology which (not coincidentally if, of course, not intentionally) is manifestly self-serving to the male-gendered subject.[80]

De Lauretis' observation points to the failure faced by many analyses of sexuality which narrowly critique phallogocentric systems without engaging the categories of sexual difference and gender that are themselves necessary, imbricated elements of patriarchy. While the prevalence of gay images and the absence of public gay subjects define Altman's conception of the state of modern Japanese homosexuality, such a paradox disappears with the consideration of gender and sexual difference as terms within the rubric of the gay boom.

De Lauretis' insistence that gender cannot be ignored in the contexts of sexuality brings us full circle to the trope of (in)visibility with which I began this essay. In the passage cited above, de Lauretis' critique is directed particularly towards the exclusion of gender in Foucault's theorizing of the discursive production of sexuality. Citing de Lauretis' passage in a fuller context illuminates the ideological tension that underlies my argument.

> Hence the paradox that mars Foucault's theory, as it does other contemporary, radical but male-centered theories: in order to combat the social technology that produces sexuality and sexual oppression, these theories (and their respective politics) will deny gender. But to deny gender, first of all, is to deny the social relations of gender that constitute and validate the sexual oppression of women; and second, to deny gender is to remain "in ideology," an ideology which (not coincidentally if, of course, not intentionally) is manifestly self-serving to the male-gendered subject.[81]

Hence emerges the importance of re-considering Sedgwick's claim to the discursive expanse of the metaphor of (in)visibility, a metaphor that Sedgwick derives from Foucault as forebear. "Gay thinkers of this century have," posits Sedgwick, "never been blind to the damaging contradictions of this compromised metaphor of *in* and *out* of the closet of privacy." Yet, when Sedgwick claims the origins of the closet in European culture, she relies on Foucault to assert that there is no room in that European closet for other metaphors. Sedgwick continues the passage.

> [The closet's] origins in European culture are, as the writings of Foucault have shown, so ramified–and its relation to the "larger," i.e., ostensibly non-gay related, topologies of privacy in the culture is, as the figure of Foucault dramatized, so critical, so enfolding, so representational–that the simple vesting of some alternative metaphor has never, either, been a true possibility.[82]

While queer thinkers and critiques may well see the complex bind that the dichotomy of (in)visibility produces, is it not also possible that this meta-vision blinds and deadens the sensory apparati to other discursive registers? Can our envisioning of Japanese male homosexuality ever escape the sexual's own force as spectacle? Shall we, other Jesuits, see anything besides the prospect of Asian men in coitus?

ENDNOTES

1. Elizabeth A. Povinelli and George Chauncey, "Thinking Sexuality Transnationally," *GLQ*, spec. issue on *Thinking Sexuality Transnationally* 5:4 (1999) 439. A similar focus on the "interrelations of sexuality, race, and gender in a transnational context" can be found in the *Social Text* special issue on *Queer Transexions of Race, Nation, and Gender*. Harper, McClintock, Muñoz and Rosen, eds., *Social Text* 52/53, 15: 3-4 (Fall/Winter 1997) 1.

2. Dennis Altman, among others, makes this apt criticism. Warner's introduction attempts to forestall this critique when he plots a homogenizing trajectory of expansion, "As gay activists from non-Western contexts become more and more involved in setting agendas, and as the rights discourse of internationalism is extended to more and more cultural contexts, Anglo-American queer theorists will have to be more alert to the globalizing–and localizing–tendencies of our theoretical langauges." Michael Warner, eds., *Fear of a Queer Planet* (Minneapolis: University of Minnesota Press, 1993) xii.

3. Intra-Asian trajectories are important concerns that I have not been able to examine in this paper. For a theoretical perspective, one can refer to Leo Ching, "Imaginings in the Empires of the Sun: Japanese Mass Culture in Asia" in Rob Wilson and Arif Dirlik, eds., *Asia/Pacific as Space of Cultural Production* (Durham: Duke University Press, 1995) 262-283. In addition, I have chosen not to theorize oppositional and experimental movements in this context. Within a Tokyo-Taipei-New York triangulation alone, Taiwanese queer director Mickey Chen's film-in-progress on Tokyo gay youth, the wide acclaim that Ts'ai Ming-liang's films have met in Japan's alternative cinema theaters, and Shu Lea Cheang's video work as it traverses U.S. and Japanese experimental, lesbian production scenes each suggest differently the many alternatives to the hegemonic routes I discuss in this paper.

4. Lisa Rofel, "Qualities of Desire: Imagining Gay Identities in China," *GLQ* 5: 4 (1999) 453 and 467. The kind of "post-national" rush that Rofel cautions against is well represented by Chris Berry, "Sexual Disorientations: Homosexual Rights, East Asian Films and Post-modern Post-nationalism" in Xiaobing Tang and Stephen Snyder, eds., *In Pursuit of Contemporary East Asian Culture* (Boulder: Westview Press, 1996) 157-182.

Rudi C. Bleys' broadly schematic history of European imaginations of homosexuality in non-European settings raises for me the need of a reverse 'ethnographic' gaze, namely more finely focused studies like Rofel's from scholars working out of non-European contexts on the reception, refraction, or rejection of European and American theories of sexuality in the nineteenth-and twentieth-centuries. Rudi C. Bleys, *The Geography of Perversion: Male-to-Male Sexual Behavior Outside the West and the Ethnographic Imagination, 1750-1918* (New York: New York University Press, 1995).

5. Andrew Parker, Mary Russo, Doris Sommer, and Patricia Yaeger, "Introduction" in *Nationalisms and Sexualities* (Routledge: New York, 1992) 2.

6. Arjun Appadurai, "Commodities and the Politics of Value" in Appadurai, ed., *The Social Life of Things: Commodities in Cultural Perspective* (Cambridge: Cambridge University Press, 1986) 4-5. Emphasis in the original.

7. Alessandro Valegnani, "Sumario de las cosas que pertenecen a la Provincia de Japon. . . ." in Tsuneo Watanabe, *The Love of the Samurai: A Thousand Years of Japanese Homosexuality* (London: Gay Men's Press, 1989) 23.

8. For a compelling discussion of sexual, racial, and national difference in film within a psychoanalytic framework, see Earl Jackson, Jr., "Desire at Cross(-Cultural) Purposes: *Hiroshima, Mon Amour* and *Merry Christmas, Mr. Lawrence*," *positions* 2:1 (Spring 1994) 133-174. The work of Frantz Fanon can also undergird such a project. For readings and critiques of Fanon's work in this respect, see E. Ann Kaplan, "Fanon, Trauma and Cinema" and other essays found in Anthony C. Alessandrini, ed., *Frantz Fanon: Critical Perspectives* (London: Routledge, 1999) 146-157.

9. Vincent Canby, rev. of *Okoge*, *New York Times* 29 March 1993, C16. Without falling for Canby's puritanical red herring, I cannot refrain from pointing out that the US Smithsonian Institute was forced to cancel its screening of *Okoge*, chosen by the Smithsonian programmers as representative of recent Japanese cinema, over complaints about the film's opening sequence and its explicit gay sex scenes. Cancellation of the film was overshadowed by the concurrent 1994-95 furor over the Enola Gay exhibit.

10. The introduction to a recent anthology of Japanese writing on male homosexuality performs this historicizing move. Stephen Miller notes the explicit presentation of male homosexuality on the television screen in the 1993 gay boom television melodrama, *Dôsôkai*. "From denial to acceptance in the course of a single television series. How could this happen? Where were the media precedents, the editorials, the marches? Can liberation really be achieved in one television program? Obviously not. Yet, the precedents were there, hidden in history, in the form of a long and well-documented tradition of 'male love.'" Miller's move from the late twentieth-century to a subsequent discussion of seventeenth-century texts raises the question of the usefulness of transhistorical categories of sexuality, especially in a cross-cultural setting. While a gay liberationist project might strategically rely on this projection into the past, the value of that tactic grows tenuous when it is removed from its immediate, cultural, political context. Although Miller's comment is made in passing and probably should not be overscrutinized, I still find it important that visibility and by extension the closet provide the key registers here, underlining both the present in its literal clarity of the television screen and a past "acceptance,"once visible but subsequently "hidden in history." The latter phrase establishes the specter of a stable, transhistorical gay male presence at the expense of an interrogation of how sexuality and gender themselves have been written into the course of modernization. See Stephen D. Miller, *Partings at Dawn: An Anthology of Japanese Gay Literature* (San Francisco: Gay Sunshine Press, 1996) 8. For a critique of this logic, see William Haver, rev. of *Partings at Dawn, Journal of Japanese Studies* 23: 2 (1997) 486-487. Director Hamano Sachi has wrestled interestingly with the question of queering historical subjects in her film on writer Osaki Midori (1896-1971). Hamano's 1998 film, *Dainanakankai hôkô: Osaki Midori o sagashite* (*Wandering in the Seventh World: In Search of a Lost Writer*), relies on structures of juxtaposition and montage to achieve this effect and on competing, contradictory organizations of time within the film.

11. Brett de Bary, "Not Another Double Suicide: Gender, National Identity, and Repetition in Shinoda Masahiro's *Shinjūten no Amijima*," *Iris* 16 (Spring 1993): 60

and 82-3. Mitsuhiro Yoshimoto, "Melodrama, Post-modernism, and Japanese Cinema," *East-West Film Journal* 5:1 (January 1991) 28. Yoshimoto's dismissal of a psychoanalytic methodology stands in opposition to de Bary's own development of its potential for Japanese cinema studies.

12. Mark Chiang, "Coming Out into the Global System: Postmodern Patriarchies and Transnational Sexualities in *The Wedding Banquet*" in David Eng and Alice Y. Hom, *Q & A: Queer in Asian America* (Philadelphia: Temple University Press, 1998) 388. The idea of "representational laundering," cited by Chiang, is Fredric Jameson's.

13. The logic here is reminiscent of Frantz Fanon's understanding of homosexuality and the Oedipus as absent from Antillean society. See Frantz Fanon, *Black Skin, White Masks* (London: Pluto Press, 1986). See also Diana Fuss, "Interior Colonies: Frantz Fanon and the Politics of Identification" in Fuss, *Identification Papers* (London: Routledge, 1995) 141-172.

14. This vision allows us to recognize racial, national, and ethnic otherness as an element of key importance in the operation of desire. While not offering an apology for the racist violence that potentially may reside in "yellow," "potato," and other "fevers," it would offer these "fevers" as perversions, in the Freudian sense, that are simply extensions of a centrally racist logic that governs desire itself, including the intra-ethnic, intra-racial, and intra-national fantasies that are normally exempt from anti-racist scrutiny. This critical project, for which David Cronenberg's *M. Butterfly* provides a persuasive prop, is one I will leave for another time, and examine here a more limited example where such a national, ultimately racist rhetoric can be brought usefully into the analysis of one plane of sexual representations–namely, the closet.

15. Chiang, "Coming Out into the Global System," 377. See also David L. Eng, "The Wedding Banquet: You're Not Invited and Some Other Ancillary Thoughts," *Artspiral* 7 (Fall 1993): 8-10. Eng, "Out Here and Over There: Queerness and Diaspora in Asian American Studies," *Social Text* 52/53, 15:3/4 (Fall/Winter 1997) 31-52.

16. Chiang, "Coming Out into the Global System," 384.

17. Chiang, "Coming Out into the Global System," 379.

18. Eng, "Out Here," 32. Martin F. Manalansan IV, "In the Shadows of Stonewall: Examining Gay Transnational Politics and the Diasporic Dilemma" in Lisa Lowe and David Lloyd, eds., *The Politics of Culture in the Shadow of Capital* (Durham: Duke University Press, 1997) 487.

19. Yukiko Hanawa, "Inciting Sites of Political Interventions: Queer 'n' Asian," *positions* 4:3 (Winter 1996) 462. Hanawa's critique is directed toward foundationalist, Asian American queer narratives of identity. Hanawa moves adeptly between Japan and the United States, as she suggests the limitations of essentialist logics of sexual identity that frequently underline arguments of visibility. For a different critique of identarian positions, readers may refer to Wim Lunsing, "Lesbian and Gay Movements–Between Hard and Soft," *Soziale Bewegungen in Japan* (Hamburg: Ges. für Natur-und Völkerkunde Ostasiens e.V., 1998) 279-310. Like Hanawa, Lunsing also targets as American the desire for fixed gay or lesbian identities. Lunsing, however, substitutes a national or cultural foundationalist logic in the place of the identarian sexual identities he decries. Lunsing's disparaging of the strategies of

political lobbying and litigation derive from his labeling that strategy part of a movement that is "hard," "American," and by implication 'non-Japanese.'

20. Eve Kosofsky Sedgwick, *Epistemology of the Closet* (Berkeley: University of California Press, 1990) 72.

21. I cite as example of these lexical complexities the following article which appeared in the now defunct *Imago*, formerly Japan's most widely-circulating journal of popular psychology and psychoanalysis. Ôya Akiyo, Shirakawa Kayoko, Nakahigashi Motoko, "Auto de aru/ni naru koto: Tôkyô rezubian gei parêdo o megutte" [Being/becoming out: On the Tokyo lesbian gay parade], *Imago*, spec. issue *Gei riberêshon* [Gay liberation], 6:12 (November 1995) 52. Only hinted at within my paper, the stakes of lesbian visibility and representation discussed in this article are in direct contrast to the media glut of male homosexual imagery. Claire Maree discusses this issue in relation to the lesbian mini-boom that followed the gay boom. Claire Maree, "Gyokai Debut: Negotiating the Closet/ Lesbians in Tokyo," unpublished manuscript.

22. Judith Butler, "Imitation and Gender Insubordination," *Inside/Out* (New York: Routledge, 1991) 16.

23. Diana Fuss, "Introduction," *Inside/Out* (New York: Routledge, 1991) 4.

24. *Epistemology of the Closet*, 72. Notable too is Sedgwick's position within the Japanese instantiation of this discourse of visibility. In the prominently figured lead article to *Imago*'s special issue on "gay liberation," Sedgwick, Halperin, Foucault, and Butler were the most regularly cited theorists within a discussion focused largely on "the closet" and Japan's gay movement. Tasaki Hideaki, "'Gei sutadi' no kanôsei" [The possibility of 'gay studies,'] *Imago*, spec. issue *Gei riberêshon* [Gay liberation] 6.12 (November 1995): 22-24 *passim*. Sedgwick's *Epistemology* was published in Japanese in 1999.

25. Sedgwick's analysis of male homosexuality is enfeebled by its overextension of the logic of the closet to explain male homosexuality *per se* and its subsumption of lesbian desire to an epiphenomenon of female sociality with the effect that female desire need not figure in her argument. See Teresa de Lauretis, *The Practice of Love* (Bloomington: Indiana University Press, 1994) 115-116 and 192-193.

26. Taking up the 1998 media explosion in Japan around marathon runner and Olympic medalist Arimori Yūko and her "formerly gay" American husband, Gabriel Wilson, I examine elsewhere the mutual imbrication of sexuality and economics as structured in tabloid representations of U.S.-Japan relations. See Jonathan M. Hall, "Shôhi suru otoko, shori sareru onna, sono aida ni kakerareta dôseiai" [A consuming man, a disposable woman, and the homosexuality bet between], *Gendai shisô*, spec. issue *Jendā sutadīzu* (Gender studies), 27:1 (January 1999) 231-237.

27. Margaret Scott, "Two New Japanese Films Explore a Once-Taboo Topic," *New York Times* 142: 2 (10 January 1993) H21. Stuart Klawans, rev. of *Okoge, The Nation* 256.17 (3 May, 1993) 606.

28. Dana Takagi, "Maiden Voyage: Excursion into Sexuality and Identity Politics in Asian America," *Amerasia Journal* 20:1 (1994): 1-17. Cited in Chiang, "Coming Out into the Global System," 386-387.

29. Michel Foucault, *The History of Sexuality: An Introduction* (New York: Vintage Books, 1990) 56.

30. Ôshima Nagisa, "Hinkon no sei: seiteki GNPshugi kara no kaihô" (Sexual poverty: Liberation from Sexual GNPism," *Tenbô* 154 (October 1971) 124. Translation from Nagisa Oshima, "Sexual Poverty," *Cinema, Censorship, and the State* (Cambridge, Mass.: MIT Press, 1992) 242.

31. I am thinking here of the homophobia of such early films as *Kôshikei* [*Death by Hanging*, 1968], and the sublimated homoeroticism of *Senjô no merri kurisumasu* [*Merry Christmas, Mr. Lawrence*, 1983] and *Gohatto* [*Taboo*, 1999].

32. Ôtake: Yappashi mô hotondo Nyū Yôku jôtai to iu koto desuka. Kamioka: Nippon mo senshinkoku no nakamairi shita. Sonna ki ga shimasu.

33. Hirano Hiroaki, "Gei-bū mu nanka iranai" [Who needs the gay boom] in Hirano, *Anchi-heterosekushizumu* [Anti-heterosexism], (Tokyo: Pandora, 1994) 23.

34. See Miller, this volume.

35. "Gei bū mu no yukue," *Shūkan dokushojin* 4 March, 1994: 1-2.

36. Wim Lunsing, "'Gay Boom' in Japan: Changing Views of Homosexuality?" *Thamyris*, 4:2 (Autumn 1997) 279-80.

37. Yodogawa Nagaharu, "Wedingu banketto" [The Wedding Banquet], *Sankei shinbun* [The Sankei shinbun], 16 November 1993. Evening edition. Available on the Internet at: http://www.sankei.co.jp/mov/yodogawa/93/931116ydg.html

38. Chiang, "Coming Out into the Global System," 376.

39. Yamane Sadao, ed., *Kannô no puroguramu pikucha: Roman poruno 1971-1982* [Program pictures of the senses: Roman porno 1971-1982], (Tokyo: Firumu āto sha, 1983) 188-89.

40. Satô Tadao, *ATG eiga o yomu* (Tokyo: Firumu āto sha, 1991) 402-3.

41. Linda C. Ehrlich, "The Debut of a Film Director: Nakajima Takehiro," *East-West Film Journal* 2:2 (June 1988) 129-134 *passim*.

42. Like *Okoge*, it is important that the male protagonist is not *fully* male. Sumio's pubescence can here be compared with the gay men's sexuality: neither representing the full figure of male heterosexuality. Bill Nichols' work on boys in their late adolescence is relevant here, but, observing the ease in which the passage is made, the contract enacted, from boy to man, I remain more skeptical than Nichols. See Bill Nichols, "Sons at the Brink of Manhood: Utopian Moments in Male Subjectivity," *East-West Film Journal* 4:1 (December 1989) 27-43.

43. Robin Wood, rev. of *Okoge*, *Cineaction* (Toronto, Ont.) 30 (Winter 1992) 76.

44. Biddy Martin, "Extraordinary Homosexuals and the Fear of Being Ordinary," *differences*, spec. issue *More Gender Trouble: Feminism Meets Queer Theory*, 6:2 + 3 (1994) 102.

45. Klawans, rev. of *Okoge*, 606.

46. The work of D. A. Miller and Lee Edelman has been critical for me at this juncture. I found crucial inspiration for this research on homophobia, the closet, and spectacle in Miller's now classic essay, "Anal *Rope*," Diana Fuss, ed., *Inside/Out: Lesbian Theories, Gay Theories* (New York: Routledge, 1991). See also Lee Edelman, "Tearooms and Sympathy, or The Epistemology of the Water Closet" and "Seeing Things: Representations, the Scene of Surveillance, and the Spectacle of Gay Male Sex" now collected in Edelman, *Homographesis: Essays in Gay Literary and Cultural Theory* (New York: Routledge, 1994).

47. Ôshima, "Sexual Poverty" *Tenbô*, 108. A slightly different wording can be found in the English translation, Ôshima, "Sexual Poverty," *Cinema, Censorship, and the State*, 242. In the English essay, Ôshima's key term *rankô* is translated as "rough sex." A more faithful rendering of the word would be "orgy." Although elsewhere in his oeuvre, Ôshima does entertain the relation between sex and violence, here his observations pertain more to an idea of indiscrete, unquantifiable sexual abundance.

48. I use the term "race" here advisedly. Tessa Morris-Suzuki usefully describes the situation as "racism without race" where "discrimination . . . produces difference just as much as difference produces discrimination." Tessa Morris-Suzuki, "Race," *Re-Inventing Japan: Time, Space, Nation* (Armonk, NY: M.E. Sharpe, 1998) 79-109 *passim*, especially 83-84.

49. "Outcast" here is the subtitled translation of 'nakama-hazure' which does not carry the specific racial or class sense that the English "outcast" with its homonym "outcaste" might do. 'Nakama-hazure' is closer to the sense of someone who has been ostracized.

50. Margaret A. Lindauer, *Devouring Frida: The Art History and Popular Celebrity of Frida Kahlo* (Hanover, NH: Wesleyan University Press, 1999) 178-9.

51. Lindauer, *Devouring Frida*, 176.

52. Irigaray and de Lauretis pun here on the aural similarity between the Greek root for sameness, -homo, and the Latin term for man, -homo. While French and American English leave room for punning, the British desire for correct diction led to debates, and a shift in BBC policy, over the root's pronunciation with a Latinate schwa or Greek long vowel.

53. Teresa de Lauretis, "Sexual Indifference and Lesbian Representation," now in Henry Abelove et al., eds., *The Lesbian and Gay Studies Reader* (New York: Routledge, 1993) 144. See also de Lauretis, "Strategies of Coherence: Narrative Cinema, Feminist Poetics, and Yvonne Rainer," in de Lauretis, *Technologies of Gender: Essays on Theory, Film, and Fiction* (Bloomington: Indiana UP, 1987) 107-115 *passim*.

54. Oswald Durcot and Tzvetan Todorov, *Encyclopedic Dictionary of the Sciences of Language* (Baltimore: Johns Hopkins UP, 1979) 276.

55. Biddy Martin, "Sexualities Without Genders and Other Queer Utopias," *diacritics*, 24.2-3, 104.

56. While criticisms of *Okoge* and other films of the gay boom have emerged among Japanese gay critics and feminists, discussions have remained limited in their scope. Analyses have critiqued the film's characters or the spectators themselves–in this case, largely women. A typical example of this approach can be found in Satô Masaki's essay "*Okoge* Girls and Eyes that *Twinkle*." Satô's camp essay is laden with misogyny. "No matter how hard getting pregnant may be, an abortion is something anyone can get done. . . . As revenge for the endless demands these idiot girls place on gay men, the *Okoge* girls just as well ought to lose their honor to such things." Satô Masaki, "*Okoge* Girls and Eyes that *Twinkle*," *Ginsei kurabu 17: kuia firumu* [Silverstar Club 17: Queer Film], (Tokyo: Peyorotu kôbô, 1993) 142-143.

57. Ôshima Nagisa, *op. cit.*, 238.

58. *Runêsansu* is also the title of a subsequent 1991 *shojo manga* by Wakuni Akisato. Set in a dystopic science fiction world, as are many of the late products of the

tradition, *Runêsansu* suggests the easy assimilation of images of male homosexuality to totalitarian systems of control that I detailed in the first section of this chapter. Matsui Midori's description of the work bears repetition here: "Homosexuality is treated as an apparatus of totalitarian control in *Renaissance*. . . . Its creator, Wakuni Akisato, describes a society controlled by the colored races after the virtual extinction of the white race by skin cancer. The name 'Renaissance' refers to the perverse project of the Japanese corporation Hara, which raises Caucasian clones in underground pastures on the moon, without giving them language, and checks them out as prostitutes to a select few of the dominant races. Despite an apparent permissiveness which allows bisexuality and homosexual marriage, the society regulates sexuality as an important means of mind control . . . the homosexual 'utopia' is constantly watched over by the rulers on the moon as an object of specular domination." Midori Matsui, "Little Girls Were Little Boys: Displaced Femininity in the Representation of Homosexuality in Japanese Girls' Comics," *Feminism and the Politics of Difference* (Boulder: Westview P, 1993) 192-193.

59. Tomoko Aoyama, "Male Homosexuality as Treated by Japanese Women Writers," *The Japanese Trajectory: Modernization and Beyond*. Gavan McCormack and Yoshio Sugimoto, eds. (Cambridge, UK: Cambridge UP, 1988) 202.

60. Merry White, *The Material Child* (New York: The Free Press, 1993) 176. For an analysis of Japanese women's magazines, see the introductory essay in Lise Skov and Brian Moeran, eds., *Women, Media and Consumption in Japan* (Honolulu: U Hawaii P, 1995) 59-71.

61. We can trace a genealogy for the *okoge* boom to its generic precursor well-established within Japanese popular fiction, *shojo manga* or young girls' comics. Their popularity unequalled in the cartoon worlds of Europe and North America, *shojo manga* commonly take as their object *bishonen*, androgynous, beautiful, young boys who precipitate dramatic tales of homosexual knabenliebe. Notable are *June*, a series which features the seduction of the beautiful heroes by nasty British aristocrats, and the *Marginal* series with its sci-fi Gothic surrealism. Other *manga* include themes of samurai boy-love, fantastic European history, or modern boarding schools with most featuring a *bishonen* involved in either homoerotic or explicitly homosexual scenarios.

62. *Crea*, February, 1991: 105. Also see, among others, *Crea* (August, 1991) and *Peach* (March, 1993).

63. *Ibid.*, 63.

64. *More*, November, 1991: 296.

65. Fushimi Noriaki, "The Possibilities of Deep, Non-sexual Relationships with Women," in *More* (November 1991) 296.

66. *Ibid.*, 297.

67. Martin, "Extraordinary Homosexuals," 103.

68. Hashimoto Osamu, "Today's Women Are Already Gay" ["Imadoki no onna wa sude ni shite gei de aru"] *Crea*, spec. issue "Gay Renaissance" Number, February 1991: 74.

69. Martin, "Extraordinary Homosexuals," 101.

70. Judith Butler, "Against Proper Objects," *differences*, spec. issue *More Gender Trouble: Feminism Meets Queer Theory*, 6.2 + 3 (1994) 9.

71. Satô Tadao, *Nihon eiga shi 3: 1960-1995* [*History of Japanese Film, 3: 1960-1995*] (Tokyo: Iwanami shoten, 1995) 305.

72. Lawrence Chua, "Queer Wind From Asia," *The Nation*, 5 July, 1993: 38-41.

73. The emergence of a genre cannot be attributed to simple tally; rather, social and epistemological forces, such as multiculturalism and orientalism, help constitute the categories through which we begin to count and assign films. While this essay is not the place to examine the North American establishment of the queer Asian genre, I suggest that it is the same tropes examined in the previous section that motivate this movement. The 1993 San Francisco International Gay and Lesbian Film Festival offered, for example, *Twinkle* (Japan), *Okoge* (Japan), *Slight Fever of a 20-Year Old* (Japan), four shorts by Hiroyuki Oki (Japan), *The Silent Thrush* (Taiwan), *The Wedding Banquet* (Taiwan), *The East is Red* (Hong Kong). More experimental Asian and diasporic Asian voices could be found in video works by Ming Yuen S. Ma, Ellen Pao, Anson Mak, Quentin Lee, and Pablo Bautista.

74. Taiwanese investment made possible Chen Kaige's *Farewell*. *The Wedding Banquet*'s description of an interracial couple was itself a collaboration between Taiwan's Ang Lee and James Schamus, screenwriter and producer of most of Ang Lee's films. Similarly, the Japanese SONY Corporation financed the Canadian David Cronenberg's film adaptation of U.S.-born David Henry Hwang's play *M. Butterfly*.

75. For a similar positioning see Berry, "Sexual DisOrientations,"165-66.

76. Dennis Altman, "The New World of 'Gay Asia,'" *Asian & Pacific Inscriptions*, Ed. Suvendrini Perera (Melbourne: Meridian, 1995) 133. Altman repeats this argument in "Global Gays/Global Gaze," *GLQ*, 3:4 (1997) 417-436.

77. Eve Kosofsky Sedgwick, *Epistemology of the Closet*, 230.

78. Dennis Altman, "The New World of 'Gay Asia,'" 126.

79. Dennis Altman, "The New World of 'Gay Asia,'" 133.

80. Teresa de Lauretis, *Technologies of Gender* (Bloomington: Indiana UP, 1987) 15.

81. See also pp. 3, 23-24 of the first essay in de Lauretis, *Technologies of Gender*.

82. Eve Kosofsky Sedgwick, *Epistemology of the Closet*, 72.

AUTHOR NOTES

The author wishes to thank Teresa de Lauretis, who has supervised the project since its inception and whose writing, as must be apparent, is its most significant inspiration. The author wishes also to acknowledge the important contributions made by Earl Jackson, Jr., Tamae Prindle, Targol Mesbah, and Andrew Grossman. Lisa Bloom's invitation to present this work at her graduate seminar on feminism and queer theory at Josai International University provided an opportunity for clarification of the argument, while Margherita Long, J. Keith Vincent, Claire Maree, Kitahara Megumi, and Elyssa Faison have been important, long-term interlocutors in discussions of sexuality and Japan. Help in obtaining stills was provided by the Stills Department of the British Film Institute in London and by the Kawakita Memorial Film Library in Tokyo. Permission to use stills from *Remembrance* and *Okoge* was granted by Takasawa Yoshinori, Aya Productions, Tokyo. The author is solely responsible for all errors. He would like to thank Andrew Grossman for conceptualizing this volume and for his unflagging efforts as editor.

The (Temporary?)
Queering of Japanese TV

Stephen D. Miller

University of Colorado, Boulder

SUMMARY. One of the primary texts of the "out" queer cinema of Japan is the television serial *Dôsôkai,* first aired in 1993. Unlike Western television shows positing queer characters, *Dôsôkai* presents its gay characters without apology or excuses, and as leads rather than as colorful appendages. At the same time, however, the show filters gay eroticism through the (hetero)normative mode of serial melodrama, at once pushing the boundaries of national permissiveness while normalizing and homogenizing homosexuality by rendering it within a conventional form. *[Article copies available for a fee from The Haworth Document Delivery Service: 1-800-342-9678. E-mail address: <getinfo@haworthpressinc.com> Website: <http://www.HaworthPress.com>]*

The deviant, in fact, is the true representative of the way people are.

–Seamus Heaney

Stephen Miller received his PhD in classical Japanese literature at UCLA in 1993. He is currently an Assistant Professor in the Department of East Asian Languages and Civilizations at the University of Colorado, Boulder. In 1996 he edited an anthology of Japanese gay literature entitled *Partings at Dawn* (Gay Sunshine Press). He is currently finishing a project on the Buddhist poems in the imperial poetry anthologies of the 11th and 12th centuries.

Address correspondence to the author at: Department of East Asian Languages and Civilizations, Campus Box 279, University of Colorado, Boulder, CO 80309 (E-mail: smiller@spot.colorado.edu).

[Haworth co-indexing entry note]: "The (Temporary?) Queering of Japanese TV." Miller, Stephen D. Co-published simultaneously in *Journal of Homosexuality* (The Haworth Press, Inc.) Vol. 39, No. 3/4, 2000, pp. 83-109; and: *Queer Asian Cinema: Shadows in the Shade* (ed: Andrew Grossman) Harrington Park Press, an imprint of The Haworth Press, Inc., 2000, pp. 83-109. Single or multiple copies of this article are available for a fee from The Haworth Document Delivery Service [1-800-342-9678, 9:00 a.m. - 5:00 p.m. (EST). E-mail address: getinfo@haworthpressinc.com].

83

INTRODUCTION

In the spring of 1999, Nippon Television Network Corporation (NTV), one of Japan's largest commercial stations, aired a twelve-week drama entitled *Romance* during prime time.[1] With lots of splashy previews and advertisements, *Romance* was a televised version of a stage play by the contemporary writer, Tsuka Kôhei. The ads for *Romance* included this single one-sentence text: "Watashi ga aishita otoko ni wa–'kare' ga ita." Translated loosely, the sentence means something like, "Along with that man I loved–came 'him'." This rather foreboding warning hinted at the homoerotic subtext to this drama.

While *Romance* was a disappointing flop for NTV, there were several hopeful signs that it would not be. The cast was young and beautiful (centered around two of Japan's newest stars, Miyazawa Rie and Ikeuchi Hiroyuki); the focus of their activities was a swimming pool which meant that many of them partially disrobed; the playwright who wrote the original stage play was a successful and popular author, particularly during the 1980s; and last but not least, NTV was following up on a previous hit with a blatantly homoerotic theme, *Dôsôkai (Reunion)*, a ten-week one-hour series broadcast during prime time in the fall of 1993.[2] While there was every reason to expect that *Romance* might draw the same high audience viewership that *Dôsôkai* did, it became clear after four or five episodes that *Romance* was a rambling and poorly executed program (admitted to me by the producer of *Dôsôkai*, an employee of NTV) that, among other things, dumbed down and then demonized the central gay character. In fact, *Romance* was so retrogressive in its conception of homosexuality, it is difficult to understand how a television station which had produced a vivid and daring view of it only six years earlier could be so ignorant and clumsy in its conception and production now.

What makes the success of *Dôsôkai* so remarkable is not that the story line was primarily gay, but that it was so explicitly, in-your-face gay. In fact, many of the scenes in the program were shot like a soft porn film with the camera lingering over partially nude men and zooming in on specific body parts when sexual acts were portrayed. One cannot help asking: how is it that such a program could be broadcast in a country in which heterosexual relationships and marriage are the societal norm, in which homosexuality is still perceived as a threat to the status quo, in which there have been few, if any, televisual precedents, in which the explicit is often eschewed for the implicit, and in which television–like television everywhere–represents the dominant–i.e., heterosexual–ideology?[3] But if broadcastability is an issue in understanding this program, so too is viewer receptivity and understanding. When the famous coming-out episode of *Ellen* was broadcast in the spring of 1997 in the United States, the media interest in and viewer responses to its broadcast were preceded by three decades of marches, legislation, demonstrations, and public debates–not to mention the airing of an episode of *Roseanne* in which Roseanne kissed another woman. So what, then, preceded *Dôsôkai*, one may ask? What sort of social and political action, public discussion, and consciousness raising prepared the Japanese audience for *Dôsôkai*? The answer, quite surprisingly, is very little. Homosexuality has never been a topic for religious debate in Japan since neither Buddhism nor Shinto, the two principal religions of Japan, have concerned themselves with the morality of sex. Moreover, since homosexual acts are not considered to be criminal behavior in Japan, the social and political implications of homosexual relationships have been met more with public silence (some might say disinterest) than discussion, debate, and theorizing (except perhaps among a few academics and only very recently).

John Fiske, author of *Television Culture*, has said, "A program is a clearly defined and labeled fragment of television's output. It has clear boundaries, both temporal and formal, and it relates to other programs in terms of generic similarity, and more essentially, of difference."[4] The reason for "*Dôsôkai*'s broadcastability and its receptivity may lie in this deceptively simple definition. It may in fact not be *Dôsôkai*'s radical approach to homosexuality that made it such a great success on television, but rather the way in which an extraordinary topic was molded into the ordinary, using all the familiar codes of social and televisual discourse. It is my contention that *Dôsôkai*, despite its apparent radicalness, portrayed a world that was acceptably Japanese in both an historical and contemporaneous sense. Acceptability, in this sense, revolves more around the social construction of Japaneseness itself rather than around ethical codes of morality. Since *Dôsôkai* was radical only *within the boundaries of Japaneseness*, it could be enjoyed–though not always understood perhaps–by a large number of viewers.

BACKGROUND

Japanese television is notoriously more liberal than American television. This is not to say there are no restraints or controls; to the contrary, there are many. But it is not too suspect to state the obvious: the Japanese television medium does, like its counterpart here, reflect what is acceptable to the majority of the Japanese citizenry. And sexuality, while socially circumscribed, does not have as much moral and religious baggage attached to it as it does in the West.

For years in Japan, the post-eleven o'clock-news slot for one of the major commercial stations has been devoted to a program in which topics such as breast size, sex toys, adult films and sexuality in all its permutations is talked about, giggled about, shown, and investigated. Full nudity is prohibited on Japanese television (and until recently in movies as well), but it is not uncommon on this program to see women expose their breasts to the cameras while the male commentators make suggestive remarks, pretend to fondle the guest, and in general act like high school teenagers. The occasional viewer might think that this program is only an excuse for male voyeurism, but in fact there are also numerous evenings devoted to topics such as impotence, the size of the male sexual organ, homosexuality (usually accompanied by outbursts like "*iya daa*"–or "that's disgusting"–from the female guests), sexual techniques, and the like. While one might be dismayed at the sheer goofiness of the presentation, there is no doubt that the topics "discussed"–if in fact that is the right word–are much more wide ranging than anything found on American television.

But what of prime time? My research has uncovered very little literature that pertains to sexuality and Japanese television. If one is to believe the authors of *A History of Japanese Television Drama*, however, there have been very few dramatic programs that have dealt with sexuality as anything other than a by-product of juvenile delinquency or boredom in the suburbs.[5] About one such program, *Maido Osawagase Shimasu*, Ôyama Katsumi says, "[This program] grabbed public attention as a new drama of manners and daily life in the way in which it dealt with problems of sex so frankly and without fuss in the relationships between high school students and their parents, although it has come under some fire for using indecent language."[6] Other than this one isolated reference, the words "sex" or "sexuality" do not appear in this book.

My own personal survey of prime time television from the 1980s and the early 1990s, while not thorough, encompassing, or expert, reveals that the topic of sex is often–as stated above by Ôyama–peripheral to the main narrative. One might see a program about a loveless marriage or teen pregnancy, but the emphasis in these stories is usually on the dissolution of family or the pathos that accompanies these experiences. In terms of homosexual or homo-erotic content, *to my knowledge* there has never been a fictionalized or non-fictionalized television program that dealt with either the phenomenon of gay male homosexuality or lesbianism *as it occurs and is manifest in Japan*.[7] What has been aired, however, are documentaries and news stories about the gay movement in the West, transsexualism, and what the Japanese call the *nyû hafu* ("new half," a word that covers both the pre-and post-operative transgendered).

The early 1990s, however, saw a cultural *buumu* ("boom") in gay visibility in Japan. Starting with the publication of an award-winning novel in 1990 (*Yes, Yes, Yes*, 26th Bungei Prize), this boom saw the release of films on gay themes (*Okoge*, 1992, and *Boys of Summer*, 1993), the start of an International Gay and Lesbian Film Festival (1991), the publication of a Japanese coming-out novel (*Shinjuku Ni-chôme kimi ni attara*, 1993), and some brave but poorly attended gay pride marches (since 1994). As meaningful as each of these cultural landmarks may have been to the gay community, nothing could have predicted the astounding success of *Dôsôkai*. As the screenwriter, Izawa Mann, said to me, "Many gay men in Japan perceive their lives in terms of pre-*Dôsôkai* and post-*Dôsôkai*." While it is difficult to prove the veracity of this, one thing is certain: *Dôsôkai* enjoyed unprecedented success throughout Japan for NTV. It turned out to be one of the most successful television dramas ever aired by this station. During its sixth week, *Dôsôkai* captured almost 20% of the audience viewership, surpassing even the highly popular nightly program "News Station."

Dôsôkai is, first and foremost, a melodrama–in the pejorative sense that we use that term–similar in many ways to an American daytime soap opera. If one does not understand this most fundamental character of the program, all discussion about it will be rendered ludicrous. One must accept the fact that the outlandish plot and production are standard fare for Japanese audiences. Everything about *Dôsôkai* is done hyperbolically: the close-up camera shots, the exaggerated lighting, the use of arias and musical crescendos, the poetic speeches of the characters, their exaggerated and quickly changing emotions, and the cliff-hanging scenes.[8] But as Wimal Dissanayake has said about Asian film, "[W]e need to constantly keep in mind that melodrama in Asia connotes different sets of associations from those obtaining in the West."[9] He goes on to exemplify this statement:

> [T]he concept of suffering is pivotal to the discourse of film melodrama in Asian cultures. We need to bear in mind the fact that most Asian cultures valorize human suffering as a pervasive fact of life and that salvation is a liberatory experience emanating from the insights into the nature and ineluctability of human suffering. Hence the metaphysical understanding of suffering becomes the condition of possibility for participating in the meaning of life. Suffering and the ensuing pathos are commonly found in Western melodrama as well; however, their place in and significance to Asian film melodramas are considerably different.[10]

Melodrama in *Dôsôkai* seems to serve two specific purposes: (1) it aestheticizes, albeit in exaggerated ways, that which might be construed as distasteful, and (2) it caricaturizes the potentially subversive elements of the plot. One of the most often-heard comments about *Dôsôkai* is that it was "shot beautifully" (*kirei ni satsuei sareta*). Even if someone has nothing else positive to say about the program, inevitably they will agree that the scenes (of partially nude men, in particular) were done tastefully. On the other hand, the melodramatic elements of the program–while common to most Japanese television dramas–also serve to soften what might be controversial or subversive. The exaggerated and cartoonish elements of the production constantly remind audiences of the story's fictional (untrue?) nature. But again, it is important to keep in mind, as Dissanayake has said, that the quality of pathos is decidedly different in Asia than in the West. What may be regarded as caricature in the West could be regarded as artistic expression in Asia.

THE STORY: THE FIRST HALF

Dôsôkai revolves around a group of twenty-something Tokyoites who all went to the same high school in a small fishing village on the nearby Izu Peninsula. Among this group, the central character is a handsome and successful builder/contractor named Fûma (written with the Chinese characters for "wind" and "horse") [Photo 1]. Fûma is portrayed as a man torn between the deep–one might even say spiritual–affection he feels for his wife, Natsuki (written with the characters for "seven" and "moon") [Photo 2], the love he feels for his best friend, Atari (written with the character for "middle" or "in between") [Photo 3], and the sexual feelings he has for a younger male lover, Arashi (written with the character for "storm") [Photo 4].[11] Fûma chose to marry Natsuki at first because she used to be in love with Atari: if he cannot be Atari's lover himself, he can get closer to him by marrying someone Atari has loved. On the other hand, Fûma is unable to consummate his marriage with Natsuki and unable, initially at least, to disclose his true feelings to Atari. The only place he can discover himself is in the gay district of Tokyo known as Shinjuku Ni-chôme (the second district of Shinjuku). Here, at a gay bar called "Splash," Fûma finds Arashi, a young, hip, bisexual boy who falls in love with Fûma and leads him onto the path of self-revelation.[12]

In the first four episodes of *Dôsôkai*, Fûma is desperately trying to lead the kind of straight life his engagement and marriage to Natsuki dictate. But while Fûma harbors secrets he cannot reveal to Natsuki, Natsuki harbors the personal terror (known to all) that came from her mother's attempted drowning of her when she was only a child. So Fûma's inability to relate to Natsuki is met with Natsuki's fear of being related to (this is the reason given for her breakup with Atari). Fûma's failure to perform his husbandly duties on their honeymoon (and Natsuki's own emotional reticence to push it) leads Fûma to become more and more desirous of Arashi and the liberating sexuality their relationship engenders.

By the fifth episode, Fûma has turned a corner. He is unresponsive to Natsuki as anything other than a live-in companion, unwilling to relate to Arashi as the kind of lover Arashi wants, and yet he still longs for the unattainable Atari. The tension between Fûma's two lives–the "straight" one he is failing and the "gay" one he is resisting–becomes taut and neurotic.

PHOTO 1. Nishimura Kazuhiko as "Fûma"

PHOTO 2. Saitō Yuki as "Natsuki"

PHOTO 3. Takashima Masahito as "Atari"

PHOTO 4. "Fûma" and Yamaguchi Tatsuya as "Arashi"

Alone and confused, Fûma visits–to the rising crescendo of Leoncavallo's *Pagliacci* ("The Clown")–one of Tokyo's gay cruising parks where under a half-clouded moon he meets a man who is described in the screenplay as "a young Western man who might be a model."[13] As the man unzips Fûma's zipper and begins to fellate him (Fûma's arms dangling Christ-like through the limbs of the tree he is leaning against), they and the other denizens of the park are suddenly attacked by a gang of gay-bashing (*homogari*) thugs. While this scenario may seem unlikely in a city regarded as safe as Tokyo is, many gay men in Tokyo claim that the scenario is not implausible.[14] Realistic or not, the scene serves three important purposes to the progress of the narrative: (1) it devalorizes anonymous sex; (2) it highlights the intolerance gay men experience in Japan; and (3) it brings Fûma's double life into Atari's world.

How the scene accomplishes the third of these purposes is as follows: Atari and some of Fûma's other high school friends have been playing basketball next to the park where Fûma is being attacked. As the basketball rolls into the nearby woods, Atari runs into a group of the gay-bashers as they are fleeing. Curious as to what has happened, Atari enters the woods and finds Fûma bloodied on the ground as he receives the last blows of his attackers. In one of the most dramatic scenes of the program, Fûma looks up at Atari, horrified that his true love has discovered both him and his secret.

The one principal character who is lost in the first three episodes of the program is Natsuki. In the attempt to establish the discursive space around Fûma as a gay man who has married for all the wrong reasons, Natsuki is presented as indecisive and floundering. She is not willing to be ignored as a wife or as a woman, but she is also not savvy enough (among all the lies, who could be?) to understand why her husband is unresponsive and absent. Natsuki's suspicions about Fûma start with their honeymoon and are frequently reinforced as he spends less time at home or she hears comments about him having been seen at a place or a time she thought he was elsewhere.

By the fourth episode, it becomes clear that Natsuki is not going to be portrayed as a stereotypical Japanese spouse who will look away as her husband leads his own wifeless life. But it is Natsuki's decisiveness that leads to her discovery of Fûma's relationship with Arashi. Aiming to help Fûma out of a difficult business situation, Atari and Natsuki visit an older man at a bar who they think, because of connections, might loan them some money. He is eccentric to the extreme, and he is accompanied by a younger and very solicitous woman. As Atari and Natsuki try to introduce themselves politely and explain the situation, the old man seems preoccupied until his young companion tells him that "some customers have come." Confused by the situation and the meaning of "customers," Atari and Natsuki look bewildered, but soon find out that the bar is an excuse for the old man to spy on young lovers having sex in the adjoining love hotel. The far wall suddenly opens up into a one-way mirror into which none other than Fûma and Arashi will come into view. Just as they are about to appear, however, Atari accidentally knocks a glass and its contents over. In a rush to clean up the glass and ignore the scene in the far window, Natsuki and Atari stoop to the floor. Looking up for just a second, however, Natsuki sees Fûma and Arashi as they fall into bed and begin kissing each other passionately. She is horrified by the sight of her husband with another man, but she is more horrified that her suspicions have been confirmed. She runs out of the bar and Atari, who has not seen Fûma but is aware that the "customers" were two men, chases after her.

Distraught by what she has seen, Natsuki seeks revenge, but she does so in a way that in the end will only bring her closer to Fûma. To quell both her anger and her loneliness, Natsuki buys the brightest red lipstick she can find and heads out to town. The person she meets, however, is none other than Arashi, selling his youthfulness to lonely women. In a twisted irony only a program like this could produce, Arashi takes Natsuki to the basement of a building Fûma's company is in the midst of constructing. Here they have sex, and afterwards, adding insult to injury, Arashi demands Natsuki pay him the equivalent of about $75. As he drives away on his motorcycle, he yells out to her that she should be more confident in herself since she was "really good" [Photo 5].

PHOTO 5. "Arashi" and "Natsuki" engaged in their sexual tryst

What is not clear from the above cursory and selective account of the first half of "Dôsôkai" is the extraordinary explicitness of many of the scenes (and the cause of great surprise among Westerners who see it). To give just one example: when Fûma picks up Arashi at "Splash" for the first time and takes him to a love hotel, there are back nude shots of both of them shower-ing–presumably before their sexual encounter [Photos 6 and 7]. When it appears that Fûma, out of fear, is going to try to leave without having sex ("Actually, I'm no good at this kind of thing," he says to Arashi), Arashi approaches him dressed only in a towel, puts his arms around him, and presses up against Fûma, forcing him to feel the desire he is trying to repress. "Why don't you just take the plunge," he asks, as we see and hear the familiar sight and sound of water splashing [Photo 8]. Needless to say, this is all such a far cry from the single kiss-scene in *Roseanne* or the coming-out episode of *Ellen* that one cannot help but be stunned by its blunt portrayal of homosexual desire.

THE STORY: THE SECOND HALF

Atari's discovery of Fûma at the gay cruising park provides the momen-tum for the second half of the program. While the first half was concerned with Fûma's attempts to repress his feelings, the second half is a meandering exploration of the consequences liberation brings. If *Dôsôkai* is radical in its depiction of homosexual desire, it is much less radical in its conception of how that desire may manifest in society.

After Atari accompanies Fûma back to his apartment, Fûma confesses–with a knife to his own throat–that he has been in love with Atari for the last twelve years since they first met in high school. Shocked by this revelation, but ready still to be the everlasting friend he has always promised to be, Atari offers himself to Fûma. In the bedroom, Atari admits it "feels strange" (*myô na kanji*) to be lying naked with a man, but he is in fact aroused [Photos 9 and 10]. The next morning, after their liaison, Atari agrees to spend four days with Fûma in the mountains–an offer that includes sexual intimacy–but with the proviso that they will revert to being "just friends" (*tada no tomodachi*) at the end of this time.

After Fûma spends his four days with Atari,[15] he returns home to Natsuki, face glowing, dressed in the kind of tuxedo one might wear as the groom to a wedding. He declares "today [his] independence day." As Natsuki carefully places the photos from their unconsummated honeymoon into a photo album, Fûma stands up suddenly and announces that he is not the kind of "human being who can be classified as heterosexual." He is, he says, more like the Greek example of Zeus and Ganymede. Natsuki, of course, knows this and tells Fûma so. She then reveals the extent of her compassion for his situation,

PHOTO 6. "Fûma" showering before his first sexual encounter with "Arashi"

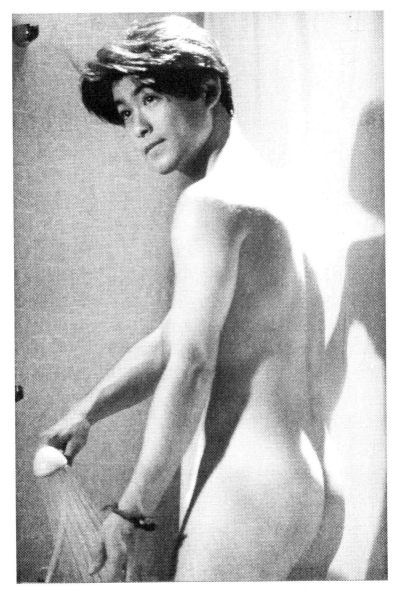

PHOTO 7. "Arashi" showering

PHOTO 8. "Arashi" embracing a reluctant "Fûma"

PHOTO 9. "Atari" kissing "Fûma" after the confession

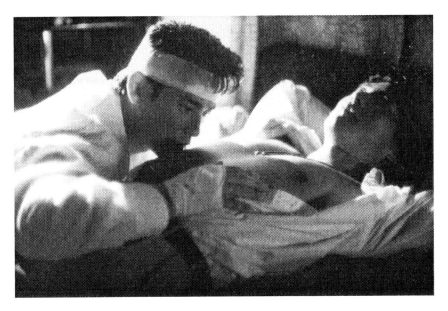

PHOTO 10. "Fûma" realizes his dream of a sexual union with "Atari"

"When I think about the lonely journey you've walked, that you've borne by yourself . . . the desolation which you carried as a cross and walked with silently: this pierces my heart." Not only does Natsuki feel compassion for Fûma, but she claims to still love him as well. And when Fûma asks her from where her happiness will come now that she knows he cannot satisfy her, she says she does not know, but that she wants to search for it with Fûma. In fact, she says, as they embrace, "Let's make tonight our real honeymoon."

While Western (and certainly feminist) audiences might groan immediately at what we would call the naivete of Natsuki's compassion, it is clear that we are meant to sympathize with and understand her altruism. Keeping Dissanayake's comments about Asian attitudes towards suffering in mind, we should remember that it is most likely Natsuki's compassion for Fûma's pain that audiences will respond to, not her willingness to stay married to a man with whom she can gain no personal sexual pleasure. About the pleasure audiences derive from television, Fiske asserts, "Pleasure results from a particular relationship between meanings and power. Pleasure for the subordinate is produced by the assertion of one's identity in resistance to, in independence of, or in negotiation with, the structure of domination."[16] This scene between Natsuki and Fûma exemplifies the kinds of televisual negotiations that occur between dominant and subordinate ideologies. For the majority of viewers to sympathize with Fûma, it is essential that, despite his declaration of incompatible sexual orientation, he remain married and loyal to Natsuki. It is essential, in fact, that to all who see them, they behave like an ordinary heterosexual couple.

Ironically, the means by which Fûma and Natsuki will create their facade of ordinariness is through Arashi. Arashi's existence is still a threat to their love, to "normalcy." Arashi cannot accept Fûma's decision to continue living without him and with Natsuki, nor can he live with his indecisiveness about his own sexuality. In an attempt to find out who he is, Arashi goes to a "host club" to sell himself. His first client, however, turns out to be a kind of mentor. He does not want to have sex with Arashi, but rather he wants to draw him. His appreciation for Arashi is aesthetic, not sexual. As he draws, he begins talking to Arashi about what he wants in life, who he is. The old man then starts naming the famous Westerners who are thought to have had homoerotic relationships or desires (Plato, Michelangelo, Napoleon, Balzac, Schubert, Mozart, Thomas Mann), saying, "These are men who have loved men. There are numerous others too." As Arashi listens enthralled, the old man continues by telling him about the tradition of male-male love in Japan, a tradition that goes back to the earliest period in Japanese history and continued, he says with some bitterness, until the Americans and their puritanism brought "morality" to Japan.

Arashi's response to this, we are led to believe, is immediate and transformative: if there is a tradition of male-male love in Japan, then his love for Fûma must be justifiable. Without a thought for the consequences of his actions, he goes to Fûma's house and calls out his name from the street in the middle of the night. It is not Fûma, however, who responds; it is Natsuki. She accompanies him into their bedroom (they live with Fûma's parents), offers him the shower, and tells Fûma that he can stay the night with him while she sleeps in the single bed nearby.

But Arashi's lesson in the tradition of Japanese homoerotic love is not over yet. The narrative strategy for connecting Arashi's behavior with this historical tradition comes in the form of a traditional *kabuki* play. Fûma tells the story of *Sakura-hime Azuma Bunshô* ("Lady Sakura, Documents from the East," 1817) by Tsuruya Namboku.[17] While the play is long and intricate and the details are numerous, the relevant parts for *Dôsôkai* concern the unbroken vow of love between two of the male characters, one who dies before the other. Reborn as a woman, the character inevitably meets the man she/he left behind, and their vows of love are rekindled. At the end of Fûma's story, Arashi says, "Then we too must have a bond from a previous life . . . "

Fûma's recounting of the *kabuki* play is obviously not only for Arashi's benefit. The audiences watching *Dôsôkai* are also being "taught" the historical rationale for this kind of behavior. To reinforce the telling of the story, Natsuki imagines Fûma and Arashi dressed in the garb of a Tokugawa period (1600-1868) samurai and his beloved young man. Awash in color, the scene strives somewhat limply for the style of a *kabuki* play [Photo 11]. In the final episode of the program, this same scene is replayed, again as Natsuki's fantasy. But as the two men gaze into one another's eyes, the following words appear on the screen: *Nen'yû: nanshoku no chigiri* (literally: "thinking of my friend: the vow of male love").[18]

This linking of Fûma and Arashi's relationship to the tradition of male-male love in the Tokugawa period is a convenient narrative ploy that conflates the past and the present by ignoring all the social and historical ruptures in between. It brings together that which can be venerated with that which is still unknown by stepping over, as it were, history itself. If the unknown has roots in the distant past, it can be made familiar, elevated, and valorized. It can be given, in other words, the authority of tradition. It can also be given another name. The Western-identified "homosexuality" or "gay" becomes, in effect, *nanshoku*, the Japanese word most commonly used to describe the erotic relationship between men during the Tokugawa period, a word that Gary Leupp translates as "male eros."[19]

The association of *nanshoku* with other oft-quoted values of the Tokugawa period–fidelity, loyalty, honor, and revenge–becomes the theme of the final three episodes of *Dôsôkai*. Fûma and Atari's four-day getaway in the mountains planted a seed of doubt in Atari's mind: if he is capable of having sex

PHOTO 11. "Arashi" and "Fûma" as lovers from the Tokugawa period

with Fûma, then perhaps he is not the person he thought he was. This doubt leads Atari to prove himself. He picks up someone who he thinks is a young woman (Hiromi), accompanies her to a love hotel, and finds out to his surprise that she is still partially a he (in fact, he is a friend of Arashi's). Enraged by the deception and what appears to be a cruel joke on him, Atari attacks Hiromi, leaving her/him dazed and injured. Several days later, when Hiromi has recovered, she/he lures Atari to a nearby empty bayside warehouse where her friends rape and sodomize him. This is the sequence of events that leads Fûma and Arashi to the same warehouse the next day to avenge the honor of their friends. Though neither of them knew the other was involved, they cannot back down from their obligations. They have no choice but to fight one another. A combination of wrestling and fist-fighting, the battle becomes increasingly erotic as they hit, grab, flail, and push up against one another. After they are both bloodied and exhausted, lying on the floor, Fûma turns over, reaches for Arashi's hand, and pulls himself on top of Arashi and kisses him (to the rising crescendo of Mozart). Fûma pulls Arashi up to his knees and they kneel in front of one another as the camera zooms in on them licking, sucking, and chewing on each others' earlobes. Arashi then pulls Fûma's head back, revealing his neck, as the following conversation ensues:

Arashi: I'm Dracula, you know.
Fûma: I'm no beautiful young girl.
Arashi: You're more beautiful than any young girl.
Fûma: Stop it!
Arashi: (as he brings Fûma's hand to his crotch) This is what you've done to me.
Fûma: Me too.
Arashi: I wonder if I'm completely homosexual now?
Fûma: It's already happened.
. . . .
Arashi: Who's better? Atari or me?
Fûma: I can't compare you two.
Arashi: Is Atari big?
Fûma: Stop.
Arashi: Do everything you did with Atari with me. And then I'll do even more than that to you. . . .
Fûma: Two men together, no matter what they do, they won't contaminate one another. I don't know why, but with a man and woman, I feel like it can be so complicated.
Arashi: I wonder why that is?
Fûma: A man's existence itself is abstract. Mutual abstractions, no matter how intertwined, are a geometrical design.
Arashi: Geometry is prettier.
Fûma: It's too pretty. Anything beyond that, there's no depth.

Arashi then tells Fûma about his first sexual experience as a first-year junior high school student. Having been seduced by a drunken and flabby neighborhood woman who smelled when he fellated her, he has always hated women–even when he desired them at the same time. He wanted their bodies, but he always felt there was something more important to him in his life.

Arashi: After I came to Tokyo, if I were invited by a university student to go home with him, I would.
Fûma: Don't say it. Jealousy seers my heart.
Arashi: But I've never given my heart to anyone . . . only to you, Fûma.
Fûma: (hugs Arashi passionately)
Arashi: Ouch. It hurts from where we hit each other.
Fûma: Pay it no mind. We're bound only by our pain.

Any retelling of this scene only seems absurd until one recalls the believability factor of any melodramatic show, soap opera, or weekly TV movie. A scene does not have to be believable to be realistic. It only has to reflect a world of reality to be believable. As John Fiske says, "We can . . . call television an essentially realistic medium because of its ability to carry a socially convincing sense of the real. Realism is not a matter of any fidelity to an empirical reality, but of the discursive conventions by which and for which a sense of reality is constructed."[20] In fact, there is nothing unbelievable about any of the following facts: (1) that Fûma and Arashi might have a fistfight, (2) that a fistfight might occur in a place where there is likely to be less interference, (3) that a fight might end up being erotically charged if the two opponents were also lovers, (4) that Arashi's confusion comes from a dislike of women, or (5) that Fûma and Arashi feel that the pain of their physical injuries should be tolerated since they caused it themselves. It is only when we try to assemble these facts under our own private umbrella of reality that believability is challenged. We might be amused or amazed or offended or confounded by such a scene, but there is nothing (at least in the ratings) to indicate that the audiences watching *Dôsôkai* turned off the TV and rejected the method in which the story was told.

The concluding two episodes of *Dôsôkai* attempt to bring closure to what has been a much more complicated story than this essay can justifiably attend. And whereas an American soap opera might take weeks to bring resolution to the narrative intricacies of a plot, *Dôsôkai* accomplishes the same thing in two hours. Having said this, however, it must also be said that the unrealistic time constraints stretch the believability of the characters for this author even more than before.

As a symbol of . . . what?–their individuality, their resolve, their willfulness?–the ninth episode contains a scene in which Atari, Arashi, Fûma, and Natsuki are all masturbating, albeit in separate places, at the same time. Atari masturbates in the shower to images of Fûma and him together (are we really to believe that their liaison together and his subsequent rape later in the series made him gay?). Arashi masturbates with the moonlight streaming through his room with pictures of Fûma scattered about on the floor. Natsuki, after closing Fûma's bedside reading (Proust's *Remembrance of Things Past*), calls out Fûma's name and then turns over to attend to her own sexual needs. Finally, Fûma, who has been awakened by Natsuki, turns over and sees Natsuki writhing on the bed across from him. Saddened by his inability to relate to her sexually, he turns over, bites his lip to stop himself from crying out, and then proceeds to join the other three in their silent *menage a trois*. Each of these scenes is interspersed with the shot of a single white rose that gradually comes into full bloom and then, after orgasm, sheds its petals one by one.

The central relationship in *Dôsôkai* is clearly the one involving Fûma, Natsuki, and Arashi. There can be no denouement until their relationship is resolved. While an earlier scene depicting the three of them in the same bed would seem to suggest a new family order, the final episode changes the dynamics of the message entirely. Natsuki has become pregnant as a result of her sexual liaison with Arashi. Though she never told Fûma about having sex with Arashi, she has no choice but to confess now. At first, Fûma is angry, but his anger quickly dissolves as soon as he understands the circumstances (circumstances he, in fact, caused) that led to Natsuki's behavior. At first, the two of them discuss abortion, but later they decide to keep the child. Fûma calls Arashi to ask him to meet him at a park so he can tell him the news. As Arashi walks through the park, he spies a young man with a crossbow aiming an arrow at a cat. He yells at the hunter, calling him a coward for trying to kill something so helpless. Then he turns away at the sound of Fûma's voice calling his name. As he walks towards Fûma, the hunter shoots Arashi in the back. Before he dies–in great melodramatic tradition–Arashi declares his love for Fûma as Fûma hugs Arashi and screams out with grief.

In the concluding scene of *Dôsôkai* (meant to take place several months later), we see Fûma, Natsuki, and their child as they are happily taking a walk: for all intents and purposes, the typical heterosexual family. Fûma glances down the street and sees a construction worker who looks exactly like Arashi (played, in fact, by the same actor). Fûma appears shocked by the resemblance and stares. Natsuki, aware of course of the similarities, approaches the man with Fûma standing next to her and invites him to join them for dinner sometime [Photo 12]. Fûma and his child turn and begin to walk away as Natsuki and the construction worker continue talking.

The similarities between the ending of *Dôsôkai* and the Japanese movie *Okoge* (*Fag Hag*) are almost too alike for them to be coincidental.[21] Released the year before *Dôsôkai*, *Okoge* is the story of a woman (Sayoko) who befriends two male lovers (Goh and Tochi) after meeting them on a gay beach. In part because she was sexually abused as a child, Sayoko feels safe with these men and provides them with safe haven for their liaisons (Goh's mother lives with Goh and Tochi is married). After Goh and Tochi break up, Sayoko tries to match up Goh with another man who comes to a gay bar they often frequent together. Goh likes this man, but he turns out to be straight (*nonke*). After several attempts at seduction, he eventually forces Sayoko to have sex with him. She resists, but gives in only when she imagines that–even if (as she does) get pregnant–she is somehow serving as a vessel for Goh's love of this man.

Okoge concludes with the formation of a "family," much like the "family" in *Dôsôkai*: Sayoko and her child come to live with Goh, after Goh's mother dies. In the final scene of the movie Goh, Sayoko, and the child are strolling through the streets of Shinjuku Ni-chôme late at night. They have become a family out of necessity. But just as in *Dôsôkai*, this is a family that recognizes that the husband cannot be responsive to the wife's needs and will need someone else to make it complete. As they pass one man on the street who

PHOTO 12. "Fûma" and "Natsuki" encounter an "Arashi" look-alike

Goh glances at, Sayoko asks if he is Goh's type. He replies, "Not particular-ly," as the credits begin to roll.

CONCLUSION

In John Storey's explication of Stuart Hall's important article on televi-sion, "Encoding and Decoding in the Television Discourse," he concludes, "There is nothing inevitable about the outcome of the process–what is in-tended and what is taken may not coincide."[22] What Storey is speaking about, of course, is the process whereby the viewers of a program make meaning(s) out of what they see. As Storey says, " . . . meanings and messages are not simply 'transmitted', they are always produced . . ."[23] Because of this, the derivable meanings of *Dôsôkai*–as with any program– are polysomic and variable. What a gay white male from Boulder, Colorado thinks *Dôsôkai* means may not coincide at all with what a mother of two children in Shizuoka, a retired fisherman from Hakodate, or a young gay schoolteacher from Okinawa thinks it means.

At a presentation of an earlier version of this essay at the University of Tokyo, a young graduate student in the newly-formed field of "gay studies" implored me to write about the everyday realities of gay men and women in

Japan. Yes, he said, it was all well and good to have homosexuality depicted on TV, but in fact how real was it? The focus of much of the activity was in a gay ghetto (Shinjuku Ni-chôme) and the outcome was nothing other than a variation on the typical heterosexual family. This was progress, he said, but it was meager and limited.

It is hard not to agree with him. But it is also hard not to hope that such depictions–in all their melodrama, in all their unreality, in all their limited fields of vision–somehow contribute to the gradual familiarization of the unknown to the known. As Atari says in one of the final scenes, "Life is splendidly confused. And somehow I've come to like that confusion. Don't we want to be impassioned by life?" Perhaps so. But better yet would be a world in which the realities of life were well balanced with its passions.

There is no doubt that *Dôsôkai* presented on prime time television a world that had never before been seen by the majority of Japanese viewers. And while it might be argued that much of this world was presented merely for the sake of titillation, there can also be no doubt that it was presented in such a way that viewers knew they were watching something based in reality. *Dôsôkai* did not attempt to make a political statement, as *Ellen* did when it was aired in 1997. Instead, it was a personal statement that focused on desire, responsibility, and consequence. And there is every indication that audiences watching it responded to its approach with enthusiasm.[24]

NOTES

1. Research for this paper was conducted primarily in Japan with the cooperation of the screenwriter, Izawa Mann (in 1997 and 1999), the director, Hosono Hidenobu (February 18, 1999), and one of the three producers, Kawahara Yasuhiko (May 12, 1999). In addition to giving the author their valuable time and expertise, they also provided him with still shots, a set of video tapes of the program, and a full copy of the screenplay. Valuable assistance was also provided by the graduate students in Ueno Chizuko's sociology seminar at the University of Tokyo. In particular, the author would like to thank Ino Shin'ichi for his valuable comments sent by e-mail after the seminar. He would also like to thank the numerous gay men in Japan who tirelessly answered his questions about the program. Photographs from *Dôsôkai* appear in this paper with permission of Izawa Mann.

2. The complete title of the screenplay is *Dôsôkai: Alumni Reunion, the Smell of Perilous Affairs Ten Years After.* The second part of this title in English is unchanged from the original and appeared thus in the opening shot of the television program as well as on the title cover to the screenplay.

3. In the author's interviews with the director and one of the producers at NTV on 2/18/99 and 5/12/99, both Hosono Hidenobu and Kawahara Yasuhiko admitted that the broadcastability of *Dôsôkai* had more to do with the sagging ratings of NTV's television dramas than anything else. Since NTV had not had a hit drama in a long while, they were willing to do almost anything to mend this situation. While both claimed to have been uncomfortable with the subject matter at first, neither of

them objected enough to withdraw their support. In fact, they both felt that, in the end, it was one of the best production experiences they had ever had and claimed to have enormous respect for the screenwriter.

4. John Fiske, *Television Culture* (London and New York: Routledge, 1989), 14.

5. Masunori Sata & Hideo Hirahara, ed., *A History of Japanese Television Drama* (Tokyo: The Japan Association of Broadcasting Art, 1991).

6. Katsumi Ôyama, "The Shôwa 50's and After," in *A History of Japanese Television Drama*, 200.

7. The one exception to this "*that I know of*" is a part of a program that Izawa Mann wrote for NTV before *Dôsôkai*. The program was entitled "Gekai, Arimori Saeko: Inochi no Jikan" ("Arimori Saeko, Surgeon: The Hours of One's Life"). In it there appeared a scene with a decidedly homosexual character. See Izawa Mann, *Gekai, Arimori Saeko: Inochi no Jikan* (Tokyo: Kadokawa Shoten, 1992), 231-275.

8. At one presentation of *Dôsôkai* made at a statewide gay and lesbian conference on the campus of the University of Colorado in 1996, the audience reacted more to the production techniques (i.e., the melodrama) of the series than they did to its explicitness.

9. Wimal Dissanayake, ed., *Melodrama and Asian Cinema* (New York: Cambridge University Press, 1993), 4. Though I am not an expert in this field, I will assume that the same holds true for melodrama in television.

10. Ibid.

11. While I am tempted to extrapolate on the Chinese ideograms used to write the central characters' names, the screenwriter insists that there were no underlying motives in their creation. On the other hand, it is hard to believe that the Chinese ideogram used for Atari's name ("middle" or "in between") does not, given the role he plays, signify his position in the relationship among Fûma, Natsuki, and Arashi. Likewise, as the young man who threatens Fûma and Natsuki's relationship, how can Arashi's name (written with the ideogram for "storm") not signify his role?

The following actors play these roles: Fûma (Nishimura Kazuhiko), Natsuki (Saitô Yuki), Atari (Takashima Masahiro), and Arashi (Yamaguchi Tetsuya).

12. All of the scenes at "Splash" were filmed at a gay bar in Shinjuku called Zip. One of the running tropes of the program is the sound of splashing water. Metaphorically, it is used to represent the daringness one needs to "jump into" this sort of relationship. This is explicitly expressed in the first episode in a scene between Fûma and Arashi at a love hotel.

13. Izawa Mann, *Dôsôkai* (screenplay, vol. 5, 1993), 52.

14. Izawa Mann himself claims that there are many unreported beatings of gay men in Tokyo. He also says that even when the beating is reported, it is necessary to read between the lines of news reports to get the full import. If a beating is reported in a well-known cruising park, then the likelihood of it being gay-related is much higher. Personal communication, January 17, 1999.

15. One of the highlights of their four days together is a sex scene in front of a large fireplace. Shot similarly to the scene of the two main characters wrestling in front of the fireplace in the film version of D. H. Lawrence's *Women in Love* (1969), Fûma and Atari are shown embracing bathed in the light of the fire. As their passion builds, we see them stand up, take off their shirts, unbutton and lower their pants as a well-placed table moves into view between them and the camera.

16. Fiske, *Television Culture*, 19.

17. A full explication of *Sakura-hime Azuma Bunshô* can be found in Donald Keene, *World Within Walls: Japanese Literature of the Pre-Modern Era, 1600-1867* (New York: Holt, Rinehart and Winston, 1976), 458-466.

18. *Nen'yû* is another word for *nenja*, meaning an older man (sometimes a monk, sometimes a man of samurai background) who sexually mentors a younger man. See Tsuneo Watanabe & Jun'ichi Iwata, *The Love of the Samurai: A Thousand Years of Japanese Homosexuality*, trans. D.R. Roberts (London: GMP Publishers Ltd., 1989), 156, and Gary P. Leupp, *Male Colors: The Construction of Homosexuality in Tokugawa Japan* (Berkeley: University of California Press, 1995), 43.

19. Leupp, *Male Colors*, 1.

20. Fiske, *Television Culture*, 21.

21. Izawa says that he had not seen *Okoge* when he wrote the screenplay for *Dôsôkai*. Personal communication, June 1997.

22. John Storey, *Cultural Studies & The Study of Popular Culture: Theories and Methods* (Athens: University of Georgia Press, 1996), 11.

23. Ibid.

24. As of the summer of 1999, *Dôsôkai* was still available for rental in most large video stores in Tokyo and Kyoto.

Two Japanese Variants
of the Absolute Transvestite Film

Julian Stringer

University of Nottingham

SUMMARY. This essay compares two Japanese transvestite films from different generations–*Black Lizard* of 1968 and *Summer Vacation 1999* of 1988. While Western transvestite conventions are usually exploited only to climactically reinforce heterosexual coupling, what binds these two films is their divergent tradition of what I call "permanent transvestism." That is, the films employ a cross-dressing which occurs extra-diegetically, is unnecessary to the plot, and which an audience may or may not be aware of depending on their geo-historical position. However, it is this non-Western tradition of cross-dressing that nevertheless imparts an aestheticization of sexual desire beyond fixed categories of "gay," "lesbian," or even our conventional ideas of transsexualism. *[Article copies available for a fee from The Haworth Document Delivery Service: 1-800-342-9678. E-mail address: <getinfo@haworthpressinc. com> Website: <http://www.HaworthPress.com>]*

The critical and commercial interest generated in recent years by such films as *The Adventures of Priscilla, Queen of the Desert* (Stephan Elliot, Australia, 1991), *The Crying Game* (Neil Jordan, UK, 1992), *Farewell My*

Julian Stringer, PhD, is Lecturer in Film Studies at the University of Nottingham. He has published essays on Asian cinema in numerous anthologies as well as *Screen* and *Cineaction.* He is currently working on a study of the history and politics of film festivals.

Address correspondence to the author at: Institute of Film Studies, School of American and Canadian Studies, University of Nottingham, University Park, Nottingham, NG7 2RD, England (E-mail: Julian.Stringer@nottingham.ac.uk).

[Haworth co-indexing entry note]: "Two Japanese Variants of the Absolute Transvestite Film." Stringer, Julian. Co-published simultaneously in *Journal of Homosexuality* (The Haworth Press, Inc.) Vol. 39, No. 3/4, 2000, pp. 111-126; and: *Queer Asian Cinema: Shadows in the Shade* (ed: Andrew Grossman) Harrington Park Press, an imprint of The Haworth Press, Inc., 2000, pp. 111-126. Single or multiple copies of this article are available for a fee from The Haworth Document Delivery Service [1-800-342-9678, 9:00 a.m. - 5:00 p.m. (EST). E-mail address: getinfo@haworthpressinc.com].

Concubine (Chen Kaige, China, 1993), *Orlando* (Sally Potter, UK, 1993), *Peking Opera Blues* (Tsui Hark, Hong Kong, 1986), and *Rouge* (Stanley Kwan, Hong Kong, 1987) demonstrates that cross-dressing in Asian and non-Asian cinema remains a subject of some analytic importance. Imaginative titles such as these explore issues of sexual ambiguity by proposing transvestism as a suggestive illustrative metaphor for the impossibility of social subjects ever securing fixed gender identities.

While some are quick to point out that the kind of movies listed above potentially disrupt existing boundary classifications, and so encourage the establishment of new ones, others have argued that gender-confusion narratives frequently work to reassert masculine privilege. Popular examples of the form may refuse to interrogate the binary relationships upon which sexual difference is constructed, or else they may neglect to challenge the implied primacy of a male, white, heterosexual (and/or Western) gaze. Either way, movies concerning cross-dressed characters are the site of real ideological contestation, the terrain upon which cross-cultural struggles over questions of power, representation, and appropriation are often played out.

In terms of Western critical discourse, the theoretically sophisticated interventions into the psychodynamics of transvestite representation provided from within Anglo-American film theory by such feminist scholars as Chris Straayer (1996), Annette Kuhn (1985), and Gaylyn Studlar (1991) are of particular interest. These three writers analyze gender masquerade by asking how cross-dressing in the movies validates the needs and desires of such subcultural audiences as midnight movie fans and gay, lesbian and queer spectators. Each starts out by identifying in dominant Western cinema a certain paradigm of transvestite commodification. According to this paradigm, the project of any individual film is to organize itself around the presence of a diegetic character who momentarily adopts a gender disguise so as to motivate and advance the narrative. Paradoxically, though, such stories are usually told in a highly conventional fashion. A character introjects into him or herself the (valued or devalued) signifiers of an opposing subjectivity; spectatorial attention becomes anchored around the fascinations of a momentary drag act; at some point along the line, the transvestite character is then compelled to reveal her or his "true" biology to both the other diegetic characters and to the film's audience; and as a result, gender ambiguities are resolved through a reassertion of the boundaries separating male from female. With varying amounts of strain and uncertainty, what Straayer calls "the temporary transvestite film" habitually ends up offering the reassurance of gender stability.

Perhaps because there are so few (Asian and non-Asian) examples to draw upon, Straayer, Kuhn and Studlar tend not to talk about films which refute altogether the narrative expediency of a character's temporary disguise. In other words, they refuse to engage with the possibility of a wholesale masquerade, wherein a man plays a woman for the whole film, or where a woman plays a man for the whole film, without necessarily even drawing attention to the fact. (Examples of what Straayer (1996: 74) terms "trans-sex casting" include Linda Hunt in *The Year of Living Dangerously*, [Peter Weir, 1983] and Divine in *Hairspray* [John Waters, 1988]). What I would like to call here "the absolute transvestite film" presents an expert drag act so as to focus on a paradox. Offering a seemingly secure representation of a stable gender identity, absolute transvestite films simultaneously throw into the air the whole nature of gender identity by encouraging a total (mis?)recognition of a successful masquerade, an "impossible" identification with the opposite sex.

It could be argued that within the contemporary US commercial cinema, the film that comes closest to exhibiting some awareness of how this might be done is *The Ballad of Little Jo* (Maggie Greenwald, 1993.) Based upon historical fact, this film concerns a woman in the nineteenth century American West, Josephine Monaghan (Suzy Amis), who successfully impersonated and lived as a man for forty years. (The community she lived among only discovered her masquerade upon her death.) However, Greenwald chooses to present the viewer with the objective knowledge that Josephine/Jo is "really" a woman right at the very beginning of the plot, thus ensuring that we carry this awareness through to the end of the narrative–hence the spectator once again delights in the fact that other characters cannot see through what we know to be a successful masquerade. While not wishing to take anything away from the film's very accomplished revision of the Western, a notoriously masculinist genre, it is telling that audiences of *The Ballad of Little Jo* are not allowed to be seduced by the protagonist's brilliant disguise in the same way that the other characters are. By refusing to experiment with a more absolute form of misrecognition, gender dynamics are once again subordinated to the thrill of a spectacular narrative revelation.

In contrast, I would like to offer a few thoughts concerning two Japanese films which manage to resist this urge to organize narrative interest around the unveiling of a transvestite's "true" biological sex. Both *Black Lizard* (*Kurotokage*, Fukasaku Kinji, 1968) and *Summer Vacation 1999* (*Sen Kyuhyaku Kyuju Kyunen no Natsu Yasumi*, Kaneko Shusuke, 1989) may be said to favor versions of absolute transvestism. Now, given the culturally specific constructions of gender operative within the Japanese theatrical and subcultural traditions they draw upon, it is not wholly surprising that my examples come from the non-Western commercial cinema. However, it is not my intention to trot out an Orientalist argument about how it is the "difference" and "otherness" of these two titles that sets them apart from comparable Western films. It is not too much of a stretch of the imagination to picture films that are just as engaging and conceptually challenging being made in North America and Europe.

I have chosen to write about these two movies, then, for three reasons. First, because I like them very much. Second, because they do things with cross-dressing that Western commercial narrative films appear not to have done yet. And, third, because in doing these things, they seem to demand a slight modification or extension of some of the critical possibilities advanced by Western theorists of cross-dressing in the cinema. Throughout the paper, I try to keep two questions in mind. What is it about *Black Lizard* and *Summer Vacation 1999* that allows them to carry off their cross-gender imperson-ations so well? Can such forms of absolute transvestism be appropriated into Western film studies in ways that are culturally respectful, critically desirable and politically useful? Before pursuing these questions, however, it is neces-sary to spend a little more time explaining how an absolute transvestite film differs from a more temporary one.

NARRATIVE

Chris Straayer defines the temporary transvestite genre as "a specific subset of transvestite films in which a character uses cross-dressing tempo-rarily for purposes of necessary disguise" (42). As already stated, the constit-uent feature of such films is that they are organized around a linear narrative dynamic. It is necessary for a character to adopt a disguise, one that is either adequate or inadequate to the job of hiding his or her biological gender; the disguise engenders a slippage of heterosexual and homosexual identities; the film's audience is clued into the disguised character's "real" gender by a manipulation of objective and subjective points of view; finally, the unmask-ing of the disguise proceeds hand-in-glove with the narrative resolution, both of which are usually structured to resonate against the final restoration of the heterosexual couple.

While it is certainly true to say that the temporary transvestite film pro-vides the liberating possibility of gender confusion, it tends to mitigate against what Straayer describes as the kind of "unexplained transvestism that subverts the convention of necessity" (45) in *Boy! What a Girl!* (Arthur Leonard, 1947). Accordingly, there must be a *reason*, a narrative justification for the transvestite's introjection of other gender signifiers, together with some kind of containment device–narrative closure–to frame, explain and regulate disturbing questions of why characters adopt the accroutements of a different sex. In utilizing a distinction made by Esther Newton between cross-dressing (which "exaggerates the opposite sex's assumed gender codes to appear obviously, inadequately disguised") and transvestism (an attempt "to pass as a member of the opposite sex"), Straayer postulates that the "generic plot" of such films is transvestite (because other diegetic characters are fooled by the disguise), while "because the disguise is inadequate to trick the film audience, its extradiegetic operation is that of cross-dressing" (47).

As a slight modification of these arguments, I would point out that the Asian absolute transvestite films *Black Lizard* and *Summer Vacation 1999* provide no "explanation" for their transvestism, that they reject the "convention of necessity," and that they construct spectators who are potentially just as unaware of the masquerade as the diegetic characters themselves. More properly, they totally reverse Straayer's schema. The generic plot of the two films may be considered cross-dressing, as no one need be fooled by a disguise when an issue is not made of that disguise, while as the technically brilliant performances of the male to female transvestite in *Black Lizard* and the four young female to male transvestites in *Summer Vacation 1999* are more than adequate to trick an unaware (cross-cultural?) film audience, their extradiegetic operations are transvestite.

Annette Kuhn elaborates on the temporary transvestite film's need to construct narrative closure when she writes that "sexual disguise must usually be accounted for, given some sort of explanation within the story. Where a character assumes sexual disguise during the course of the narrative, this move typically constitutes a disruption that sets the story in motion" (57). Once again, it is suggested that the form taken by such films will embody a master-slave dialectic, as the plausibility and pleasures of the disguise will always be subordinated to the forward march of the narrative. Titles like *Victor/Victoria* (Blake Edwards, 1982) and *Tootsie* (Sydney Pollack, 1982) need to guide their viewers through the processes and justifications of transvestism because "explanations . . . often constitute a central element of plot, sometimes even activating the narrative. In this sense, these films construct cross dressing as in varying degrees culturally 'strange'" (59).

For Kuhn, too, stories can differ in how they let audiences know of such disguise through objective or subjective narration, through how much more knowledge than the other characters is possessed by the viewer. Kuhn introduces the useful concept of the "view behind" (62) a cross-dressed character, namely a secure vantage point occupied by the spectator that lets him or her know when a character is masquerading. On the other side, in the two Japanese films I look at, the view behind the masquerade is extended into a more distant perspective that circulates around the cult of stardom. *Black Lizard* and *Summer Vacation 1999* transfer gender intrigue from what Roland Barthes (1974) terms a narrative's hermeneutic code, or the linear code of enigmas (Why does s/he adopt a disguise? Will other characters recognize it? When will the unmasking occur?), to the wider social knowledge associated with what Barthes calls a text's symbolic and cultural codes. Given the homosexual inclinations of the two films, such re-focusing of audience competencies around less "obvious," more covert material is entirely appropriate. And as Robin Wood (1986: 19) points out, "the richer and more complex the semantic/symbolic structure, the finer the film."

Gaylyn Studlar writes about a series of American midnight movies–*Pink Flamingos* (John Waters, 1970), *The Rocky Horror Picture Show* (Jim Sharman, 1975), and *Liquid Sky* (Slava Tsukerman, 1982)–which, through gender ambiguity, concern themselves with "the deeply problematic construction of femininity in patriarchal culture" (143). According to Studlar, such titles resolutely fail to challenge fixed male (white, heterosexual) spectator positions through their "unwillingness to be perverse enough" (141–to which one might respond, perverse enough for *what?*). For her, all three titles expose male anxieties about femininity. Writing about Divine in *Pink Flamingos*, for example, she asks, "is our awareness of Divine's maleness, like that of any female impersonator, the unalterable difference that inevitably makes his/her sexual jokes and representation of female sexuality 'a form of male aggression upon the woman he personates?'" (143). Her article ends by calling for a popular narrative cinema (one that does not exist yet) that would be delightfully perverse in the extreme.

Maruyama Akihiro's transvestism in *Black Lizard* is not like the work of any celluloid female impersonator I can think of, and while it is certainly possible to argue that the whole basis of *Black Lizard* is a joke on being female, it is also possible to read the film as being perverse enough through its very accessibility. Escaping the marginal, safely regulated zone of the midnight movie show and subcultural arena, Fukasaku's detective thriller places absolute transvestism squarely in terms of popular culture.

I am not about to argue that *Black Lizard* and *Summer Vacation 1999* provide a simple subversion of all the limitations of the temporary transvestite film–clearly, they are caught up in some of the problems isolated by the critics mentioned above, and they demand to be read in more than just the terms I choose to advocate here. Even though I am happy to think of the two works being appropriated by Western spectators through acts of productive re-contextualization, I would also warn against the temptation to try and increase the political use value of such films (as well as the cultural capital of individual spectators) by viewing them solely through the lens of an exclusively Western camp and/or queer interpretation. Culturally alien readings should not be superimposed onto Asian cinemas too casually.

In addition, it is worth bearing in mind that part of the reason why *Black Lizard* and *Summer Vacation 1999* are so striking to the distant observer is because they are also somewhat striking within Japan itself. The distinction of both films is to exist within the heartland of "official" Japanese culture, while also flirting with its "unofficial" margins. The former does this through a self-conscious affiliation with a gay male subculture, the latter through the evocation of a barely submerged lesbianism.

BLACK LIZARD

Black Lizard, which plays like a camp Japanese *film noir*, appears not to have been shown in the West until featured as part of the 1984 Edinburgh International Film Festival's pioneering retrospective of twenty-five years of Japanese cinema (Rayns, 1984). Since then, it has been unspooled at various gay and lesbian film festivals, exhibited in a short run at New York's Film Forum in 1991, and distributed widely in the US on videocassette.

The film has the air of a knowing cult item. Shot by a veteran director of yakuza pictures, Fukasaku Kinji, starring a famed transvestite and nightclub host, Maruyama Akihiro, and written by Mishima Yukio, noted gay artist, political extremist and suicide obsessive, whose shocking death by *seppuko* in 1970 still makes ideologues of official Japanese culture queasy, *Black Lizard* has been written out of English-language histories of the national cinema. The film doesn't quite seem to fit, not even as a footnote to a recognized Kabuki/transvestite classic like *An Actor's Revenge* (Ichikawa Kon, 1962). As far as I can tell, David Desser (1988: 96) is virtually alone among Western scholars of Japanese cinema in pointing out its tangential relationship to the New Wave cinema of the 1960s, and in recognizing its unusual fascinations.

Certainly, the plot itself is perverse enough. A famed detective named Akechi (Kimura Isao) enters a secret nightclub and encounters its owner, the master criminal Black Lizard (Maruyama Akihiro). Employed by the jeweller, Iwase (Usami Junya), to stop the theft of his priceless diamond, The Star of Egypt, Akechi manages to thwart Black Lizard's attempt to kidnap Iwase's daughter, Sanae (Matsuoka Kikko). After a second, successful kidnap attempt in Tokyo, Black Lizard is tracked to her hideout by the disguised Akechi, then foiled in her attempt to kill Sanae and turn her beautiful body into another one of her bizarre human statues (Mishima plays her prized possession). Humiliated because Akechi has listened to all her private declarations of love for a detective who has such "a deep and romantic attachment to crime," Black Lizard commits suicide. Akechi mourns the impossibility of their love, proclaiming with great feeling that Black Lizard had the heart of "a true diamond."

Aside from featuring a transvestite villain who is given no "justification" for dressing up, and who never has her "true" biology revealed or even hinted at by the narrative, *Black Lizard* features a dazzling collection of presentational metaphors about the illusionary nature of gender. All the main characters adopt disguises. Akechi starts out as the kind of salaryman who fuelled Japan's post-war economic renovation, but soon adopts the disguise of an old hunchback so as to catch the villain; Black Lizard evades Akechi's clutches in Osaka by herself dressing as a man in a suit; when Sanae is kidnapped a second time in Tokyo, it is revealed that the villains have only succeeded in snatching an impostor, a look-a-like; finally, the young man who falls in love first with Sanae, and then with Sanae's double masquerades as a young businessman, a bearded seaman, and as Black Lizard's slave. Indeed, part of the fun of the film lies in the fact that all the actors appear so eager to camp it up by trying on as many different costumes as possible. In addition, the director enhances this illusionism through a number of stylistic choices, such as mirror shots and paralleled tracking shots. And to top it all off there is the beauty of Mishima's elusive, poetic dialogue, which beckons and winks like The Star of Egypt itself.

Described like this, *Black Lizard* resembles a mix of the serious and the trivial, a modern-day fairy tale for adults. For the purposes of this paper, I would like to suggest how its mix of camp and knowing subversion comes about through the interlocking of three authorial points of view. Happily, the end result of this fortuitous collaboration is an exposure of some of the anxieties characteristic of Japanese male subjectivity. Indeed, we might say that the joining of these three perspectives marks a refusal of consensus politics in favor of doubt and subversion–just as the film's refusal of temporary transvestism is marked in favor of absolute transvestism.

The first authorial discourse revolves around the extremely popular works of mystery writer Edogawa Rampo, whose original book, *Black Lizard*, was adapted by Mishima for the stage play that became the basis for the film. Rampo (a Japanization of Edgar Allen Poe) was responsible for creating the famous detective, Akechi, whose exploits have been read about by a young, predominantly female Japanese audience. Rampo is sometimes criticized for being "too Western" because his work is caught under the sway of the late nineteenth century American and European decadent imaginations. Transposing the grotesque imagery of a Poe or Oscar Wilde to a Japanese setting (and getting into trouble with native censors in the process), Rampo found a wide readership but little critical support. Tellingly, his genre pieces have tended to be passed over by standard histories of modern Japanese literature, while histories of Japanese cinema fail to discuss movies based on his work, such as *Black Lizard* or Tanaka Noboru's 1976 *roman-poruno-eiga* (romantic-pornographic film), *Stroller in the Attic (Yaneura no Sanpo Sha)*. (The success of Okuyama Kazuyoshi's *The Mystery of Rampo* (1993), at more or less the same time as the release in Japan of other Rampo adaptations, indicates that this situation may be changing.)

Edogawa Rampo provides an interesting example of how a Western-influenced decadent imagination can be put in the service of an exploration of modern Japanese subjectivity. As with Poe, there is a level of psychosexual and familial anxiety in the writer's concerns, one that works against the uniquely homogenizing tendencies of Japanese nationalism in the post-Meiji Restoration period. If the first collection of Rampo's stories published in English, *Japanese Tales of Mystery and Imagination* (1956), is anything to go by, his fictions are habitually concerned with the shape-shifting terrors of male loss and lack. One of them, "The Hell of Mirrors," provides an interpretation of the mirror-phase of subject development that would make Jacques Lacan spit in jealous rage. In this story, a man who has a fetish for anything capable of reflecting an image traps himself inside a mirror-laden metal ball and goes mad.

Similarly, of course, male to female transvestism is often read as an act of loss, of emasculation, as it entails a wilful identification with the culturally devalued feminine. Maruyama Akihiro's absolute transvestite performance in *Black Lizard*, however, suggests more than the kind of fetishistic attachment to the image of a phallic woman that might alleviate the castration anxieties of male spectators. To explain why this is so, let us consider the film's opening scene.

Black Lizard starts out with a brief explanatory voice-over by Akechi describing his thoughts on first entering a secret nightclub festooned with Aubrey Beardsley prints. After Black Lizard's star entrance, the credits begin to roll over her performance of a torch song, while shots of her singing are intercut with Beardsley's illustrations for Oscar Wilde's interpretation of the *Salome* myth. Throughout these opening images, the credits represent Japanese nostalgia for the kind of *fin-de-siecle* Western decadence that Rampo Edogawa emulated and that also seduced Mishima.

However, the credits show a keen awareness of the gender subversion suggested by this specific choice of art-historical reference matter. Even though Akechi meets Black Lizard in a club frequented by heterosexuals (it is full of scantily-clad female go-go dancers being ogled and groped by businessmen in suits), the entire film works to codify a gay seduction—from Akechi's opening voice-over ("This was a new experience for me") to the declaration by the detective and the criminal of their mutually impossible love for each other. As Charles Bernheimer (1993) and others have suggested, Beardsley's illustrations for Wilde themselves provide a subversive gender spin on the sexual dynamics of the Biblical story. The illustration used most prominently in the film (to back the director's credit, for example) is the Medusan imagery of Salome floating in the air while holding the severed head of Jokanaan, which Bernheimer claims, for both Beardsley and Wilde, became "a stimulus to sexual inversion, confusion and parody, rather than a horrifying symbol of emasculation," as it could easily have been. On these terms, Salome's decapitation celebrates "the many suggestions of deviant sexual practice that suffuse this image," and the film utilizes its significations as if to emphasize that we must throw the phallocentric logic of castration theory "on the compost heap of history" (73).

Further, *Black Lizard* everywhere celebrates the kind of deviant sexual practices that Edogawa Rampo delights in. By turning the author's fondness for a male figure who is seduced by a criminal female into a transvestite's seduction of a straight man, the film highlights the illicit nature of Japanese homosexuality. On a broader level, too, the movie dramatizes the female impersonator's appropriation of femininity, which is literalized through an allegory about a master criminal kidnapping a young woman three times so as to take her feminine beauty for herself. As in a fairy tale, the gender dynamics are only thinly veiled; the theft, or "hijacking," of feminine gender is needed so as to empower and beautify a (cross-dressed) man.

It is not exactly clear to me whether or not the film's audience, either Japanese or Western, is meant to realize that Black Lizard is played by an expert female impersonator, which is to say that if the film presents an absolute transvestite masquerade it does not impose any absolute recognition on the viewer's part. The view behind the transvestite image that Annette Kuhn talks about is not offered up to the knowing spectator through narrative signalling of Maruyama's biological gender (although the use of costume–high collars that hide his adam's apple oscillating with the shock of an open neck–may help). Yet as the work of Rolanda Chu (1994) indicates, the provocative meanings of a star image such as Maruyama's can provide a "view outside" of the view behind cross-dressing.

Ian Buruma (1984: 117) has noted that Maruyama Akihiro (Miwa Akihiro) hosted a famous night club where her female impersonation act was the main attraction. Maruyama's transvestism was commodified as serious entertainment for a cultured audience, while "to a Western observer all this is the highest of Camp":

> Camp rests on a sense of irony: the irony of a serious attempt to reach an impossible ideal, the gap between human inadequacy and the grandiose goal . . . the point is, though, that there is no gap between attempt and ideal in Miwa's club or the Kabuki theater or the Takarazuka: people do not pretend that the ideal has anything to do with reality. They enjoy seeing Lady MacBeth played by a famous Kabuki star, precisely because it is more artificial, thus more skilful, in a word, more beautiful.

David Desser (96) elaborates on this observation, first by rejecting (a little too quickly, in my opinion) the obvious Western response to *Black Lizard* ("While camp may be a positive value to some, there is something a bit condescending in such a judgement. Maruyama Akihiro's image, as Ian Buruma notes, is not camp"), and then by claiming that in the film "sex roles are deliberately theatricalized, highlighted in their social essence, and so provide a starting point for a radical critique of the dominant culture's attitudes toward sexuality."

While not wishing to diminish the technical brilliance of Maruyama's performance as a manifestation of the culturally beautiful, the point should also be made that Maruyama's socially mobile nightclub success carries an obverse set of meanings. On one hand, Buruma describes his routine's weirdly unexpected cultural effects: "'Oh, she's looking lovely tonight', says an elderly gentleman to his wife. And a tear rolls down the scarred cheek of a tough-looking character immediately recognizable as a member of the gangster community" (87). On the other hand, this success has as its repressed other Maruyama's apprenticeship, in the words of Mishima's biographer, Henry Scott Stokes (1974: 151) as "the most celebrated female impersonator of his day" in the gay bars of Tokyo (such as the Brunswick, where he first met Mishima). As such, this dazzling transvestite performance is at once an extremely stylized theatrical *tour de force*, and an extension of private feelings and subcultural affiliations.

If *Black Lizard* had been written by virtually anyone else except Mishima Yukio, this fact might not have seemed quite so important. For Edogawa Rampo's detective narrative and Maruyama Akihiro's transvestite skills are politically energized by Mishima's presence. Mishima wrote the part of the master jewel thief for his cross-dressing friend in between making his own appearances in macho yakuza films. Given all this, the question remains: What kind of mind would produce such an absolute transvestite image?

The question can be slightly recast: How can this absolute transvestite image co-exist with the masculinist nature of Mishima's thought and public image at this time? Mishima's fascination with the possibilities of gender confusion are evidenced both by his interest in the official *onnagata* tradition of male transvestism on the Kabuki stage (the ostensible influence for Maruyama's style) and in his own "unofficial" nocturnal wanderings as a denizen of Tokyo's gay bars.

Produced only two years before Mishima's spectacular death, *Black Lizard* dramatizes the ambiguous and contradictory masculinist logic that led up to Mishima's very public act of *seppuko* in 1970. The toying with issues of illusionism, bodybuilding, voyeurism and violence are all familiar from his writings. In addition, the author's appearance in the film functions like a prequel to how he wanted his own body remembered–as an idealized art object. Yet for all the official public recognition Mishima enjoyed, he met Maruyama in the gay clubs. Moreover, he was often seen closing the latter's performance of a cabaret number ("The Sailor Who Was Killed by Paper

Roses") with a gay kiss that made it into the Japanese tabloid newspapers as "shocking" behavior for a married celebrity to be indulging in public.

A thinly-veiled version of that tender act makes it into *Black Lizard*, as the eponymous villain plants a kiss on her beloved embalmed statue, played by Mishima. Significantly, this particular kiss is highly over-determined because it is privileged as being the only moment repeated twice within the film. It is also followed by a reaction shot of a woman, Sanae (or rather Sanae's double) recoiling in horror, as if she were to be taken as representative of the scandal-ized Japanese public. In other words, at this moment the view behind the transvestite image (which has never been presented to the spectator, but which we may or may not have taken up) is collapsed together with the view outside, and the skilful, beautiful tradition of the *onnagata* is mixed in with the memory of a gay bar kiss. Simply put, while the Kabuki stage sanctions an official version of transvestism, Mishima and Maruyama here takes its unofficial shadow out of the subcultural sphere by throwing a challenge to the national viewing subject.

Push the absolute transvestite logic of *Black Lizard* one step further and Mishima's own obsession with preserving his beautiful body begins to re-semble a masquerade, a drag act. In light of the film's narrative concerns–a thief wants to preserve beautiful bodies as living statues–it is impossible not to read its gender dynamics outside of the knowledge of what Mishima did to his own body on November 25, 1970. Black Lizard's diegetic desire to embalm beautiful living dolls is matched by Mishima's own philosophy on the preservation of masculinity. Mishima is a unique figure in twentieth century media history in that he pushed the logic of what Susan Jeffords (1994) terms the masculine "hard body" way past breaking point. After spending a decade building his muscles up, he refused to see them waste away through the process of ageing. Instead, his solution was to preserve his ideal hard body through ritual suicide. He disembowelled himself with tre-mendous enthusiasm, ensuring that his body image would live on in popular memory as a force to be reckoned with.

The director Shinoda Masahiro (quoted in Mellen, 1975: 243) once noted, somewhat cryptically, that Mishima felt that "being a living thing, a flower must cease to exist. He thought that in order to obtain an eternal flower it is best to make it an artificial or 'Hong Kong' flower . . . he never believed that his flower was a real one. Therefore, he had to shed his own blood to make it real. I wonder then why Mishima so ardently needed to make a plastic flower into a real flower and then into an eternal one." *Black Lizard* embodies this strange philosophy in two ways. First, its presentation of Maruyama's abso-lute transvestite performance aspires to turn an imitation woman into a real one and then into an eternal one. Second, the view outside the film is caught up with Mishima's own body image as it would become immortalized through *seppuko*. As a result, the film's refusal to compromise with the viewer through letting her or him *know* the terms of the transvestite masquerade signals a refusal to compromise with the kind of agreed, polite consensual understandings of Japanese society Mishima himself kicked against.

SUMMER VACATION 1999

Kaneko Shusuke's *Summer Vacation 1999* is influenced by a different tradition of Japanese absolute transvestism, namely the female to male cross-dressing performances of the Takarazuka theater. All the roles in this story of the adolescent longings, fears and desires experienced by four young boys at boarding school are played by young girls aged between fourteen and sixteen. If male to female absolute transvestism of the kind practiced in *Black Lizard* raises the question of why a man would want to introject into himself the devalued signifiers of femininity, female to male transvestism of the sort presented by the Takarazuka Revue raises the possibility of a feminine appropriation of masculine privilege through gender imitation.

A collection of established stars and new faces, the four young leads of *Summer Vacation 1999*, Miyajima Eri, Nakano Miyuki, Otakara Temeke, and Mizuhara Rie, pull off their imitations of boyhood adolescence with a brilliance that fully demonstrates the technical skills and affective possibilities advanced by the Takarazuka Revue. The film is set in a deserted school where four barely pubescent boys are holed up for the summer. It opens with the apparent suicide of the lovesick Yu (Miyajima) after his rejection by the cold-hearted Kazuhiko (Otakara). Three months later a new boy, Kaoru (Miyajima in a double role), who bares an uncanny resemblance to Yu, arrives and starts to open up old rivalries and passions. Jealousies erupt between the two as well as between the other boys, Naoto (Nakano) and Nario (Mizuhara). The possibility that Kaoru may or may not actually be Yu brings the various adolescent homoerotic longings out towards the verge of another tragedy.

As with *Black Lizard*, *Summer Vacation 1999* nowhere points narratively to its gender masquerades, and it can be said to be open to persistent and absolute gender misrecognition by "naïve" viewers. Appropriately enough, the film works through an elaborate series of paradoxes and uncertainties. While the four female actors all give utterly solid and convincing performances, the presence of a number of unresolved narrative enigmas (Is Kaoru really Yu? Which of the young boys is providing the retrospective voice-over narration?), together with a brilliantly subtle use of symbolism, points to nothing but doubt and incoherence. Again, the film undermines gender distinctions through a consistent concern with illusionism. (While it is set in an identified future, a lot of the cute gadgets and gizmos used in the school appear to have come from out of the past.) There are no female characters, and the boys speak in masculine speech patterns, yet the primary color compositions are light and delicate, and the stunning musical score for piano and strings connotes classical "female culture."

With this film, the narrative hermeneutics of the temporary cross-dressing film as discussed by Straayer, Kuhn and Studlar–When will the moment of revelation come? How will the disguise be broken? Will it be comic or tragic?–are replaced by the viewer's cultural appreciation of professionalism in terms of performance. Jennifer Robertson (1989: 53) has provided an analysis of the Takarazuka Revue's rationale, which decrees that the aim of any individual female participant is to "eliminate what is different yet to display as much difference as possible . . . she must, through technologies of gender such as clothing, speech, gestures and ambience, signify 'male' gender in such a way as to make it, and her very person, appear uncoded or 'natural'." Female performers in this tradition strive to represent a socially valued masculinity at the same time as they work to overcome the devaluing of femininity.

Robertson also points out that the Takarazuka Revue provides an important outlet for the development of lesbian relationships (both among actresses and among star-audience identifications) which challenge the silence surrounding explicit representations of love and sex between women in Japanese culture. It might be emphasized that this challenge is powerfully carried by absolute transvestite representation; after all, while a temporary transvestite hermeneutic can be explained away as "just a phase," a brief disruption of the normative order, *Summer Vacation 1999* fixes gender masquerade and imitation as the norm itself.

Like *Black Lizard*, the film comes out of a mix of official and unofficial cultures. While the all-female theatrical revue is internationally celebrated, Kaneko has claimed that he based *Summer Vacation 1999* partly on his own childhood experiences of alienation, and partly on Hagio Moto's quasi-gay graphic storybook from the 1970s, *Toma's Heart* (*Toma no Shinzo*). Like many other examples of *shojo manga* (*manga* aimed at girls), Hagio's work depicts male homosexuality for a young female audience. Indeed, she was one of a group of female artists who revolutionized the comic book form in that decade by portraying the sensual actions of male heroes existing in all-male worlds (e.g., *The November Gymnasium*, or *Juichigatsu no Gimuna-jiumu*, set in an all-male boarding school in Europe).

Transferred into the terms of a commercial film, Kaneko's script (co-written by Rio Kishida, who used to collaborate with avant-garde film and theater director Shuji Terayama) has the distinction of working through a circular logic rather than a strict cause-effect chain. As befits a narrative about the confusions between past, present and future, there is no strong resolution and clear tying together of all loose ends, but rather an associational mix of shifting identities and problematics that mimics the serial narratives of the comic book form itself.

Moreover, because *Summer Vacation 1999* is concerned with that moment of subject development between childhood and adulthood when, according to "traditional" Japanese aesthetics, a boy or girl can be considered most "perfect" (like a cherry blossom, his or her beauty will soon wither and fade away), its narrative presents a form of chaste androgyny rather than the gay bar associations of *Black Lizard*. However, Kaneko's film has something in common with Fukasaku's in that it is also organized around the shock of a sexualized kiss. Towards the end of the film, Kaoru finally seduces Kazuhiko when the two embrace on the cliff overlooking the lake that is the location for both the narrative's opening and closing moments. Again, because of its homosexual implications, the scene provides a challenge to the viewer. As with Sanae's shocked response to Maruyama's planting of a kiss on Mishima in the earlier film, this jolt is registered by the reaction of a diegetic character–this time Naoto, who is jealous of Kaoru.

What the centrality and similarity of two such kissing scenes in these otherwise very different absolute transvestite films suggest are a range of interesting questions. What is the connection between diegetic and non-diegetic reactions to same-sex kisses in Japanese cinema? Are these codified as appropriate reactions for a (male/female) national viewing subject? Does the kiss in absolute transvestite narratives serve the same kind of narrative function as the revelation of gender masquerade in temporary transvestite films? Has the long-standing prohibition on the depiction of genitals in Japanese media meant a slight modification of how transvestite revelations can be depicted? Does all of this constitute a different aesthetic of the erotic than we may be used to in Western countries?

While this is not the place to consider these much wider issues, I want to end by pointing to one marked instability in the status of *Black Lizard* and *Summer Vacation 1999* as absolute transvestite films, namely the highly tentative and ambiguous nature of their respective voice-overs. In both cases, the seemingly objective knowledge given on the soundtrack at any one moment is subverted the next through the voice-over's disappearance, or else through its sudden transferral to another character. In other words, even if the films construct absolute gender (mis)recognition, the soundtracks still encourage temporary (shifting, transitory) identifications. At the same time as I wish to acknowledge and celebrate the absolute transvestism of these two films, I find it interesting that even such wholesale masquerades end up gesturing towards the ultimate fragility of all gender representation.

REFERENCES

Barthes, R. (1974). *S/Z*. New York: Hill and Wang.

Bernheimer, C. (1993). "Fetishism and decadence: Salome's severed heads." In E. Apter and W. Pietz (eds.), *Fetishism as Cultural Discourse*. Ithica: Cornell University Press, pp. 62-83.

Buruma, I. (1984). *Behind the Mask: On Sexual Demons, Sacred Mothers, Transvestites, Gangsters, and Other Japanese Cultural Heroes*. London: Penguin.

Chu, R. (1994). "*Swordsman II* and *The East is Red*: The 'Hong Kong film', entertainment and gender." *Bright Lights*, 13, pp. 30-35, 46.

Desser, D. (1988). *Eros Plus Massacre: An Introduction to the Japanese New Wave Cinema*. Bloomington: Indiana University Press.

Jeffords, S. (1994). *Hard Bodies: Hollywood Masculinity in the Reagan Era*. New Brunswick: Rutgers University Press.

Kuhn, A. (1985). *The Power of the Image: Essays on Representation and Sexuality*. London: Routledge and Kegan Paul.

Mellen, J. (1975). *Voices from the Japanese Cinema*. New York: Liverlight.

Rayns, T. (1984). *Eiga: 25 Years of Japanese Cinema*. Edinburgh: Edinburgh International Film Festival.

Robertson, J. (1989). "Gender-Bending in paradise: Doing 'female' and 'male' in Japan." *Genders* 5 (Summer), pp. 188-207.

Stokes, H.S. (1974). *The Life and Death of Yukio Mishima*. New York: Farar, Straus and Giroux.

Straayer, C. (1996). *Deviant Eyes, Deviant Bodies: Sexual Re-Orientations in Film and Video*. New York: Columbia University Press.

Studlar, G. (1991). "Midnight s/excess: Cult configurations of femininity and the perverse." In J.P. Telotte (ed.), *The Cult Film Experience: Beyond All Reason*. Austin: University of Texas Press, pp. 138-155.

Wood, R. (1986). "Notes for a reading of *I Walked With a Zombie*." *Cineaction!*, 3-4 (January), pp. 6-20.

Obscenity and Homosexual Depiction in Japan

Udo Helms
Tokyo University

SUMMARY. This essay serves as an historical introduction to the problem of film censorship in Japan, a country which, despite an often liberal sexual history, continues to impose baffling and even irrational censorship standards on both its domestic and imported cinema. However, whereas sexual censorship in the West is often the result of religious dogmatism, Japanese film censorship may in fact revolve around political struggles whose import is not the censoring of offensiveness *per se,* but is rather authoritarianism's basic yet desperate desire to assert itself in an increasingly liberal political climate. Furthermore, Japanese censorship has had the unique side effect of creating safe spaces of sexual fantasy (for children, for example) that most countries, in what is in fact a greater form of censorship, refuse to create at all. *[Article copies available for a fee from The Haworth Document Delivery Service: 1-800-342-9678. E-mail address: <getinfo@haworthpressinc.com> Website: <http://www.HaworthPress.com>]*

INTRODUCTION: THE TÔGÔ CASE

When Tôgô Ken, publisher and editor of the magazine *The Gay* and a well-known figure of the gay community in Japan,[1] returned to Tokyo from

Udo Helms, a PhD student, graduated in Japanese and Media Studies with a thesis on the self-regulation system of the Japanese movie industry at Free University of Berlin in 1999. He is currently a PhD research student at the Institute of Socio-Informative Communication Studies (ISICS) at Tokyo University. His previous publications include the translation and analysis of taiyou no kisetsu ("Season of the Sun," 1956) at Humboldt University Berlin in 1999. (E-mail: ahyra_matsda@hotmail.com).

[Haworth co-indexing entry note]: "Obscenity and Homosexual Depiction in Japan." Helms, Udo. Co-published simultaneously in *Journal of Homosexuality* (The Haworth Press, Inc.) Vol. 39, No. 3/4, 2000, pp. 127-147; and: *Queer Asian Cinema: Shadows in the Shade* (ed: Andrew Grossman) Harrington Park Press, an imprint of The Haworth Press, Inc., 2000, pp. 127-147. Single or multiple copies of this article are available for a fee from The Haworth Document Delivery Service [1-800-342-9678, 9:00 a.m. - 5:00 p.m. (EST). E-mail address: getinfo@haworthpressinc.com].

127

San Francisco one February morning in 1987, he was in for an unpleasant surprise. Customs officials at Haneda Municipal Airport confiscated a number of gay magazines and tapes he had bought in the States, claiming these contained obscenity (waisetsu). Considering this incident–a regrettable but insignificant nuisance–Tôgô gave in to the confiscation, only to find himself additionally charged with "the attempt to import obscene goods into Japan with the possible purpose of redistribution," which in his case carried a fine of 84'000 ¥. It was this "criminalization" that made him search legal assistance.

Japanese trials are lengthy in general, especially when they run through all institutions such as this one did. In the first instance, Tôgô was found guilty; since he edited a gay magazine, it was found that the "risk" of redistribution of the obscene materials was indeed high. Tokyo High Court overruled this decision in 1995, however, arguing that the magazines and tapes had been in his private possession; Tôgô had built his defense on §19 of the International Declaration of Human Rights, which claims the superiority of the private right of freedom of expression over any national law limits, and §21 of the Japanese Constitution, which guarantees freedom of expression as well as the prohibition of censorship (Asai 1995: 10f.). The decision made Tôgô's trial a landmark case; the importing of obscene goods for private possession would henceforth be allowed. Customs was not willing to give in to this however, and went in revision to the Supreme Court, which reverted to the guilty verdict in 1997 and sentenced Tôgô to pay the fine, and the cost of his litigation, which had exceeded the fine by four times that amount already in 1995 (ibid.).

To western understanding, this incident may appear utterly bizarre at first: How can one of the most advanced nations of the world possibly cling to a criminal charge as ancient as "obscenity"? One may wonder whether this incident has an antihomosexual touch, and whether heterosexual "obscenity" is equally persecuted. Since the problematic aspects of the articles in question obviously referred to the depiction of the male body in the nude, and the depiction of male-male sex, there is also the question whether obscenity applies more to gay than heterosexual erotica.

This paper will try to answer these questions; it will not try to construct a legal theory of discrimination of homosexuality in Japan, however. Contrary to most western nations, there have neither been legal prohibitions–nor protections–of homosexuality in Japan, which features a longstanding, if today obliterated, historical record of male homosexuality.[2] Discrimination is mostly related to social or economic aspects, and when evident in the media rather cultivates clichés than endorses contempt.[3] However, I will argue that given the factors and measures applied to the legal interpretation of obscenity today, there is a technical disadvantage of gay film if it involves the depiction of the male sexual organ–the only piece of imagery whose unobstructed depiction in whatever context is to this day prohibited without exception.

CALL IT RIGHT, CALL IT WRONG:
OBSCENITY STANDARDS AND AUTHORITIES

A look at *Badi*, the most popular gay magazine in Japan, suggests that as far as the contents of pornography in Japan is concerned, anything goes: there are countless depictions of the male body in the nude. These include images of male-male sex variations such as mutual masturbation, oral and anal intercourse, as the penetration of orifices with devices or limbs, sadomasochism including bondage, strangulation and flagellation, and soft paedophilia.[4] Nowhere, however, is the penis depicted unobscured; in photos, the shape of the penis is mostly blackened, in videos covered with a mosaic effect or white dots. In manga, the penis is not fully designed, so that it remains an outline, or the graphic design shows the act of penetration in close-up, so that the full sexual organ is not visible. Most puzzling to the western observer might be that variations of sex that are generally thought to be much more graphic remain unobscured, such as the insertion of limbs or enemas in the anus and sadomasochistic torture. It is quite apparent that the penis is obscene, whereas the arse is not. So what is the legal concept of obscenity?

WHAT IT IS ALL ABOUT?
THE DEFINITION OF OBSCENITY

Officially, censorship does not exist in Japan, which is–next to Germany– the only country which constitutionally forbids it. In both countries, the Allied occupation forces were instrumental in establishing a constitutional freedom of expression to guarantee the development of pluralism in its main adversaries of World War II. However, the Japanese government tried from the very first to obstruct this freedom, fearing its abuse by communist or other unwanted elements. When the Japanese government transmitted a draft of the new constitution to the Allies in 1946, the corresponding §217 bore a limitation: "Lawful measures to control vulgarities in literature, theater, film and broadcast shall be allowed in order to protect youth and the high public standard of civil behavior."[5] On screening the draft, this was crossed out by pen, with the remark: "Dangerous, since this could justify police observation." The desired limitation expresses the paternalistic attitude of Japanese authorities, which was to succeed over the intentions of the Allies in the course of the Chatterley trial (Kudo 1987: 106f.).

In early 1950, publisher Oyama Hisajirô and translator Itô Sei of the Japanese version of D. H. Lawrence's *Lady Chatterley's Lover* were charged with distribution of obscenity. Oyama was fined 250,000 ¥ in first instance on January 18th, 1952, but Itô was found not guilty. The court did not define the book as obscene per se, but just twelve passages from it. The next instance upheld Oyama's fine and additionally asked Itô to pay 100,000 ¥. The Supreme Court refused on March 13th, 1957 to omit these charges (Maki 1964: 3).

The defense referred repeatedly to § 21 of the constitution, i.e., that even if freedom of speech had to be limited for the sake of "public welfare," there would have to exist a definition of obscenity before the offense; otherwise persecution would be necessarily arbitrary. The Supreme Court rejected this argument, however, since judges would have to consider the interest of the general public, not the right of individuals to err. It justified its decision on the basis of a common sense of shame, which would make "normal" people feel uncomfortable when confronted with descriptions of sexual acts (ibid.: 10). It was acknowledged that the work in question was a piece of art, but at the same time it was determined that art and obscenity would not exclude each other (ibid.: 11).

The definition of obscenity which was developed from the verdict is:

> That which produces a sense of shame in a "normal" Japanese person who encounters, in public, an image or text whose primary intention or effect is to stimulate sexual desire. (Beer in Allison 1996: 149)

This definition is so vague that there is a lot of leeway for authorities to decide what is obscene and what is not–indeed so much leeway that they usually refer to precedent cases as a basis of justification for decisions (Okudaira et al. 1986: 130). Nevertheless–or maybe just because of that–the *Chatterley* verdict was repeatedly used to explain justiciary decisions, as in Tôgô's case.

The most puzzling fact about the *Chatterley* trial is, however, why the Occupation Forces allowed its initial start, and even passed sanctions themselves in its context,[6] considering their willingness to guarantee constitutional freedom of speech without limitations as described before. In the year the trial began, GHQ overruled the prohibition of the translation of Norman Mailer's *The Naked and the Dead* because there would have been no reactions in the United States upon the release of the book which would have justified such a move (Kudô 1987: 100). However, this was exactly the case with *Lady Chatterley's Lover*, which was prohibited in the U.S. until 1959, too.[11]

Lawrence's work was thereafter adopted to the collection of classic literature of the British publishing house Penguin, which is available internationally (including in Japan). Since this edition contained only text, it was not censored by Customs, which is only responsible for the passing of images. That means that since 1960–three years after the *Chatterley* verdict–the English version of the book has been available in Japan, whereas the Japanese translation does not contain the twelve "obscene" passages until today. The leading expert on freedom of expression in Japan, Okudaira Yasuhiro, thinks that this absurdity may be the reason for the persistence of §175 Penal Code,[8] which serves as the key reason to justify the Supreme Court's decision to prohibit these twelve passages. Its demise would therefore mean to admit a mistake (Okudaira et al. 1986: 91).

WHO DOES WHAT TO FILM?
CENSORSHIP AUTHORITIES

There are three authorities which are more or less entitled by law to monitor obscenity in film. The Administration Committee for the Motion Picture Code of Ethics (Eiga Rinri Kanri Iinkai, short Eirin), the body of self-regulation of the Japanese film industry, reviews all domestic and imported films intended for theatrical release. Eirin is a private institution, i.e., submitting films for classification is "voluntary,"[9] whereas Customs' (Zeikan) inspection of imported films is not; it directly relates to the prohibition of obscenity, although limited to visual material. Even if one or both of these authorities passes a film, the Metropolitan Police (Keishichô) may confiscate this item if it is considered obscene, and therefore a violation of §175 Penal Code–for example, when decisions of Eirin are thought to be too soft or a film is screened in an unauthorized version.

Most problematic is Customs censorship; it is impossible to determine exactly what this institution considers obscene, since there are no rules for the inspection. This means that distribution companies of imported films cannot be sure about possible claims beforehand (Baba 1993: 7). When confronted with this issue, Customs usually replies that sentences of the Supreme Court, most importantly the *Chatterley* verdict, would have explained what obscenity is–Customs only has to locate it (Shimizu 1997: 48).

Since there are no rules, the Customs Tariff Law of 1910 is the foundation of Customs' inspection; it was reactivated right after the end of the occupation in 1952. Section 61 of the law states the obligation to declare imported goods, §111 settles the punishment for a violation of this order: a fine of up to 350,000 ¥ or up to three years in prison (Nomura 1970: 274). Section 21 of the law[10] says that "books, pictures, sculptures and similar things which could endanger public order and customs" must not be imported to Japan. Examples are weapons or opium, but not obscenity, which is forbidden due to §175 of the Penal Code. In relation to film, the inspection office (Chôsakan) of Customs explained the following:

> Obscene articles are forbidden. In principle, these contain sexual depictions of a non-public character not suitable to normal people, like sexual organs, pubic hair, intercourse or other sexual acts. (Kuwahara 1993: 73)

This is the only explicit formulation in regard to Customs' film inspection, but not available in official print. Violations carry penalties of a fine of up to 550,000 ¥ or up to five years in prison (Nomura 1970: 275). Until 1957, only Customs inspected imported films, but due to the protests of Eirin, both organs were entitled to carry out inspections–which means that an imported film is revised twice. Another result of the quarrel between these two institutions was that Customs was to rely on "persons of learning and experience" for its decisions; therefore, the "Discussion Group of Films and other visual materials" (Eiga yunyû tô shingikai) came into being in 1961. This counseling body has no veto right to the decisions of the "Film Office" (Eiga bu), however (Beer 1984: 337).

Customs does not perceive itself as an organ of censorship, since it never reviews a film that has not already been censored; when a print arrives in Japan, it is handled by a Customs broker until being passed. Under the responsibility of this company, the print is transported to a laboratory where the distributor has to permit blurs (bokashi), mask effects (masuku gake) or mosaics of "obscene" body parts. Usually the distributor will follow the advice of the technicians who work on precedent without contradiction, which would result in loss of time and money for a second run through Customs if its inspectors should object to the depictions. After this "treatment," the Customs broker asks for the import certificate; the film is reviewed and, if not objected, passed (Cote 1993: 29).

There are several reasons for this complicated system. First, the system allows Customs to claim that it does not censor, since the distributor delivers the print "voluntarily" to the lab, which receives no specific orders for cuts. Second, if these were passed, the Ministry of Finance would be responsible for an unconstitutional definition of what is obscene and what is not. Third, due to the prolongation of this process, distributors are under considerable financial and schedule pressure and are thus unlikely to challenge Customs' decisions. Finally, the nonexistence of specific rules and a responsible organ for them ease censorship for the authorities, while artists, industry, or the public find it hard to protest against it (Cote 1993: 27b).

However, following a slow retreat of Customs from film censorship, its officially responsible body Eirin has come under increasing pressure from the film world, mainly because of its high fees and a number of arbitrary decisions. Eirin was created in response to the constitutional freedom of speech, which had come into effect in 1947. The Allies asked the Japanese film industry to introduce a regulation system based on the Production Code of the United States (Itô 1973: 46). A first draft of a film code was already passed in summer 1947 on a meeting of all studio bosses, who founded the "Sustaining Committee for the Motion Picture Code of Ethics" (Eirin Iji Iinkai) which is still responsible for changing the regulations. Eirin started to work in 1949, but Allied film censorship continued until the end of the occupation. In 1956, a series of juvenile delinquency-themed films called taiyôzoku-eiga ("Sun-group-films") triggered massive public protest against the leniency of this organ, which up to then was only composed of members of the industry. Eirin was reformed: its principles became more detailed, its chairman being a former Minister of Education, Takahashi Seiichirô (Kuwahara 1993: 54f.). Nevertheless, Eirin has been the focus of constant criticism by both official and pressure groups, blaming the committee of doing too little, and increasingly by the industry itself, regarding the unsatisfactory classification system, its high fees, and its Code of Ethics, which has not been substantially revised since 1959.

In 1996, a series of irritations caused a group of Japanese directors headed by Wakamatsu Kôji, himself one of the most notorious film-makers of Japan,[11] to issue a "memorandum against censorship in the name of self-regulation," according to which 90% of directors are of the opinion that Eirin should be dissolved:

> In a theater, which is separated from the public space, everyone should get what he wants for his entrance fee (. . .). What is the reason for bokashi, if you still see a naked couple on the screen? They only guarantee that a film is "officially" not obscene. This has nothing to do with the real impression a depiction has. If all films are treated the same and directors are forced to abstain from certain depictions, it is no miracle when audience figures decrease (. . .). Almost every film is nowadays produced independently. It may have been alright in earlier times that Eirin, which was founded by the big studios, revised their films. But today, these studios almost entirely distribute and exhibit independently produced films. (Wakamatsu 1997:123f)

The key reason for the "out-of-touchness" of Eirin's regulation rules is that the committee has not only been criticized by authorities for lenient interpretation of its standards, but also persecuted itself by the Metropolitan Police Department (Keishichô). It does not review films, but has the legal authority to confiscate tapes or films screened in public whenever these are found to be obscene. This happened most prominently in 1965, when two reviewers of Eirin were sued for distribution of obscenity along with director Takechi Tetsuji of the "Anti-American" porn "Black Snow" (kuroi yuki), and in 1972, when three reviewers were charged for passing the films of the Nikkatsu porn trial (1972-80).[12] Especially during the latter case, Eirin restricted visual expression drastically–not by amendments to the code itself, but rather by additions to its technical considerations for reviewers. A new chairman in 1978, Arimitsu Jirô, also from the Ministry of Education, introduced rules that quasi-ordered bokashi and decidedly forbade pubic hair, which up to then had been a common understanding (Kuwahara 1993: 238f). What followed was the so-called "Ice Age" of the Japanese film industry: Although the defendants of the Nikkatsu trial were eventually acquitted in 1980, the sheer length of the trial made most pornography producers–the vast majority of the independent film world–compromise with both Eirin's and Customs' standards. Bokashi, which had been introduced as a means to increase audience interest,[13] became a standard procedure to avoid obscenity charges, and many films imported from abroad–where the depiction of sexuality in general and homosexuality in particular gained a more serious character–suffered from it.

WHAT DO THEY DO?
TREATMENT OF (HOMO)SEXUAL FILM IN THE "GAY BOOM"

There were not many gay-themed films in Japan prior to the 90s, although the establishment of a gay scene dates back to postwar times.[14] Gay-themed films, as in the west, often exploited homosexuals or stereotyped them to entertain a predominantly straight audience, though there already existed a substantial gay pornography segment.[15] This changed with the emergence of the so-called "Gay Boom" in 1991, triggered by a special issue of the woman's magazine CREA on homosexuality (Lunsing 1997: 252f.). As other magazines picked up the topic, Fushimi Noriaki's *Private Gay Life* became the first gay-themed bestseller, followed one year later by Kakefuda Hiroko, who founded the first (and only) lesbian magazine *Labrys* (which did not survive, however). Also in 1992, a series of gay-themed independent films appeared, which took a new turn on the (previously rather racy) subject by stressing human relationships. Most notable were *Karakara hikaru* (*Radiant Light*, by Matsuoka Joji), in which, after an arranged marriage, a woman allows her husband to carry on his gay relationship; and *Okoge*[16] (by Nakajima Takehiro), in which a woman befriends gays and eventually allows them to have sex in her apartment. Even gay porn had its first critically acclaimed feature, *Soshite bokura wa kawatta* (*That's When Things Changed*, by Yamazaki Kuninori), which depicted the relationship of two gays in a construction group rather honestly, but still regarded them as disadvantaged (Weisser 1998: 431).

Of biggest public interest was, however, the TV drama *Dôsôkai* (*Alumni Association*), screened in autumn 1993 on Nihon Terebi (Lunsing 1997: 275f.). Its success paved the way for directors who identified themselves as gay through their works, which depicted homosexuality from the inside, such as Hashiguchi Ryosuke's *Hatachi no binetsu* (*Slight Fever of a Twenty Year Old*, 1993) and *Nagisa no Sindbad* (*Like Grains of Sand*, 1995). The latter film won the Grand Prix at the Rotterdam Film Festival in 1996, and thereby placed gay films from Japan in international discourse. Another gay director who managed to obtain international recognition was Oki Hiroyuki, who rose from the porn business to make both erotic and introverted video films such as *Anata ga suki desu* (*I Like You Very Much,* 1994).

THE "HAIR BOOM":
CUSTOMS BATTLING FOREIGN OBSCENITY

In 1991, the much discussed "Hair Boom," a series of photobooks which exposed the pubis of more or less famous actresses, led to the legalization of pubic hair and thereby inaugurated a slow retreat of Customs from film censorship. Interesting enough, this occurred at the same time as the "Gay Boom"–and was even a part of it, since male nude photo books were for the first time retailing in major bookstores and advertised in subway trains. These photos showed male pubic hair, but not their organs, which were considered too risky by the publishing companies. Therefore, the official definition of the penis as obscene remained unchallenged, whereas the definition concerning pubic hair vanished.

Jacques Rivette's *La Belle Noiseuse* was the first theatrically released film with pubic hair, which was altered at only 18 places, a result reached after lengthy discussions between the distribution company Comstock and Customs/Eirin (Cote 1993: 28). Shortly after its unprotested release, Eirin changed its regulations in October 1992, adding the words "in principle" to the prohibition of pubic hair in order to be able to allow their depiction case by case; critics were of the opinion that Eirin tried to keep track with Custom's liberalization (Baba 1993: 7), and the Metropolitan Police made clear that there was no abolishment of the pubic hair prohibition (Shimizu 1993: 74).

The result was a widespread confusion about what was allowed and what was not; Eirin passed a series of controversial decisions on Japanese films, which sparked debate on the accuracy of its examination practice and led to the aforementioned attempt to disband the organ altogether. Customs sometimes agreed, but more often refused to pass films uncut which depicted pubic hair; the majority of the latter were mainstream gay-related films, with the possible reason that the "Gay Boom" was in full swing, and these films were likely to find a (straight) audience. The most regrettable incident, occurring in March 1993, related to Neil Jordan's gay-(sub)themed film *The Crying Game*. Despite personal requests from the director, the film's pivotal moment–the main character realizing upon undressing his love interest that she is in fact a transsexual, he thereupon throwing up in shock–was masked, thereby rendering the whole scene and topic of the film incomprehensible to the Japanese audience.[17]

However, in the same 1993, a film with an equally transgendered context was the first to pass Customs' censorship unchanged. After lengthy debates with its distributor Furansu-eiga-sha, *Orlando* (directed by Sally Potter) kept its pivotal sex change shot, in which actress Tilda Swinton regards her newly female body in a mirror. The Ministry of Finance might have allowed this due to the demise of Kawakita Kazuko, head of that company, on June 7th (its approval came two weeks later). Kawakita had been a dominating force in the Japanese film world, always eager to improve its conditions, so that the fulfillment of her last request may have been an act of condolence. Also, the scene involved the female pubis, whereas the passing of *The Crying Game* would have allowed the showing of a penis.

Another case is linked to yet another obscenity litigation connected to homosexual art, even more debatable than in Tôgô's case. In 1992, distributor Uplink had to fog a scene in *Looking for Langston* by Issac Julian (1988), in which a male nude by Robert Mapplethorpe hung on a wall–at the cost of 200,000 ¥. The irony in this case was that there was at the time a Mapplethorpe exhibition with exactly that photograph in Tokyo (Asai 1995: 8). Nevertheless, Yamashita Yukio, who sent the Whitney Museum's Mapplethorpe catalogue privately from New York to Japan via DHL that year, found himself confronted with obscenity charges after the carrier's Japan branch office opened the mail and delivered its contents to Customs. Yamashita challenged a guilty verdict in October 1994 (Asai 1995: 12f.), but it was upheld by Tokyo High Court in October 1995 and is pending decision in the Supreme Court.

A MATTER OF FACE: EIRIN'S TROUBLE IN DEFINING A NEW ROLE

Occasionally, it was not Customs who blocked (homo)sexual depictions, but Eirin after Customs had these depictions passed, which occurred more frequently after *Orlando*. Pubic hair remained an issue for Eirin, although–or because–it lost its importance for Customs. In particularly confrontational 1996, which saw quite a few alienations of Japanese directors by Eirin,[18] a number of imported art films were hit with this issue, most notably *Beyond the Clouds* by Michelangelo Antonioni and Wim Wenders, whose protests against Eirin's claims led to their withdrawal of the film, and *Total Eclipse* by Agnieska Holland, in which not the homosexual relationship between poets Paul Verlaine (David Thewlis) and Arthur Rimbaud (Leonardo di Caprio) was the problem, but a three-second shot of pubic hair of Verlaine's wife. Since distributor Nippon Herald had already fogged male sexual organs at four places on behalf of Customs, the company was not ready to invest even more money in a "correction" that was thought to be completely irrelevant. Still, the shot was cut to obtain a general classification,[19] which was an economic necessity due to the popularity of di Caprio with juveniles (Baba 1996).

Equally hard hit was the (partially) homoerotic *Pillow Book* by Peter Greenaway, of *Prospero's Books* fame. Although the present head of Eirin, Shimizu Hideo,[20] mentioned in an interview with the author in June 1995 that such an aesthetic depiction of the male nude could be screened in Japan without any problem, the film–which features primarily Japanese men in full frontal nudity–was filled with numerous bokashi.

The reason for Eirin to change pubic hair shots even if these are not blocked by Customs seems to be rivalry at first: as far as imported films are concerned, Customs decides when to allow more leniency, while Eirin can only adopt or not adopt these changes. Not claiming any bokashi of a film coming from Customs may result in a loss of face which would eventually make distributors wonder what authority this organ has to press them into a costly second examination of their prints for gaining access to exhibition; indeed, independent distributors not represented in the Eirin Sustaining Committee thought about establishing their own body of self-regulation in 1997 (Asai 1997: 42f.).

However, there is more to this, since the pubic hair changes were said to have been brokered between Customs and Eirin (Cote 1993: 29). If one institution behaves erratically, the other may benefit from a rise of reputation in the film world, which nowadays generally blames Eirin for being the one who is out of touch. As Customs is perceived less strict than Eirin, the question of whether the former's censorship is not more unconstitutional than the latter's becomes more abstract. This allows Customs to insist upon its own standards whenever desired, in the face of a society that has become totally open to just about any kind of sexual expression. Eirin gets the chance to promote itself as a "guardian of society" instead of an alibi for film makers to do whatever they want–an accusation that was brought against the committee whenever a film caused public debate. It thereby strengthens its legally unprotected status by pleasing the authorities, and survives due to their acceptance in spite of being oblivious to the real standards of Japanese society.

THE LAST LINE OF DEFENSE: MALE GENITALIA

The fact that the depiction of male genitalia remain prohibited without exception spurned what was probably the biggest controversy on Customs censorship in the 90s. In October 1997, a film dealing with Dutch colonial rule in Indonesia, *Mother Dao*, was censored prior to its exhibition at the Yamagata International Documentary Film Festival. The scene in question showed Chinese forced laborers under a shower, exposing their genitals. Director Vincent van Monnikendam commented on the incident in a press conference of the Festival:

> This must be the first time that film material of more than thirty years of age is censored (. . .). To a documentary, which is supposed to show reality, censorship does the utmost harm (. . .). I am indeed very displeased that a scene which so obviously serves to show the misery of forced laborers is cut in the name of "obscenity." (Yamanouchi 1997: 42)

The incident shows the crucial dilemma of Customs censorship: on the one hand, it has become more liberal in the course of the 90s as far as nudity and pubic hair are concerned; on the other hand, one piece of imagery was chosen to be unequivocally forbidden, having at least one clear asset that is obscene, the male sexual organ. It has become, so to speak, the last line of defense for Customs. If it were not rigorously censored, the concept of obscenity—which has been narrowed down from nudity to pubic hair to genitalia over the past decade—would collapse.

In relation to the censorship of *The Crying Game*, Laurent Allary, representative of the French film export union Unifrance in Tokyo, declared that "a naked woman is more easily accepted as artistic. A naked man is perceived as more unnatural and more aggressive, and it is difficult to convince old-fashioned censors, who are not used to seeing such things, that it is art" (Regelman 1993: 68). This is an idea that is obviously shared by many Japanese artists as well, since genitalia were never exposed in male nudes of the "hair boom," contrary to the pubis of women. This disadvantage is easy to explain. Pubic hair hides female genitalia; were it shaved, or were the crotch shot in a position that clearly exhibits the vulva, it would still be considered obscene. But as long as pubic hair in itself causes an erotic sensation, this is unnecessary. A nude male body, however, cannot be shot without its protruding genitalia; therefore, changes to the image are necessary and more likely to be automatically ordered, whereas the degree of explicitness of female nudity gives room for discussing these decisions. This is the technical disadvantage of gay films I mentioned in the introduction, although it may just as well apply to lesbian film. In recent years, the Tokyo International Gay and Lesbian Film Festival had only one film, a lesbian film, stopped at Narita airport. The reason for this might be that the Festival tries to work pre-emptively, advising its guests to conceal films they anticipate to be problematic, constantly pondering the odds and risks of sexual expression—just like artists in the gay video and film scene, who try to find means of

telling their stories and/or showing as much as possible without really challenging the system.

This is by no means a unique Japanese phenomenon–the depiction of a
penis is still unthinkable in Hollywood, too. It was not possible for director
Paul Thomas Anderson to have his star Mark Wahlberg display his real penis
in the final shot of *Boogie Nights* (1998). Instead, internal Hollywood standards forced him to use a bogus penis for that scene. In the Japanese version,
however, this artificial penis was–as anyone might expect–blurred, which
made many spectators believe that Wahlberg was a, well, truly impressive
actor. At present, even an artificial penis cannot be brought upon the Japanese
public.

SO WHAT'S THE POINT OF IT ALL?
EXPLANATIONS FOR THE OBSCENITY ISSUE

The official explanation of the prohibition of obscenity, protecting the
moral values of Japanese society in respect to an individual sense of shame in
"normal" people, is of course very incoherent considering the fact that Japan
is a country in which virtually every aspect of sexuality is highly commercialized. From animated ad cards for hostess clubs lying around in telephone
boxes to TV shows which have the camera peeking up girls' skirts while
playing basketball. Contrary to pornography in western countries, the Japanese variants are both more playful and more available, and are therefore less
likely to reek of forbidden pleasures. They are a part of Japan's everyday
culture. So what makes authorities decide that genitalia are too much? One
possible approach claims that this is because they are authorities, which need
to effectively demonstrate their existence to prove–or fantasize–that they
have a say in the creation of society.

THE AUTHORITY ARGUMENT

The Japanese Constitution of postwar Japan had censorship abolished,
like any other means by the state to suppress freedom of expression.
Only one means erroneously remained: §175. It is therefore no surprise
that the state clings so desperately to this article: It is its only means to
prove its authority and deny the people freedom of expression. (Oshima
1988: 210)

These were the closing phrases of Oshima Nagisa at his obscenity trial,
which concerned a book with the script and stills from his film *The Realm of*

the Senses (1976),[21] though not the film itself, which had been vigorously cut by Customs on its reentry to Japan–where Oshima could not have his radical vision of erotic obsession processed without risking persecution. Having studied law in his student days, Oshima willingly searched for a confrontation with the authorities, to whom he wanted to issue a definition of obscenity in regard to film; he did not succeed, but used the platform of the trial to deliver a speech which all but shattered the public perception of obscenity as vice, and almost ruefully declared that self-regulation cannot work under such circumstances:

> If we look at the history of repression of police and persecution against cinema, we find two characteristic patterns: First, justice always strikes as soon as a new form of sexual expression appears. (. . .) Second, with every incident of this kind they gain ground (. . .). It seems that the Metropolitan Police arrives more and more at changing the organ of film censorship (i.e., Eirin) and to bring it under its control. (Oshima 1988: 206)

This corresponds to the previous idea that Eirin and Customs may actually pretend to their antagonism over the pubic hair issue in order to strengthen each others' positions. For scholars like the aforementioned Okudaira Yasuhiro, censorship has not the aim to protect society, but to secure the authority of its institutions against the public in a way that is visible in mainstream culture (Allison 1996: 155). The more sexuality is present, the more its lack of genitalia is obvious, the more everybody knows who is running the show– in striking contrast to western countries, where censorship tries to hide and remain hidden. This may explain why it is easier to attack censorship there, since it is easier to question the justification of authorities who want to remain in the dark–as they want certain things to remain dark–as opposed to those who act in public.

THE ECONOMIC ARGUMENT

The packaging of bodily exposure that decenters or obscures genitalia (. . .) is big business. It sells products and is productive itself of a construction of leisure that is sold to Japanese consumers as escapist recreation. (. . .) The state has in fact endorsed and encouraged a sexual economy of a particular order, one that evades the state surveillance of pubic realism and therefore constructs the stimulation and simulation of sexuality as a fantasy (. . .). Such mass sexual tropes as voyeurism, infantilization, and sadomasochism are something other than "obscene" and other than "real." (Allison 1996: 150)

This definition makes it possible to regard Customs censorship as a means of protection of the domestic sexual fantasy market. On the one hand, by denying products which violate obscenity rules access to the Japanese market of sexual fantasies, the domestic contributors to this market are protected–and are therefore maybe all too willing to accept the accompanying compromises on what they can and cannot broker to the public. On the other hand, the cultivation of a domestic culture of sexual fantasies makes it harder for foreign products to appeal to Japanese customers, which explains the genuine plethora of "typical" Japanese products in both hetero-and homosexual pornography, far outweighing the representation of porn from abroad. And with a reason: If the degree of stimulation is much higher in the domestic product, why turn to the imported product if all it offers is the unobstructed sight of an item anyone knows?

In addition, although it is certainly unconstitutional, censorship in Japan has not led to any more regrettable effects than the liberation of pornography in western culture, especially in gay context. Whereas sexualization has deeply penetrated gay communities to a degree that personal identification with the sexual preference has become a paramount public image–if not to say, ideal–of homosexuals, the Japanese economics of sex as fantasy have helped to expand the possibilities of what is acceptable for the majority. For example, both hetero- and homosexual persons in western countries may feel confronted with the necessity to draw a line between what he/she prefers or tolerates and what he/she rejects within the realm of sexual fantasies, such as the moral dilemma of paedophilia, because these fantasies are perceived–via pornography, news or other means–as real. In Japan, however, where the reality of the sexual act is obscured, the readiness to tolerate or enjoy such fantasies–but not the real thing–is higher, which means they can be effectively marketed:

> By restricting one bodily sight/site, the state permits and stimulates the mass production of a host of others. Restrictive laws are actually a boost to the big business of sexual fantasy-making in Japan, which, in the format of "fantasy," can be marketed to children as well as adults. (Allison 1996: 150)

This has the positive side-effect that childhood and sexuality are not artificially separated from each other, as illustrated by the extremely popular anime *Sailor Moon*, which contains homosexual lead characters.[22] In the dubbed versions distributed in the west, these characters' sexuality has been unequivocally changed, indicating that western broadcast stations are shying away from the topic of homosexuality in a children's program, whereas Japanese do not. Sex is not considered as harmful to juveniles in Japan, which explains why sexually stimulating photos of adolescents are printed in gay magazines like *Badi* without any problem (Lunsing 1997: 275)–and the obscenity issue might assist in that. The problem with this is that fantasy justifies a sexual abuse, however docile–just like gays accuse lady's manga, a subgenre of comics aimed at women in their 20s, of abusing homosexual themes for satisfying women, who counter that this would be a fantasy, and fantasy should be allowed to be free (ibid.: 274).

CONCLUSION:
IS THERE A HOMOPHOBIC INTENT
IN OBSCENITY LAWS OR NOT?

There are two ways in which the obscenity laws influence homosexual imagery, as they influence sexual images in general: directly suppressive, by prohibiting the depiction of genitalia and, if considered obscene, pubic hair; and indirectly creative, by urging the industry to substitute genitalia with graphic violence, androgyneity, or other means. As stated before, this does not necessarily have to be regarded as bad; as outmoded as the prohibition of genitalia may seem in regard to the plethora of Japanese sexual fantasies, it might have helped to enable the playfulness of Japan's sexual culture, which, while certainly abusing and stereotyping its objects, at least prevents sexual frustration. This could explain why there is far less sexual violence, though arguably more harassment, in Japan than in the United States, for example.

To answer the initial question of whether there is a "line" into obscenity that applies more to homo- than heterosexual film: yes and no. The problem is that as soon as a film is described as gay-themed, Customs will automatically assume that it will show a penis; and since that would be obscene, the authorities will inspect gay films closer than others. That means, if the day should come that a penis can be shown in Japan, it is unlikely to pass in a gay-themed context. Thus, by assuming the worst from films of this genre, one might say that there is a disadvantageous treatment of homosexuality in film.

However, the abundant presence of homosexual topics in Japanese culture for women–as in lady's manga–does not allow to interpret this caution as a discrimination against homosexuality as such. It is clearly directed against the penis, and the problems with homosexuality are limited to that issue–as the often daring story contents of gay films in Japan shows, Eirin's concern is directed to the same issue.

Apart from the fact that the penis is the ultimate obscenity, there is no particular suppression of homosexuality as such. The limitations are enforced within the frame of the obscenity regulations; at least officially, there is no difference between the depiction of the male body in heterosexual or homosexual acts. In practice, however, different treatments of male/female genitalia (as in *Crying Game* versus *Orlando*) suggest a homophobic intent, that is, to prevent the sexualization of the male body to a degree similar to that of the female body. Japan is paternalistic, and male authority is not just exposed by docile female behavior and prevalent sexual harassment; it is represented by men who feel they have the responsibility to protect themselves and their peer group from any tendency that might put the values which placed them in power of society.

ENDNOTES

1. Tôgô Ken, born 1935, is the only Japanese "politician" who outed himself. He founded the party Zatsumintô to protest the discrimination of homosexuals in Japanese politics. His magazine *Za Gei* (*The Gay*) is the most political among Japanese gay periodicals (Hoshino 1992).

2. In feudal Japan, clerical, military and commercial male homosexuality was abundant; see, i.e., Leupp, Gary P.: *Male colors*, Berkeley: UP California 1995, or most recent: Pflugfelder, Gregory M.: *Cartographies of Desire: Male-Male Sexuality in Japanese Discourse, 1600-1950*; University of California Press 1999. Due to the "westernization" of Japan which made homosexuality appear shameful, there was a law against homosexuality at the beginning of the century, which was however never enacted and later abolished (Furukawa Makoto: Dôseiai no hikaku shakaigaku: rezubian, gei sutadiizu no tenkai to nanshoku gainen ("Comparative social studies on homosexuality: Lesbian-gay studies and the concept of nanshoku"), in: Inoue Toshi/ Ueno Chizuko et al.: *Sekushuaritei no shakaigaku*, Iwanami Shoten, pp. 113-130.

3. Social pressure may contain the severance of family ties because of the refusal of fathering or bearing children, economic pressure may contain harassment by colleagues or administration, i.e., refusal of family-orientated wage increases and/or promotions or bullying (Hoshino 1992: 47). A good example of gay stereotyping may be the issue on homosexuality of one of Japan's most successful TV shows, Koko ga hen da yo Nihonjin ("That's Weird, Mr. Japanese") hosted by comedian and filmmaker Kitano Takeshi, aired September 1, 1999 on TBS network. A group of rather intolerant foreigners attacked a group of rather docile Japanese homosexuals in a staged-looking confrontation which put the blame of discrimination conveniently on the foreigners' side, insinuating that such prejudices would not exist in Japan (Badi 11, 1999: 38).

4. That is, video ads of teenage boys who are partially in the nude out of sexual context, i.e., swimming. There are more graphic textual and animated images of paedophilia. Hetero-and homosexual porn often tries to stress "innocence" by having its characters wear school uniforms, regardless of the real age of the protagonists.

5. Text of §21 Constitution.

6. The Allied Headquarters had Oyama Publishing closed because the translation of *Lady Chatterley's Lover* had not been authorized (Kudô 1987: 116)

7. In 1954, import of *Lady Chatterley's Lover* had been refused by New York customs. After a lengthy trial concerning other cases as well, in 1959 the Supreme Court passed a verdict that federal state censorship laws would be unconstitutional

whereupon the ban was revoked (Nomura 1970: 274). It is therefore possible that Lawrence's book was instrumental in liberating the First Amendment in the United States, whereas it had the reverse effect in Japan.

8. For text of §175 Penal Code; see Appendix.

9. However, theater owners who are members of the National Entertainment Association (Zenkôren) are expected to show only films passed by Eirin due to the Healthy Environment Law (Kankyô eisei hô) from 1957, the same year when the re-formed committee started to operate. Therefore, Eirin's regulation is indirectly obligatory to film producers and distributors, since they could not retail their product otherwise, as nearly all theater owners are Zenkôren members (Beer 1984: 343).

10. Text of §21 Customs Tariff law; see Appendix.

11. Wakamatsu Kôji's films since the 60s contain frequent abuse and torture of women. He had already founded an interest group for sexual liberty in film in 1970 (Hiraoka 1970: 280).

12. After Japan's oldest film studio Nikkatsu reverted to porn production exclusively in 1971, police confiscated three videos and four films of their "romantic porn" (roman poruno) productions; for more on the Nikkatsu porn trial see Itô 1973, Kuwahara 1993, Oshima 1988).

13. Bokashi were artistically used in *Emanuelle* (by Just Jaeckin, 1974) to avoid cuts, resulting in the film's enormous success (Kuwahara 1993: 226). The same distribution company Nippon Herald also used this technique with *Caligula* (directed by Tinto Brass, 1980), which achieved a B.O. result of U.S. $3 million in spite of its 450 bokashi (Kuroda 1981: 282). The company claimed that bokashi were more attractive to the Japanese audience than cuts (Bornoff, Nicholas: *Pink Samurai. Love, Marriage & Sex in Contemporary Japan*, New York: Pocket Books, 1991, p. 406).

14. Gay bars date back as early as the 20s, but regular gay bars came into being in Hibiya, in part due to gay U.S. military. Tokyo's Shinjuku Nichome district became the epicenter of the gay scene in the late 50s/early 60s. The first gay periodical *Rose group (barazoku)* went into print in 1971, and gay rights groups have been active since 1976 (Hoshino 1992: 56f.)

15. Gay sex films, called barazoku eiga after the first gay magazine, developed in the 70s. It came into full swing in the early 80s, in part because of the Osaka-based subdivision ENK of then porn major Nikkatsu, which specialized in gay porn (Weisser 1998: 263). The aforementioned Tôgô Ken made *Mansion of Roses: Passion of Men (Bara no yakata: otokotachi no passion)* for this company in 1983 (ibid.: 266). But also straight pornographers like Sato Hisayusu made gay films, like *2nd Mad Ballroom Gala (kurutta butokai 2*, 1988), which won the 1993 Berlin Gay and Lesbian Film Festival (ibid.: 466).

16. Okoge literally means "rice sticking on the ground of a pot" and refers to women who stick to gays, who are derogatively called okama, "honorable pots," in reference to a pot in the shape of the anus (Cherry, Kittredge: *Womansword*, Tokyo: Kodansha 1989, p. 35).

17. Film expert Donald Richie reported overhearing the conversation of two Japanese women wondering about what had caused the man's sudden repulsion, one of them stating that she may have had leprosy (Allison 1996: 168).

18. Japanese directors who had trouble with Eirin in 1996 included Iwai Shun-ji–one scene in his *Swallowtail Butterfly* was said to bear the risk of inciting juvenile delinquency; his *Picnic* had to wait one year on the grounds that it violated medical ethics, since it contained a relationship between a nurse and a mentally disturbed person. A similar claim was made against Sai Yôichi's *Maakusu no yama*. Most controversial, however, was the classification of Hosono Tatsuoki's *Shabu gokudô* (*Vicious Path of Shabu* [a drug]) as an adult film; it was the first time Eirin based such a decision on violence. It was assumed that Eirin wanted to set an example with this film, since it starred the biggest Japanese actor, Yakusho Kôji (of *Shall We Dance* fame, Baba 1996).

19. Prior to 1998, there were only the classifications general, restricted (from 15) and adult (from 18'); recently, a PG13 category has been introduced, which had been pursued by Eirin's chairman Shimizu Hideo since he took office 1990 (Shimizu 1997: 56).

20. Shimizu Hideo is professor of law at Aoyama Gakuin and one of the most famous media law scholars of Japan.

21. *The Realm of the Senses*–in Japanese *Ai no koriida* (*Corrida of love*)–was produced and processed in France, but shot in Japan. The trial (1976-78) concerned passages from the script and stills in a book on the film; Oshima was charged for writing the script and authorizing its publication (Oshima 1988: 202f.).

22. The characters Zoisite and Kunzite are male homosexuals in the original. The dub changed Zoisite to a woman. Sailors Uranus and Neptune (female) have a romantic affiliation in the show, with Uranus displaying some "butch" behavior. Haruka and Michiru (female) are also clearly in a relationship. Fish Eye (male) looks almost exactly like a woman and regularly dresses as one–this type of gay character is common in anime and manga aimed at girls.

REFERENCES

Allison, Anne
1996 *Permitted and Prohibited Desires. Mothers, Comics, and Censorship in Japan.* Boulder/Oxford: Westview Press.

Asai Takashi
1995 *Waisetsu tokushū: Poruno wo kôjin yunyū suru jiyū* ("Obscenity special: The Right to Import Porn Individually"). In: Saikoro-Dice, No. 9 April 1995, Uplink, p. 7-18.
1997 *Eiga fuan oyobi kankeisha hisshū kamoku: jishu kisei kôza Eirin hen* ("Indispensable Summary for Film Friends: a Course on Self Regulation by Eirin"). In: Saikoro-Dice No. 21 (Sep. 1997), Tôkyô: Uplink, S. 29-43.

Baba Hideshi
1993 *Meisaku wo kaku "hea kisei"* (The unclear "hair rules"). In: Asahi Shinbun 14.11.1993, p.7
1996 *Nenrei seigen no minaoshi wo kentô* ("Examining the correction of classification"). In: Asahi Shinbun 10.11.1996.

Beer, Lawrence W.
1984 *Freedom of Expression in Japan.* Tôkyô/San Francisco/New York: Kodansha.

Cote, Mark
1993 *Blurred Vision–Film Censorship in Japan.* In: Japan International Journal Vol. 3, No. 3, March 1993, Tôkyô: JIT Publishing.

Hiraoka Masaaki
1970 *Kokka to waisetsu, in: Sei-shisô. seido. hô* ("Sexuality: Essays, system, law"). Jyurisuto special issue Nr. 5, Tôkyô: Jyurisuto 1970, S. 278-284.

Hoshino Hiroaki (Ed.)
1992 *Bôifurendo-gei handobukku* ("Boyfriend; gay handbook"). Shônensha 1992.

Itô Tatsuo:
1973 *Eirin: rekishi to jiken* ("Eirin-history and incidents"). Tôkyô: Perikansha.

Kudô Yoroshi
1987 *Nihon koku kenpô* ("The Japanese Constitution"). Tôkyô: Yûhaikaku.

Kuroda Toyoji
1981 *A Japanese film history.* In:Variety May 13, 1981, Los Angeles, S. 259ff.

Kuwahara Ietoshi
1993 *Kirareta waisetsu: Eirin katto shi* ("Obscenity gone: Eirin's cut history"). Tôkyô: Yomiuri Shinbunsha.

Lunsing, Wim
1994 *"Gay Boom" in Japan–Changing views of Homosexuality?.* In: Thamyris Vol. 4, pp. 267-293.

Maki, John M.
1964 *Court and Constitution in Japan,* Seattle: University of Washington Press.

Nomura Keizô
1970 *Zeikan ken'etsu to sei ni kan suru hyôgen no jiyū* ("Customs censorship and the freedom of sexual expression"). In: Jyurisuto: Sei-shisô. seido. hô ("Sexuality Essays. System. Law."). Special issue Nr. 5, Tôkyô: Jyurisuto, S. 272-277

Ôshima Nagisa
1988 *Die Ahnung der Freiheit* ("The Premonition of Freedom"). Frankfurt: Fischer.
Okudaira Yasuhiro/Tamaki Shôichi/Yoshiyuki Shinnosuke
1986 *Sei hyôgen no jiyū* ("Freedom of sexual expression"). Tôkyô: Yûhaikaku
Regelman, Karen
1993 *Will Tokyo Tame the Crying Game?.* In: Variety 22.3.1993, S. 1 + 68. Shimizu Hideo
1993 *Masumedia no jiyū to sekinin* ("Freedom and responsibility of mass media"). Tôkyô: Sanseidô.
1997 *Yajiuma monogatari* ("Memoirs of a leatherneck"). Tôkyô: Sanseidô. Wakamatsu Kôji (mit Shimizu Hideo)

1997 *Kaitai? minaoshi? Eirin vs. Eiga kantoku kyôkai no gekiron* ("Dissolution? Correction? A heated debate between Eirin and the Director's Association"). In: Tsukuru April 1997, S. 122-131.

Weisser, Thomas and Yuko
1998 *Japanese Cinema Encyclopedia–The Sex Films*. Miami: Vital books, 640p.

Yamanouchi Etsuko
1997 *Kiroku eiga wo okasu ken'etsu* ("Censorship attacks documentary film"). In: Shûkan kinyôbi 14.11.1997, S. 42.

APPENDIX

1. Texts

1.1. Prohibition of obscenity of §175 Penal Code (Keihô)

§ 175: On the distribution of obscene literature a.o.:

> A person who distributes, sells or exhibits in public obscene writings, pictures or other objects, shall be punished with prison and forced labor for up to two years or pay a fine of up to 5,000 Yen. The same applies to persons who possess such material with the purpose of selling it.

1.2. Prohibited imports of §21 Customs Tariff Law (Kanzei teiritsu hô)

The following freight shall not be imported:

1. Narcotics, hashish, opium or similar means of stimulation (. . .).
2. Devices for the forgery, alteration or imitation of bank notes, shares, or receipts.
3. Books, pictures, sculptures and similar things, which would harm public morals and order.
4. Articles which violate copyright law (and related laws).

The Rise of Homosexuality
and the Dawn of Communism
in Hong Kong Film:
1993-1998

Andrew Grossman

SUMMARY. I have designed this essay as a general overview of the self-evident trend towards queer subject matter in the past decade in Hong Kong film, a trend that not only coincides historically with the 1997 handover to the Mainland but also frequently comes equipped with parent-child relationships that can be read as allegories for the colony's future as the "child" to its mother country. Queerness in HK films has both alternated between and combined indigenous forms of queerness and the imported Western variety; by charting courses through internationalized concepts of homosexuality, HK films have posited their queerness not only as an existential allegory of (post)colonialism but also as a claim (or hope) for a utopian sexuality *cum* utopian international politics. *[Article copies available for a fee from The Haworth Document Delivery Service: 1-800-342-9678. E-mail address: <getinfo@ haworthpressinc. com> Website: <http://www.HaworthPress.com>]*

It is commonly said that political subjects in Hong Kong cinema are anathema, taboo. Both fearful of Mainland Communist reprisals after 1997, and subservient to the triad-controlled film industry which prefers predictable profit margins over risky social controversy, explicit political criticism in

Andrew Grossman, MA, studied film and philosophy at Sarah Lawrence College, followed by a Master's Degree in English and Creative Writing from Rutgers University. He is currently working on writing projects that attempt to cross and synthesize the genres of avant-garde theater, the screenplay, and cultural criticism. His writing has appeared in *American Book Review*. (E-mail: morgold@webtv.net)

[Haworth co-indexing entry note]: "The Rise of Homosexuality and the Dawn of Communism in Hong Kong Film: 1993-1998." Grossman, Andrew. Co-published simultaneously in *Journal of Homosexuality* (The Haworth Press, Inc.) Vol. 39, No. 3/4, 2000, pp. 149-186; and: *Queer Asian Cinema: Shadows in the Shade* (ed: Andrew Grossman) Harrington Park Press, an imprint of The Haworth Press, Inc., 2000, pp. 149-186. Single or multiple copies of this article are available for a fee from The Haworth Document Delivery Service [1-800-342-9678, 9:00 a.m. - 5:00 p.m. (EST). E-mail address: getinfo@haworthpressinc. com].

Hong Kong film is rare at best, and disastrous at worst.[1] But consistent exposure to the film culture reveals this idea to be both misguided and myopic: in so many films, as in everyday life in Hong Kong before 1997, there were casual yet anxious references to the imminent reversion to Communist dominion, an omnipresent awareness that the existential historicity of Hong Kong itself is a political contention. In a sense it had been redundant for Hong Kong film-makers to posit their work within a frame of political extrospection (or outright propaganda) since their lives are already implicitly freighted with the foreknowledge of a preordained and unwilling political transformation. Any aggressive proselytizing would be rendered not mute but actually superfluous by the numbing uncertainty of daily reality.

Rather, instead of specific films created to instigate socio-political upheaval, the problematic had ingrained itself into the unconscious of the film culture itself, such that countless films can be interpreted as allegories–knowing or unconscious–of the former colony's doubtful future. What is generally referred to as HK's fear of "Communism" in the international media–of which these films must also be a part–must be qualified, however. The idiomatic use of the word "communist" has become a code word to ambiguously (and even euphemistically) designate China's generically totalitarian nationalism, such that the fears China instills would not be too different from those of any oppressive regime. Now that 1997 has passed and we have not yet seen another "Tiananmen Square," we have the luxury of rethinking the years immediately before the handover. But for HK film-makers in the 1990's, handover anxiety was irresistible and irrepressible.

Great Britain's lease on Hong Kong (from 1842, following the Opium War) had offered the world a unique, inverted parody of the traditional colonialist problematic. Instead of the standard progression of premodern national autocracy to modern colonial exploitation to an uncertain post-colonial democracy dependent on first-world support, Hong Kong has moved from the feudal oppression of Dynastic Chinese rule to the Western democracy of British colonialism to an uncertain post-colonial communism predicated on nationalist isolationism. The "climax" of this lineage, then, rather than a chance for autonomy, is the colony's reintegration into its original host country, from monarchy to communism, without fortuitously intersecting with the sole significant attempt at *some* sort of attempted Chinese republicanism (1911-49, following the victory of Sun Yat-sen to the fall of Chiang Kai-Shek). Immediately after 1949, HK was a refugee's paradise; but as 1997 approached, those ex-refugees became refugees once more.

Throughout the new-wave period (roughly 1978-late 80s/early 90s), indigenous film productions were dominant at the Hong Kong box-office. By 1993, following an ever-increasing exodus of emigrants to the West, the cheapening of film production values coupled with increased video pirating lessened the financial returns of HK films, and Western (Hollywood) films for the first time reigned supreme.[2] By the mid-1980's, new-wave Hong Kong film had become almost pathologically trendy,[3] a practice which paved the way for a new trend to emerge in what we can call the "post-new wave" period of 1993 onwards: the gay-themed film. A new openness regarding gay and lesbian themes loosely ties together the end of the HK new wave and the beginning of the post-new wave (1993-4 onwards). However, whereas the subgenres instigated by new-wave films such as John Woo's *A Better Tomorrow* (1986) or Ching Sui-Tung's *A Chinese Ghost Story* (1987) updated old, constant themes and stories with a new style, the gay/lesbian trend, ushered in at the end of the new wave, standardized a new homosexual content (not a new style), and a uniquely political one. The 1997 deadline slowly ticking away, liberal (and liberating) homosexual subject matter became one of Hong Kong cinema's primary allegories for the dread of the Mainland's homophobic version of "communism"–could Hong Kong continue its path to politico-sexual liberty, or would HK's reversion dash its hopes for freedom?[4] Thus the cinematic allegory was crystallized: the feared "nonexistence" of individual freedom post-1997 became mirrored in Mainland China's official line on the "nonexistence" of Chinese homosexuality. Political freedom became sexual freedom, as homosexuality–and by extension trans-sexuality/ transgender–became *the* metaphor for individual freedom. Of course, Hong Kong had inherited the 20th century's homophobia as much as Mainland China or anywhere else[5]–but the pro-gay about-face of HK films in the mid-90's was quite revolutionary compared to the mainstream films of any other country. In practice, homophobia in Mainland China may not be so different from the homophobia encouraged by other political hegemonies. The difference, however, is that China has a well-documented literary and historical pedigree of homosexuality that most Western countries do not. For China, looking back is–by Western standards of homosexuality–looking forward.

If one must cite the catalyst for the gay-themed film trend, it would most probably be Chen Kaige's *Farewell My Concubine*, a 1993 co-production between HK and the Mainland. A story of the unrequited homosexual love between two Peking opera actors[6] (one played by Leslie Cheung, whose own homosexuality is the stuff of HK tabloids), the film was banned in the Mainland for the crime of condoning and glorifying homosexuality, allegedly an infectious symptom of "Western decadence." *Concubine's* status as a Mainland-HK co-production crystallizes each side's contentious interpretation of history.[7] The outrageous lengths the Cultural Revolution went to deny the history of China, and its homosexuality, seemed to have instilled a mass-amnesia in the Chinese censors. As a character in Stanley Kwan's[8] *Full Moon in New York* (1990) points out, "China has a long history of homosexuality . . .

you should read the 'Records of Han,'" referring to the dynasty (202 b.c.-220 a.d.) in which a disproportionate amount of the emperors were homosexual.[9] This posits the cultivation of a homosexual *ethos*, evoking an ideal of specifically conventionalized aesthetics rather than the homosexuality of a neutered late 20th century anti-essentialism. It was also during the Han Dynasty that Buddhism was imported from India, and, along with the non-discriminatory philosophies of Taoism,[10] asserted a somewhat popular alternative to Confucian hierarchical conservatism. Although occasionally encountering some resistance from Neo-Confucianism centuries later, homosexuality has only been totally condemned in China in this century. The Chinese had overanxiously adopted Western prejudices (then recently codified by late 19th century Germanic medical quackery) wholesale along with Western technology in an endeavor to keep pace with modernization/industrialization. That the Communists should then object to homosexuality in a film about Chinese opera is a ludicrous denial of common historical fact. As Tao-Ching Hsu remarks in *The Chinese Conception of the Theater*:

> The vogue of the admiration for feminine beauty in men in the context of Chinese opera had several causes . . . the official attitude towards homosexuality facilitated the propagation of such a taste–"public quarters" of young boys were openly operated and patronized.[11] [157]

Or, as A.C. Scott says in his essay "The Performance of Classical Theater":

> It was common practice to use boy apprentices [in Chinese theater] as male prostitutes in Chinese intellectual circles.[12] [120]

The famously homosexual environment of Chinese theater was both decadent and economically driven, with Peking Opera boys being sold into servitude. As Mackerras says:

> Acting was not the only function which these boys fulfilled. It was no secret in Peking that most of them soon became homosexuals . . . In fact with the passage of time many people came to regard the *hsiang-kung* [the servile opera boys] as male prostitutes . . . In 1913 the new republican government ordered their suppression on the grounds that they were harmful to public morals . . . however, the *hsiang-kung* did not disappear in Peking for about another decade. In some parts of China the practice of enslaving boys for theatrical training was not finally eliminated until the communists came to power.[13]

It was perhaps following the *Farewell My Concubine* controversy that Hong Kong film-makers saw gay-themed filmmaking as a way of recognizing the sexual possibilities of the past that the Mainland would not, for only in the mutuality and solidarity of a commonly acknowledged past would there be a future for HK and the mainland. Obviously, homosexual slavery is hardly liberal; but the content of this widespread historical acceptability of homosexuality in itself–which the communists wanted to suppress *not* for primarily economic reasons–could be freed by a (not necessarily Anglocentric) democratic (re)form. Although economically and politically hierarchical, Dynastic homosexuality stood as a high aesthetic standard, and one predicated on behavior and not pigeonholed self-identity–despite the perception that the stage performers who often embodied it were thought to have low morals, either heterosexual or homosexual. (Here, morality and aesthetics do not necessarily inform each other.) The recovering of homosexuality as a lost symbol of Chinese diversity would be the means to acknowledging a Chinese past within the context of HK's democratic dilemma. "China" as represented in these films–and also as a general cultural idea–is not a geopolitical designation but a cultural one that should ideally unite racial, geographic, and sexual diversities.

It should come as little surprise, then, that many of HK's gay films should deal with intergenerational or parent-child relationships, with the mainland posing as the senior aspect ("motherland"/"fatherland") and HK the junior. The parental figures will come to stand for China's pre-communist ancestral roots (*ur*-parents), who knew more about homosexuality than even the capitalistic influences which are now peddled in China currently know. Although mainstream HK films had included sympathetic, if not exactly progressive, portrayals of gay characters as a new convention since circa 1993, following *Concubine* (and the belated decriminalization of homosexuality in 1991)[14] it was at first done peripherally, or within the overall context of a prying heterosociality.[15] It was Shu Kei's *A Queer Story* (1997) that first presented two major male stars–George Lam and Jordan Chan–as lovers in a *mainstream* film[16] universe whose erotic choice is exclusively homosexual. Lam, still closeted, is in his forties, a father-figure to the younger Chan, whose character is in fact named "Sonny." The film's Chinese title actually translates as "Gay Man 40,"[17] the specification of Lam's age bringing to mind a well-known passage from Confucius's *Analects*:

> At fifteen, I set my heart upon learning. At thirty. I had planted my feet firmly on the ground. At forty, I no longer suffered from perplexities. At fifty, I knew what were the biddings of Heaven. (II., iv.)[18]

The irony, of course, is that at 40 he is still plagued by the same perplexities that stifled him as a child–such would be the case, presumably, for all closeted gay men laboring under a heritage of Confucian (patriarchal) hegemony. Euphemistically labelled a "pervert" in grade school, Lam has now been living a private life with the openly gay Sonny for eight years. Like communist China unable to accept its homosexual past and denying its history with a mask of face-saving conventionality, Lam plans on masking himself through a marriage to his old platonic girlfriend, with whom he had had intercourse but once, under coercion. Director Shu Kei has seen that Lam should have the most ironic vocation possible: a marriage counsellor, projecting his fantasies of heterosexual normalcy by masochistically reinforcing the hegemonies that constrict him. He at one point declares to a client: "Hypocrisy, appropriately dispensed, is a virtue." On one level the remark is a seeming cop-out, paying lip service to the very "don't rock the boat" type of conventionalism in which Lam's character is trapped. However, a questioning of the phrase "appropriately dispensed" may reveal a hidden irony. If one questions the definition of "appropriate," the apparent superficiality of this quote becomes ironic, for if hypocrisy taken "appropriately" follows through logically to look back upon itself, its "appropriate" dispensation becomes a self-negation, and only then is it "virtuous."[19] If hypocrisy is itself hypocritical, it cancels itself in a double negative; indeed, there is nothing virtuous about the lies Lam lives, nor the society that compels him to do so.

Lam's anguished client suspects (accurately) that her husband is having a gay affair across the Mainland border in Shenzhen. Despite its pro-gay stance, and happy ending, this is a rare pro-gay film that also accounts for the torment of a wife unwittingly trapped in a bogus marriage to a closeted gay man, suggesting the novel argument that acceptance of homosexuality is in the best marital interests of potentially cuckolded heterosexuals. The irony of having the mainland be the locus of homosexuality instead of presumably liberal Hong Kong suggests that the dissolution of normative sexual and gendered borders parallels the dissolution of national borders. The Mainland will sooner or later have to own up to past history and present reality: homosexuality is, and has been, an integral part of mainland China, in Shenzhen as in everywhere else. If China wishes to dissolve the borders of its fractured nationhood, all its borders, including its contentious sexual ones, should be subject to the same logic of dissolution, for sexuality must not be divorced from the national identity China seeks to construct.

Dragging Lam into the fray, the wife takes a taxi to Shenzhen to spy on her husband: "Comrade, please take us to Yee Kung Gardens"–to which Lam replies, "These days only gay people call each other 'comrade'." This is the now-common slang usage of *tongzhi* ("comrade"), subversively appropriated here to signify the defiant camaraderie of homosexuals. The "bordered" irony is further complicated by a linguistic co-option and subversion: because language fundamentally creates politico-sexual prejudices, it is now language that must destroy them. After grappling with whether or not to come out as a gay man after the funeral of his friend, a professor who dies of

AIDS,[20] what forms the climax of the story is not if he will come out, but *to whom* he will come out. Logically, it is his father, the openly gay intergenerational relationship of Lam-Chan ironically doubled in the closeted relationship between Lam and his own father, who seems both stricken yet unsurprised at the revelation of his son's gayness. Importantly, the symbol of honesty in both intergenerational relationships is not the elder but the younger, a genealogical reversal in the passing down–or, in this case, the "passing up"–of wisdom. The cosmopolitan HK, blessed with the youth of democracy, must instruct its elders on how to reclaim their own lost youth and national history.

After Lam's futile attempt at marriage, his would-be wife sees through the charade and instructs him, "You're not a child . . . why can't you face reality?" There is a double paradox: youth knows the enlightened wisdom of the times, but Communist Chinese are themselves "children" in the scope of the nation's history (fifty years of Communism versus five thousand of dynasticism), whose denial of China's homosexual history exposes a pathological infantilism which is incapable of a self-correcting self-consciousness (or even knowing how to dispense hypocrisy "appropriately"). Youth must become old (the "new" homosexuality must be recognized as historical, and not new or Western at all) and the old youthful (the liberalization of prejudicial hegemonies). Meanwhile the Communist regime that is perceived as authoritarian is in fact a very recent development.

Shu Kei's immediately previous film, *Hu-Du-Men*[21] (1996), offers a more ambitious (if also more romanticized) critique of Chinese homosexuality, as well as providing a showcase for Josephine Siao Fong-fong, in the role of a contemporary Cantonese opera singer who specializes in *mun mo-sung* (male martial and scholarly roles). The opening explanatory title informs us:

> Hu-du-men is a term from Cantonese opera. It refers to the imaginary line between the stage and the backstage areas. When actors cross the hu-du-men they should forget themselves and become their roles.

Because the role-playing involves the practiced, educated cultivation of institutionalized transvestism, the idea of *hu-du-men* suggests that gender performativity may not necessarily be a gestured mediation of desire, but that desire is itself a learned "education" or practice. Thus, "performance" would no longer carry the neutered, stigmatic value of post-Butlerian queer theory; that high social approbation is awarded to sexual performance suggests that the highest level of desire is that it is a thing performed, a ritualized socialization, gay or straight. It may also be true that this represents personal desire as a *public* construction in a non-individualistic, non-Western society. That this artistic ideal is traditional, and is still practiced in mainstream opera today (whereas, for example, conventional performers of Shakespeare no longer use cross-dressing as a necessity of their craft), contradicts the notion that performativity is a product of contemporary Western post-structuralist subjective disjunction, for in fact much of what is mistakenly dubbed "post-modern" ideology is actually ancient in many cultures.[22] Unlike the North American post-Stonewall politics of *A Queer Story*, *Hu-du-Men* longs for a recognition of the grand antiquarian traditions of homosexuality's social legitimacy (nae, glorification) that render recourse to post-Stonewallisms moot by comparison.

If the *hu-du-men's* removal of sexuality from the domain of Self causes Siao to doubt her own sexuality, it causes her legions of exclusively female fans hardly any doubt at all. Of one Siao says, "I can't stand this one . . . she really thinks I'm a man and wants to marry me." The artificiality and manip-ulativeness of performativity mesmerizes the "performees" more than the performers; more than merely questioning the integrity of the subject, the *hu-du-men's* transformations inform and define the object's desires as well.[23] When the object is itself a mass-consciousness (i.e., an audience), it is the conventionality of the masses that is at stake–a gendered illusion that might be dispelled before a self-conscious audience of one becomes "reality" by dint of the individual's surrender of identity to the *polis*. The illusion of the *hu-du-men*, combined with the illusion of mass-identification, reconstructs gender alignments, creating a new construction no less valid than its prede-cessor–since the moral value of gender constructions is arbitrary anyway. The receptive illusions of the *hu-du-men* are ready-made for the illusions of an audience's mass-identity.

The plot of *Hu-du-men* centers, again, around the parent-child binary. In order to pursue her opera career, Siao was forced to give up her son for adoption–the dissolute, unstable gendering of the theater denies the legitima-cy of heterosexual motherhood. Meanwhile, the love affair of Siao's lesbian teenage stepdaughter (from Siao's perspective, homosexuality is not biologi-cally generated, on stage or off) is only to the angst of her natural father. To complete the thematic mix, Siao and her husband are planning on emigrating to Australia before 1997: the issues of sex, gender, parenthood, and nation-hood intersect and unify. To placate the homophobic husband, Siao speaks with her stepdaughter's somewhat butch girlfriend, asking, "Why do you dress as a boy?" "So do you," the girlfriend answers, to which Siao replies, "Only on stage–off stage I'm 100% woman." The girlfriend answers back with an insight beyond her years (again, the passing "up" of wisdom): "How do you know the men who admire you aren't gay?" As a woman, she is asexual; only as a man–as an artistic conceit–is she sexualized, and it is thus the *hu-du-men* itself that is the sexual catalyst, transmogrifying the latent into the actualized with its scale of irresolute identity. Sexuality becomes a living art–attractive only as a work of art (as opposed to a work of biology), performance is desire. She is a better "man" than a biological man because art can acquire a social value beyond biology's mere neutrality. Worshipped as a man *offstage* by heterosexual women, the subject's gender is objectified as a man whose identification is re-subjectified to the allegedly heterosexual female spectator. Both self and other, the subject and the object, are heterosexual females engaged in an entirely sincere lesbian charade, the greatest achievement of whose aesthetic is the losing of the performer's gender and the transformation of the spectator's sexual object choice. Although Chinese opera actors–like actors in the West–were thought to have low moral standards in their personal/sex lives, the public standards embodied by their performance reinforce a morally gendered typology. The sexual aesthetic is not only separate from the moral aesthetic, but the former actually becomes the more active and powerful of the two. As performers, opera actors would impersonate heterosexual moral archetypes–the virtuous hero, the wicked villain, the female beauty, etc. Yet these normative types are presented for the purpose of subverting them through their trans-sexual reception.

This is not comparable to a drag show, whose parody of gender typologies expressly appeals to the self-consciousness of its audience, and in which the masquerade's hyperbole calls attention to the inadequacy of its realism. The whole point of a drag show is the audience's self-consciousness of the art of illusion. In Cantonese opera, the *hu-du-men* mandates a loss of self-awareness and a discovery of unconsciously reconstructed desire. Also, unlike a drag show, the gendered opera characters represent morally correct archetypes, which are superficially acknowledged but then soon subverted through the audience's internalization of the *hu-du-men* the actors project. Of course, on some level the audience *is* aware of the masquerade, but its success as artistic convention requires that the audience, as an extension of that convention, lose themselves in the moment. This is comparable to Aristotelian catharsis–on some level, the audience of a Greek tragedy is obviously aware it is engaged in a rational artistic contract when it enters the theater, but in order to experience the emotionalism of catharsis the audience must suspend its self-awareness that what it watches is a fiction.

Furthermore, contrary to positing sexuality as inherently masculine, here heterosexuality is diminished to a necessary but intermediary station in lesbian desire (Siao's fans on some level *are* aware that she is female), and as an historically accepted convention. Masculinity is a stop on sexuality's sliding scale, a stop which must acknowledge the masculinist constructions and hegemonies in and through which such heterosexually-typed performances occur (the means), before moving on to the actual object of the lesbian desire (the ends). Because Siao can be a better man than a real man, lesbianism is a better form of "heterosexuality" than real heterosexuality. Simply, performance is not a mere means to a sexual end, but embodies that end within itself. The lesbianism activated by the *hu-du-men* is also subversive because, within an overarching patriarchy, it posits masculinity and male tropes as the exotic "other." Through this "othering" of patriarchal types, masculinity is effeminately sexualized to engage female homosexual interplay, subverting the masculinism that forces the need for such games in the first place. Like the crossing of the Shenzhen border in Shu Kei's *A Queer Story*, the *hu-du-men*'s sexual limbo also mandates the transgression of a border whose first explicit designation is gender, not nationality, but which ultimately conflates the two as a necessary criterion of China's original cultural history.

In *Hu-du-Men*, Siao's character acts in a new opera production directed by "Mr. Lam," an American-born Chinese, "neither Western nor Chinese" (just as performers are neither male nor female), who is seen as anti-traditionalist in the eyes of the troupe's most stalwart actor. The director explains that the very organism that is Cantonese opera is characterized by its adaptability and ongoing transformation, that a facet of its traditionalism is its progressive developmental betterment. Paradoxically, maintaining the status quo would be anti-traditionalist. "The all-male cast has given way to a mixed-cast," he concludes;[24] the fact that in the mixed cast the women play men, that cross-dressing is continued despite the absence of its practical necessity, indicates the desire (either conscious or a continuance of a culturally indoctrinated unconscious) to maintain the unfixity and instability of gender definitions as a high-honored cultural achievement. The conventionality of cross-dressing in a mixed cast is the rare case of a subversive convention: though entirely unnecessary, the convention has given way to unconscious desire, and is exploited as an inverted pretext to continue a tradition which draws extensively on homosexuality (as Mackerras, etc., notes). It is crucial that this speech is given by Lam, whose Westernized democratic perspective directs the progressive/liberal dimension of the film's politics towards the future of a non-democratic HK. In a sense, the aesthetics of the practice of *unnecessitated* cross-dressing disrupts constructivist theory's notion of gender fluidity and role-playing. Here, there is fluidity *between* genders but not *within* them. It is easy to artificially transform into either gender, but once you have transformed, you are stuck within morally circumscribed gender archetypes (hero/villain, etc.). You can be a man or woman, but only a certain and "correct" type of man or woman. However, that is all that is required to activate homosexual desire. The moral typology is the real disguise, not the gender, and the secret yet ulterior desire to subvert impossible moral ideals is also the desire to subvert those ideals' heterosexual imperative.

Under this aesthetic, it is at first biology, and *not* sociology, that is fluid. What is essentialist are the moral heterosexual tropes (hero, villain, the beauty) performed by male or female personae, regardless of the performer's gender. This moral essentialism conspires to make it seem that gender "naturally" follows from moral archetypes and, in turn, gender propriety from those archetypes–but of course the moral basis is itself hegemonically manufactured. This typology reinforces heterosexual tropes but its practical performance activates homosexual desire because the audience's desire is artistically transformed from an attraction to the gender of the trope to an attraction to the gender of the *performer*. So while it may seem this is homosexuality performed (or justified) as heterosexuality, the subversion of heterosexuality also subverts the morality in which it is manifest (classical character types). It was indeed also well-known that many opera performers–from modern Cantonese lesbian Yam Kim-fei to the old Peking Opera boys–were homosexual in real life, suggesting that the heterosexuality of moral tropes was a self-conscious pretext, and that Chinese opera's homosexual agenda was more than a mere fantasy.

Siao's character eventually meets her prodigal son (through a bit of Dickensian coincidence, he is her protege's boyfriend), but cannot reveal her identity on a condition of the adoption. Her natural son must remain a fond mystery–she, multi-gendered in the performance of China's history, has lost her heterosexual child not in favor of a deviance but in the pursuit of that child's own history, in this case a theatrical history which eliminates sexual boundaries. Rather, Siao will content herself with her adopted daughter, a lesbian whose (homo)sexual identity simultaneously looks forward to a democratic future and acknowledges the (pre-Westernized) historical past (Siao's biological son is, alas, forever lost). In the end, Siao and her husband do not emigrate to the West, but the daughter is sent to boarding school in Australia– a child caught between Western influence and the encroaching communism of an uncertain East, the West is required to foster her identity. China may have its history, but the modern Chinese may not want it.

What perhaps prefaced the boom of politically "out" gay films, such as Shu Kei's, was the renaissance of the traditional device of cross-dressing in period costume films, whose fantastic conventions had temporarily suffered at the hands of the new-wave's early (and, by the mid-1980s, mostly abandoned) attempts at naturalism. By the early 1990s, cross-dressing had once again standardized itself as a popular trope in HK films, in part because of the tireless (and occasionally tiresome) efforts of director/producer Tsui Hark. There has perhaps been no (heterosexual) commercial director in the past twenty years so obsessed with transvestism, and yet he has been at the same time ever-afraid of pushing his obsession into the homosexual terrain to which it is naturally tantamount. His gorgeously photographed *The Lovers* (1994, aka "Butterfly Lovers"), based on a traditional Chinese legend previously filmed as *The Tragic Story of Leong San-pak and Chuk Ying-toi* (1958), tells the ancient star-crossed tragedy of a girl who disguises herself as a male so she can be a scholar (a pursuit restricted to males, of course). On the one hand, this could be analogous to, say, Olivia's equally opportunistic cross-dressing in *Twelfth Night* in the Western canon. On the other hand, the overwhelming popularity of the martial period film in the early 1990s,[25] in which cross-dressing came to be a predictable, predetermined convention allowing free play with sex/gender, created an omnipresent phenomenon which dwarfs the contemporary commercial popularity of Shakespeare in the West, another "period" conceit (even when the cross-dressing is performed with a mixed cast, as Shakespeare now is).

Yet Tsui's and other director's period costume films from this period did not employ the extra-diegetic transvestism of the *hu-du-men*'s opera world, and the opera-films popular in the 50s and 60s based on that same conceit.[26] In that opera world, cross-dressing is external to the dramatic diegesis and occurs offstage, so the audience cannot make a "before-and-after" comparison of the actor's gender roles. But HK's new-wave films, perhaps in their Westernism, reject this premodern homosexual idea in favor of a diegetic CD which, because it occurs "onstage," invites such before-and-after judgments. It is thus ironic that the post new-wave's pro-gay films, such as Shu Kei's, should have been so immediately and bluntly preceded by period-costume cross-dressing films whose reversion and allegiance to the conservative homophobia of Western transgender representations–which are always "onstage" and demand re-transformation before the end–ignores the *hu-du-men*'s more subversive Chinese traditions.

Diegetic cross-dressing became not merely accepted but seemingly obligatory in many period films 1992-4, suggesting again the paradox that conventions need not always be so conservative. Cross-dressing was indeed popular enough to transcend generic boundaries, and found its way into comedies too. Transgender became so acceptable that, while never quite "normative" in itself, it was popular enough to challenge the idea of gendered normativity. Lin Ching-hsia, for example, enjoyed the greatest popularity of her career as the transsexual "Asia the Invincible" in the second two installments of the *Swordsman* trilogy (1990-93). These two are the only recent HK films in which gender transformation does not occur "onstage"–but nor does it occur offstage. It instead happens in the imaginary spaces between the installments of each sequel–but the male actor from the first film is replaced in the second by Lin, so it is sort-of cheating and not strictly in keeping with the *hu-du-men*'s loss of self-consciousness. Indeed, unlike Chinese opera, in which actors "become" their character's gender, cross-dressing in these films is self-conscious within the diegesis and plot of the film. Nevertheless, because HK cross-dressing had become an accepted category, and not relegated to single, gimmicky drag stories as in the West, the difference between extra- and intra-diegetic transvestism may be partly mitigated. Perhaps unable to deal to with modern homosexuality directly on a large scale (at least until two or three years later, in the mid-90s), the rediscovery of the cross-dressed period film in the early 90s became a convenient historical displacement (and relegation) of politico-sexual ideology to a past both safely costumed and more sexually adventurous than post-1997 HK's probable future.

In *The Lovers*, the disguised-girl and a fellow male student begin as friends but slowly fall in love–either in spite, but presumably *because*, of gender confusion. Sleeping in the same bed, he tells "him," "I am worried that you are another Tong Mung Chun," a former homosexual student. "Who was he?" she asks. "He isn't 'real'." "What is real?" she asks back. "A man can do anything to a woman . . . kiss . . . make love." She, disguised, concludes, "I see . . . this is called 'real . . . '" Not, mind you, it is real, merely that it is called such, and the joke is obviously intentional. (Carried a step further, that this story is a cherished Chinese archetype, and that one of its characters now claims homosexuality to be somehow not quite "real," may be an ironic stab at the Mainland officials who claim homosexuality has no natural or epistemic "reality" in China.) Nevertheless, he is attracted to her/him; yet confused, he homophobically whispers to himself at night "Don't become a sissy" repeatedly. The overdetermined heterosexual resolution of the conservative transvestite romance (compare, again, to *Twelfth Night*, etc.) uses its false, pre-ordained coda to reinforce normative (i.e., closed) subject-object gender identification: the disguise does not dictate desire, essential sexual personality does. Naturally, the difficulty in disguised transvestite-romance plots is that one is never sure if the lover is unconsciously "seeing-through" the disguise to the "real" gender, and thus falling in love with that (a fictive wish-fulfillment which reinforces hegemonic heterosexuality); or if, even if the climax's wish-fulfillment is the happily heterosexual unmasking of gender (dispelling the illusion of performance art), it is nevertheless that the male becomes attracted to the female *as* a male, and because of same. While the "sissy" monologue in *The Lovers* seems to indicate the latter, it is nevertheless the familiar Western idea that gender mobility gravitates towards the female, and sexual mobility towards the male; the necessity of female gender-play is identical to the neurotic fear of male sexual-play (or mobility). Here, homophobia impedes the *hu-du-men*'s subversive sexual mobility, creating a unidirectional scale whose conservatism preserves the phallic male as sexual origin/initiator. Not only would male homosexual transgression be forbidden, it is the only type of homosexuality that exists *to be* forbidden (patriarchy does not recognize even lesbianism). As a vehicle to reinforce heterosexuality, the experiment of diegetic or "onstage" female transvestism provides only a smokescreen for the male, the questioning of whose gendered hegemony is far more socially, politically, and economically at stake. Yet in the case of *The Lovers*, this is Tsui (a

Western-schooled director) imposing a twentieth-century brand of Western homophobia on a pre-modern text.

The *Lovers*'s dramatic irony in the discussion on the "real"[27] foreshadows the audience's preconceptions about generic-dramatic conventions of cross-dressing itself, acknowledging that "reality" is only that which is called such (lingually constructed). Yet Tsui's *The Lovers* (and all of his conservative drag-works in general) must deny the possibilities that it purports to explore–the actual crossing of the gender line into real homosexuality is for *other* people, or for *other* director's stylish (re-)interpretations of famous Chinese legends. The mechanics of the plot do indeed see that gender is reassuringly unmasked only for the couple's rival families to selfishly forbid their union. (The film's cross-dressed first half is comic, while the conventionally-dressed second half is abruptly tragic: as usual, farce reigns supreme as heterosexuality's favorite defense mechanism). The "mask" of transvestism may have been what stood between their sexual union, but the disguise was also necessary to thwart, albeit temporarily, the sad codings of Confucian familial tyranny which stood between them. Unable to unite in this world, they both die and are reincarnated as butterflies in the next, fluttering away together from the hands of a Buddhist monk. That the appeal to Buddhistic/metaphysical freedom–the rejection of categorical materiality for a natural *cum* supernatural Becoming–should be enacted as such an impotent escapist fantasy, however, only proves the ultimate immobility of sexual hegemony.

The other big transvestite romance of 1994, and the most successful one to push cross-dressing into contemporary times, was Peter Chan Ho-san's popular *He's a Woman, She's A Man*. It approaches heterosexual transvestism with only slightly more daring than *The Lovers* (even though it is modern dress), as a pop idol named "Sam" (Leslie Cheung) must cope with his own unwanted affections for his supposedly male protege, Wing (Anita Yuen)–unbeknownst to him a girl in male guise. After finally mustering the courage for a passionate kiss, he is soon revolted by his seemingly homosexual transgression. The happy ending sees Sam, in climactic enlightenment, declare he "doesn't care" if she is male or female, but by this point it has already been established to him that she is indeed female, and therefore "acceptable." The director's ostensibly liberal intentions are undercut by his own timidity–wouldn't the statement be stronger if he was still unsure of the gender, and expressed his devotion nonetheless? As it is, the ending can be seen as both moot and marginally hypocritical. As in *The Lovers* (and countless other drag-romances), the man falls in love with the woman *as* a man, as if a forbidden homosexuality were necessary to both activate and "excite" otherwise banal heterosexual desire.

Chan's sequel, *Who's the Woman, Who's the Man* (1996), though less popular, is actually the richer and more complex of the two films which, taken as a whole, constitute a veritable essay on gender performance. The sequel begins exactly as the original had ended, with Sam and Wing embracing in the elevator whose stalls had previously caused Sam claustrophobic panic. At the end of the first film, the elevator stalls and Sam proclaims he no longer is afraid of being stuck in the (metaphoric) elevator–i.e., he has overcome the "compartment-alization" that phobically separates male from female. Yet the elevator is no metaphoric closet, for in the second film he will regressively reassert the homophobia we thought the trials of the first film had dispelled. (We presume Sam's admitting he doesn't care if Wing is male or female in the climax of the first film is tantamount to an admission of bisexuality, but the sequel regresses his character to re-tread the issue.) Wing is now a successful pop star in her own right, but since her fans think she is male, Sam is afraid of being seen as a public gay couple. Angry with Sam's image-consciousness and his renewed homophobia, the now sexually confused Wing falls in love with her musical idol, the legendary, reclusive singer Fan-fan (Anita Mui), who is also ignorant of the Wing's true gender identity and for whom Sam has his own intentions. Playing in a cross-dressing film together, Fan-fan dresses as a man, and Wing enacts a woman-as-a-man-as-a-woman (their scene parodies Rhett Butler and Scarlett O'Hara, no less). Sam, spiteful and jealous, reveals the secret of Wing's gender to Fan-fan, making her too shocked to complete her kissing scene with Wing. Meanwhile, Wing herself is confused by her own lesbian attraction to Fan-fan, her idol. Whereas it is a common literary trope to symbolize male homosexuality by having one man be attracted, transitively, to the other man's woman, here a lesbian attraction–yet ironically performed in *heterosexual* drag–mediates Wing's and Sam's suppressed *heterosexuality*!

But Wing and Fan-fan, vengefully defying Sam's scheming, do eventually embrace, and sleep together, to the latter's shock. Their actualized lesbianism *finally* breaks diegetic cross-dressing's limitation of sexual bounds, transgressing the generic separation of homosexual form from heterosexual content (in *Twelfth Night*, homosexual formalism is required to actualize heterosexual content, but as a mere vehicle the homosexual structure has no value in itself beyond the transformative). Here, however, the usually heterosexual romantic content, too, threatens to become homosexual, as form and content could become mutually inclusive. But, frustratingly, director Chan will not allow them to enjoy their lesbian transgression for even a moment, as he would also not allow Sam to profess his love to Wing before he knew the latter's true gender in the prequel. The fact that the lesbian kiss occurs in a cross-dressed film *within a cross-dressed film* seems to ironically comment on the popular cowardice of most transvestite romances, the latent homophobia of which it will now, finally, transgress. But that it occurs within a meta-performance robs it of its reality–the kiss was perhaps indeed only a

performance (designed for Sam, not themselves). Their lesbianism would not
have been actualized in any other way, because the unreality of this way will
later allow them to conveniently dismiss their transgressive conduct. This is
ironic considering the many gay and lesbian supporting characters in both
films, whose "out"-ness frames and explicates the homosexual import of
Wing's cross-dressing.[28]

Indeed, after taking this bold step, *Who's the Woman* reverts to the formula
of its prequel by having Wing and Fan-fan (like Wing and Sam in the prequel) repudiate their homosexual conduct. The two anxiously regret their
transgression, and Wing naturally winds up back in the arms of Cheung. By
placing the lesbian transgression within a meta-performative space further
removed from reality, what the transgression achieves is only the regaining of
the level at which it began, the performance of the film proper (they have
only dug themselves out of the meta-film). Although Wing and Fan-fan do in
fact sleep together after the kiss (although we only see them waking up
together in the same bed), that the original kiss was a conscious performance
allows all that followed from that premise to be also merely performed. The
film also seemingly tries to parody filmic drag conventions by suggesting
that in film worlds where cross-dressing is the "norm," it is heterosexuality
that is repressed because the daily surface of the world is non-heteronormative performance. Yet *diegetic* cross-dressing conventions don't really go this
far, and are not really subversive enough to pose much of a threat. By having
Fan-fan and Wing regret their lesbianism, the films seems to subvert the
homosexual conventions of a cinematic drag sub-genre not really deserving
of such a subversion. The film is so obsessed with performance–such that
even its boldest transgression is only a play-act without sociopolitical merit–that it winds up negating sex instead of liberating it.

As Sam and Wing, reunited, fly to the supposed artistic inspiration of the
paradisiacal Africa, Cheung dreams about (a land of "primitive" heterosexuality?), he experiences the same pangs of claustrophobic anxiety on the plane
that he had on the elevator. His claustrophobia–like all phobias–symbolizes a
loss of environmental control, in this case his inability to control his own
sexual identity. The joke that the film begins where it ends is frustratingly
pessimistic; the structural circularity creates the illusion that the very
hegemonic categories of sex-gender identity the film superficially attempts to disrupt are, in the end, resistant to subversion anyway. What
remains is only the empty shell of performance, not an end unto itself nor
even a means to a foreseeable end–the film intentionally sabotages itself. The
climactic joke is not satire or anything at all subversive–the humor there stems
from the ironic repetition of cycles, the simple recognizability of conservative structures, and the nihilistic knowledge that the individual is powerless to
overcome them. The film's unfortunate allegiance to this conservatism–indeed

the basic heterosexist conservatism of romantic comedy as a genre–only lends unnecessary support to the sad Butlerian idea that performance is a circular "trap," a means without an end. The momentary transgression of the lesbian interlude is denied liberating value in and of its own content–the "shame" and "unmentionability" attached to it turn it into a homosexual formalism the function of whose romantic content is hypocritically hetero-sexual. In *The Lovers*, Tsui Hark at least had the luxury of conservatism by using a well-known legend; Chan, by locating his two films within democrat-ically politicized spaces, has no such luxury. *He's a Woman* was made in 1994, and can be seen as a necessary middle point in the progression from the cross-dressed period films of the late new-wave to the modern-dress "out" gay films a couple of years later; but by 1996's *Who's the Woman*, it is frustrating that Chan's themes have not been shorn of their own reluctances, even considering the post-new wave's trend to the contrary.

Director Chan has even said that his aim was not to make homosexual movies with his *He's A Woman . . .* films. "It's really not about homosexual-ity, the movie's not about that. The movie's about two people connecting on a very platonic level."[29] (236) But, for better or worse, these films *are* about homosexuality, the director's own bewildering claims notwithstanding. Or, these films are *not* about homosexuality to about the same degree that Spike Lee's films are not about race relations, but are simply about people who "just happen" to be different races and who still try to get along. We must ask, "Are the heterosexual love stories that have filled the screen for the past century films that are not really about *heterosexuality* per se, and could also *equally* appeal to homosexual audiences?" Because the answer is such a stupefying "no," because traditionally heterosexist cinemas have only re-cently recognized their homosexual audiences, because standardized film romances have indeed been about progenitive heterosexuality *per se* and could not under different circumstances have been about homosexuals, we must dismiss Chan's naive comment and instead ask him why he would enact his "platonic" romance within gender-performative spaces that necessarily invite homosexual politics? These performative spaces do not just "happen to be," they are constructed for a social purpose. But what purpose is that, if not a political one–to merely window-dress this admittedly enchanting love story with "exotic" sexuality? But Sam's homophobia in both films does, in fact, politicize them sufficiently, so we might assume director Chan is reluc-tant to publicly admit the possibilities that the films themselves make ob-vious.

Most of HK's "out" films, more or less beginning around 1994, eschew cross-dressed subtextual games in favor of presenting a mildly explicit *textu-al* sexual politics, often woven into a romantic comedy–a "progressive" assimilation of homosexual choice into the democratic socio-sexual fabric.[30]

Writer-director Cheung Chi Sing's *Love and Sex Among the Ruins* (1996) indeed attempts to push romantic seriocomedy into more political territory but, although diverting and often complex, the film turns squeamish at the end. A film that at first suggests ideal Communism may solve sexual discriminations, it ultimately and hypocritically, and even unintentionally, posits male homosexuality as an insurmountable taboo in its pseudo-Marxist/utopian plan. The film's male homophobic hero, "Man-cheung," is impotent, the result of one unfortunate night in his endless womanizing in which his partner sprays his penis with a substance that results in impotence–the film's punishment for his callous heterosexuality. Despite the erotic lavishings of an equally heterosexual policewoman, "Ron," who makes it her goal to cure his impotence, his condition fails to improve. Since it was heterosexuality/heterosexism that got him in trouble in the first place, Ron's reinforcement of such evil strategies will not do the trick. Cheung-man is friends with a bisexual woman who is having an affair with a lesbian ("Billie"); the bisexual's Marxist-bohemian husband is a Mainland Chinese, recently returned from the Mainland and in the process of securing his emigration papers to HK. The joke, presumably, is that the only people who want to emigrate *to* HK before 1997 are Mainlanders.

The husband is fascinated by his wife's same-sex affair and even draws sketches of their lesbian embrace, aestheticizing their love into an objectified frame both humanized (the camera's own perspective–one of dramatic valorization–is here also the husband's) and dehumanized (it is nevertheless rendered "unreal" by dint of its artistic framing). In an amusing scene, the husband remarks to the impotent hero, "Affairs are required to enrich marriage, according to Frederich Engels." "Who is he?" the hero replies. "Don't you know him? How can you live here after 1997?"–satirically pointing out the disparity between the ideal Marxism of the 19th century and the corrupted communism of Mainland China, whose uncritical adoption of Western culture, including its homophobia, has more in common with Western bourgeois moralism than it might care to admit.[31] The husband responds, "He was a good comrade and friend of Marx." "Oh, a comrade?" laughs Cheung-man, echoing the gay appropriation of the word (*tongzhi*), as in the similar dialogue from *A Queer Story*. The joke that Marx, as a "comrade," was metaphorically homosexual (by way of being communally sexual) would seem to inform the film's probable political thesis–but director Cheung will flinch at the end.

The husband soon grows threatened by the lesbian affair and tells his wife to make a choice between them–he is ultimately not a truly "communal" communist just as China is not truly communist, both paying only lip service to Marxist ideas. The husband is both angry and jealous that the wife, in order to pay for his emigration to HK from China, worked as a hostess (i.e., hooker) in lesbian Billie's bar–it is on this capitalism that their lesbian affair was predicated. The wife's indebtedness to the lesbian is seen as a capitalist advantage by the husband; indeed sexual capitalism is the way of Western HK, a force his comic attempts at sexual communism will try to resist throughout the film. Experimenting, the husband–in female drag–tries to seduce the lesbian, with risible results; the husband is refused not only because of his poor performance[32] but because of the transparency of his pursuit's cold intellectualism. It is a performance that pretends to be nothing more than a performance; perhaps the husband's failure is this "out" film's own rejection of the overly coy drag-film universe of the late new wave period. Regardless, as a transparent joke, this drag has little to do with desire. Failing this, the husband turns his attentions to the impotent hero, and attempts to sketch his flaccid penis–to the latter's objections and an ensuing interval of situational comedy. Previously, lesbian love scenes had been presented with both solemnity and eroticism, albeit from the titillating view of a male director; the prospect of gay male contact, however, is still cinematic taboo,[33] requiring comedy's fearful denial. Even as distanced art (sketching), homosexual contact is disallowed, unlike the previous significance of the lesbian portraiture.

The hero's emasculation will ironically be the catalyst for his climactic and reinvigorating experience of female love–but with Billie. By having sex with a lesbian, he avoids defensively polarized heterosexual binaries and discovers a masculinity he *never* had, even before his impotence: as he recognizes his partner as a human and not just a sex object, his erection symbolizes his new sexual humanity. This is a utopian sexual communism, in which people can be truly and sexually equal and compatible, regardless of *both* gender and sexual object choice. The film can sneakily avoid any male homosexual contact by justifying the solution to the hero's problem as one in which *neither* party is sexually attracted to one another, but they do it anyway–out of humanistic-communistic attraction. (Presumably, the experimental husband might enjoy a bisexual encounter with Cheung-man.) Male sexuality is simply polarized into either biological functionality (or lack thereof) or cold intellectualism (the husband). The interim of actualized desire is female domain, and the actualization of that desire also becomes *actualizing*, even for a male partner. The aggressive, diametric female heterosexuality of the policewoman will also not cure the hero–it has no inspiring revelation of polymorphous sexual possibility, only reinforcing the hegemonic strategies that initially led to the hero's impotence. The bisexual wife's aegis was sullied through her sexual capitalism as well as through her semi-heterosexuality. Only through the sexually disinterested emancipation of the lesbian can he become potent again–sexually and humanistically. In their brief sex scene, "I can't take you as a woman," she says to him, both drunk. But he takes her as one, and immediately he regains his erection. Only through the recognition of the other as a human being–as opposed to a dehumanized object–is his potency reinstated; only through an experience with a lesbian, an experience neither strictly nor conventionally heterosexual (or strictly homosexual) can his humanity be regained. Likewise, the husband's earlier attempt at cross-dressing failed because it was self-interestedly disingenuous. But the husband now comes to bond with the lesbian as well by sleeping with her too, and to him she is no longer a mere *object d'art*. However, the "otherness" of lesbianism may restore the hero's humanity, but it cannot overcome the film's own male homophobia.

The one sexual possibility for which the film will not permit closure is homosexuality between the two men.[34] After giving a speech about Marxist communal sexuality, the husband attempts to broaden his communal horizons by "experiencing" the formerly impotent male hero, taking off his pants and comically miming a position of sodomy. That both (as opposed to only one) of the sexual encounters between the males are buffered with comic denial, whereas lesbianism is both sanctioned and free (and yet still objectified and "othered" as a sort of polymorphous heterosexuality by a male director, and in a film about deobjectification, no less), betrays both sexism and cowardice on the filmmakers' part. In a supposedly enlightened (and admittedly enter-taining) film, the taboo of the inviolable male body remains intact.[35] The male body's inviolability is "proof" of its superiority, suggesting the familiar argument that (male) homophobia is really a psychically displaced sexism.

The most publicized "out" gay film of the post-new wave has been Wong Kar-wai's *Happy Together* (1997),[36] a cosmopolitan gay romance seemingly free of apology, whose mostly suffocating, brooding atmosphere is dispelled in a climax of life-affirming energy. It is a film which at once wants to wear its homosexuality on it sleeve and simultaneously purport to be simply sexual rather than homosexual. Like Peter Chan, director Wong runs from the possi-bility of being attached to a product labelled "homosexual": " . . . the couple could just as well have been about male and female relationships, but they just happened to be men."[37] (268) But if they just happened to be men, why wasn't this "unisexual" film made years ago, before HK's cinematic climate warmed up to homosexual possibilities? Obviously, it couldn't have been, because politics informs the lives–and artistic representations–of all homo-sexuals living under hegemonic regimes, the apolitical insistences of particu-lar film directors notwithstanding (political apathy is not the same as utopian-ism). Regardless, because it would feature two major HK male stars (Tony Leung Chiu-wai and Leslie Cheung, natch) miming slightly explicit sex. Wong chooses to open his film with *the* sex scene, an obvious gesture de-signed to placate a mainstream audience's presumably nervous expectations regarding such a taboo. With the obligatory sex scene "out of the way," such a sight need never recur, and the (straight) audience can now rest at ease. Wong's *Days of Being Wild* (1991) was the story of a sadomasochistically heterosexual man (Leslie Cheung) whose affairs are a substitute for the female "gap" in his life left by the mother he never knew: his parental estrangement manifested itself in nihilistic sexuality. In *Happy Together*, the two male lovers (Leslie Cheung and Tony Leung Chiu-wai) are both sadoma-sochistic–alternatively ostracizing each other and reconciling–and the es-tranged parental love object, a theme familiar from so many HK gay films, is displaced to the literal homosexual desire of the father (as opposed to the mother in the heterosexual *Days*). Although Cheung's sexuality in *Days* was also largely characterized by sadomasochism, that film is apolitical. In *Happy*, Cheung is once against sadistic (at least initially), toying with Leung's emotions and cheating on him with rich (non-Chinese) patrons. His character's national exile in *Happy* is left unexplained in the text, so we must presume homosexuality's necessarily political baggage is sadomasochistic explanation enough, and that their sexual S/M is an internalization of the homophobic social sadomasochism responsible for their national exile. If this is true, then the film is indeed about homosexuality *per se*, and how homo-sexuality allegorizes the alienated binary relations represented in the film by Leung's estrangement from his father.

The first image in the film is of a passport[38]–political exile becomes nomadic (homo)sexual freedom. Leung and Cheung, after a presumable rou-tine of parting and reuniting, establish a base in Argentina. After soon break-ing up again, Leung spitefully accepts Cheung back into his cramped, dingy apartment[39] after the latter has been beaten by the man for whom he had left Leung. The isolation of the apartment is not merely their social alienation, but their mutual alienation, as they enact a series of games of romantic depriva-tion, unwilling to forgive previous transgressions of loyalty. Leung first takes a job at a kitchen, then at an abattoir, where the washing away of blood echoes the lost sexuality of the tumultuous Iguazu Falls which they once planned on seeing but never did–the purity of the Falls reddens to the blood of heartbreak. Eventually, they separate permanently, but Leung has hidden Cheung's passport, and refuses to give it back–he is a political, as well as romantic, refugee. Now Leung is the sadist, although the film does not seek to moralize either side of the relation. A conflation of sexual freedom and political freedom, the politico-sexual power the passport symbolizes has been stolen by the sadistic Leung, who internalizes and redirects the external social masochism of their exile into a private sadism whose object is Cheung. In one shot, the camera's perspective is upside-down (as in all of Wong's films, style and content are inseparable); the literal joke that Argentina is on the opposite/upside-down hemisphere as HK restates the theme of parental estrangement. Here, the West is represented by neither colonial HK nor the U.S., but a South

American West as exotic to China as China is still to the U.S., compounding the alienation by one additional degree of variability. Leung wishes to reunite with his father in HK and leaves Argentina, leaving Cheung's sadism, and hopefully his own, behind. He stops in Taiwan, and by coincidence meets the family of a boy he fell in love with and thought would never see again (the happy ending, escaping his sadomasochistic relationship). "On Feb. 20, 1997, I'm back on this side of the world," he says. On television, Leung watches a report about the death of Deng Xiao Ping, whose progressive reforms opened China to the (less sadistic?) West. With Deng gone, he can optimistically wonder what will be China's next step, a wonderment joined with the optimistic promise of meeting again with his non-sadistic new boy-friend. China is, perhaps now, one step closer to the West, and the reunification with his father(land) is also perhaps one concurrent step closer, and hopefully several steps less sadomasochistic. As *Happy Together* was made in early 1997, he wonders (as do we) who will follow Deng as the audience wonders what will follow for HK.

Besides *Happy*, the other high-profile HK "homosexual" film of 1997 by an individualistic (i.e., "art film") director was Yim Ho's difficult but lovely *Kitchen* (1997), from the novel by Banana Yoshimoto. Yim had previously explored the democracy/communism binary in his underappreciated *King of Chess* (1991, co-directed/meddled-with by Tsui Hark), in which cautious optimism shaped the allegory of HK-China cooperation. *Kitchen*'s allegory is far more obtuse than *King*'s, and perhaps the only HK film in memory to seriously deal with a transsexual as a main (and most interesting) character.[40] Aggie, shocked by her grandmother's recent death, becomes mute, and is taken in by a young man (Jordan Chan) and his transsexual father, Emma (comic actor Law Kar-ying superbly cast against type). Emma blames himself for his wife's death and has since undergone surgery to recapture and subsume his wife into himself–both husband and wife, father and mother in one. "He kept his wife's spirit alive in his new, female body," Louie explains to Aggie. Emma has a businessman beau, who yet seems unable to grasp Emma's gender identity; in a drunken stupor, he declares women live without the social pressures placed on men, and Emma jokes he should undergo a sex-change. In the film's turning point, a baroquely stylized scene shot in filtered red, he stabs Emma to death. Immediately before, Emma had said "He thought I was joking . . . he knows I'm not joking now," and we realize Emma's sexual identity has only just been revealed to him. Before, Aggie had regained her voice after discovering a new-found productivity in the kitchen; the blue, desirous moon reflected in her knife from the kitchen's window, a connection took hold between reattaining reality and wish-fulfillment. But in the murder scene, the knife represents not domestic (feminine or "kitchen-ly") sustenance but its own destruction: a murder-suicide, as the boyfriend cuts his own throat after he murders Emma (perhaps a gendered parody of Japanese ritual suicide, in which it is the woman who traditionally slices her own throat).

Aggie flees to China, secretly hoping Louie will demonstrate his love by following her. He eventually does, and they return to reunite in the ivory space of the kitchen to start anew. The film's final image is of a red rose against the kitchen's whiteness, the overwhelming crimson of Emma's murder scene relocated into a now manageable and diminished perspective. Earlier the film had cited the locus of ostensible sexual horror not in gender per se, but in its transformation, when on television plays David Cronenberg's *The Fly* (1986), the story of a man who turns from human purity into a monstrous, subhuman hybridity–indeed, the Cantonese term for transsexuals literally translates as "human monsters." The "monstrousness" of sexual impurity horrifies the murderous boyfriend because transsexuality challenges simplistic binary valuations by unifying the self and other–in patriarchal heterosexuality, "self" is male and "other" is female. This utopian subject, a combination of self and other, would theoretically be both signifier and referent in one, making any discrimination impossible. If the easy subject-object distinction is denied, values will become valueless (the frightening denial of value causes the shocked boyfriend to kill Emma)–or such would be the view of those so threatened by gender reconstruction.

Because Emma is also the strongest, most dominant figure in the film even after his death, we measure the remaining characters against the memory of his wise character, whose extraordinary life makes the two young lovers seem bland by comparison. Emma's strength, too, allows Aggie to regain her Self, as he becomes the generational/ancestral substitute for Aggie's dead grandmother. Here, transsexuality actually denotes fully characterized humanity, an appreciation of female-male (yin-yang dualism). Throughout, Yim Ho's transitional technique of choice is, tellingly, the fade-out; repeatedly ticking clocks fade in and out (the film was made only months before the 1997 handover). Meaning and identity are unstable, merely transitional "fades" on an endless yet blind search for closure to a meaning that is in fact meaningful only when open, when transgressive potential is available. Transsexuality, symbolic of the dissolution of the most primal biological foundation of discrimination, is a utopian ideal–but it will be destroyed in the end by those who ironically fear utopianism as a threat to the status quo (which it is literally–the paradox is that what is really utopian is undesirable, or, more simply, that egalitarianism is scary).

Although *Kitchen* has no espoused political agenda, it again fixes the sexual problematic in the parental figure, which we have previously associated with mainland China, or more generally in this instance China's legacy/influence. Aggie and Louie are reunited across the border in China, suggesting that their two-person reincarnation of Emma (Emma's flawed heterosexuality re-manifested into utopian transsexuality transformed again into an improved and more realistic youthful heterosexuality) is within China's rightful sexual boundaries. Reuniting in the ancestral homeland, or father-land, they also re-unite the transsexual father, and reform him in their own bodies. *Kitchen* resists the usual homophobic interpretation of parental China, however, not because it reconstitutes transsexuality as heterosexuality (indeed, as Chinese theater has shown, China has an unremovable history of sexual ambiguity), but simply because parental Emma is the most vital and positive force in the film–and it is this vital force the two lovers inherit.

The film opens with a title: "Planet Earth has only one woman" and ends with another: "Planet earth has only one thing–the two of us." Transferring this to nationality, Emma's vital unified polysexuality (Emma is the one woman, since it must necessarily be the mother who gives life/birth)–is motherland/fatherland China at her/his most liberated and enlightened. The "one thing" of unified Emma becomes the dual bodies of Aggie and Louie, "the two of us." They are inheritors of Emma's sexual energy and now possessed of historico-sexual ancestry, and will have children to continue that legacy. Emma's singularity, by her murder, is reincarnated into the binary heterosexuality of Louie and Aggie. This can be seen as a highly symbolic rendering of what Stephen Teo cites[41] as *chengxian qihou*–"to evoke the past so as to inherit its legacy," and thus inspire the future. In terms of first causes, Emma's omnisexuality makes him/her a God whose heterosexual children will populate the earth. The God must then be destroyed (murdered) so its memory can be infused and mythologized while being simultaneously invisible, as homosexuality still is in China. *Kitchen*, however, posits this mythology as hopeful, deeply personal, and directly familial, and not as an oppressively static received/hegemonic idea.

Perhaps the first major film to locate homosexuality within the context of China's democratic future was Stanley Kwan's *Full Moon in New York* (1990), foreshadowing the popular gay/lesbian boom by a few years. It is the story of three women who each symbolize one of the three "Chinas": Maggie Cheung is Hong Kong, Siqin Gaowa is the Mainland, and Sylvia Chang is Taiwan. Like Evans Chan's haunting *Crossings* (1994), it locates New York as the migratory crossroads of the East and West and posits seeing relative cultural differences as humanistic samenesses as the solution to overcoming boundaries.[42] If one of the three must be a lesbian, it should come as no surprise that it is HK representative Cheung, whose sexual dilemma is, unsurprisingly, aligned with political ones.

The three women cement their friendship in Chang's Chinese restaurant, the Chinese restaurant being the most visible vehicle of Chinese assimilation and acceptance in the U.S. The first half of the film delineates the crisis of each woman. Taiwanese Chang, an actress, is unsatisfied with both Chinese and American lovers, and feels alienated from each national system. Siqin Gaowa, from the Mainland, is married to an American-born Chinese who has adopted too much of the capitalist mentality. And Cheung's lesbianism translates into a social isolation which occasionally explodes into neurosis and cruelty (she explodes in anger when a passerby brushes against her on the street; once Changs' landlady, she cruelly threatened to evict her). This social isolation also comes to stand for the national-cultural isolation the three women share, and thus it is Cheung's lesbianism that can allegorize the totality of their immigrant experience. The second half of the film brings those issues to a head: Siqin Gaowa's "ABC" husband exploits the Chinese immigrant labor in his NY factory, not considering that he, too, is Chinese; Chang's father exploits a woman who suffered in the Cultural Revolution to further his career (the male object in Chang's story goes from lover to father); Cheung, attempting to become Americanized, unites capitalism and heterosexuality by attempting to woo her male business partner. No solution is offered to any of these problems–the unification of East and West will be a compromise, instilling various degrees of transformation and assimilation. Chang, an actress hoping to win the role of Lady Macbeth in a multicultural production, is asked why she, as a Chinese woman, thinks she is qualified. In an earlier scene, Chang was dehumanized, forced to mime the actions of a horse; now, she recites the story of a female tyrant during the Han Dynasty who murdered the emperor and grotesquely tortured her rival, actions which make Lady Macbeth look kind. The Westerners, simply, do not realize the painful universality of the human condition.

Although Cheung's lesbianism is downplayed (Kwan was not yet "out" as a gay director and HK films were still generally homophobic in 1990), it is a lead-in to the homosocial bond in which the three leads can take their only refuge. The final scene shows them in drunken reverie, hardly shorn of their woes, yet toasting to both themselves and their female union. The final shot of the film is their broken liquor bottle, its shards reflecting the distant, if romantic, hope of the Western moon. Yet, as the Chinese sarcastically say, "the moon is rounder in the West,"–that is, things in the West are not as rosy as they seem, even if that moon is "full." The "full moon" of the title is the Chinese notion of a union (or totality/fullness), yet this union will occur only abroad (in NY), as if to suggests the West, despite its flaws, will nevertheless be the democratic pole towards which China's future will eventually gravitate. These problems of national exile, and ambivalences about cultural hybridity, will not be redressed with individual solutions–rather than treating each character as a subplot to be partly closed as the film's clock ticks away, the women's trials are joined in a homosocial solidarity that offers an optimistic reading of their transnational subjectivity. The realization of this solidarity itself is the climax and conclusion, a union which paradoxically ends their alienation from China by joining them in a foreign land–the group humanism of mobile female solidarity replaces anti-humanist group national-ism. The problems they must solve may necessitate a compromise between East and West, but the union that will empower them to do so is itself uncompromising. In New York, Cheung can be an open lesbian (whereas in 1990 Stanley Kwan himself could not be out in HK), yet as an alien with no home. The female union among the three, then, substitutes for and becomes lesbian Cheung's parental *cum* ancestral home (her lesbianism is the same as that of her Chinese ancestors), yet one of progressive, unlimited spirit and not bounded geography. The film's romanticism is thus sort of a precursor to that of *Hu-du-Men* and *Kitchen*, as all three films idealize the unknown political future in terms of the known sexual past.

Since reversion to the Mainland, production of gay-themed films in HK has abated, but has not stopped.[43] Some post-1997 films, gay or otherwise, have attempted to (often depressingly) ape Hollywood[44]–perhaps the new endeavor to unify East and West will not be the metaphor of homosexuality but the capitalist reality of cross-cultural homogenization. But it could not have been a coincidence that the rise of homosexual representation in HK films immediately preceded the moment when HK's immediate future hung in the balance, or that this representation should have been so frequently coupled with the issues of parentage, parental alienation, emigration, and nationalist boundaries. If Yim Ho's *Kitchen* and Shu Kei's *Hu-du-men* can be seen as an example of *chengxian qihou* (the invocation and subsumption of the past for the good of the future), equally important are *A Queer Story* and *Love and Sex Among the Ruins*, which seeks to come to terms with homo-sexuality in present-day China, and Wong Kar-wai's *Happy Together*, and Stanley Kwan's *Full Moon in New York*, which move beyond China to postu-late an international subjectivity that situates China in the ongoing process of historical discovery and transformation. The question of parentage (and by extension, common ancestry or "original" parent) in these films has been interpreted as the quest for recovering one's own history in light of the Communist handover, for only in recognizing the bonds of the pre-commu-nist (pre-1949) past will there be hope for the democratization (but not necessarily or strictly "Westernization") of China. But another question lin-gers: If China is Hong Kong's parent, who is China's? In order to overcome the nationalist problematic, we must realize that all nations begins at a point of artificial construction, an arbitrary origin of no actual value.

Stanley Kwan's most recent film, *Hold You Tight* (1998), offers a post-1997 addendum to our issue of transsexual transnationalism, one fraught with problems of its own. Chingmy Yau plays dual roles: the sexually dissat-isfied HK housewife "Yeut Man," and her Taiwanese counterpart "Rosa," recently divorced and without custody of her only daughter. The two do not exist simultaneously in the film's temporal-spatial diegesis, except for one brief moment. It is only when Yeut Man boards a plane and mysteriously dies (or disappears) that the character of Rosa appears; their substitution is enacted when they cross paths momentarily in an airport, from HK to Taiwan. This intersection of geographical boundaries–a post-1997 progression from formerly democratic HK to still-democratic Taiwan–is the mysterious, flash-forward image that opens the film.

Yeut Man has died, and her husband Wai is in mourning. Wai is befriended by a gay realtor (Eric Tsang, performing a more sophisticated version of his openly gay role in *He's a Woman, She's a Man*), who is only interested in a platonic friendship. Read politically, homosexuality now is equated with "home," (he is a *realtor*), whereas the heterosexual bargain–Yeut Man/Rosa in international transition–is, ironically, the one defined by unstable, shifting boundaries. We can see this as Kwan's stubborn post-1997 positioning of HK as a permanent and free home of sexual choice, an apolitical choice above and apart from China's internal boundaries. In extended flashback, we are introduced to Siu, a young man who represses his homosexual attraction for Wai, and who will shadow him following the death of Wai's wife, Yuet Man. (Homo)sexually repressed Siu flirts instead with Yeut Man at the pool where he is a lifeguard, after rebuking the advances of some gay teenagers. Masturbating in the shower afterwards, the object of his fantasy is unclear. Does he fantasize about Wai, a homosexual desire the teenagers provoke, or Yuet Man–or is she, in that familiar formula, just Wai's intermediary? He eventually seduces Yeut Man, but his gift to her of *men's* cologne belies his sexual desire's true object to be male–the husband Wai–with Yeut Man personifying, yes, the safely transitive heterosexual buffer between the two men. Her wearing of men's cologne reminds her of Siu, but to Siu she becomes Wai through the cologne's sexual aegis–it is as if her masculinization will allow her to be a gay male, a gay version of her husband Wai. Cologne is a unisexual stimulant, and the excitement its unisexuality elicits is not objectively fixed in either sexual desire nor biological gender. It is a polymorphous sexual signifier which realizes formerly abstract or neutered sexual desire according to the subject that experiences it, not the object that wears (or "performs") it.

By sleeping with the wife of his love object, he will attain knowledge of the desired object through the un-gendering of an intermediary (the "role" of "spouse," but not a female *per se*). A construction of the object's gender through subjective desire only, this is the opposite of performance. The subject does both jobs, imagining a performance and receiving only the projection of its own imagination. It is an irrational confusion borne not really from the irrationalism of Siu's repression, but from that of the hegemonies that caused that repression in the first place (Siu's repression is only an effect, not a cause). Yet this privileging of subjectivity can also be liberating. Perhaps this is the film's post-1997 idea that empowering the individual (the subject) must be extreme–as crazily extreme as the homophobic Mainland authoritarianism which seeks the subject's disempowerment and its concurrent desexualization.

But Yeut Man soon leaves for Taiwan, never to return (she disappears when her plane crashes), and we catch up to the present. Wai, previously more interested in his (asexual) computers than his wife, now mourns; Siu stalks Wai, hoping to understand his own true feelings. They officially meet through the mutual friend of Tsang's gay realtor character, whose symbolism of "home" (i.e., country/nation) facilitates what will ultimately intimate the climactic connection with their own homosexual "home." After getting drunk at a bar, Siu carries the sleeping Wai to his apartment, and sprays him as he sleeps with the cologne he gave to Yeut Man. Before, Siu had said to Yeut Man that the cologne will symbolize himself, as a sentimental token. Now, as he holds the bottle, he is at once homosexually spraying "himself" onto Wai and simultaneously homosexualizing, through his own subjectification of the cologne, the heterosexuality of Yeut Man's idea of the cologne. It is one step closer to realizing his homosexuality, yet still tied up in conflicting symbols, as he himself is still conflicted.

Yet, as Yeut Man left Siu, Siu now leaves for his native Taiwan, there meeting Rosa, Yeut Man's doppleganger. Rosa is one degree more estranged than Yeut Man, for she is divorced from a marriage rather than being merely frustrated in one, yet unlike Yuet Man she is also parent to a daughter, albeit one whose "ownership" is being contested in the divorce. After 1997, the only "democratic China" left is Taiwan, so we can guess that Rosa is what Yuet Man *would have been* had HK not reverted to the Mainland–the futuric/optimistic child is now democratic Taiwan, not HK. The question of freedom for China's literal progeny is also moved to Taiwan–she is divorced, as is Taiwan from China, and possession of her futuric child is in contention. It is in democratic Taiwan, furthermore, that Siu will own up to his own individual homosexual identity. Although Siu is initially drawn to Rosa, the gaping disparity between her and Siu's true object, Wai (Rosa is twice removed from Wai, once by gender and once by nationality), causes him to break down and confess his true feelings to Wai, in the form of a message on his answering machine. In the film's final shot, Tsang's comforting realtor and Wai, still broken-hearted over his wife's death and yet unknowing of Siu's message that awaits him at home, tentatively drive across a bridge cloaked in night.

The bridge to be traversed, perhaps, is that between sexual objectivity (authoritarian sexuality *cum* homophobia) and subjective longing (individual sexuality). The terrain over which this bridge stretches is not simply the unknown but also seems to be irrational. After all, that Siu treats Yeut Man as a man does not make her one, nor does it make her want to be one–it doesn't account for the object's desires (the cologne, i.e., sexual activation, is controlled by the subject). But if those objective desires are hegemonic and unchallenged, we cannot be sure they are legitimate as free desires in the first place, since they are indoctrinated desires, and not chosen from a personal experience of *all available* sexual options. Thus Siu's (and the film's) "irrationality" is really more or less the same metaphoric utopianism of modern-day films such as *Kitchen* or *Love and Sex Among the Ruins*. Both use a variation of this idea of re-subjectification to enlighten, humanize, and trans-sexualize heterosexuality. In *Kitchen*, the subject and object (both heterosexuals) became unified in Emma's transsexuality, as a new futurist subject that unites binaries and thus negates their discriminatory capabilities. In *Love and Sex*, the hero was both cured of his impotence and humanized by heterosexual sex with a lesbian, an act which presumably requires *both* parties to subjectively reimagine the object's gender as an empowering act of fantasy. This fantasy is not stigmatized–it is a positive recognition that because all sexuality is subjectively experienced, it can only be constructed as subjectivity as well. In the schema of classical opera worlds, as in *Hu-du-men*, it is the object which performs its gender. But in the modern worlds of *Kitchen, Love and Sex*, and *Hold You Tight*, it is the *subject* which performs, acquiring the power of metaphoric transformation by receiving its own performance. It is a fantastic and private performance which may not even be disclosed to the "performee." In an era when sexuality is homogenized by government (or corporate) structure, this internalization of performance may be a defiant act of individualism. Its individualism may be also, indeed, all the more valuable in a Chinese culture where political individualism is often a foreign import, perhaps an over-compensatory import now required to re-mind Communist China's "amnesia" regarding its own homosexual history.

Unlike the pre-1997 *A Queer Story, Hu-Du-Men, Kitchen, Happy Together*, to a lesser extent *Love and Sex Among the Ruins*, and Kwan's own *Full Moon in New York*, the post-1997 *Hold You Tight* makes no explicit reference to either the parent-child binary and/or Mainland Communism. *Hold You Tight* does not frame the issue of sexuality's democratization as one being pulled between HK and Mainland. Rather, HK is now once again part of China, and its internal challenge to the Mainland is contrasted with Taiwan's external challenge–while the Mainland's specter necessarily looms above nonetheless. (It is a variation of the geopolitical triad of Kwan's *Full Moon*, with the Mainland reduced to an implicit presence.) The movement does not recognize external Anglo democracies, as does *Full Moon*, but sets up a movement between the two "Chinas" poised to lose their democracies, a movement positivized by the hope, still uncertain, of its "movers." The diegetic ignorance of the Mainland in a HK gay film may suggest that Hong

Kong's future lies in the appreciation of itself as a cultural entity whose (homosexual) history will fall victim to neither its Communist predicament, nor be rejected for still-imperfect Western democracies. As the island of Taiwan lies precariously between these two poles, it may come to be that the parent-child relationship is reversed: the "parental" Mainland, denying the diversity of its own history, may indeed become the stubbornly close-minded infant, as "small" Hong Kong rises the level of its own free politic, inheritor and pedagogue of its true and ineluctable sexual legacy.

Now, after 1997, the last democratic outpost in China is indeed the Taiwan of *Hold You*, and Taiwan lives with the same burdens that did HK. Taiwanese director Tsai Ming-liang's film *The River* (1997), however, is perhaps more optimistic (while certainly less commercial) than any of its HK counterparts. The story of an incestuous family, and told in Tsai's typically reserved, minimalist style, the film's optimism is perhaps obscured by its spare anti-emotionalism. The three family members–mother, father, son–are alienated from one another: the father always eats alone, they have no conversations that exceed a few banal sentences. They are so blindly alienated that they would not even *know* if they were incestuous, treating each other as if they were strangers. They will be incestuous because of their alienation, not in spite of it.

It begins with the son, in his early twenties, being convinced by a film director (played in a cameo by HK director Ann Hui On-wah, cast as if to recognize what should be the shared political causes of HK and Taiwanese film) to act as an extra in her film–he will play a corpse floating in the titular "river." The river, visibly polluted to the naked eye, will come to symbolize both a border (as it is superficially a geographical border) *and its own cross-ing*–yet first it is a pain so great it is mistaken for disease. The son, days after floating in the river for only a minute (as a film extra), begins to experience severe pain in his neck and shoulders–the result of the river's unnamed "disease," or unease. He showers, but cannot expel the river's stench from his body. He meets an old girlfriend, and, although we will discover he is not exclusively heterosexual, they have sex in the dark–all sexual experience in the film occurs in almost total darkness. Sex is not an escape from alienation, but a desperately blind retreat further into it. We fade out from this darkness to another image of darkness: the father in a gay bath-house cruising for men. This darkness, the commonality of the sexual unknown, will eventually unite the two in person as it unites them now as cinematic technique. But their familial relations also occur within alienated spaces (those of their apart-ment), such that the alienations of both sexuality and the family are conflated. The father and mother rarely speak to each other; later, the mother, coming home drunk one night, attempts to make love with the sleeping son. The son will soon also have a sexual encounter with the father; significantly, the only sexual relation not explored in the film's diegesis is the traditional heteronormative one between father and mother.

The son's pain grows worse and, in addition to going to a Western hospital, the family tries all means of Chinese medicinal treatments: acupuncture, massage, herbs, and finally a spiritual healer. "His body is possessed by a foreign element," the healer says. The sickness is explicitly of the body, yet Tsai homoeroticizes this into a sexual pain–indeed, the aching son is shown in his underwear or partly nude in nearly every scene. Meanwhile, the apartment's roof is continually leaking water, and although we are not sure why, the dirty water must manifestly symbolize the river entering their house. The river, a sexual symbol too, is a conduit through which truths will be realized–the painful "disease" caused by the river is the pain of the truths laying dormant in the sexual darkness. From the perspective of the faith healer, the seeming disease is a foreign (i.e., non-Chinese) element. From this, it may at first seem that such a foreign (i.e., democratic/internationalizing) element is required to re-enlighten a now enshrouded Chinese homosexuality. But we cannot accept the healer's simplistic and superstitious nationalism at face value. Because of the coming revelation of incest, an "internal" action, the "pollution" must be the resurfacing of that which has been repressed and buried *internally*. Yet the river is not bad–it may appear bad to the superstitious eye, but the pain with which it infects its host is the necessarily painful path to ultimately salutary truth. The river negotiates not the geography of the apparent world, but the hidden sexual spaces beneath it, the spaces which alienate the family from within.

One night the son follows a man–unknowingly a male prostitute his father had been with–back into the bath-house his father is still in. In the identity-sheltering darkness, the son enters the father's room and the two have sex, both unknowing of the other's identity. Only when the light comes on does the father realize what has happened; he slaps the son (who does not fight back), although he had no more prior knowledge about his father's identity than the father did about his. When the father returns home, the house is now entirely flooded via the leaking roof–the river is the knowledge of homosexuality, as water is also a (drippingly semenic) sexual symbol. The river, and the homosexual knowledge it portends, has entered their house; because its intrusion is now complete and impossible to ignore, it *must* be crossed–the border between the father and son must be crossed in the new and truthful terms of their literally shared homosexuality. If we continue the Mainland/Territory allegory of the Parent/Child relationship of HK gay films, here Taiwanese director Tsai is far more subversive by suggesting it is the Mainland (father) who is secretly and hypocritically gay, and whose failure of owning up to its own homosexuality causes the (national) "family" to be alienated, fractured. The father slaps his son not because their behavior was taboo, but simply because he is angry his secret was revealed. (For it to have been taboo, they would have had to have acted like a family in the first place.) Unlike George Lam's marriage counselor overcoming his hypocrisy in A *Queer Story*, here the hypocritical father is in a sense closeted even to himself, attempting to excuse his own transgression behind the thin mask of self-righteousness his role as father conveniently provides.

The father overcomes his anger and they continue on their journey to alleviate his son's river-induced sickness. In the end, the master faith healer from whom they have been receiving advice and for whom they continue to wait for guidance seems to give up (or the spirits have told him to do so), telling the father and son to return home and see a (Western) doctor. After the father tells this news to his son, the son opens the window of the hotel room where they lodge, and for the first time healthy, bright light floods the film's darkness, a brightness similar to the final shot of *Kitchen*, in which the blood red of a rose is controlled by the illumination of the kitchen's ivory. They no longer need to see a doctor because, in the accidental dark, they have already seen one–that is, they have seen *themselves*. Because such dark secrets will eventually explode into light, the darkness that alienated them also facilitated their incestuous reconciliation, a realization that yes, they are of the same family, of the same cultural/sexual identity, after all. It is a realization literally groped in the darkness, one through and about homosexuality.

The river does not symbolize "foreign homosexuality" because the father is *a priori* homosexual. The "foreign-ness" of the river is the foreign-ness of alienated interior truth–the strangeness of national-familial unions based on sexual understanding. Changes in the Chinese body politic will be painful, so it will be easy to misinterpret this pain as a disease, the foreign homosexual disease perceived by the Communist party line. The fractured pieces of China, then, will truly reunite only through progressively disclosing this "painful" secret: the secret that the father, the original China–indeed the hegemonic authority–is gay, too.

NOTES

1. For example, the banning in Hong Kong of the anti-communist, anti-Mao *China Behind* (1974) and *If I Were For Real* (1980), or even the initial financial disappointment of John Woo's *Bullet in the Head* (1990).

2. The demarcation of the HK new wave is slightly arguable; I am using the rise of university-schooled directors such as Ann Hui On-Wah and Tsui Hark, circa 1979, until the financial decline of indigenous film's supremacy at the box office, circa 1993. I designate post-1993 as "post new-wave."

3. *Jurassic Park* was HK's number one box office draw in 1993, and *Speed* was number two in 1994; these are, of course, the most conspicuously commercial Hollywood films of their years.

4. For example, the entirely derivative subgenres that have been constructed around the popularity of Ricky Lau's *Mr. Vampire* (1985), John Woo's *A Better Tomorrow* (1986), Ching-siu Tung's *A Chinese Ghost Story* (1987), etc. However, this is phenomenologically no different from such generic catalysts as *The Godfather* (1972), *Jaws* (1975), or *Star Wars* (1977) in Hollywood.

5. According to Article 5 of Hong Kong Basic Law, after 1997 Hong Kong is a "Special Administrative Region" (SAR) of the Mainland, operating under the same legalist and capitalist system (with the addition of the People's Liberation Army) it had under British rule, and not subject to full subsumption for another 50 years. Of course, there has been a question as to whether or not the Mainland will one day violate this "one country, two systems" agreement.

6. Examples of homophobia in HK film before the mid-1990s are legion, and are at least as crude as those found in films from any other country. A representative example would be an allegedly "comic" scene in Dean Shek Tin's *The Family Strikes Back* (1986), in which a police captain is afraid of catching AIDS by sharing a drinking cup with a man only suspected of being gay. Admittedly, however, this attitude is similar to the non-politically correct positions of HK film on race and gender throughout the 1980s.

7. The tragic ending of Chen Kaige's film version of *Farewell My Concubine*–in which the gay protagonist effectively commits suicide in a mirror image of the opera he performs, consummating art's tragedy with life's–is not present in the source novel, which may suggest the gay character's (Leslie Cheung) martyrdom is at the hands of the hypocritical Mainland unable to remember its own homosexual history.

The idea of a rich male patron (such as Ge You in *Concubine*) courting actors specializing in cross-dressing roles is a common trope, employed previously in HK films such as Sammo Hung Kam-bo's 1982 *The Prodigal Son* (in which the patron is too dumb to understand the true gender of his love object), *Peking Opera Blues* (1986, Tsui Hark), and the underrated *Laishi, China's Last Eunuch* (1987, Jacob Cheung Chi-leung). That these films are all from different genres–martial arts, action-comedy, and melodrama respectively–demonstrates how pervasive, familiar, and socially expected this trope is when it comes to Chinese opera.

8. It is also probable that director Chen Kaige knew that his film would be censored in the Mainland, and thus intended it for Hong Kong and other foreign audiences.

9. Stanley Kwan Kam-pang was HK's first openly gay male mainstream director. Before his "out" gay films (beginning with *Yang and Yin: Gender in Chinese Cinema*, 1996), he had specialized in "women's" films, most conspicuously *The Women* (1985) and *Center Stage* (1992). Gay subtext is first introduced in his *Rouge* (1987), in which Anita Mui performs in a cross-dressing scene. It is while she is dressed as a man that the male hero's attraction to her is activated. It is worthwhile noting that *Yang and Yin* is generally unavailable in Chinatowns and comes equipped with an English-language narration, suggesting that it was not primarily intended for Chinese audiences.

10. See Tsai Yung-Mei and Ruan Fang-Fu, "Male Homosexuality in Traditional Chinese Literature." *Journal of Homosexuality*, Vol. 14, 1987. Also see: Hinsch,

Bret. *Passions of the Cut Sleeve: The Male Homosexual Tradition in China.* University of California Press, 1990.

11. Particularly in Chuang Tzu, although Taoism in general avoids discriminatory, Aristotelian categorizations.

12. Hsu Tao-Ching. *The Chinese Conception of the Theater.* Seattle: University of Washington Press, 1985.

13. Scott, A.C. "The Performance of Classical Theater." *Chinese Theater,* ed. Colin Mackerras. Honolulu: University of Hawaii Press, 1983.

14. Mackerras, Colin. *The Chinese Theater in Modern Times.* Amherst: University of Massachusetts Press, 1975.

15. After the Law Reform Council first broached the subject in 1980, the HK Legislative Council decriminalized homosexuality in 1990; decriminalization was officially enacted under the Crimes Amendment Bill of 1991.

16. As representative examples, see Derek Chui Sung-kei's *Oh! My Three Guys* (1994), Lawrence Cheng Tan-shui's *He and She* (1994), or Peter Chan Ho-san's *Tom, Dick, and Hairy* (1993), all of which plead for bourgeois acceptance of gays and lesbians while simultaneously grounding gay characters in effeminate typologies which only reinforce their "otherness" (effeminacy represents psychic deformity). *Oh! My Three Guys,* although positing its sympathetic gay characters as the leads and not as supporting players, stupidly continues in the outmoded Freudian supposition that a gay man is simply an "un-actualized" heterosexual who has never met the "right" woman.

17. *A Queer Story* is roughly analogous to Jonathan Demme's propagandistic *Philadelphia* (1994) within the realm of mainstream commercial Hollywood film, minus that film's *de rigueur* martyrdom.

18. Presently, the common word in Cantonese for gay is *gay-lo* ("gay man"), whose modern adoption of the English may implicitly side it with Western political awareness.

19. Confucius, *The Analects.* Trans. Arthur Waley. New York: Random House, 1989.

20. I am reminded of a passage from Nietzsche's *Twilight of the Idols*: "Nothing seems rarer today than genuine hypocrisy . . . Hypocrisy belongs in the ages of strong faith when, even though constrained to display another faith, one did not abandon one's own faith." Lam's character is at first such a genuine hypocrite, who does not abandon his own homosexuality; eventually, the seed of this ingenuousness will *overtake* his hypocrisy. The "negative" aspect of hypocrisy will, opposite to Nietzsche's formula, negate hypocrisy's lies and not its truths when it turns back on itself–thus the homosexual truth is freed. "Skirmishes of an Untimely Man," No. 18, *Twilight of the Idols.* Trans. Walter Kauffman. New York: Penguin, 1982.

21. The professor dying of AIDS even plans on producing a public-relations film about AIDS before his death, to the dismay of his longtime companion, who believes such a film would simply reinforce the stereotype that AIDS is only a gay issue. The inclusion of this sequence perhaps self-criticizingly acknowledges director Shu Kei's own second thoughts about how *A Queer Story* itself, as a film intended to redirect bourgeois sensibilities of tolerance, might be seen only as a form of contrived pleading.

22. Based on the stage play by Raymond To Kwok-wai.

23. For example, contemporary social constructivism, Skinnerian Behaviorism, and post-structuralist literary criticism were arguably prefigured by Taoism's radical championing of nurture over nature and positing the objectification of the subject. In particular, I am thinking of Chuang Tzu's "Discussion on Making All Things Equal."

24. Comparatively, the homosexuality of the opera world in Chen Kaige's *Farewell My Concubine* is apparently essentialist, with characters filling in male or female roles appropriate to their innate personalities rather than their roles defining their personalities *a posteriori*. It may thus be a criticism of *Concubine* that its sexual philosophy is socially conservative or anti-sociological.

25. In the 1920s, the all-male and all-female Cantonese opera troupes were consolidated into mixed troupes, and the bearded warrior role (*mo-sung*) was replaced by the clean-shaven scholarly warrior (*mun mo-sung*). We might presume the more recent *mun mo-sung* is actually more ready-made for gender confusion than his bearded ancestor.

26. Cross-dressing (usually in period costume) is a standard trope in Tsui Hark's work, although he usually exploits only its comical functions, repeatedly treating its sexual implications with irritatingly predictable coyness (his eye is on the box office). See his *Peking Opera Blues* (1986) and the Tsui-produced *Swordsman Pts. 1-3* (1990-93), *Dragon Inn* (1992), and *Magic Crane* (1993). Sex comes a little more to the fore in director Tsui's somewhat underrated *Green Snake* (1993), in which it is not humans but female snake-spirits who dress as women to seduce men–it is notable that Tsui's most sexual film should also be the one which suggests that what lurks beneath gendered disguise is terrifyingly otherworldly.

27. The recrudescence of the period martial-arts films in the early 1990's may be generally credited to the success of the multiple-directored *Swordsman* and its immediate sequel (1990, 92), and Tsui Hark's non-cross-dressed *Once Upon a Time In China* series, which updated the old Wong Fei-Hung series of the late 1950's-60's, bringing the pro-nationalist agenda to the fore.

28. For example, Yuen Kwei's *Fong Sai Yuk Pts. 1-2* (both 1993), in which unknowingly lesbian romantic entanglements brought about by cross-dressing are compounded with the Oedipally comic story of a virginal martial hero whose first love is his mother; in Part II, it is the mother who enacts the "damsel-in-distress" posture for her own son at the film's climax. In part I, a woman in love with the male-dressed mother dies while still thinking she is a man; dying in the mother's arms, the mother perpetuates the woman's happy deathbed fantasy rather than dispelling her own gendered illusion. This is a rare case in which drag is not dispelled–at least as far as that one diegetic character is concerned.

29. It would be interesting to investigate whether or not the *hu-du-men* operates more successfully in live performance or on film. However, since the opera-films of the pre-new wave period are basically filmed plays in which the transvestism is permanent and begins off-stage, I am considering them as effectively equal to stage performances.

30. Interviewing Tsui in his documentary *Yang and Yin: Gender in Chinese Cinema* (1996), director Stanley Kwan expresses puzzlement over Tsui's choice of the

184   *QUEER ASIAN CINEMA: SHADOWS IN THE SHADE*

words "real" and "unreal." Tsui responds defensively, saying he had no intention of
being homophobic by calling homosexuality "unreal."

31. Although *Who's the Woman* features many openly homosexual characters in
supporting roles, it is their marginality *per se*–as subsidiary characters–that is their
chief characteristic. The supporting characters of the lesbian assistant or the gay
house-painters in the film, for example, are included to flesh out the film's "colorful" spectrum of liberal sexuality, and do not represent the homophobically centered
sexuality audiences are invited to identify with.

32. Stokes, Lisa Odham and Hoover, Michael. *City on Fire: Hong Kong Cinema*.
New York: Verso, 1999.

33. See note 16 above.

34. Taiwanese director Edward Yang's *A Confucian Confusion* (1994) casts this
"Capitalism versus Confucianism" issue in terms of a post-Tiananmnen Square capitalist economy and *heterosexual* group-dynamics. Director Yang would first include
"out" gay characters amongst his usual intersection of personages in his subsequent
Mahjong (1996); this is perhaps an awareness that gay characters in contemporary
democratic Chinese films were now not only allowed but seemingly "necessary" to
represent a cross-section of democratic life.

35. The same "man-cross-dresses-to-seduce-a-lesbian" ploy is also used in Peter
Chan Ho-san's *Who's the Woman, Who's the Man* (1996). In a sub-plot, an adamant
heterosexual (Jordan Chan) in drag seduces a beautiful but stubborn lesbian as she
sleeps–we are given to assume that in the subconscious state of unguarded sleep she
will be more accepting of his advances, which she had previously rebuffed. They
have intercourse, but she decides it was a failed experiment. It may be inferred that
director Chan's politics have become somewhat more "politically correct" since
1993's *Tom, Dick, and Hairy* (see note 16 above).

36. The taboo of male homosexuality combined with the husband's fascination
with lesbianism only reinforces the sexist idea that lesbianism is unconsciously designed for the delectation of the male heterosexual. After the implementation of a
ratings system in 1988, a flood of "category 3" (in terms of the M.P.A.A. censorship
ratings, this could run the gamut from a "hard R" to an "X") films were released
that displayed lesbianism for a straight male audience. Gay male pornography, however, is still largely unavailable in commercial video stores (even after the 1990/1
decriminalization laws). One presumed exception, which I have not seen, may be a
transsexual exploitation entitled "She-Male's Passion" (1994). The original title in
Chinese literally translates, however, as *A Woman That Has X/Yau X Dik Nui Yan*–
even assumedly targeted to a specific community, trans-sexuality is designated as an
unknowable "X" rather than a positive and achievable destruction of boundaries.

The category 3 film can also earn its rating for violence, and while the category 3
sex film reinforces institutionalized heterosexuality, the more notable (and more
written-about) category 3 violence film often assaults the institution of the patriar-
chal-heterosexual family unit with a vengeance. Here, violent assault substitutes for
homosexual subversion as anti-family loners (i.e., "homosexuals") lash out against
society. As 1997 anxiety has been cited to explain seemingly all HK phenomena, one
can stretch the point and posit that the destruction of the family is tantamount to challenging the Mainland Chinese Confucianist family ideals which threaten future HK

liberty and sexual freedom. Particularly, Billy Tang Hin-sing's *Run and Kill* (1993) and Herman Yau Lai-to's *The Untold Story* (1993) gleefully break taboos by revelling in the gory, onscreen murder of small children; the latter was considered respectable enough to earn star Anthony Wong a Best Actor award at the HK Film Awards, further testimony to differences between Eastern and Western acceptabilities. These two films present single, asexual males as their villains. In Lau Kai-ming's *Daughter of Darkness* (1993), it is the institution of the family itself which is sadistically (and satirically, in its villainous excess) punitive and must be revenged upon–ultimately by castrating the father (he is shot repeatedly in the genitals), denying the Family its progenitive socio-sexual dictatorship. In this distaff variant, the female killer is oversexualized, the object of numerous rape scenes. In this sub-genre, male sexuality's octave runs only from heterosexual to rapist, while nevertheless representing the anti-family position homosexuals are thought to embody. Female sexuality's octave, however, ranges from hypersexual to "normally" sexual. Of course, this is basically the same homophobic patriarchy which resists the male homosexuality of *Love and Sex Among the Ruins*.

37. A similar, if indeed lesser, hypocrisy features in Leonard Heung Lap-hang's *Love Recipe* (1994), an otherwise genial, lyrical comedy. Among its four romantic principals, a gay man is included, whose sexual life is active, complex, and encouraged by his friends (one of whom even procures a "stud" for him). However, the film's epilogue provides post-scripts for all the principals save the gay character, suggesting his participation may have been mere tokenism after all.

38. It is interesting to note that the poster and video box art for *Love and Sex Among the Ruins* features a depiction of the five principal characters in heterosexual alternation (girl-boy-girl-boy-girl) behind a large beach towel. The film's ostensible subject of sexual transgression and self-discovery is contradicted by the heterosexual conventionality of its advertising. That said, it may also stand as a testament to the gap between artistic intention and the advertising industry's self-preservational conservatism.

39. *Happy Together* is indeed the most written-about gay film recently from HK. Its high recognizability-quotient even accounts for a comic scene in which the two male heroes of Wong Jing's action-comedy *We're No Bad Guys* (sic) (1997) innocently rough-house while a poster of *Happy Together* hangs on the wall behind them. When one of the heroes' mothers interrupts them and notices the poster behind them, the comedy that ensues has her naturally assume they are gay, a relationship she liberally encourages. As of this writing, *Happy* is also the only major HK gay film available on North American home video, a fact more attributable to director Wong Kar-wai's trendiness than the film's gay subject matter.

40. Stokes and Hoover, ibid.

41. Compare to director Watanabe Takayoshi's *Hong Kong Nightclub* (*Hon Kon Daiyasokai: Tatchi & Maggie*, 1997), a HK-Japan co-production which also uses the "passport" as a conflated symbol of political exile and sexual power. Its *Some Like it Hot*-type story concerns a predatory gay reporter who goads his young male assistant into cross-dressing in order to effect a disguise from the mobsters whose killings they had witnessed. This gleeful film, in which homosexual and heterosexual desires are for once perfectly equal, was made only months before the 1997 handover. It ends

with a uniquely explicit on-screen statement (before the roll of the final credits) propagandizing the hopefully autonomous political future of HK; it is likely that its unafraid liberalism is the product of its Japanese (not Hong Kong) writer and director, who can obviously afford a greater risk.

42. The insular claustrophobia of the apartment as the site of homosexual sadomasochism may invite some comparison with James Baldwin's *Giovanni's Room*.

43. The only HK narrative film (i.e., not strictly pornographic) with real transsexuals I have come across is the "category 3" *Hero Dream* (1993), a low-budget action-exploitation affair filmed in Thailand. The ridiculous plot has the machine-gun-wielding "Transsexual Gang" team up with a straight male hero to defeat the Thai gangsters who murdered the latter's pregnant wife. The film alternates heterosexual couplings with explicit sex scenes between male-to-female transsexuals. One of the transsexuals falls in love with the hero, and with guns blazing comes to the hero's rescue when he is outnumbered by the villains; the transsexual is fatally wounded and on his deathbed professes his love to the somewhat sympathetic hero. It is a fascinatingly subversive moment that transsexually conflates the martyrdom of a male-bonding movie (in which one male sacrifices his life for his buddy) and the tragedy of an ill-fated heterosexual romance. Of course, the transsexual dies quickly enough and the hero falls in love with a Thai nurse.

The most visible example of 90's transsexuality is, again, *Swordsman 1-3*, in which the nationalistically dubbed antihero "Asia the Invincible" gradually transforms, supernaturally, from male to female over the course of the series, and in parts 2-3 is played by a cross-dressed Lin Ching-hsia. Part II climaxes with Asia's apparent death, leaving the male hero unsure as to whether or not he slept with the polygendered Asia or his/her female consort in a darkened room.

44. Noted in reference to Allen Fong Yuk-ping's seminal new wave film *Father and Son* (1981), in Teo's *Hong Kong Cinema: The Extra Dimensions*. London: British Film Institute, 1997.

Happy Alone?
Sad Young Men in East Asian Gay Cinema

Chris Berry

University of California, Berkeley

SUMMARY. This essay chooses as its texts three films representing contemporary gay male subjects from each of the "three" China's: HK, Taiwan, and the Mainland. Relocating the homoerotic image of the "sad
young man," a trope popular from Hollywood rebellion films of the 1950s
and 1960s, to contemporary China, I discuss how this masculine icon has
been transformed from one of heroic rebellion to one of existential isolation. Indeed, as the politics of both the outmoded Confucian family and
fractured Chinese nationhood intersect, what the sad young (gay) man rebels against is a political fluctuation which is no longer fixed; as the young
man's opposition is no longer fixed, so too does he become alienated even
from his own rebellious cause. *[Article copies available for a fee from The
Haworth Document Delivery Service: 1-800-342-9678. E-mail address:
<getinfo@haworthpressinc.com> Website: <http://www.HaworthPress.com>]*

Chris Berry, PhD, teaches in the Film Studies Program at the University of
California, Berkeley. He has written widely on Chinese cinema, and has a strong
interest in the media and the sexuality in the Asia-Pacific region. He is the author of
A Bit on the Side: East-West Topographies of Desire (Sydney: EMPress, 1994), and the
co-editor of *The Film-maker and the Prostitute: Dennis O'Rourke's "The Good Woman
of Bangkok"* (Sydney: Power Institute Press, 1999), and *Australia Queer* (Melbourne: Meanjin, 1996). He has co-authored a chapter on lesbian/gay/queer internet
use in Taiwan and Korea in *Web Studies* edited by David Gauntlett (London: Arnold,
2000), and written about Tsai Ming-Liang's *Vive L'Amour* in *Falling for You* edited
by George Kouvaris and Lesley Stern (Sydney: The Power Institute, 1999). His piece
on the Seoul Queer Film and Video Festival appears in the Web journal *Intersections*
(*http:// wwwshe.murdoch.edu.au/hum/as/intersections*). (E–mail: chrisberry82@hotmail.
com or c.berry@latrobe.edu.au).

[Haworth co-indexing entry note]: "Happy Alone? Sad Young Men in East Asian Gay Cinema." Berry,
Chris. Co-published simultaneously in *Journal of Homosexuality* (The Haworth Press, Inc.) Vol. 39,
No. 3/4, 2000, pp. 187-200; and: *Queer Asian Cinema: Shadows in the Shade* (ed: Andrew Grossman)
Harrington Park Press, an imprint of The Haworth Press, Inc., 2000, pp. 187-200. Single or multiple copies of
this article are available for a fee from The Haworth Document Delivery Service [1-800-342-9678, 9:00 a.m. -
5:00 p.m. (EST). E-mail address: getinfo@haworthpressinc.com].

187

It is natural to be part of a collective, anxiety-provoking to be apart.[1]

In his essay "Coming Out as Going In" Richard Dyer investigates the gay stereotype of the sad young man that he encountered growing up in the 1950s and 1960s as "complex, varied, intense and contradictory, an image of otherness in which it is still possible to find oneself."[2] Among the star images he cites are James Dean, Dirk Bogarde and Montgomery Cliff. Recently, a similar (and similarly complex) type has also begun to circulate through East Asian films. Unlike the roles played by most of the actors Dyer cites, it is usually clear that these sad young men are gay. And so, although they are also socially alienated and often unhappy, at the same time they also participate explicitly in the cinematic imagination of a sexual identity that has been largely absent from East Asian cinema prior to this decade, except possibly as a comic bit-part. This essay examines these sad young men using Wong Kar-wai's *Happy Together* (1997), Tsai Ming-Liang's *Vive L'Amour* (1994) and Zhang Yuan's *East Palace West Palace* (1996) as its primary examples.[3]

Feature films have long been globalized commodities. So the images Dyer writes about may well be part of the lineage for the East Asian examples considered here. However, my interest is less with the global than with the regional and the local. For my contentions here are that the East Asian sad young man is a local reinvention that draws upon and resonates with regional cultural antecedents, and that each such reinvention derives its particular meanings from its local context. At the risk of oversimplification, the impossible relationship in *Happy Together* echoes the uncomfortable circumstances of Hong Kong's transition period. *Vive L'Amour* communicates the alienation and contingency of Taiwan's existential condition as a place of exile through its focus on three characters without families and an empty apartment. And *East Palace West Palace*'s tale about the criminal who tries to seduce a cop is about what it takes to achieve personal fulfillment in a police state. All three films prop their locally specific meanings upon the widespread modern interpretation of the broad Confucian family-based culture as one where space outside family and family roles is dystopic and anomic rather than liberating. Why this might have a particular relevance for young East Asian audiences in the nineties is interesting to speculate about. So is the question of what these internationally circulating representations of the gay as sad young man type have to offer actual gay/lesbian/queer people in and out of East Asia. To return to Richard Dyer's formulation, why might people want to find themselves in these films today?

We can begin by focussing on the regional cultural and cinematic context in which this type has appeared in the last few years. The Asian sad gay young man is found in films that circulate not only locally but also internationally through film festivals and art-house cinemas. Within the global perspective generated by international circulation, these films are sometimes grouped together as "Asian Queer Cinema." In fact, as I pointed out in an earlier essay written when the phenomenon was still relatively new, even then the films were highly heterogeneous. They included short films and videos like Ellen Pau's tribute to Cantonese opera female stars *Song of the Goddess* (1993); documentaries such as Nakata Toichi's *Osaka Story* (1994) in which he comes out to his family; experimental films like Oki Hiroyuki's symphony of a city film *Heaven 6 Box* (1995); and independent features. There were also higher budget features made by (professedly) heterosexual directors for a general audience like Chen Kaige's *Farewell My Concubine* (1993), and also no-budget videos made by g/l/q directors for g/l/q audiences. They were made in a wide range of countries, including amongst the diaspora outside Asia itself. And although films about men predominated, some were also focussed on and or made by women.[4] All this is still true.

What was also true earlier this decade is that almost all the larger budget features being made for a general (i.e., not specifically gay, lesbian and queer) audience came from East Asia and they dealt with the contemporary emergence of gay identity as a family matter. That is to say, they considered being gay as something with ramifications for the blood family and as a family narrative, not the narrative of the gay individual alone. As well as the international hit from Taiwan, *The Wedding Banquet* (1992), examples include *Okoge* (1992) and *Twinkle* (1992) from Japan, and *Broken Branches* (1995) from South Korea. Other types of film were more diverse, although the blood family was by no means absent.[5]

It is this pattern that more recent East Asian features including *East Palace West Palace*, *Happy Together* and *Vive L'Amour* break. Their lead characters are shown outside the context of blood family. In many cases, we have no idea whether or not they maintain any links to their families and we rarely if ever see them interacting with family members, even on the phone. However, they are also represented as alone. They are not members of the emergent gay and lesbian communities that have sprung up in many Asian metropolises over the past decade and more.[6] Nor are they represented as members of gay and lesbian "chosen families."[7]

East Palace West Palace focuses on a young man called A Lan and the cop he hopes to seduce during his nightlong interrogation. A Lan's mother appears in a few flashbacks, but there is no sign of any present connection. *Vive L'Amour* is an ironically titled film that traces the lives of three lonely young people without family or friends, one of whom appears to be grappling with his homosexual desires. In *Happy Together* the contrast between gayness as a solitary condition and family is clearest. The film follows a gay couple from Hong Kong as they fight their way through a trip to Argentina. Leslie Cheung plays Ho Po-wing as the more impulsive, irresponsible and flamboyant of the two–the more stereotypically gay partner. In the only sex scene, he is the bottom. This character has absolutely no connection to blood family and ends up stranded and alone in Argentina. His partner, Lai Yin-fai, played by Tony Leung, is represented as what is conventionally considered more responsible. When they run out of money, for example, Lai gets a normal job whereas Ho lives off other men. Towards the end of the film, Lai is shown phoning home to Hong Kong. He wants to make up with his father, who he fought with about stolen money before leaving Hong Kong; when this fails, he writes his father. Towards the end of the film, we understand from his voiceover while in Taipei that he is still on his way home, loyal to his father (and having abandoned Ho without returning his passport to him). Only the third character, Chang from Taiwan, is implied to maintain a good relationship with his family. He is drawn to Lai, but they do not have sex. Within this array of characters, distance from conventional heterosexual male behavior stands in direct relationship to distance from family, solitude, failure and despair.

Given that the last decade and more has seen the development of larger and more publicly visible gay communities throughout East Asia, why is it that these lonely figures predominate among feature film representations of gay men outside the family? Part of the answer to this question must lie in the particular connotations attached to the individual without a family role and the specific understandings of self-hood prevalent in East Asian cultures. The writings and debates about the conception of the self in East Asia are numerous and complex.[8] But they tend to agree that in pre-modern cultures heavily influenced by Confucianism, the self was understood not as an autonomous and internalized personality or character but as a socially and relationally defined role that one tried to assume. Furthermore, the hierarchy of blood family roles formed the archetypal model for these roles throughout society, so that even on an imperial scale the Emperor was understood as a father to his subjects.[9] Within this system, the only place of the individual outside family roles is that of the outcast, the exile, the social derelict. To refuse a familial role is not only to be unfilial within domestic space–it is also to be without wider social status. Perhaps this is why in pre-modern fictions, the only way to accommodate fantasies of escape from the family system was through the construction of the mythical *jianghu* "rivers and lakes" environment inhabited by heroic but lonesome outlaw heroes in martial arts legends and the like.[10]

This history in the mainstream cultures of the region goes some way to explain the two large patterns in East Asian feature film representations of gay identity so far. Either it appears within the codes of family melodrama as something struggling to find a role within that relational structure, or it appears in modern-day realist portrayals of the lonely romantic such as those under consideration here. However, to leave it at that would be inaccurate. For it would conjure up a binary model of cross-cultural "exchange" between two static "Western" and "Oriental" cultures and conceptions of self. Within such a model, the individual outside the family appears statically fixed as only ever a mythic impossibility or a foreign imposter. This fails to acknowledge the dynamic and violent impact of both imperialism and the modernizing responses to it upon East Asian cultures and societies, and the crucial role of the importation of concepts and ideas as part of that ongoing transformational process.

The concept of the monadic "individual" subject has already been circulating within the syncretic post-colonial environment of East Asia for at least a century now. Lydia Liu prefers not to describe this process as importation, as this fails to adequately acknowledge local agency and change. Instead, she suggests the term "translingual practice," pointing out that, "Meanings . . . are not so much 'transformed' when concepts pass from the source language into the target language as (re)invented within the local environment of the latter."[11] For example, early twentieth century depictions of the individual have been traced in Chinese May Fourth plays as would-be agents of modernization, simultaneously heroic and yet often struggling vainly against the deeply entrenched social structures of relational self-hood.[12] Alternatively, there are the altogether more triumphant images of Communist Party cadres in socialist realist and revolutionary romantic literature and art. For the most part they also have no visible blood family or any romantic entanglements, and in this sense are monadic. Yet, presumably because the Party itself has taken over the functions of the hierarchical family and socialism sets itself up against individualism, their individuality has been subordinated to the Party and its collective modernizing project.

With this history in mind, it would be wrong to simply see the sad gay young men under examination here as representations of some sort of inevitable failure of the individual in an East Asian context because such a conception of the self is inauthentic. Instead, these representations have to be seen as the latest in an ongoing series of East Asian constructions of the individual outside the family. To understand them properly, we need to try to attend to their particular social and historical construction and function.

Turning first to Zhang Yuan's *East Palace West Palace*, the specificity of being gay in the People's Republic is written into the very title of the film, which is drawn from Beijing gay slang. On either side of the Forbidden Palace on the north edge of Tiananmen Square there are two public toilets that have long been popular as gay cruising spots. These are the "east palace" and the "west palace." Most of the narrative takes place in a park, which is also a typical gay cruising zone in this city with few commercial venues for gays. Although there are no laws specifically against gays, more general laws prohibiting hooliganism and so forth legitimate regular police sweeps on the population of the park.[13] This is how A Lan and the cop come to spend the night in the little police station in the park, where the cop's interrogation ironically enables A Lan to tell his story and attempt to seduce the policeman.

Although there is no question that there are many local references in the film and in A Lan's story, the particular picture that emerges in the film of A Lan as a contemporary Beijing gay man is far from being a positive image. In addition to the unappealing general context of police harassment, A Lan's "confession" becomes a cross between a coming out story and a case history. In it, he presents his character and its formation as a cross-cultural melange of perversions, neuroses and general failures of conventional masculinity. His flashbacks invoke Freudian pop psychology-style accounts of excessive mothering by showing him not only as growing up in a single parent household but also being breastfed at a very late age. When he seeks out older men at a relatively young age, this is implied to be a search for a father substitute. (He tells of the family friend who suggests he should not be alone on Chinese New Year's Eve–a traditional family time in China–and then seduces him.) At the same time, his fantasies are full of the female Beijing Opera characters that were sung by men. In recent years, this has been reified as a trope for local homosexual traditions, as displayed for example in *Farewell My Concubine*. He identifies with the female role, as indicated by his frequent return while under interrogation to an opera about a female prisoner and her executioner. This figure also connects to his sense of suffering and his sexual tastes, which are shown to have evolved out of repeated abuse into masochism.[14]

Zhang Yuan has responded to concerns about this very negative image in the first gay feature film to come out of the People's Republic of China by claiming realism. "I interviewed many, many people, including my own friends and also sociologists who have carried out investigations of gay life in China," he explains. "In China there is no visible gay culture and no one understands gay people. It is very hard to find any gay friends who are living a happy, well-adjusted life under these circumstances. . . ."[15] Although there is little doubt that what Zhang says is accurate, the appeal to realism sidesteps the issue of what the broader signification and function of this image is. After all, Zhang was not compelled to make a film about gay life at all. And furthermore, had the furtive and difficult circumstances of gay life in contemporary China not suited his purposes, perhaps he could have chosen the life of a gay Chinese living overseas. Ang Lee seems to have done just that with *The Wedding Banquet*.

Perhaps a clue to the appeal of the marginalized and harassed gay men for Zhang can be found by looking at his other work, which also often focuses on marginalized people. Zhang is one of the younger generation of film-makers who graduated from China's only film school, the Beijing Film Academy, in 1989. In the highly controlled political culture that followed the Tiananmen

Square Massacre, new film-makers such as Zhang had to choose either to submit to the mainstream system or to go it alone. Taking the latter route was a political step whether the film-makers themselves liked it or not. For in a country where the regime continues to assert control over the "ideological area" at the same time as it allows a market economy to develop, working independently is provocative. It was also a risky step, as is indicated by the fact that Zhang is the only independent director to have maintained consistent output in the nineties. In *Mama* (1990), he looked at the disabled and social neglect of them. In *Beijing Bastards* (1992), he examined the rock subculture, and *Sons* (1995) dealt with alcoholism and unemployment. As a marginalized film-maker whose independent films cannot be screened in the People's Republic because the regime will not consider films produced outside the state system for an exhibition certificate, perhaps it is not surprising Zhang is so drawn to the disadvantaged and despised in Chinese society.[16]

However, beyond auteurist interpretation, there is a further and specific metaphorical reading of *East Palace West Palace* available to those spectators who are sensitive to subtextual possibilities in a highly policed and censored society and culture. As A Lan battles to survive, he learns to become a masochist. Here, the policeman finds himself confronted with a most unusual phenomenon. A Lan is a member of the public who actually wants to be taken in for questioning and to be punished. In these circumstances, punishment is no punishment at all. If the park is a heterotopic representation of the People's Republic itself then the film seems to imply that in a police state masochism is the only surefire road to fulfillment.

Happy Together is set in Argentina, a distance that ensures it is not a realist portrayal of contemporary gay life in Hong Kong. However, Argentina functions as a heterotopic metaphor for Hong Kong in *Happy Together* just as surely as the park in Beijing is a metaphor for the People's Republic in *East Palace West Palace*. Perhaps the comparison of Argentina to Hong Kong is encouraged most explicitly when Lai notes that Argentina is on the other side of the earth from Hong Kong, setting it up as a reverse of Hong Kong. Then the camera shows us upside down images as if to give us the view from Hong Kong.

As the film was released on the eve of the "return" of Hong Kong to the People's Republic in 1997, Lai and Ho's journey and the question of whether to return home conjures up the whole period of the transition and response to 1997. It is not that one of them represents the mainland and the other Hong Kong. Rather they represent two sides of Hong Kong, two different impulses unable to reconcile. Ho stays on the road at the end of the film, without a passport, just as Hong Kong Chinese are without a real British passport. He becomes the representation of eternal exile and diaspora, neither reaching the Iguazu Falls the couple had determined to visit nor returning home. Lai, on the other hand, reaches the waterfall and then returns home, unsure of whether his father will welcome him or not. This uncertainty suggests considerable ongoing ambivalence on his part about the return home. And Ho's desire to get his passport back implies that he is also ambivalent about his place in the diaspora, and that he would like ideally to leave it and return home, too.

The larger symbolic connotations of Lai's father are even clearer when one notes that the Chinese word for "motherland" is in fact a kind of fatherland. *Zuguo* means "land of one's ancestors." But here "ancestors" is defined as patrilineal ancestors. The fraught relationship between Lai and Ho, who is always suggesting "let's start over," echoes the agonized and divided response to 1997 that dominated Hong Kong culture with an ever-growing urgency from the moment of the 1984 agreement between Britain and the People's Republic.[17] In these circumstances, making Ho and Lai a gay couple deploys the conventionally accepted fundamental difference of gender to write them as two sides of the same coin rather than as two distinct people.

My earlier discussion of the way in which the film's carefully graded structure of degrees of gayness equates to degrees of aloneness and despair already suggests that this deployment of the gay as sad young man trope in *Happy Together* may be homophobic. Certainly, Ho and Lai's abusive, jealous, and unstable relationship is not a pretty picture. But, perhaps the most compelling (in every sense) reason for such an interpretation lies in the representation of the Iguazu Falls themselves. At the beginning of the film and again towards the end when Lai actually reaches the waterfall alone and without Ho, a bird's-eye view of the waters thundering down from all sides into a black abyss is repeated. As with Wong's other films, *Happy Together* is dominated by medium shots and close-ups. The few other long shots are mostly empty shots of the flatlands the couple drive through when unsuccessfully trying to reach the waterfall together. The dynamic birds-eye long shot of the falls is therefore singularized, and its repetition turns it into a motif further drawing attention to it and suggesting it has more significance than as a tourist snapshot.

The equation of male homosexuality with the anus, and the depiction of the anus as a black hole leading to death is a persistent one in homophobic heterosexual cultures,[18] and this shot seems to confirm that quality in *Happy Together*. Yet, homophobia itself is a complex phenomenon. This pronounced rejection is not generated by indifference, but instead such an excessive defense structure must be seen as an attempt to repel something that has a certain attraction. In the case of *Happy Together*, the bird's-eye angle above the falls suggests vertigo. At once frightening, the magnificent image is also compelling, and one is not sure whether to run or to throw oneself into the waters. Furthermore, the Iguazu Falls lie on the border of Argentina and Paraguay. Therefore, like Argentina itself in the film, they offer themselves up for interpretation as a metaphor for Hong Kong's no-man's-land status between China and Britain or the West in general as a place of transit. Add anality, and Hong Kong becomes a sort of two-way orifice.[19]

These references to the predicament of transitional Hong Kong are typical of Wong's films. In this light, Ho and Lai are not exceptional characters, but rather the latest in a series of isolated, anomic individuals. Within any visible kinship relations, unable to make appointments, sustain relationships or reach destinations, they all seem to be figures for transitional Hong Kong, orphaned between Britain and China in the post-Declaration, pre-Return period. For example, in *Days of Being Wild* (1991), Leslie Cheung is Yuddy, dumping his girlfriend and his foster mother to search in the Philippines for his real mother, who only refuses to see him. *Chungking Express* (1994) traces flirtations between two different cops, each with two different women, switching narratives as swiftly as they switch women. In each case, the first girl jilts them, and the connection with the second one is composed of fleeting moments that certainly do not amount to stable commitment. In the very absence of any narrative completion or stable personal connection, without a sense of a future or even a secure base in the past, the characters live in a heightened present, fetishizing dates, numbers, sensations, looks and glances.[20] This effect is heightened by Chris Doyle's cinematography, with its manipulations of speed, color and distance simulating emotional intensities and the ebb and flow of subjective attention. Furthermore, just as Ho and Lai are doubled in *Happy Together*, so these two cops are twinned in *Chungking Express*, for the uncanny similar-but-different character is a common trope in Wong's films expressing the unsettled and contradictory personality engendered by the contradictions of the transition itself.

Links to other characters in other films by the same director also apply to the sad young man at the center of *Vive L' Amour*. But in his case, the continuity is even more obvious. For what seems to be the same character played by the same actor (Lee Kang-Sheng) has appeared in all of Tsai Ming-Liang's films to date. In *Rebels of the Neon God* (1992), the film made prior to *Vive L' Amour*, he appears as a teenager profoundly alienated from his parents, who are simultaneously warring with each other. He finds a projection for a wide range of his emotions by developing an obsession with a slightly older man on a motorbike. The same family configuration appears again in *The River* (1997), the film made after *Vive L'Amour*. Only this time, we discover that his father spends his time seeking out casual sexual encounters in the semi-dark of Taipei's saunas, a habit that has unforeseen consequences when he bumps into his own son there one night.

In *Vive L'Amour* this character appears without any family. Although he is as alienated from other people as ever, he is not alone. Rather, there are two other characters also without visible family or friends. One is a single woman in her late twenties who sells real estate and lives alone in a small apartment. He steals a key to an empty luxury apartment on her books one day, and goes there to kill himself. The third character is a young clothes hawker. The woman happens to pick him up one day and take him back to the very same apartment for a one-night stand. Although they are unaware of it, they disturb the other young man's suicide attempt. A farce-like comedy ensues, during which the would-be suicide experiments with a little cross-dressing and pecks the other young man on the cheek as he sleeps.

Unlike *Happy Together's* distant evocation of Hong Kong by way of Argentina, *Vive L'Amour* is quite specific in its inscription of Taipei. However, unlike *East Palace, West Palace*, which shows us gay Beijing, *Vive L'Amour* avoids Taipei's burgeoning gay, lesbian and queer society and culture by making its sad young man not just closeted but so deeply unsure of his sexuality that he would never connect with that world. Instead, the specifics of Taipei are used to inscribe a metaphor of homelessness. And, by virtue of a double meaning in Chinese, homelessness extends to lack of family. For, in Chinese, the word for family, *jia*, is also the word for home. To be without a home is to be without a family.[21] In this particular case, then, the sad gay young man helps to signify homelessness and lack of family excessively and redundantly.

The empty luxury apartment that the real estate agent is trying to sell is a symptom of a construction boom fuelled by speculation that was a feature of Taipei at the time the movie was made. But in the film, these luxury homes without families (or *jia* without *jia*) are symbols of unfulfilling financial success, much as the real estate agent herself seems quite well off but deeply lonely. The young hawker she picks up on the street is also not poor. At the beginning of the film he is shown returning by air from overseas with suitcases of clothes to sell. But he works from a sheet spread out on the sidewalk rather than a shop. This so-called "spreading a carpet" (*bai ditan*) mode of selling is characteristic of Taipei, like the apartment boom. Because it is illegal it is also transient and ephemeral. Finally, in this film, the sad young man at the center of Tsai's films' job is also related to a local fashion. He sells columbaria, or niches for funeral urns. At one point, we hear another salesman's patter. He promotes these niches as homes away from home. By buying one now, although it will be empty, in the future you and your loved ones can be together. He goes on to suggest that friends can arrange columbaria close to each other so that they can visit easily and play mahjong with each other in the next life.

In this film, the sad gay young man connects with an array of signifiers specific to Taiwan. And much as he is used to say something metaphorical about the People's Republic in *East Palace West Palace* and combined with Argentina to say something about Hong Kong in *Happy Together*, here he is part of an excessive significatory complex implying the Taiwanese condition as an existential homelessness. For Taiwan is the island to which the Nationalist Chinese KMT retreated after their defeat by the Communists in 1949. Ever since, they have maintained that they are there temporarily, that they will return to the mainland, and that Taiwan is not a country in itself but only a province. In other words, the younger generations of Taiwanese depicted in these films have grown up being told the place of their birth is not home but exile, or rather that home is exile and vice versa.

As I hope I have shown, *Happy Together, East Palace West Palace* and *Vive L'Amour* all deploy the sad young man trope in locally specific ways. Furthermore, those locally specific meanings are propped up on a broader general East Asian signification of this individual without a role in the traditional family system as a lonely outcast. Now, by way of conclusion I would like to return to some of the questions and observations I began with. First, if we are to follow Lydia Liu's suggestion and understand constructions of the individual in twentieth century Chinese culture as historically and socially specific (re)inventions, why has this particular trope of the sad gay young man appeared at the same time in these films from Hong Kong, the People's Republic of China and Taiwan? Beyond the specific local conditions, is there anything broader linking them together?

In response to this question, I would note that not only are the sad gay young men located amidst other similarly isolated and lonely characters in the films of Wong Kar-wai and Tsai Ming-Liang, but also that these characters are young members of a new generation. Furthermore, whereas the early and mid-twentieth century range of examples of individuals outside the family cited above were all, in their various ways, symbols of the modem, I would argue that these alienated young people are symbols of a post-modern era. In *East Palace West Palace*, neither A Lan nor the cop enter into long discussions about the socialist project. Indeed, this modernist, progress-oriented teleological model of development seems to be largely forgotten, and instead we simply have A Lan grappling with his present needs. In *Happy Together*, any Hong Kong free trade modernist progress is replaced by aimless journeys, inability to reach destinations and difficulty returning. The future and the past are gone and replaced by the savoring of the present in all its delights and horrors. And in the Taiwanese example of *Vive L'Amour*, there are only disconnection and temporary homes, and again there is no sense of any modernist progress towards destination. Perhaps this is best expressed in the final scene of the film when the real estate agent walks through a mudscape of unfinished park, and, itself another local site familiar to Taipei filmgoers at the time and symbolic of unkept civic promises. There, she sits down alone and weeps. No one comforts her, just as no one in the film connects with the gay young man to alleviate his sadness.

This then leads me on to my other question. What is the value of the sad gay young man trope for viewers today? Maybe it is possible to see how it might appeal to spectators who are not gay, lesbian or queer because of its symbolic functions as a local or even generational metaphor for alienation and a figure for the times.[22] But how much help is it to the gay, lesbian or queer spectator to have become a sort of image of existential anomie for straight people? However, before one jumps to self-righteous protestation, perhaps we should recall that for many young lesbian, gay and queer spectators in China, Taiwan and Hong Kong today, being lesbian, gay or queer is not much easier than it was for Richard Dyer growing up in England in the fifties and sixties. Maybe, just as the trope offered him a complex and ambivalent way to find himself it might ring true enough for them, too. At a very minimum, even though the East Asian sad gay young man seems to have been mostly invented for mainstream culture rather than by and for gays themselves, it does add to the range of circulating and visible potential models and images of oneself to negotiate with and work off.

NOTES

1. Chinese sociologist commenting on boarding preschools, cited in David Y.H. Wu, "Self and Collectivity: Socialization in Chinese Preschools," in Roger T. Ames with Wimal Dissanayake and Thomas P. Kasulis (eds.), *Self as Person in Asian Theory and Practice* (Albany: State University of New York Press, 1994), p.243.

2. Richard Dyer, "Coming out as going in: The image of the homosexual as a sad young man," in *The Matter of Images*: *Essays on Representation* (Routledge: London, 1993), p. 74.

3. No standard method of romanizing Chinese characters has been adopted here. There are different systems in use in Taiwan, Hong Kong and the People's Republic, along with individual idiosyncratic spellings preferred by some individuals. In these circumstances, it seemed foolish to impose one system across the board, and instead I have used the spellings found in subtitles and credits fences. The only exception is the transcription of the original titles of films in the filmography at the end of the essay. Those that were originally in Chinese characters are given there in pinyin romanization.

4. Chris Berry, "Sexual Disorientations: Homosexual Rights, Fast Asian Films, and Post-modern Post-nationalism," in Xiaobing Tang and Stephen Snyder (eds.), *In Pursuit of Contemporary East Asian Culture* (Boulder, CO: Westview Press, 1996), p. 167.

5. For a more detailed description and analysis of these films, see Chris Berry, "Asian Values, Family Values: Film, Video and Lesbian and Gay Identities," *Journal of Homosexuality* 39:34 (1999).

6. See, for example, Dennis Altman, "The World of 'Gay Asian'," in Suvendrini Pereira (ed.), *Asian and Pacific Inscriptions*, a special book issue of *Meridian*, 14:2 (1995), pp. 121-138.

7. For a discussion of this term and phenomenon, see Kath Weston, *Families We Choose*: *Lesbians, Gays, Kinship* (New York: Columbia University Press, 1991).

8. See, for example, Francis L.K. Hsu, "The Self in Cross-cultural Perspective," in Anthony J. Marsella, George De Vos, Francis L.K. Hsu (eds.), *Culture and Self: Asian and Western Perspectives* (New York: Tavistock Publications, 1985), pp. 24-55; Michael Harris Bond (ed.), *The Psychology of the Chinese People* (Hong Kong: Oxford University Press, 1986); and Donald J. Munro, *The Concept of Man in Early China* (Stanford: Stanford University Press, 1969).

9. Tu Weiming, "Self-hood and Otherness in Confucian Thought," in Marsella, De Vos and Hsu, op.cit., pp. 231-51.

10. Seekam Tan has explored the way in which Hong Kong queer culture and homoeroticism intersect with these spaces in both martial arts films and the contemporary generic equivalent, the Hong Kong action movie in "Delirious Native Chaos and Perfidy: A Post-Colonial Reading of John Woo's *The Killer*," *Antithesis* 6:2 (1993), pp. 53-71.

11. Lydia H. Liu, "Translingual Practice: The Discourse of Individualism between China and the West," *Positions* 1:1(1993), p. 165.

12. Tam, Kwok-kan and Terry Siu-han Yip, "The Self in Transition: Moral Dilemma in Modern Chinese Drama," in Roger T. Ames, Thomas P. Kasulis and Wimal Dissanayake (eds), *Self as Image in Asian Theory and Practice* (Albany: State University of New York Press, 1998), pp. 200-218.

13. For further details on gay life in China, see Paul Richardson, "Subcultural Revolution," *Attitude* 1:10 (February 1995), pp. 68-74. and Wan Yanhai, "Becoming a Gay Activist in Contemporary China," in Peter Jackson and Gerard Sullivan (eds.), *Emerging Lesbian and Gay Identities and Communities in Asia* (forthcoming 1999).

14. That a gay man in contemporary Beijing might imagine himself in such a matrix is made more plausible when one bears in mind that articles and books published since the late eighties on homosexuality construct just such cultural and psychological lineage. See for example Li Yinhe and Wang Xiaoba, *Tamen de Shijie* (*Their World*), (Hong Kong: Cosmos Books, 1992, originally published in China), and bang Beichuan, *Tongxinglian* (*Homosexuality*), (*Jinan*: *Shandong Kexue Jishu Chubanshe* [Shandong Science and Technology Press], 1994).

15. Quoted in Chris Berry, "*East Palace West Palace*: Staging Gay Life in China," *Jump Cut* 42, p.86.

16. For more detailed discussion of Zhang and his young colleagues, see Berry, op.cit.

17. Ackbar Abbas, *The New Hong Kong Cinema: Culture and the Politics of Disappearance* (Minneapolis: University of Minnesota Press, 1997).

18. Leo Bersani, "Is the Rectum a Grave?" *October* 43 (1988), pp. 197-222.

19. For a far more detailed reading of how *Happy Together* queers transitional Hong Kong, see Audrey Yue, "What's So Queer About *Happy Together*," *Inter-Asia Cultural Studies Journal* 1:2 (forthcoming, 1999). As Audrey's doctoral thesis supervisor, I am sure my thinking on this film has been informed by her remarkable insights in more ways than I am aware. I am deeply grateful to her.

20. For further discussion of the loneliness of Wong's main characters, see Jean-Marc Lalanne, "Images from the Inside," in Jean-Marc Lalanne et al., *Wong Kar-wai* (Paris: Editions Dis Voir, no date), pp. 9-27. On page 22, Lalanne notes "The charac-

ters belong to only one generation, from twenty to thirty years old, and the preceding generation, that of their parents, seems to have disappeared."

21. For a closer examination of the construction of loneliness in this film and the spectatorial relation it implies, see Chris Berry, "Where Is the Love? The Paradox of Performing Loneliness in *Vive L'Amour*," in Lesley Stem and George Kouvaris (eds.), Caught in the Act: Performance in the Cinema (Sydney: Power Institute Press, forthcoming 1999).

22. Indeed, the young Korean filmmakers whose short films were shown at the Seoul Queer Film and Video Festival in 1998 not only made it clear they themselves were straight, but also proclaimed this as the reason for their interest in gay, lesbian and queer characters. For a report, see http://wwwsshe.murdoch.edu.au/hum/as/intersections/current2/Berry.html

FILMOGRAPHY

Beijing Bastards (Beijing Zazhong), dir: Zhang Yuan, People's Republic of China, 1992.

Broken Branches (Naeil ui Hyahae Hununun Kang), dir: Park Jae-Ho, South Korea, 1995.

Chungking Express (Chongqing Senlin), dir: Wong Kar-wai, Hong Kong, 1994.

Days of Being Wild (A Fei Zhengzhuan), dir: Wong Kar-wai, Hong Kong, 1991.

East Palace West Palace (Donggong Xigong), director: Zhang Yuan, People's Republic of China, 1996.

Farewell My Concubine (Bawang Bie Ji), director: Chen Kaige, People's Republic of China, 1993.

Happy Together (Chunguang Zhaxie), dir: Wong Kar-wai, Hong Kong, 1997.

Heaven 6 Box (Tengoku no Muttsu no Hako), dir: Oki Hiroyuki, Japan, 1995.

Mama (Mama), dir: Zhang Yuan, People's Republic of China, 1990.

Okoge, dir: Nakajima Takehiro, Japan, 1992.

Osaka Story: A Documentary, dir: Nakata Toichi, UK, 1994.

Rebels of the Neon God (Qing Shaonian Nezha), dir: Tsai Ming-Liang, Taiwan, 1992.

The River (Heliu), dir: Tsai Ming-Liang, Taiwan, 1997.

Song of the Goddess, dir: Ellen Pau, Hong Kong, 1993.

Sons (Erzi), dir: Zhang Yuan, People's Republic of China, 1995.

Twinkle (Kira Kira Hikaru), dir: George Matsuoka, Japan, 1992.

Vive L'Amour (Aiqing Wansui), dir: Tsai Ming-Liang, Taiwan, 1994.

The Wedding Banquet (Xiyan), dir: Ang Lee (Li An), Taiwan, 1992.

The Cross-Gender Performances of Yam Kim-Fei, or The Queer Factor in Postwar Hong Kong Cantonese Opera/Opera Films

See-Kam Tan

Nanyang Technological University

SUMMARY. This essay is designed as a brief historical examination of the Cantonese female cross-dressing star Yam Kim-Fei, whose hundreds of films and opera performances in the '50s and '60s have made her one of the century's most celebrated transvestite artists. While her craft has often been relegated to studies of gender alone, I assert that the traditions of Chinese operatic transvestism she employs are not merely a relativist historical-artistic mode without political relevance but can be justifiably reclaimed for the purposes of queer interpretation and spectatorship–for indeed their original intent coincides very well with what we call "queer" today. *[Article copies available for a fee from The Haworth Document Delivery Service: 1-800-342-9678. E-mail address: <getinfo@haworthpressinc.com> Website: <http://www.HaworthPress.com>]*

Although no longer in production, the Cantonese Opera Film–that is, movies adapted from Cantonese opera–was one of the major genres of postwar Hong Kong Cantonese cinema (mid-1940s to late 1960s). The heyday of this cinema was in the 1950s: it accounted for one-third of the 500 or so Cantonese films produced during this period.[1]

See-Kam Tan teaches and researches at The School of Communication Studies at Nanyang Technological University, Singapore.

[Haworth co-indexing entry note]: "The Cross-Gender Performances of Yam Kim-Fei, or The Queer Factor in Postwar Hong Kong Cantonese Opera/Opera Films." Tan, See-Kam. Co-published simultaneously in *Journal of Homosexuality* (The Haworth Press, Inc.) Vol. 39, No. 3/4, 2000, pp. 201-211; and: *Queer Asian Cinema: Shadows in the Shade* (ed: Andrew Grossman) Harrington Park Press, an imprint of The Haworth Press, Inc., 2000, pp. 201-211. Single or multiple copies of this article are available for a fee from The Haworth Document Delivery Service [1-800-342-9678, 9:00 a.m. - 5:00 p.m. (EST). E-mail address: getinfo@haworthpressinc.com].

© 2000 by The Haworth Press, Inc. All rights reserved.

201

One of the foremost actors of this genre was the late opera diva and film actress, Yam Kim-Fei (1912-1989), a/k/a Yam Kim-Fai (in *pinyin*: Ren Jian-hui), also deferentially referred to as "*Yidai Yiren*," or "The Artist of a Generation."[2] Of the 300 or so movies attributed to her, most were Cantonese opera pictures.[3] Although she also acted in Cantonese modern drama features, another primary genre of Cantonese cinema, this was more the exception than the norm. Movies featuring her in female roles were equally rare since, as a specialist cross-gender performer, her forte was to play "man." (So too was the case of her opera works.)

Cantonese Opera Film Retrospective, a bilingual catalogue first published in 1987, and then revised in 1996, is probably the most comprehensive attempt to study the genre. Yet none of the papers in the catalogue offers an exclusive study on Yam, or her works. Nonetheless they acknowledge her contributions to the genre, often in venerated terms.[4] While frequently lauding her work as a renowned cross-gender performer, they invariably stop short of framing it in queer terms.

My paper principally addresses this oversight. In doing so, it reclaims Yam and her works for queer discourses. Here, the term "queer" generally corresponds to that commonly understood by queer theorists in that it similarly challenges supposedly stable binaries such as male/female, gay/straight, and sex/gender. More specifically, my paper seeks to locate the queer factor in Yam's cross-gender acts (and by extension, Cantonese opera and its cinematic equivalent). Yam's professional trafficking at the borders of gender lends itself to Queer Theory, that which Paul Burston and Colin Richardson espouse. For Burston and Richardson:

> Queer Theory is both "Political" and "Cultural": political, because it seeks to expose and problematize the means by which 'sexuality' [has been] reduced to the definitions and relations of gender; cultural, because just about everything we might call Queer Theory concerns itself with the ways in which cultural texts–books, films, television, magazines, etc.–condition understandings of sexuality.[5]

While Yam's role-specialization as a cross-gender performer is arguably queer (as we shall see), it should be stressed that cross-gender performances are by no means unique to Cantonese opera films, or opera from which such films derived their conventions. Mandarin films featuring Ivy Ling Po or Chen Pei Pei, two movie queens of the Shaw Brothers studio in the 1960s, would readily dispute all suggestion to the contrary. Ling and Chen acted extensively in Huangmei opera films and swordplay flicks, respectively. In their pictures, they frequently played the male protagonists, while women invariably acted the female protagonists, as in Yam's movies (as well as her opera works). Cross-gender performances are likewise not an exclusive preserve for actresses in Cantonese or Mandarin films. In the history of postwar Hong Kong Cantonese and Mandarin cinemas (not to mention their Teochew counterparts), it is indeed not uncommon for the gender line to be crossed, or breached, by actors of either sex. Actors have been known, albeit relatively scarcely, to be professional gender-benders too–for example, Banri An (1904-1964), who was well-known for his parts as old women (or in opera terminology: *laodan*).[6]

As far as traditional Chinese theater is concerned, specialist cross-gender performers are hardly peculiar. Mei Lanfang (1894-1961) would probably count as the most famous of such performers in the twentieth century.[7] Mei came from a family of theater artists: like his grandfather and father, his stage specialty was to play *dan* (female) roles in Beijing opera. Mei differed from Yam (or other female-to-male opera performers) in several fundamental ways. Sex (in the biological sense) was one: the former was a man, while the latter was a woman. Role-specialization was another: the former was a *dan*, while the latter was a *sheng*. Finally they belonged to different schools of Chinese opera. In opera terminology, *dan* and *sheng* are two of the four primary role-specializations, the other two being *chou* and *jing*. The four terms are also vocational designations for performers specializing in corre-sponding role-types, or character-types: *dan* (female), *sheng* (male), *chou* (jester or clown) and *jing* ("painted faces").[8] The former two types may be played by male or female actors, while the later two types are usually male parts, and often played by male actors. In addition to gender, the four role-types, or character types, all have age and class markers–for instance, young or old; and poor or rich. Additionally they each have distinct singing style, speech pattern, stage movement, costume convention, and make-up. Finally the practice of role-specialization in Chinese theater does not necessarily reduce performers to stereotypes because, as Elizabeth Wichmann points out, they play characters who:

> may be good or bad, strong or weak, intelligent or stupid. Role-type specialization produces patterns (*guilü*) of performance technique rath-er than dramatic characters with stereotyped personalities. [Besides] performers of each role-type specialize in the display of certain selected performance skills.[9]

Functioning as a system of signification then, the actors not only bring to-gether a kaleidoscopic array of theatrical elements which consist of story, music, voice, movement, makeup, costume, and stage properties, but their characters also speak a number of registers: class, gender, sexuality and erotic style.

Although playing to different audiences, Yam was a much more accom-plished film actor than Mei, a consequence arising from her experience with working in movies which were largely made for commercial exhibition and public consumption. Mei's film works were less so, being primarily non-commercial film documentations, or straightforward records, of his stage repertoires. However, Mei was no less a celebrated cross-gender opera performer than Yam: their respective rendition of *dan* and *sheng* characters enthralled audiences both at home and abroad. In the specific case of Mei, his tours in Japan, United States, Europe, and Russia during the 1930s helped establish Beijing opera as a revered theatrical form in the international artistic, dramatic and literary community.[10] They also made him an eminent figure in this community. It was around this time that the German dramatist Bertolt Brecht saw him perform. Tremendously impressed by what he saw, Brecht wrote (for example), "[By] comparison with Asiatic acting our own art still seems hopelessly parsonical."[11]

Elsewhere, the drama theorist Faye C. Fei articulated the significance of Mei's contributions to Chinese theater differently from Brecht's. In particular she was interested in the cultural and social implications of cross-gender performances in relation to discourses of gender. "Among his many contributions to Beijing opera," she wrote:

> Mei was credited for upgrading the literary standards of the plays with strong women characters and for combining and developing techniques for better showcasing the performers' versatility in singing, dancing, movement, speech, and acrobatic skills. As a result, Mei helped to turn the young female characters on the stage into more respected, intelligent, talented, cultivated, and dignified human beings.[12]

Yam's cross-gender acts similarly showed the malleability of gender. They likewise revealed that gender was a cultural construct. By achieving eminence in her chosen profession, she also helped elevate the status of female performers in the cultural industry, as well as extending the paradigm of their acting repertoire. Furthermore, her works not only improved the general standard of, but also set *the* standard for, Cantonese opera and opera films of her day. Or, as Sek Kei puts it, Yam's renditions brought unprecedented "romance and beauty to the Cantonese opera film," and in doing so, "elevated the genre to heights of neo-classicism."[13] Neo-classicism reworked the classicism of Yuan and Ming plays by infusing it with "strong dramatic plots"; "extravagantly romantic" lyrics that, while "classical," were "never anachronistic or esoteric"; and finally refreshing melodies that, while having an "unflinching sense of nostalgia" for classicism, were in actuality not classicism.[14]

The neo-classic turn in postwar Hong Kong Cantonese opera films may be attributed to a fruitful partnership between Yam and her two collaborators, Pak Shuet-xin (1926–), a/k/a Pak Suet-sin (or in *pinyin*: Bai Xuexin) and

Tong Dik-san (in *pinyin*: Tang Disheng (1917-1959).[15] In 1956, Pak and Yam co-found the Cantonese opera troupe, *Xianfengming Jutuan* (literally meaning Cries of the Fairy Phoenixes Opera Troupe). At the time, they were both riding the pinnacle of their separate yet connected careers as opera divas and film actresses. By installing themselves as the respective resident *sheng* and *dan* of their troupe, Yam and Pak as the fairy phoenixes gave eight sensational seasons of opera over the next two years, primarily performing the neo-classical pieces written by resident librettist Tong. The Yam-Pak-Tong collaborations yielded instant opera "classics," which when adapted into films, became movie "classics" as well.[16] Phonographs–7-, 10-, and 12-inch discs–based on their opera/film works were also made. Regardless of the form, their works–invariably featuring Yam and Pak as the male and female leads respectively–were, in general, popularly successful.[17] It is not known exactly how many operas Yam and Pak co-acted in, countless probably, but during their separate yet connected careers, they cut 33 phonographic albums together and co-starred in 60 movies, most of which were Cantonese opera films.[18]

Popular cultural artifacts such as these thus constituted Yam's achievements as awesomely impressive. They variously worked to position her centrally within the prevalent cultural mythologies of, and from, the postwar era. The recent enormous success of *Sentimental Journey* (1999), a musical-play based on Yam's life written by Hong Kong playwright Raymond To Kwok Wai, bore testimony to the continuing influence Yam had on the popular consciousness of present-day Hong Kong. This was all the more so when the musical-play makes box-office history by having the longest run ever.[19] The musical "filled in the gaps of memories [for Yam] and created a marvelous recall of [her] era," enthused one viewer.[20] That playwright To would eulogize Yam in revered terms was thus not surprising. As Janet Ho and Wong Ah Yoke reported, in the musical-play, the diva was portrayed as "totally devoted to her art" to the extent that she was "determined to be better at playing a man than the male actors themselves."[21] Incidentally and interestingly, Chan Po-chu/Chen Baochu, one of Yam's disciples, played her mentor.[22] Following the footsteps of her mentor, she took on male roles. Later she went on to act in films–but usually as female leads. Throughout most of the 1960s, Chan reigned the Cantonese screen and earned the nickname "Princess of the Movie Fans" for her widespread popularity, one which was comparable to Yam's a decade earlier when she was dubbed, "Lover of the Opera Fans." In this way (and others), the legends of Yam live again in contemporary Hong Kong.

TOWARDS A THEORY OF THE QUEER FACTOR
IN CANTONESE OPERA/OPERA FILMS

The above general discussion of Yam provides the discursive context for my ensuing theorization of the queer factor in Cantonese opera/opera films.

This theorization is predicated upon Yam's specialist work as a cross-gender performer. It also involves playing on the idea that while biologically a woman, Yam was–by profession–a man.

As mentioned before, Yam was–by profession–a *sheng*; or more appropriately, a *wenwusheng*, that is, a *sheng* whose specialist repertoire primarily comprised the following character-types: *wensheng* (learned man), *wusheng* (military man), and *wenwusheng* (learned military man). In other words, she was a *fanchuan* actress whose forte was playing all three character-types. Here the term *"fanchuan"* is used more in its colloquial sense than its "proper" meaning. The latter generally refers to actors who *occasionally* act in parts outside their specialization. This may entail acting across the gender line–for instance a *sheng* in a *dan* part. The performance may also require such actors to cross the age and class line. The "proper" meaning of the term thus implies a multitude of possible "crossings" along the gender, age and/or class continuums. As such it is not strictly gender-specific, as opposed to the colloquial sense of the term which specifically refers to performers who specialize in cross-gender roles, or who especially act in roles whose gender does not correspond with their biological one. In short, *fanchuan* performers are specialist gender-benders. (Unless otherwise stated, the term *"fanchuan'* henceforth is used in its colloquial sense.)

As a *wenwusheng*, Yam's specialist repertoire was playing the "straight" man, a role-type paradigm consisting of filial sons, gentle husbands, kind fathers, or benevolent emperors. It also comprised the various roles of a poor but charming and diligent (male) scholar, or those of a brave and chivalrous (male) warrior. In all of these cases, Yam's characters would possess the seductive charm of a talented man which beautiful women somehow found irresistible. Over and over again, they would fall in love romantically, even desperately, with their female counterparts. Yam's love-objects on stage, and in celluloid, range from mortals to spirits, from ghosts to fairies, and would invariably be women. They are also always played by female performers, one of whom was Pak. Sometimes Yam's characters would woo the heroine elegantly. Sometimes, the heroine would court them gracefully. The hero (Yam) and heroine might fall in love on first sight, or they might secure it through extravagant plans. Their love might transcend class, or be constrained by it. It might conclude happily or tragically. If the latter, the star-crossed lovers in death would experience rebirth as immortals or fairies, and live happily as a couple in eternity. Representative examples of such instances would include films (or for that matter, their opera counterparts) such as *The Tragic Story of Liang Shanpo and Zhu Yingtai/Liang Zhu Henshi* (dir. Li Tei, Zhili, 1958) and *Tragedy of the Emperor's Daughter/Dinü Hua* (dir. Long Tu, Dacheng, 1959).[23] Although infrequent, Yam would play the "straight" woman, as in *Two Naughty Girls/Yidui Yanzhima* (dir. Wu Hui,

Chengchang, 1952) and *Blessings come in Pairs/Haoshi Chengshuang* (dir. Yang Gongliang, Qunsheng, 1955). In these movies, Yam acted as "modern woman." Yam's repertoire as a woman also contained reverse cross-dressing characters. Here her film debut, *The Handsome Hero Perplexed by Love*, a/k/a *Love Traps Warrior Panan/Qing Kun Wu Panan* (dir. Chen Pi, Haoguang, 1951), would serve as a good illustration of such characters.[24] In this film, Yam played a commoner/woman-warrior (*wudan*) who, for the most part, cross-dressed as a male martial hero (*wusheng*). The film ended with the Empress adopting her: as a princess, she married the male protagonist. Playing reverse cross-dressing parts was similarly rare for Yam. In any case, her woman-characters–like her man-characters elsewhere–would likewise have to endure the test of ("heterosexual") love. In surviving its many trials and tribulations, they would eventually reconcile with their beloved and then live happily ever after, often partaking in heterosexualesque activities such as delightful marriages and blissful family lives.

Yam's various *fanchuan* impersonations highlight what I call "performative transsexualization," a performance process which enables (cross-)sexual transcendency. Huang Zuolin's study on the cross-gender art of Mei Lanfang throws light on what that process entails.[25] According to Huang, Mei's success as a female impersonator stems from his mastery of three interrelated performative elements: "*xieyi*," "introspection," and "representation." *Xieyi* literally means "writing essences." It rejects realism as a defining principle for creativity, but not in toto, for its manifestation stems from a critical engagement with realism, this being a way of getting at, and eventually to, the *heart* of the matter that *xieyi* seeks to depict. That is, it endeavors to capture "the essentialism of life, . . . not life as it is but life as extracted, concentrated, and typified."[26] To put this in another way, it basically demands that art forms (including opera) be a refinement of life itself so that life becomes art, and art becomes life.[27] To achieve this, it must exceed not only real life but also real time and space. The excess "frees" the life-in-art from the constraints of real life, thereby lifting art to the level of the sublime.[28] According to Huang, Mei's performative art demonstrates *xieyi* in action. This accounts for the gender transcendency that makes his *fanchuan* performances credible and convincing. Huang also observes that the transcendency further rests on a masterful synthesis of two acting styles on the part of Mei: "the 'inner technique' of introspection" and "the outgoing techniques of representation."[29]

Huang does not elaborate on the two acting techniques, but they may be deduced from the following conversation between a *fanchuan* actor and his admirer in the eighteenth century:

> In the year 1747, a dignitary once asked an actor whom he really admired: "There are so many of you in your profession; why are you

the only one who is really good on the stage?" The actor replied: "When I impersonate a female on the stage, I not only try to look like a female in my physical appearance; I also try to feel like a female in the depth of my heart. It's the tender emotions together with the sweet and delicate demeanor of a female that enthralls the audience. If I keep my male feelings, even just a trace, it will betray my true self; then how can I compete for the audience's affection for feminine beauty and guile? When I play a chaste female, I fill my heart with purity and virtue, so, even if I am having fun joking and laughing I do not lose my chaste inner core. When I play a morally loose female, I fill my heart with lust, so, even if I am sitting stately, I cannot hide my loose nature. When I play a noble female, I fill my heart with dignity, so, even if I am dressed in plain clothes, I retain my nobility. When I play a plebeian female, I fill my heart with pettiness, so, even if I am outfitted in grandeur, I still personify vulgarity. When I play a kind female, I fill my heart with loving tenderness, so, even if I am angry, I do not behave harshly. When I play a fiery female, I fill my heart with willful hot temper, so, even if I am obviously in the wrong, I cannot be humble in my words. I always put myself in the shoes of my characters, completely identifying with their emotions: happiness, anger, sorrow, or joy as well as kindness, resentment, love, or hate. When I don't simply play the role but really live the part of my character, the audience accepts me as such too. The reason I am the best on the stage is because I am different from the other female impersonators, who may look and move like their female characters but do not feel like them."[30]

The actor's reply, indeed a lengthy one, offers an insider's perspective to the performative trans-sexualization that characterizes cross-gender impersonations in Chinese theater. It makes it clear that successful cross-gender performers are thoroughly aware of their audience, and treat them as intelligent, demanding and discerning, that they do not play stereotypes. Total identification with the characters they play is essential. This requires self-reflexivity (or "introspection" as Huang might call it); a critical process which involves a self-conscious eradication of the "self" in the performer. This process also demands a heightened self-awareness of the constraints of one's (biological) gender/sex, and of the need to "free" oneself from such constraints in order to get to, as it were, the other side/sex. The "freeing" of oneself is related to the principle of *xieyi*, which aids "introspection," and which gives form (or "representation" as Huang might call it). Finally, performative transsexualization clearly goes beyond sartorial transvestitism.

To be sure, sartorial transvestitism is a characteristic of all *fanchuan* performances since "clothes maketh the man"–or for that matter, the woman as well. In the specific context of Chinese opera, vestimentary codes, that is, clothing as a system of signification, are one primary way to distinguish the various role-types, or character-types. Other codes include singing styles, speech patterns, stage movements, and makeup. So *fanchuan* performers should be distinguished from other types of cross-dressers in opera/films. They differ in the following ways. Firstly, *fanchuan* performers are not only specialist gender-benders but, according to their professional calling, also "full-time" cross-dressers. As such they are not cameo-drags; that is, performers who, throughout their career, play an *occasional* gender-bending role or two. By contrast, for the *fanchuan* performers, doing cross-gender impersonations *is* their career. In addition, their work is not simply drag-acts. That is to say, *fanchuan* performers are not drags who simply pretend to be, or parody, the opposite sex. By the same token, they are not transvestites who have a "fetish" for sartorial disguises. They are less a case of "gender confusion" (as the terms "drag-acts," "transvestites," etc., might connote) than that of a "third" gender-in-performance. The "third" gender is–performatively speaking–more that of a transsexual (but in reality not) than a transvestite's because *fanchuan* performers cross-dress not in order to *pass* as the other sex but, literally and metaphorically, to *become* the very "sex" which they impersonate, and which they attain performatively. Ultimately this "sex" speaks not just one sex, or two, but a register of them. It invites "polymorphously diverse"[31] identifications. Such identifications in turn characterize the queer gaze that locates *fanchuan* performers within a spectrum of "fluid" genders: male, female, both or neither. Finally *fanchuan* performers should be differentiated from *fanchuan* roles; the latter being drag-acts performed by cameo-drags, while the former referring to specialist gender-benders. They should also be differentiated from *fanchuan* characters; that is, narrative figures who cross-dress and switch gender in accordance to the plot, or story-line. Thus for *fanchuan* performers such as Yam, she is a man to start with, once on stage or in celluloid.

In sum, for *fanchuan* performers (as opposed to cameo-drags, drags and transvestites), sartorial transvestitism serves more than a conduit for the performative transsexualization: it enables, and at the same time disguises, the crossing from the biological sex to the performative one. Interestingly, despite their apparent vestmentary transvestitism, and implied transsexualism, *fanchuan* performers–as evinced by the opera/film works of Yam–are comfortable being "full-time" cross-dressers, and professional cross-gender impersonators. In their works, it is apparent that there is nothing perverse with, or weird about, trafficking at the borders of gender. Recognizing this, they celebrate what they do, *sans* justification. Herein lie the cultural specificities of the queer art of *fanchuan* performances in postwar Hong Kong Cantonese opera, and opera films.

NOTES

1. Li Cheuk-to, "Introduction," in *Cantonese Opera Film Retrospective*, Hong Kong, Urban Council, 1987, p. 9.

2. Lu Ziying and Liu Yufen, eds., *The Artist of a Generation: The Theater and Art of Ren and Bai–A Pictorial/Yidai Yiren: Ren Bai Xiqu Yishu Huace*, Hong Kong, Ciwenhua, 1990.

3. See Wu Liren, *Yam Kim-Fei: A Biography*, p. xxx, and 125-141; and Lu and Liu, eds., *The Artist of a Generation*, p. 93-99.

4. See the following articles in *Cantonese Opera Film Retrospective*: Sek Kei, "Thoughts on Chinese Opera and Cantonese Opera Film," p. 14-17; Ng Ho, "Some Primitive Reminiscences: Myth, Sorcery and the Opera Film," p. 25-28; Michael Lam, "The Last Sorrow of the Purple Hairpin," p. 38-42; and Li Cheuk-to, "A Director Speaks: Li Tie on Opera Films," p. 70-73.

5. Paul Burston and Colin Richardson, "Introduction," in *A Queer Romance: Lesbians, Gay Men, and Popular Culture*, eds. Paul Burston and Colin Richardson. London, Routledge, 1995, p. 1.

6. For a general discussion of Banri An works, see Ji Er, "Larger than Life: Liang Xingbo and Banri An," *Cantonese Opera Film Retrospective*, p. 53-57. For a brief biography of Banri An, See *Cantonese Opera Film Retrospective*, p. 96.

7. See for example Colin Mackerras, *The Chinese Theater in Modern Times: From 1840 to the Present Day*. London, Thames and Hudson, 1975, p. 59-62; and Huang Zuolin, "On Mei Lanfang and Chinese Traditional Theater," in Faye Chunfang Fei, trans. and ed., *Chinese Theories of Theater and Performance from Confucius to the Present*. Ann Arbor, University of Michigan Press, 1999, p. 154-158.

8. For a discussion of the various role-types in Beijing opera, see for example Elizabeth Wichmann, *Listening to Theater: The Aural Dimension Beijing Opera*. Honolulu: University of Hawaii Press, 1991, p. 7-12. Although Wichmann discusses these role-types with specific reference to Beijing opera, her description of them applies to Chinese opera in general.

9. Wichmann, *Listening to Theater*. p. 7.

10. Mackerras, *The Chinese Theater in Modern Times*, p. 60.

11. John Willet, trans. and ed., *Brecht on Theater*. New York, 1964, p. 94.

12. Fei, ed. and trans., *Chinese Theories of Theater and Performance*, p. 143.

13. Sek Kei, "Thoughts on Chinese Opera and the Cantonese Opera Film," p. 17.

14. Ibid.

15. For a brief biographical details of Pak, Tong and Yam, see *Cantonese Opera Films Retrospective*, p. 95 and 110-112.

16. Their partnership was sadly cut short by Tong's untimely death during the premier of what turned out to be his last completed libretto, *The Reincarnation of Red-Plum/Zaishi Hongmei Ji* (1959). In its aftermath, Yam and Pak were grief-stricken. It would take some two years before they resumed working, and staged the troupe's final season. In 1961, Tong's partially finished libretto, *The New Legend of the White Snake/Xin Baishe Zhuan*, was thus showcased.

17. Examples of their "multiple-media" works would include *Dream of the Peony Pavilion/Mudanting Jingmeng*, *The Purple Hairpin/Zichai Ji*, *The Gold-Braided Fan/Chuanjin Baoshan*, *Triennial Mourning on the Bridge/Sannian Yiku Er-*

langqiao, The Fairy of Ninth Heaven/Jiutian Xuannü, Tragedy of the Emperor's Daughter/Dinü Hua, Butterful and Red Pear/Dying Hongli Ji and *The Happy Wedding/Kuafeng Chenglong*. For synopses of these films, see *Cantonese Opera Films Retrospective*, pp. 119-124.

18. These figures include works that ensued from the Yam-Pak-Tong collaborations. See Lu and Liu, eds., *The Artist of a Generation*, p. 97 and 100-107. It is estimated that Yam and Pak made more than 300 and 200 films, respectively. Pak's film debut was in a Cantonese opera film, *Wife in the Morning, Sister-in-Law at Night/Chenqi Musao* (dir. Hong Zhonghao, Yuzhou, 1947). Yam also made her film debut in a Cantonese opera feature. It was called *The Handsome Hero Perplexed by Love*, a/k/a *Love Traps Warrior Panan/Qing Kun Wu Panan* (dir. Chen Pi, Haoguang, 1951). In 1968, both Yam and Pak retired together. Their screen swansong was *Tragedy of the Poet King/Lihouzhu* (dir. Li Chenfeng, Xianfengming, 1968).

19. Janet Ho and Wong Ah Yoke, "Life! Section: The Longest Run–The Legends Live Again," *Straits* Times (Singapore), (10th April 1999), p. 1-3.

20. Cited, Janet Ho and Wong Ah Yoke, "Key Players in the Musical," *Straits Times* (Singapore), (10th April 1999), p. 3.

21. Ibid.

22. Jade Li, "Cover Story: Chan Poh-chu–"I felt useful doing nothing," *The Singapore Women's Weekly* (April 1999), p. 14-17.

23. For a synopsis of these films, see *Cantonese Opera Film Retrospective*, Hong Kong, Urban Council, 1987, p. 118 and 123.

24. This film was adapted from a well-known Cantonese opera, *Three-door Street/Sanmen Jie*. According to Yam's biographer, numerous film producers approached Yam with offers, hoping to capitalise on her attraction as an opera star. Initially none succeeded in persuading her to make the transition from stage to screen. Then Chen managed to do so. He had two advantages over the others. Firstly, he had a good knowledge of opera, having himself worked in the medium. Secondly he knew Yam personally. Most importantly, his offer to Yam–that is, the part of Mo Poon-on–agreed with her role-specialization. See Li, esp. chs. 2 and 6.

25. Huang, "On Mei Lanfang . . . ," p. 154-158.

26. Huang, "On Mei Lanfang . . . ," p. 158.

27. Cf., A Jia, "Truth in Life and Truth in Art," in Fei, *Chinese Theories of Theater . . .* , p. 146-153.

28. Huang, "On Mei Lanfang . . . ," p. 156.

29. Ibid., p. 157.

30. Fei, *Chinese Theories of Theater and Performance . . .* , p. 89-90.

31. Caroline Evans and Lorraine Gamman, "Reviewing Queer Viewing," in *A Queer Romance*, Burston and Richardson, eds., p. 13-49.

Farewell My Fantasy

Sean Metzger

University of California, Davis

SUMMARY. In this essay, I seek to place Chen Kaige's *Farewell My Concubine* not solely within the Chinese matrix of its production but within the transnational matrix of its distribution and viewing; indeed, the film may well have been intended for international audiences, to which the film's numerous awards testify. Yet China, too, has been fascinated with Western ideas, with Freud one particular example. So here I use a Freudian interpretation of the film's rationalization of homosexuality in terms of beating and childhood sexuality, a rationalization that diverges from the Lilian Lee novel on which the film is based. *[Article copies available for a fee from The Haworth Document Delivery Service: 1-800-342-9678. E-mail address: <getinfo@haworthpressinc.com> Website: <http://www. HaworthPress. com>]*

A sweltering summer morning in the Haidian district: Insofar as I had imagined the Chinese capital, I had failed to consider the seasonal heat. How was it that Gong Li never seemed to wilt in this smog-filtered sunshine? I wondered if she too had felt miserable when she walked to the Central Academy of Drama, across town from the school where I taught. My thoughts often drifted to China's most-beloved actress, not only because she

---

Sean Metzger is a PhD student in Twentieth Century Performance and Culture and a member of the Theater and Dance department at the University of California at Davis. He is working on a dissertation entitled "In the Realm of the Rice Queen: Fetishism, Diaspora and 'Chineseness.'" His published writing can also be found in the pages of *Theatre Journal.* (E-mail: sametzger@ucdavis.edu).

The author would like to thank Dominic Cheung, Peter Feng, Andrew Grossman, Karen Shimakawa and Selena Whang for their comments on various versions of this essay.

[Haworth co-indexing entry note]: "Farewell My Fantasy." Metzger, Sean. Co-published simultaneously in *Journal of Homosexuality* (The Haworth Press, Inc.) Vol. 39, No. 3/4, 2000, pp. 213-232; and: *Queer Asian Cinema: Shadows in the Shade* (ed: Andrew Grossman) Harrington Park Press, an imprint of The Haworth Press, Inc., 2000, pp. 213-232. Single or multiple copies of this article are available for a fee from The Haworth Document Delivery Service [1-800-342-9678, 9:00 a.m. - 5:00 p.m. (EST). E-mail address: getinfo@haworthpressinc.com].

213

glossed the front page of magazines in every store and newspaper stand, but also because she had helped to frame my perceptions of the PRC before I ever set foot in it. Screened projections of the Forbidden City and similar locales had always dominated my conception of China. But whoever edited those visuals had somehow erased the palpable pollution and steady streams of sweat that envelop Beijing in July. How ironic, then, that the most recent portrait I had stored in memory was that of a group of boys on a hillside, singing in the snow! That shot comes straight from a film, of course, starring Gong Li. But this image was one of many frozen impressions to melt away over the course of my stay in northern China. On this particularly blistering day, I appeared in class, dripping with perspiration, Gong Li on my mind.

I intended to discuss the disparities between representations of China that circulated via transnational media and my students' own impressions of their country. Rather than seeking an "authentic" vision of China, my goal was to find out what national fantasy of authenticity might emerge among these well-to-do Beijingers. In the midst of introducing this topic, I happened to mention Gong Li. Students suddenly became animated; speculation spouted forth. We had found a figure with whom everyone in the room could identify, an actress who crossed national borders, a signifier of . . . of what? "I think she has played every woman who has had a difficult life in China," one of the women in my class offered. And everyone laughed, and everyone agreed. Indeed, one of the female participants in the discussion approached me three and a half hours later, at the end of class, only to reinforce this point. The people you mentioned (Chen Kaige, Zhang Yimou and Gong Li), she told me, all portray the darker side of China. No one has any interest in how China has helped people. And I thought, is this a shadow before me, falling over the rainbow of my culturally-specific Judy Garland?

My consumption of Fifth Generation films has always involved a very specific set of fantasies.[1] I have always viewed them with an impulse to construct some kind of originary narrative, something like, "this is the culture from which half my family came." I engage in this activity, conscious of the fact that national culture is imaginary and that any national mythology is fractured, with the stories varying according to the voices and positions of the tellers. Moreover, the China inherited by the Fifth Generation film-makers markedly differs from what my grandparents understood as China back in the early decades of this century. But I still look for some point of identification. Thus, when Chen Kaige's Farewell My Concubine ran through U.S. art houses, I was instantly hooked. What more could I ask for than an epic narrative with a timeline that could include my family in its scope, a seemingly same-sex oriented lead male obsessed with theater and, of course, Gong Li?

My specific investment as a transnational, U.S.-based consumer of Farewell My Concubine is, thus, very particular. Moreover, the film itself has circulated in different versions in different locales; my own thoughts pertain to the U.S. theatrical release (1993), which runs about fifteen minutes shorter than the one distributed in Hong Kong. As Sheldon Hsiao-peng Lu has pointed out, the "reading, reception, and interpretation" of the Beijing Fifth Generation film-makers "is always already of a transnational nature" because of the status of their texts as international co-productions and, as I have just illustrated, as commodities differently distributed in the international market (11). Lu elaborates, writing that "[b]esides suggesting new relations between nation-states and capital, transnationality also alludes to the *trans*versal, the *trans*actional, the *trans*lational, and the *trans*gressive aspects of contemporary behavior and imagination that are incited, enabled, and regulated by the changing logics of states and capitalism" (4). A transnational viewing position, then, serves not to delimit but rather to expand possibilities opened up by the global circulation of filmic texts in the international marketplace. I want to narrow my own viewing position as one manufactured out of a partially phantasmatic identification with the Chinese diaspora and argue that my viewing practice is, therefore, transnational in the sense of transhistorical. In other words, I desire to establish a connection to China across temporal as well as spatial boundaries.

The irony here is that such a desire is predicated on a very heterosexual coupling of diaspora and cultural transmission. Jeeyeun Lee has critiqued this "naturalized equation of kin with diasporic community" in "Toward a Queer Korean American Diasporic History," (195). She forcefully contends that "[t]he history of a queer and diasporic homeland is not about the Truth. It is about present-day investments and motivations" (199). Lee begs the question of what might be gained from my examining and writing about Chen Kaige's text. My contention is that the film exposes the heterosexual underpinnings of transnational production and consumption in a specific context and that it simultaneously points toward other ways of imagining gendered relations and their effects on cultural transmission.

Having garnered the Palme d'Or at Cannes and an Oscar nomination as well as the Golden Globe, New York and Los Angeles Film Critics' awards in 1993, Chen Kaige's *Farewell My Concubine* has achieved far more attention than its source material, Lilian Lee's nearly eponymous novel. In adapting the pages to a filmic medium, the film-maker changed the story considerably, particularly its depiction of sexuality. Jenny Kwok Lau has noted that Chen has expressed his desire to involve "the consideration of the audience and commercialism" through productions such as *Farewell My Concubine* (19). In other words, Lau contends, "Chen consciously made an effort to popularize his work" (21) using, in this case, "opera and homosexuality as two . . . selling points" (22).

This drive toward mass appeal, however, is not directed at audiences in the

PRC, for, as scholars and critics have observed, "frustration abounds among Chinese film-makers because many . . . new works cannot be shown to domestic audiences" (Nickerson and Lappin, 56). Indeed *Time* magazine has even quoted Chen saying, "I am a Chinese director who finds himself making films for the international market" (Corliss, 66). In his book *Chinese Modernism in the Era of Reforms*, Xudong Zhang goes so far as to say:

> I see the post-1989 internationally oriented Fifth Generation as a departure from, if not a betrayal of, the Fifth Generation as modernist experimentation . . . the most recent festival-going, award-winning films bear the stamp of a production system based on international capital, global distribution networks, and multi-cultural audiences. (207)

Following the work of Lau, Zhang and others who have traced the means by which films of the post-Tiananmen Fifth Generation respond to the exigencies of consumer desires, mass-distribution and marketing, I will argue that *Farewell My Concubine* creates not only a dangerous but also a generative ambivalence in its representations of sex and gender. These descriptions, I contend, play on specific cultural fantasies that the film mobilizes in both the maintenance and erosion of a heterosexual scaffolding of Chinese diaspora. Thus, I specifically intend to examine the ways in which the film negotiates homosexual and transgender identities within an international framework and the possibilities enabled and eclipsed by the work's reception in the U.S.[2]

Although films ranging from Ang Li's *The Wedding Banquet* (1993) to Wong Kar-Wai's *Happy Together* (1997) have increased cinematic images of Asian (homo)sexuality, these works have not achieved the popularity and critical currency of Chen Kaige's work. Perhaps the specific gender representations in the text account for this transnational appeal. *Farewell My Concubine* not only limits its depiction of homosexuality in comparison to the novel but also participates in the same erasure of transgender subjectivity as the book; these representations indicate, in one reading, the degree to which heterosexual normativity continues to structure gender discourse and thus evacuate certain identities.

The novel's opening line "Prostitutes have no heart; actors have no morals" sets up a juxtaposition in the book that informs its thematic scope. In contrast, these lines neatly encapsulate the principal themes and plot of the film. The cinematic text opens with a shot of an empty corridor in soft focus, a result of the chiaroscuro lighting. Cheng Dieyi (Leslie Cheung) and Duan Xiaolou (Zhang Fengyi) round the corner and move towards the camera, which now pulls back to maintain its spatial distance from the actors. A superimposed title indicates the time and locale: "1977. Beijing, China." For the viewer who has forgotten the significance of this time (one year after the death of Mao, in the wake of the Cultural Revolution), the ensuing dialogue reminds us of its significance. As the actors pass through the corridor and into a gymnasium-like auditorium, a mechanically enhanced voice from outside the frame asks, "Who are you?" The film cuts to the characters in a long shot, allowing us to see them illuminated in the light emanating from the hallway. Cutting back to a medium shot, the dialogue continues in one long take.

> Xiaolou: "We're with the opera troupe."
> disembodied voice: "It's been over twenty years since you've performed together, hasn't it?"
> Xiaolou: "Twenty-one."
> Dieyi: "Twenty-two."
> Xiaolou: "Yes. Twenty-two years. And it's been ten years since we last saw each other."
> Dieyi: "Eleven . . . eleven years."
> Xiaolou: "That's right . . . eleven years . . . yes."
> voice: "It's due to the Gang of Four and the Cultural Revolution."
> Dieyi: "Isn't everything?"
> voice: "Things are better now."

The dialogue continues until the voice offers to turn on the lights. After another cut to a long shot, a spotlight arcs down from the top of the frame; rhythmic music from the Beijing opera starts. Then the image fades to black. The film cuts to the title shot: bold red letters on a tapestry showing the final scene of the opera from which the film takes its name. Replacing these words, the credits begin with the three principal actors: Leslie Cheung, Zhang Fengyi and, of course, Gong Li.

This opening sequence thus condenses the narrative and thematics of the entire film in a tight summary. The text traces Dieyi's journey as it intersects with his acting partner Xiaolou. A third element, the disembodied voice (representing the former prostitute turned wife and now deceased Juxian [Gong Li]), interrogates and challenges the relationship between the two principal actors. Thus, the three voices that we hear in this scene represent the three principal players in the film, whose names appear only moments later. The mise-en-scène of the vacant auditorium raises a question as to the whereabouts of the audience; the voice assigns responsibility for their absence to the Cultural Revolution. In addition to stripping the opera stars of their livelihood, this movement has also apparently segregated the two thespians (since they last met during the revolution's peak in the late 1960s). Their stilted speech patterns suggest an awkwardness in their relationship. Reinforcing this theatrical convention, the formal aspects of this sequence maintain a distance between spectator and actor that mimics the perceptible emotional space between Cheung and Zhang's characters.

By this point, the text has already introduced one of the most salient changes from the novel to the cinematic text. In the book, the character of Juxian is relatively minor. Casting Gong Li in such a role, however, necessarily evokes intertextuality resulting from the star discourse that surrounds her. She has appeared in nearly all of Zhang Yimou's internationally successful works, most often, as my students so accurately observed, playing a disenfranchised woman who suffers at the hands of a patriarchal Chinese system (as in *Ju Dou* [1990] and *Raise the Red Lantern* [1991]). Thus, her presence in the text connotes a concern with sexual differentiation that both hinders and reinforces the problematic issues of gender raised by the transvestite character, Cheng Dieyi. Both of these effects result from the expansion of Juxian's role.

On the one hand, Juxian helps to introduce a historical theme alluded to but not foregrounded in the text. If we accept, as Ben Xu does, Barthes' notion of the Oriental transvestite as a translation of femininity, "a cultural invention . . . that claims its distance and difference from life," then Dieyi serves as the Chinese icon of this femininity in male-dominated society (Xu, 166). As the dan, Dieyi embodies man's ideal woman, particularly in his role as Concubine Yu, the character from the film's operatic inspiration who expresses a willingness to sacrifice herself for the love of her master.[3] Thus, the film's emphasis on the prostitute, Juxian, whose "circulation value lies only in her corporeality," functions as a counter to the idealized Dieyi "a female more perfect than nature can ever produce" (Xu, 165). This juxtaposition finds its parallel in the history of the theatrical genre.

> One of the primary themes in late-imperial Chinese representations of the actor is the rivalry between actor and courtesan for the ground of femininity . . . The feminization of actors was an artifact not only of cross-dressing in performance, but of the sexual availability of actors to elite men. (Volpp, 139)

Thus Gong Li as Juxian enriches the text, which uses a figure whose acting career signifies the patriarchal oppression of Chinese women and its partial subversion (for Gong has achieved financial independence and the freedom, because of her reputation, to make artistic choices). Moreover, the opposition between Juxian and Dieyi complicates notions of prostitution, as Xu has deftly demonstrated in his article.[4]

At the same time the employment of Gong Li's character accomplishes a certain enhancement, "the inflation of Juxian's role prevents the film from dealing with Dieyi's homosexual feelings for Xiaolou; in fact, it helps evade the issue altogether" (Rayns, 42). Questions that the figure of the dan might otherwise raise become subsumed by the overdetermined discourse of femininity; Juxian puts Xiaolou into a heterosexual matrix that eclipses any other possibility that might have emerged in his relationship with Dieyi. In other words, *Farewell My Concubine* insists on reading the dan within the binary of male and female sexual possibility. The film positions Dieyi as the fantastic concubine vying for her king's attention against Juxian, the base woman whose very physicality defines her.

The childhood narratives in the story further reinforce this delimitation of Dieyi's sexual identity in male and female terms. An analysis of the erotic possibilities introduced in the first part of the film thus merits pursuit, since such a study illustrates the progressive manner in which the later sections of the text foreclose a discussion of homoerotic desire and queer subjectivity. Before taking their stage names, Dieyi and Xiaolou answered to the appellations Douzi and Shitou, respectively. After the introductory prologue described earlier in this essay, the film shows Douzi's mother, a prostitute herself, attempting to drop off her child with Master Guan's opera troupe. Tinted in soft sepia tones, the film resembles old photographs in its coloration. The transition to color film occurs while Master Guan beats Laizi, one of his protégés who had tried to run away from the troupe. The young boy, lying prone on a wooden bench with his pants down, spots Douzi and his mother. From mother and son, the film cuts to a close-up of Douzi's face followed by Laizi's reaction shot. The change in visual style quite literally highlights Laizi's suffering. The exchange of glances between the two boys that follows, however, reveals a certain mutual curiosity. That the text links this male curiosity to a slightly sadistic and perhaps even masochistic image foreshadows the punishment doled out to boys who take a certain scopophilic pleasure in regarding one another.

In order for Master Guan to accept Douzi, Douzi's mother must chop off an extra digit on the child's left hand. Before taking this action, she offers herself if only Guan will take her child, begging him not to scorn them. The master replies that actors and prostitutes are "equally despised by society." This scene establishes a number of significant narrative elements. The master's words link Douzi's future to his mother's profession, although the mother relinquishes her son precisely because the brothel has no room for so grown a boy. His ejection from one site of prostitution and entrance into another underscores the link between prostitution and theater, so blatantly referenced in both the novel and the film. Furthermore, Douzi's acceptance into the theater requires his castration, an act that, among other functions, prefigures his later selection as a dan and the relinquishing of his body to his patrons.

After the mother's departure, the text cuts to Douzi's entrance into the boys' sleeping quarters. Being mocked for his status as the son of a whore,

Douzi burns the cloak his mother had left him, the only physical reminder he has of her besides his absent finger. This ritual burning separates Douzi from the carnality that his mother represents; however, this physicality will continue to haunt him. Douzi will not only lose Xiaolou to another prostitute (Juxian) who earns a living with her body, but he will also become a sexual object for various opera patrons because he is, as an idealized woman in an effeminate male frame, just physical enough for them. Finally he will die in maintenance of his rapport with Concubine Yu, who, as a legend, is not physical at all.

Filled with naked and half-naked boys, the children's candle-lit sleeping area exists in a state of bedlam until the arrival of Shitou. As the apparent leader of the youth, Shitou insists that Douzi have a place to sleep. He offers a place next to himself as he approaches Douzi and suggestively wraps his arm around him. To complete his initiation, the text implies that Douzi must engage in some sort of sexual activity with the elder boy. Douzi rejects the offer. The scene ends with Shitou telling Douzi how the urine "froze on the tip" of his penis. Shitou then extinguishes the candle.

Shitou's frozen penis foreshadows his later relationship with Douzi. The latter boy's early attachment to Shitou will eventually give way to Cheng Dieyi's obsession with the stage brothers' adult relationship. Once Shitou ages, however, the erotic play in which the two boys participate as children ceases. His frozen penis serves as an apt metaphor both for Xiaolou's lack of desire for Dieyi as well as the figurative impotence that allows Juxian to take control of his life and lead him away from Dieyi.

The next scene shows us Douzi forced into the splits, a position he maintains with the help of two concrete blocks that pin either leg. Shitou, displaying concern for the whining Douzi, kicks one of the blocks out of the way during his exercises. While temporarily relieving Douzi's discomfort, this action results in Shitou's punishment. From Douzi's retrieval of his master's sword, the flat side of which is used to spank the bare buttocks of misbehaving opera trainees, the film cuts to Douzi's reaction shot. The soundtrack overlays this image with a "thwack" and Shitou's subsequent cries of pain. This aural cue sets up the next image: Shitou sprawled out on a bench with his pants pulled down. After a suitable cry, he gives Douzi a knowing wink and sly smile, suggesting that his screeching is a pretense meant to please the masters. Again, the text cuts to Douzi and then Shitou, who continues the act until being released.

From these exercises the film cuts again to an image of Shitou outside in the snow; above his head, he holds a plank upon which rests a bowl of water. The narrative position of this shot suggests that Shitou's action functions as further atonement for his attempt to help Douzi. Its narrative importance will become apparent later in the film when another opera student of the next generation finds himself in a similar situation. When Shitou finally enters the boarding room, Douzi runs over to Shitou in order to hug him with a blanket. The film cuts to a shot of the two boys sleeping in each other's arms.

Although the boys' affection for one another does not take the form of graphic sex, the film suggests very strongly their physical relationship. Indeed the image of the two youths sleeping together recalls hundreds of Hollywood love scenes that culminate in similar shots (the suggestive illustration of the "morning after"). To read this scene as non-erotic, I would contend, requires that we do not ascribe any sexuality to these kids. Not only does Shitou's earlier reference to his penis call attention to such an elision in its implication of children's lewd jokes, but it also reminds the spectator that the objects of the camera's gaze are often the naked bottoms of little boys. A contradiction, at least for American audiences, exists here. Age of consent laws as well as child abuse and kiddie-porn scandals that often dominate headlines in the U.S. reveal much about how we view children and sexuality. Jim Kincaid has explored these issues in detail, arguing that the American media idealizes the child as pure even as it constantly eroticizes it.[5] The idea that children have any subjective sexuality is near-anathema to American culture. That this film, intended for the international, Hollywood-dominated market, sexualizes its children enables the work to subvert the master discourse and to use it simultaneously to deny its depiction of childhood (homo)sexuality, a phenomenon that Hollywood film can visualize but also one which it cannot admit. In fact, much of the critique surrounding this film, as the previous citation from Rayns attests, mentions the absence in the film of the clear homoerotic element found in the novel. But I would suggest that, rather than "evad[ing] the issue altogether," the cinematic text encloses the bulk of the homoeroticism between the protagonists in their pre-adult years. This enclosure functions as a safety mechanism to avoid offending the film's international consumers and thus ensures its success. The ambiguity of the sexual discourse allows spectators to see whatever they like in the film.

Whether we see childhood sexuality or not, child beatings occupy much of the first forty minutes of the film. Laizi and Shitou both receive some form of corporal punishment when asked to recite opera selections from memory. Master Guan and his assistants subsequently hit Douzi in the same manner, a thrashing on the palm of the hand with a wooden ruler. Laizi receives two more subsequent beatings before his death, and Shitou both receives and performs some sort of physical violence before the film moves forward in time to 1937.

To understand the significance of all these beatings, Freud's essay, "A Child Is Being Beaten" proves instructive. However, I do not mean to invoke Freud in a universalist manner. Zhang Jingyuan has labored extensively to reveal the extent to which Freudian ideas penetrated China in the first half of the twentieth century, a time period which corresponds to the male protagonists' attainment of maturity. Zhang has indicated the extent to which Freudian discourse has existed as a steady, if non-dominant, intellectual current in China throughout much of this century. Such importation should evoke little surprise, since, for example, the May Fourth Movement drew on the writings of other Europeans, such as Ibsen and Shaw. In each case, the Chinese intellectual community often borrowed concepts and altered them for their own purposes. Because Chen Kaige is our transnational contemporary, however, I would suggest the appropriateness of my U.S.-centered Freudian analysis. My interest is, after all, in western fantasies manufactured through Chen Kaige's text. Moreover, Freud's construction of the unconscious has permeated western thought, including the technologies of film that China also, we should remember, imported.

Freud's work delineates children's early fantasies of being beaten in two or three phases, divided along gender lines.[6] Girls, he argues, fantasize about physical punishment in three successive stages. In the first stage, the young female recognizes that "My father is beating the child" (Freud, 185). This observation reinforces the child's egoistic interests by indicating the father's lack of love for another youth and thus suggesting, by default, his affection for his daughter. The second level in which the child acknowledges that she is "being beaten by . . . [her] father" emerges during the course of analysis and reflects the daughter's guilt over her incestuous desire. As Freud explains:

> This being beaten is now a convergence of the sense of guilt and sexual love. It is not only the punishment for the forbidden genital relation, but also the regressive substitute for that relation, and from this latter source it derives the libidinal excitation which is from this time forward attached to it. (189)

Thus, this second phase contains a masochistic component; because recognition of this phase occurs only in the process of analysis, however, this masochistic urge is unconscious. The final stage generalizes the girl's specific experience and projects it outward (curiously enough, always onto boys). The fantasy thus concerns boys being beaten, and "the child who produces the phantasy [sic] appears almost as a spectator, while the father persists in the shape of a teacher or some other person in authority" (Freud, 190).

In contrast to this model, Freud writes of only two stages for boys. The first level corresponds to the girl's second stage. Masochism in this case, that is, a son's taking pleasure from his father's beating, signals a homosexual desire that the child must repress. Thus, in the third phase, the boy changes the identity of the beater to the mother in an attempt to evade the homosexuality suggested earlier. However, the boy still remains feminized as the passive recipient of the beating.

All of these developments, as one familiar with Freud would expect, occur very early in the patients' lives. What the film may provide us, then, is a visual reenactment of the characters' fantasies of being beaten. The implications of such a reading are twofold. First, this theorization allows us to understand the emerging subjectivities of the boys in the film. Second, the cinematic spectator becomes implicated in the text's process of on-screen subject formation.

In the first scenario, Douzi seems the most likely candidate for analysis, since his life's trajectory directs the narrative in the film. Assuming that the events in the representation of his childhood portray, in part, an enactment of his fantasies, we find that his development does not readily adhere to either model of beating suggested in the Freudian paradigm. As a boy, Douzi's "father" (Master Guan) does indeed hit him, but this aggression is no illusion. Freud himself, however, noted that violence inflicted by the father "was consciously remembered" in at least one of his male subjects.[7] However, the replacement of the father by the mother never occurs for Douzi. Although Juxian may eventually fill this role, she does not actually beat Douzi in any direct manner, and, while the mother chops off Douzi's extra finger, this amputation occurs before anyone from the Opera troupe has a chance to strike him.

Freud's trajectory of the female beating fantasy, then, seems closer to Douzi's experience. Recall that upon his entry into the opera-training courtyard, Douzi sees Laizi in the process of being spanked. Thus Douzi can identify with either the master or his mother as figures of benevolence, for they do not initially hurt him. The color transformation at that juncture further emphasizes a kind of shift in the film; this change is, at least partially, one of perspective, for the camera begins to take us away from the mother's viewpoint to Douzi himself. Only moments later in the narrative, however, Douzi's mother hacks at his hand with a butcher's knife.

Remember that the next violent scene is that of Shitou's beating, after he has kicked away Douzi's blocks. That scene contains a masochistic element that fits Freud's fantasy for girls except for two factors: Shitou is male, and Douzi is not the "I" being beaten. In regards to the latter issue, the boys seem to endure their beatings simultaneously. The attitude of Shitou enables Douzi to persevere in spite of the pain. Thus, the individual subject formation that Freudian theory posits becomes obscure as the demarcation between Douzi and Shitou dissolves in this scene. That Shitou is male further clouds the gender dichotomization upon which Freud insists. While the novel occasionally refers to the absent mothers of these artists in training and thus enables a stronger Freudian interpretation, the film almost completely elides this issue. Therefore, the film does not allow these boys to displace their erotic attachments onto their mothers.

While logic would suggest that these boys must then circulate in a homo-erotic economy, I would contend that such an explanation fails to account for everything occurring here. As I mentioned before, Douzi and Shitou occasionally find themselves treated as one unit as opposed to differentiated subjects. Certainly this attitude becomes apparent after Douzi and Laizi run away. They return to find all of the boys on benches with their pants down. On the one hand, Douzi thus comes back to Freud's group of boys being beaten. That Douzi replaces all these young men as the recipient of the punishment underscores this point, for Freud argues that all the boys are mere substitutes for the child with the fantasy. However, when Douzi refuses to beg for mercy, Shitou actually attempts a counterattack on Douzi's behalf. For his efforts he receives a cut over the eye. The scar that this cut leaves forever differentiates Douzi from Shitou; Shitou thus resists the passivity of being beaten and his simultaneous feminization. Douzi, on the other hand, takes beatings. Whereas Shitou becomes the aggressor by the end of the childhood scene, actually harming Douzi, Douzi remains feminized and passive. The beatings that initially encourage a reading of homoeroticism in the text, end up reinforcing a subject distinction that mimics gender differentiation. As the dan, Douzi is female; Shitou is his male counterpart.

Chen Kaige's version differs from Lilian Lee's original in this section of Douzi's return. The film only obliquely references the torment inflicted on Douzi by the other boys in the novel. As a result of Douzi's playing female roles, one of Douzi's peers teases, "He isn't really a boy. That's why the Master always has him play girls. Let's see what's inside his pants. Come on, everybody" (48). In trying to defend his friend from this massive sexual exploration, Shitou obtains the scar on his forehead by falling onto a rock. Shitou thus maintains Douzi's private sexuality in the book whereas, in the film, his actions further feminize Douzi.

The boys' performance also receives different treatment in the cinematic medium. Throughout both the novel and film, Douzi expresses great difficulty in memorizing a line from one of the more difficult operas. He constantly mixes up "I am by nature a girl not a boy," reversing the terms girl and boy. Indeed the first time that we see him fail to execute these lines properly, he receives the previously mentioned thrashing on the hand. So terrible is this particular beating that, by the end of the day, he holds up his extremity to reveal it coated in his blood.

Such a visual image recalls, of course, the scene in which a younger Douzi first examined his hand, shorn of its extra digit. The fact that the lines he cannot memorize deal with his perceived sexual identity (his biological sex versus the role that the master wants him to play) indicate, without any subtlety, the extended process of Douzi's castration. The spectator observes him become a "woman" as a result of the external pressures around him.

However, earlier in the film, after the near destruction of his hand by the overzealous master, the text mitigates against the overt feminization of Douzi. From the ruler scene, the text cuts to a bath tub scene. Pairs of boys occupy various tubs; Shitou and Douzi share one between them. Positioned behind Douzi, the larger and older boy grabs his friend's wrist and thrusts it into the water, so it will heal. Shitou's position behind Douzi and his physical manipulation of him on the one hand reinforce Douzi's passivity and his vulnerability. The text foreshadows, through the placement of the two boys, Douzi's later sexual subservience to various patrons. At the same time, Shitou's own sexuality receives questioning; his identity at this point in the film is not clear.

Thus, when Shitou takes the role of beater towards the conclusion of the childhood sequence, he finally locks the boys into the gender roles that they will inhabit for the rest of the film. When Master Ni comes to visit and wishes to hear a brief excerpt, Douzi, in spite of the punishment he has received, switches the gender of "I am by nature a girl, not a boy." Disappointed, Master Ni begins to leave the courtyard. In a rage, Shitou approaches Douzi; his stage brother accuses Douzi of ruining their opportunity to secure a major patron. In a form of lex talionis, Shitou inserts a metal pipe into Douzi's mouth (which Douzi passively receives) and violently injures him, causing blood to drip freely from Douzi's lips. After receiving this punishment from his most beloved friend, Douzi recites the opera perfectly, securing the future patronage of Master Ni.

This scene, absent from the book, further reinscribes a gender dichotomy onto Shitou and Douzi. When the two performers bask in the success of their performance later at the invitation of the old eunuch, Shitou will finally indicate their sexual division verbally. While admiring a particular sword (an object that connotes both the physical power attached to Shitou's role as well as an aesthetic artifact that symbolizes the achievement of financial success), Shitou says, "If I were emperor then you'd be queen of the palace." Thus, no question remains as to Douzi's particular role.

However, *Farewell My Concubine* then provides a scene that once again obscures the relationship between the opera duo. In a scene common to both the novel and cinematic text, Douzi eases the pain that Shitou feels as a result of smearing grease paint onto the scar on his forehead. "With great concern, Xiao Douzi cupped his friend's face between his hands and touched the open cut with his tongue. He sucked at it gently until it stopped hurting" (55). This very intimate act once more suggests the homoeroticism between the two boys, suggesting that they are two individualized subjects sexually involved with each other. Because Douzi is the active agent at this point, the film allows Douzi a measure of (stereotypically masculine) assertiveness.

Almost immediately, the text undercuts this suggestion. In another alteration from the novel, the scene in which the eunuch and Douzi meet becomes a rape. The old man, dressed in dark breeches, a white shirt and a translucent white robe, releases the female concubine from his grasp and moans and motions for Douzi to come closer. The eunuch's lips stained red with lipstick and his disheveled gray hair (he is quite old) combined with the man's dress primarily in a color that suggests death and mourning marks him with a certain vampire-like quality. The eunuch in fact proceeds to pursue Douzi around the room in a brief chase until Douzi finally succumbs to the old man on the bed. Here the film gives us a medium long shot of Douzi sprawled on the bed with his patron descending onto him.

In the novel, Master Ni engages in sexual activity with the boy.

> Master Ni beckoned Xiao Douzi to come closer and set him on his lap. Tenderly but playfully, he began stroking Xiao Douzi's face and pinching his buttocks in an almost maternal fashion . . . he suddenly lost his sense and put the boy's penis in his mouth. He sucked and sucked. Xiao Douzi's eyes widened and his mouth was dry. (56-57)

The fellatio in this scene occurs after Master Ni watches the young boy urinate into a jade white bowl that the man holds specifically for that purpose. While both scenes may connote some level of exploitation, the film clearly strips Douzi of any agency. His frantic fleeing contrasts strongly against the parallel point in the book that serves as a marker of Douzi's awakening homosexual desire as much as it does Douzi's sexual abuse.

In denying Douzi agency, the filmic text uses a traditional model of gendered opposition that codes the feminine figure as passive and the male as assertive, if not aggressive. The beating scenes in the film further reinforce this differentiation, but they also contain a contradiction. As a male, Douzi most closely exemplifies the female beating fantasy; a disjuncture thus occurs between theory and representation. However, the possibility remains that Douzi embodies both female and male as a transgender figure. Chen Kaige's work seems to insist on the denial of this possibility with its constant referral to sexual polarities. Furthermore, the bulk of play that does occur between the two opera stars happens when they are children. The intimacies that Xiaolou and Dieyi share as children stop almost entirely when the film jumps to their adult lives. Even the playful squeeze that Dieyi gives his stage brother, as an adult, occurs before Juxian's entrance.

Thus the significance of Juxian's entrance lies in its timing in the film. Almost immediately after the boys become men, Juxian appears. Her arrival eclipses the homoerotic overtones that pervaded the childhood sequence and further strengthen the gender differentiation between the men. In an ever-increasing manner, the film suggests that Xiaolou's earlier affection for Dieyi was familial in nature. Juxian thus acts as the counter that determines the fate of Xiaolou's sexuality. At the same time, Dieyi's sexual role becomes more tightly bound to the opera and decadent, if necessary, art. Dieyi maintains this art (as opposed to homosexuality) in what becomes a political narrative structured over gender.

The film exposes this prioritizing at various key moments. When Master Guan dies leaving one of his apprentices, Xiao Si, holding a plank on top of which sits a basin of water, Dieyi takes him in (much as he had held Shitou at a visually parallel scene in the text). However, whereas the novel makes it quite explicit that Xiao Si assumes the role of a subordinate to Dieyi in both artistic and sexual terms, the film elides any overt discussion of Xiao Si's sexuality. This elision serves to enable Xiao Si's unproblematic castigation of his benefactor once the Cultural Revolution begins.

In Dieyi's trial for singing for the Japanese in order to obtain Xiaolou's release, the film deletes another key phrase present in the novel. Lee's text allows Dieyi a powerful assertion that "art does not recognize the limits of nationality" (159). With these words, Dieyi demonstrates the potential power of the transgender trope. As Marjorie Garbor observes in *Vested Interests*, "transvestism is a space of possibility structuring and confounding culture" (17). Because the transgender crosses boundaries of sexual division, he (in this case) is also the perfect figure to represent the permeable boundaries of nations and the very intercultural nature of art that enables it as a force of unity in times of political upheaval.[8] In Chen's work, the best that Dieyi manages is to assert that no one beat him, although he also hates the Japanese. By weakening Dieyi's claim, Chen maintains a denunciation of the Japanese invasion of China, but he also limits the possibilities that Dieyi's gender possibilities create.

A similar move occurs near the conclusion of the film when Juxian, Xiaolou and Dieyi march out in the streets for public ridicule under the orders of the Red Guard. At the conclusion of the degrading parade, the three characters must confess their crimes against China. Xiaolou takes his prized sword (that Dieyi had obtained and presented to him on his wedding night) and throws it into the flames. In the book, Dieyi recovers this symbol of his partner's heterosexuality. In the film, the sword that Dieyi received as a gift from one of the patrons who successfully courted him, lies in the flames until Juxian rushes in to retrieve it. Thus she serves as the preserver of phallic masculinity for her husband even while she maintains Dieyi's memory of prostitution by reclaiming the object for which he had sold himself and which had served to maintain the relationship between the two men.

This scene also parallels one from the childhood sequence when Douzi replaces Shitou and the other boys as the bearer of punishment.

> In the childhood episode, each of the two boys hastens to shield the other by bearing the punishment himself. In the later episode, each instead vies to heap the blame on the other This, then, is the film's indictment against the Cultural Revolution. (Chen, 86)

The film finally then comments on the destruction of kinship ties valued in Confucian society at the same time that it allows Juxian to reinforce Dieyi's position as a decadent homosexual, whose transvestite tendencies become implicated in the characters' declines.

Finally returning to 1977 when the film began, Chen Kaige once again alters Lilian Lee's text. Whereas the novel allows the two opera stars a final chance reunion in Hong Kong that ends in Dieyi's returning to China, the film concludes with one final reenactment of *Farewell My Concubine*. Dieyi finally blurs the distinction between himself and his fantastic role by taking his own life at the end of the number. This melodramatic ending suggests that the transvestite figure, finally unable to become the idealized woman, takes his own life in frustration. Thus, the neat and tidy conclusion avoids the problematics of dealing with an alternative gendered subjectivity. Chen Kaige's film, then, prepares itself for an international market in which complicated notions of gender are subsumed by larger discourses of politics that elide, and perhaps even eliminate, the potential ruptures offered earlier in the film. The narrative's tracing of the emergence of China as a nation-state in its current form thus coincides with the assertion of heterosexuality.

Identification with this particular film, therefore, potentially situates a spectator in a heterosexual frame of reference. The inflation of Gong Li's character transforms the novel's narrative of two men and their relationship into Dieyi's challenge to heterosexual normativity, which the text uses to ground the advent of the communist revolution. Such a positioning imbues the text with a political valence that plays on a western, particularly Hollywood-derived, tradition of anti-communism, even as it critiques the older Chinese regime for its decadence. The transnational attention that this film received, then, seems linked to the foregrounding of gender dynamics that conceal a strongly anti-Chinese political undertone.

In the U.S., the gendered thematics of the film occupy the bulk of commentary on the text, for representation and sexuality are highly contested ground in our national context (the NEA debates in the early nineties provide evidence of this fact). We must therefore ask, what is at stake in the highlighting or occlusion of sexuality in these gender discussions? Writing in *The New Yorker* for example, Terrence Rafferty asserts that "These men aren't lovers, but Cheng is fiercely possessive; he obviously believes that their offstage lives should reflect the exclusivity of their on-stage relationship as concubine and king" (122). In a similar vein, a review in *Maclean's* argues that *Farewell My Concubine* is "the story of a lifelong bond between two male opera stars," and continues on to my favorite moment of the critics' reviews: "their platonic relationship unfolds against a shifting panorama of upheaval . . . The two men are the Lennon and McCartney of the Peking Opera and she [Juxian] steps in like Yoko Ono" (Johnson, 928).

In contrast, looking at the same film, *Newsweek* describes it as a "frank look at homosexuality" (Ansen et al., 74). *Commentary* writes that "Dieyi, "a homosexual, wants to be Xiaolou's concubine in real life" (Grenier, 51). If we are not yet confused by these divergent opinions, *Commonwealth* adds that "it is as a 'female' that he [Dieyi] is forced to function both off stage and on" (Alleva, 16). Often mired in misogyny and homophobia, the reviews often contradict themselves, that is literally within the same article, in attempting to locate Dieyi's sexuality. The artistic Dieyi comes to stand for traditional Chinese art that is at once oppressive and decadent albeit committed to a high aesthetic standard. In contrast, his former partner represents the submission to a communist government that also seems oppressive and overzealous albeit committed to a strong political stance.

The point here is not to chastise the critics so much as it is to point out the ambiguities generated by this text. Chen's intertwining of gender and politics confounds superficial analysis. Perhaps, what the American critical audience knows is that, as one voice in *New York* magazine opines, sex is something "about which the film-makers seem rather confused" (Denby, 84). The ambiguity in regard to sexuality in this film enables, as I have pointed out, certain political representations to run in the background. The problem, of course, as the aforementioned reviewer notes, is that "[t]he way the movie-makers present it there's something creepy about homosexuality itself; the film-maker portrays a shocked attitude toward sex. At least gay sex" (Denby, 85). Chen Kaige has, of course, heard similar criticisms and has responded by saying "it was not his movie's central subject–betrayal was" (Zha, 35). Such a statement, however, still leaves the audience with some unsettling impressions of what same-sex eroticism might mean in China.

Recall that, of the three main characters, the only one left standing at the film's conclusion is the heterosexually-defined Xiaolou. Embedded in the construction of heterosexuality, even tragic heterosexuality, the transmission of modern (that is, post-1949) Chinese culture rests with him as the credits roll. Women and men of deviant sexuality have been wiped out, murdered in the scope of the epic. As one who tries to identify with that deviantly-delimited sexual character, a representation of such a fantasy seems bleak indeed.

But I remember that Xiaolou has also suffered in a labor camp. The former king has also, to some extent, fallen in this narrative. The target of Chen's critique, therefore, seems to be a Chinese government that allows for no deviation from a norm. As a former artist, who betrothed a prostitute, Xiaolou might thus fall into the category of the oppressed. Recognizing the irony of this assertion, I would like to suggest that yet another review, this time from Lawrence Chua writing in *The Nation*, suggests a way forward. Chua notes, that "As boys, the two are lovers . . . While Chen's camera shies away from the physical dimensions of Dieyi's sexual relationship with Xiaolou, the film does allow for a more emotional concept of identity, one that refuses to be colonized by European and American notions of queerness" (38).

Although I think Chua's conclusion is a bit too idealistic, I also realize that his comments serve to mark the boundaries of my own study. Thus, a way forward for me involves acknowledging *Farewell My Concubine's* ambivalence in its representations of sexuality. I would suggest that the very contradictions among the reviews register the complexities of viewing this transnational cultural product.

Whatever the film says of gender, however, its critique of the government is not so subtle. *Farewell My Concubine* had difficulty in reaching the Chinese audience because of a difference in perceptions, one might say of fantasies, of what constitutes the "real." What I have found after examining this film is that placing myself in my grandparents' "homeland" to claim a certain identity also failed because of differing notions of what constitutes Chinese-ness. Their China is historically-specific, tied to an era that no longer exists. My attempt to connect to that culture through transnational media images or a direct, historically-specific experience must always, therefore, be a misrecognition. But if such transhistorical representation is primarily possible through fantasy, then is diaspora necessarily contingent on kinship? *Farewell My Concubine* suggests that the answer is no and gives fantasy a constitutive role in transnational identity production.

NOTES

1. The "fifth generation" are all graduates of the 1982 class of the Beijing Film Academy. They are the first class to graduate in the post-Mao era and, because of this, their films make a stylistic and thematic break from the previous social realism that dominated China's national cinema. The fifth generation's best known representatives are Chen Kaige and Zhang Yimou.

2. "Transgender" is a fluid category independent of sexual orientation. People who fall into the "transgender" category include cross-dressers and transvestites as well as pre-operative, post-operative and non-operative transsexuals (the last group consists of those individuals whose gender identities do not match their biological sex, but who do not, for whatever reason, wish to have an operation in order to physically alter themselves).

3. The "dan" is the name given to male actors who play female parts in Beijing Opera.

4. See the "works cited" for the citation. Xu argues that Concubine Yu "becomes an aesthetic figure of the affinity of prostitution and the Peking Opera" (165). Because "Dieyi offers himself promiscuously to all regardless of national or ideological difference . . . his dedication to art emphasizes the prostitutional nature of art" (Xu, 165). Juxian, on the other hand, becomes in this analysis "a prostitute in the worst sense of the term. She is an abominable creature . . . doomed to be contaminated and contaminating, a disfiguring social threat regardless of whether or not she is a dedi-

cated wife to Xiaolou. Thus the film works with and against the social presentation of prostitution as an irreversible descent into degradation, and the prostitute as irreparably fallen" (Xu, 167).

5. For detailed discussions of children's sexuality, see the work of James Kincaid, specifically *Erotic Innocence: The Culture of Child Molesting* (Durham and London: Duke University Press, 1998) and *Child-Loving: The Erotic Child and Victorian Culture* (New York: Routledge, 1992).

6. As is typical for Freud's work, this paper evolved from observations of a paucity of case studies (six, to be exact).

7. Since Freud's paper is based on only two males and four females, Douzi's experiences may not be as exceptional as they initially seem.

8. I do not mean to suggest that the transvestite is always a figure of liberation. Male domination of the stage in Beijing opera reveals the lowly status assigned to women, who were unfit for the theater. For purposes of this argument, however, I am interested in the circulation of *Farewell My Concubine* in the U.S., to an audience largely unfamiliar with historical stage conventions and their reasons for being.

WORKS CITED

Alleva, Richard. "Behind the Red Curtain: Chen's 'Farewell My Concubine.'" *Commonwealth* 120.21 (1993): 15-16.

Ansen, David, Deirdre Nickerson, and Marcus Mabry. "The Real Cultural Revolution." *Newsweek* 122.18 (1993): 74.

Chua, Lawrence. "Queer Wind From Asia." *The Nation* 257.1 (1993): 38-41.

Chen, Pauline. "History Lessons." *Film Comment* 30.2 (1994): 85-87.

Corliss, Richard. "Asian Invasion: The film world embraces a bonanza of new talent from Taiwan, Hong Kong and mainland China." *Time* 146.7 (1995): 62-66.

"The Death of Hsiang Yu." Trans. Burton Watson.

Denby, David. A Half-Century at the Opera. *New York* 26.42 (1993): 84-85.

Garbor, Marjorie. *Vested Interests: Cross-dressing and cultural anxiety.* New York: Routledge, 1992.

Grenier, Richard. "Enter the Chinese." *Commentary* 97.5 (1994): 49-52.

Johnson, Brian D. "The Red and the Restless: Soap opera unfolds in the Peking Opera." *Maclean's* 106.46 (1993): 928.

Kincaid, Jim. *Erotic Innocence: The Culture of Child Molesting.* Durham: Duke University Press, 1998.

_____ . *Child-Loving: The Erotic Child and Victorian Culture.* New York: Routledge, 1992

Lau, Jenny Kwok Wah. "Farewell My Concubine: History, Melodrama, and Ideology in Contemporary Pan-Chinese Cinema." *Film Quarterly* 49.1 (1995): 16-27.

Lee, Jeeyeun. "Toward a Queer Korean American Diasporic History," in *Q & A: Queer in Asian America,* ed. David L. Eng and Alice Y. Hom. Philadelphia: Temple University Press, 1998.

Lee, Lilian. *Farewell to My Concubine.* Trans. Andrea Ligenfelter. New York: William Morrow and Company, Inc., 1993.

Lu, Sheldon Hsiao-peng, ed. *Transnational Chinese Cinemas: Identity, Nationhood, Gender.* Honolulu: University of Hawaii Press, 1997.

Nickerson, Deirdre L. and Todd Lappin. "Frustration in Peking: Chinese directors win acclaim abroad but not at home." *Far Eastern Economic Review* 156.32 (1993): 56-57.

Rafferty, Terrence. "Blind Faith." *The New Yorker* 33 (1993): 121-123.

Rayns, Tony. "Ba Wang Bie Ji (Farewell My Concubine)." *Sight and Sound* 4.1 (1994): 41-42.

Volpp, Sophie. "Gender, Power and Spectacle in Late-Imperial Chinese Theater." *Gender Reversals and Gender Cultures: Anthropological and historical perspectives.* ed. Sabrina Petra Ramet. London and New York: Routledge, 1996.

Xu, Ben. "Farewell My Concubine and Its Nativist Critics." *Quarterly Review of Film and Video* 16.2 (1997): 155-170.

Zha, Jianying. "Chen Kaige and the Shadows of the Revolution." *Sight and Sound* 4.2 (1994): 28-36.

Zhang, Jingyuan. *Psychoanalysis in China: Literary Transformations, 1919-1949.* Ithaca: Cornell University Press, 1992.

Zhang, Xudong. *Chinese Modernism in the Era of Reforms.* Durham and London: Duke University Press, 1997.

The Outcasts:
A Family Romance

Timothy Liu

William Paterson University

SUMMARY. The following short impression is meant to be neither academic nor comprehensive. It is, rather, just that–an impression, a series of floating thoughts on a film that sticks in the mind. *[Article copies available for a fee from The Haworth Document Delivery Service: 1-800-342-9678. E-mail address: <getinfo@haworthpressinc.com> Website: <http://www.HaworthPress. com>]*

Founded on Confucian principles, the family unit plays a central role in Chinese societies. If one cannot govern at home, then peace and prosperity can hardly be expected to abound abroad. Likewise, to be thrown out of one's house is tantamount to being exiled from one's homeland. This is the condition Li Ching finds himself in at the beginning of *The Outcasts*[1] (Taiwan, 1986, directed by Yu Kan-ping). Expelled from high school after being caught by a security guard *in flagrante delicto* in a chemistry lab, this adolescent bottom boy is subsequently run out of his home by a screaming father

Timothy Liu's book of poems, *Vox Angelica* (Alice James Books), received the 1992 Norma Farber First Book Award from the Poetry Society of America. His subsequent books, *Burnt Offerings* (Copper Canyon Press, 1995) and *Say Goodnight* (Copper Canyon Press, 1998) were both finalists for a Lambda Literary Award. He is the editor of *Word of Mouth: An Anthology of Gay American Poetry* (forthcoming from Talisman House) and contributes frequent reviews to *Art Papers, New Art Examiner* and *Publishers Weekly*. Liu is currently an Assistant Professor of English at William Paterson University.

[Haworth co-indexing entry note]: "*The Outcasts:* A Family Romance." Liu, Timothy. Co-published simultaneously in *Journal of Homosexuality* (The Haworth Press, Inc.) Vol. 39, No. 3/4, 2000, pp. 233-235; and: *Queer Asian Cinema: Shadows in the Shade* (ed: Andrew Grossman) Harrington Park Press, an imprint of The Haworth Press, Inc., 2000, pp. 233-235. Single or multiple copies of this article are available for a fee from The Haworth Document Delivery Service [1-800-342-9678, 9:00 a.m. - 5:00 p.m. (EST). E-mail address: getinfo@haworthpressinc.com].

233

who thrashes him with a rod. Shivering under a blanket of newspapers in the corner of a park, A-Ching is rescued at nightfall by Master Yang, a gay father figure *cum* role model who has not infrequently brought home such stray boys, much to the consternation of Man Yi, a likeable maternal fag-hag landlady that Yang rescued years earlier form her heroin addiction. Adopted into this new family, A-Ching eventually heals from his disgrace, and following the death of Yang, returns to his own father–an imposing Job-like figure who has lost both his wife (to adultery and disease) and his other son (to pneumonia) by movie's end. What started out as a dysfunctional family of four gradually gets reduced to a prodigal pair. What then has become of our Confucian family ideal?

An image that recurs throughout the movie is that of a lone crane flying across the sky but never landing. Often accompanied by music and voice-overs, this crane comes to represent not only an outcast homosexual but anyone who is also searching for comfort and rest to no avail. The need to belong becomes more of a journey than a destination. Indeed, the only sure destination is that of the grave–everything else is up for grabs. At the heart of *The Outcasts* lies our common enemy: passionate living. It is lust that lures A-Ching's mother away from family and home. It is a jealous rage that makes the Dragon stab the tattooed heart of the ill-fated A-Feng. Without a sense of moderation or clear proportion, things tend to run amok. We witness A-Ching's father hurling down the clay urn filled with his wife's remains. But we also watch Man Yi lay down the household laws of chores and rent in order to bring stability back to their newfound adoptive family. Even after Yang's fatal heart attack, we observe the surviving members of his "family" burning incense and paying proper respect to his departed spirit. What *The Outcasts* seems to suggest is the necessity for accepting certain Confucian forms and virtues even if such virtues also form the basis for intolerance.

Throughout the film, we encounter flashlight-wielding security guards, whether in a high school chemistry lab (designed for educational "experiments") or a public park rife with cruising (a quasi-religious site where the Dragon offers up his human sacrifice). Both the religious and scientific aspects of homosexuality are hinted at in these contexts. Even at the police station, an interrogating officer seems fixated on classifying each boy as either a "yin" or a "yang"–apparently a kind of Taoist Taiwanese slang for a "bottom" or a "top." Our last encounter with the police takes place at the Blue Angel, Mr. Yang and Man Yi's newly-opened gay bar wherein the madly jealous and drunken Dragon King is restrained from cutting up another patron with the jagged neck of a broken bottle. Here, the presence of the police seems protective rather than punitive. Indeed, the Blue Angel exists as a kind of heavenly abode which not only keeps our boys employed and off the streets but creates and environment where homosexual love is nurtured rather than outlawed. The turning point is amplified by the Dragon's wish for A-Ching to be his "little brother" rather than another doomed lover (A-Ching's own little brother, Tiwa, was beloved by his mother after all). With both the Dragon and Man Yi in his life as surrogate brother and mother, respectively, A-Ching is able to return to his own father bearing gifts.

NOTE

1. With *The Outcasts* (1986), director Yu Kan-ping was considered to have made Taiwan's first commercial gay feature film. The film's English title is also sometimes known as "The Outsiders." (Ed.)

Homosexual Men (and Lesbian Men) in a Heterosexual Genre: Three Gangster Films from Hong Kong

Andrew Grossman

SUMMARY. Of the East Asian film genres that have captured the attention of film goers internationally, it should be of little surprise that martial and heroically masculine genres have been the most popular, for violent action translates well into any language. Although it has been no secret that male martiality often leaks into homoerotic desire (on the part of the audience, too), three Hong Kong films from 1998 have finally explicated the generic homosexuality that the action genre has been (defensively) ashamed to admit all along. However, rather than posit this textual homosexuality as transgressive, the generic forces under which these films operate rewrite their homosexualities, both gay and lesbian, into generic modes fashioned around regressive oppositions of gender, and not progressive liberations of sexuality. *[Article copies available for a fee from The Haworth Document Delivery Service: 1-800-342-9678. E-mail address: <getinfo@ haworthpressinc.com> Website: <http://www.HaworthPress.com>]*

Both in the East and West, homoerotic male bonding has been such an historically ubiquitous feature of action film genres that its "activation" into open homosexuality was probably only an eventuality. From the self-professed male love story of Howard Hawks's *Red River* (1948) to the *chambara's* chaste samurai homosocially devoted to his patriarchal lord, action

Andrew Grossman, MA, studied film and philosophy at Sarah Lawrence College, followed by a Master's Degree in English and Creative Writing from Rutgers University. He is currently working on writing projects that attempt to cross and synthesize the genres of avant-garde theater, the screenplay, and cultural criticism. His writing has appeared in *American Book Review.* (E-mail: morgold@webtv.net)

[Haworth co-indexing entry note]: "Homosexual Men (and Lesbian Men) in a Heterosexual Genre: Three Gangster Films from Hong Kong." Grossman, Andrew. Co-published simultaneously in *Journal of Homosexuality* (The Haworth Press, Inc.) Vol. 39, No. 3/4, 2000, pp. 237-271; and: *Queer Asian Cinema: Shadows in the Shade* (ed: Andrew Grossman) Harrington Park Press, an imprint of The Haworth Press, Inc., 2000, pp. 237-271. Single or multiple copies of this article are available for a fee from The Haworth Document Delivery Service [1-800-342-9678, 9:00 a.m. - 5:00 p.m. (EST). E-mail address: getinfo@haworthpressinc.com].

genres have frequently pitted their male heroes against the presumably stifling roles of heterosexuality.[1] Of course, these are two different classifications of homosexuality, the American Western hero a protocapitalist who is
alienated and individuated from the demands of familial (heterosexual) civili-
zation, and the samurai the very product of a conventionalized hierarchy,
which, unlike Western systems, celebrates male same-sex bonds. The patriar-
chally sexist effects of Eastern and Western homosexualities are practically
similar; for our purposes, the main difference is not the primary cause *per se*
but the legality or illegality of the context in which homosexuality is enacted
and rationalized. In 1998, three crime films in particular from Hong Kong
embodied and redefined the tropes of homosexuality and its (il)legality within contemporary HK action genres: Johnnie To Kei-fung's *A Hero Never
Dies*, Clarence Fok Yiu Leung's *Cheap Killers*, and Raymond Yip Wai-man's
Portland Street Blues.[2] These three films, and especially the two latter,
though partly derived from Chinese generic modes, transcend boundaries of
causation to become effectively valid across international genre axes. The
theses of these films, then, will become equally valid for the American (or
Indian or Mexican or Philippino, etc.) action films whose effects, if not
causations, they share.

   The normative constructions of the gangster-crime genre[3] have paradoxically afforded male homosexual play within its already deviant and legally
transgressive parameters, while compensating for and limiting the dangers of
that play by defining heroic masculinity in terms of a fundamental, knee-jerk
homophobia. A swordsman, cop, cowboy, gangster, or wanderer, in infinitely
legal or illegal sociohistorical contexts, may temporarily shift his gaze from
the ostensible heterosexual love interest the conventional genre film foists
upon him to the male co-star whose companionship he will embrace, but the
genre in which he is constructed will always pull out the rug from under him.
It is as if the genre sadistically plays with the ambiguity of the hero's
constructed masculinity and then becomes threatened by its possible implications–lest that homosexual play become *too* free, such that the hero will
revolt against its generic creator and actualize the homosexuality he is being
forced to repress. In the end, heterosexuality (or sexual abstinence, as in the
Hollywood Western) always triumphs, and homosexuality remains but a
subtext to be analyzed and proven with only painstaking measures. The
repression of the male homosexual code is perhaps epitomized in a surprisingly open dialogue between the two young heroes of Poon Man Kit's *City
Kids* (1989): "We date together, go to prison together. We may even die
together." The other hero jokingly asks: "Are we gay?" to which the other
responds, "Gay? Besides my dad, you're my only choice." But jokes, subtexts, and semi-denials may be a thing of the past. *A Hero Never Dies*, though
still operating in subtext, satirizes the homophobic formula by enacting it

with embarrassing transparency, exposing the nakedness of its skeleton; *Cheap Killers* and *Portland St. Blues* go beyond poker-faced satire to openly (textually) transgress the genre with militantly homosexual outlaw heroes. In terms of a progressive homosexuality, the only value of genre normativity is that it can be transgressed, for the rules of genre film-making are themselves a "legality" which oppresses invisible filmic minorities, even more so than the normativity of the practical society that film-making reflects and perpetuates. The avowed functions of genre are a mirror of society's legal functions–genre is law. Or, the artistic conventions of genre film are tantamount to the foundations of conventional (social) law–especially since many social taboos are illegal not because they are innately wrong but because sociologically determined aesthetics (such as religion) construct them as such.

In most "progressive" mainstream gay films, homosexuality must be defended against a society which seeks to illegalize it. In the crime film, a subcategory of the action film, the argument of homosexuality's legality is enacted within the already illegal, antisocial underworld of criminals: here, homosexuality is meta-criminality. It is taboo, or "illegal," both in legal society and the illegal gangster society that exists within (or beneath) it. Theoretically, legal society's equation of criminality with homosexuality might allow (male) homosexuality to exist more freely in an already transgressive (criminal) society populated by outcasts who may be sympathetic to homosexuals. Realistically, however, organized crime systems react against the anarchic possibilities of absolute illegality and erect quasi-legal statutes of their own similar in form (if different in content) to the social laws they oppose, thus creating an antisocial law. As part of a film genre, the morality of the outlaw hero must balance the scales of his criminal status, such that his noble subjectivity will be valued over the morality of the law he violates. The outlaw hero wins the audience's hearts because his personal code of ethics is morally higher than society's, either despite or because of his law-breaking. The gangster-hero's morality must be excessive, lest the romanticization of the gangster be nihilistic.

In individualistic Hollywood films, the gangster hero must live by a high set of personalized ethics to compensate for his illegality–or pay the consequences. Thus, in Hawks's *Scarface* (1930/2) or Walsh's *White Heat* (1949), Muni and Cagney must die because their incestuous desires are *too* transgressive, and do not bespeak of the kind of personal morality required to tip the scales in their favor. The non-individualistic (cinematic) Hong Kong gangster, however, lives by *yi*, a sworn code of martial brotherhood and loyalty usually not found in legal society. If he fails to abide by *yi*, he must face the grave consequences of his selfishness–for example, Waise Lee's villain in John Woo's *Bullet in the Head* (1990), who fatalistically places gold above friendship. Yet the genre's own morality superseding the (im)morality of its hero, should his transgressions become too extreme, can also adjust to the relative politics of the times: "Bonnie and Clyde" in Penn's atypically liberal gangster film (1967) must die not because of their free sexuality,[4] but because they are responsible for civilian deaths, an obvious taboo during the Vietnam War era. Organized legality can also enact the same morality from the opposite side of the mirror: in John Woo's *Hardboiled* (1992), Tony Leung is an undercover cop who walks, and eventually trips over, the thin line between crime and law. When he accidentally yet unforgivably shoots a cop in the film's climax, we know it will be he and not his perfectly superheroic partner Chow Yun-fat who will be martyred in the end, as an example of how *not* to enforce laws.

In Johnnie To's *A Hero Never Dies* (1998), the heroes do in fact die because they are too homosexual. Homosexuality, the most eternal and unchanging of the genre's taboos, intersects on the axis of illegality (taboo) for both organized lawfulness and organized crime (in reality as in films). Because the perceived status (and attractiveness) of criminality revolves around active male potency and strength, organized crime must overcompensate for the threat of illegal or "weak" sexualities (in an already illegal world) with a safety net of overdetermined and overdemonstrative heterosexuality. In genre film, relationships are divided into the hegemonically strong or the transgressively weak. Homosocial friendships must be in terms of rivalry (strength), not erotic love (weakness), the ostensible prize always being a normatively objectified woman (or money, which is the means to get women).

Within the criminal underworld's reactionary masculinity, homosexuality is a legal transgression within a host universe of *a priori* legal transgression. Because transgression itself is necessarily anarchic, a meta-anarchy (or meta-transgression) will involve the uncontrollability and unpredictability of two variables (the anarchy of homosexuality compounded with the anarchy of criminality). It is only within this two-variable system that homosexuality will be allowed enough free play to be able to transgress the irrationalism of genre's prejudices. The 'threat' of homosexuality will take advantage of the unpredictability of a 2-variable equation to "sneak out" into the open. Thus it is in the crime film that the action genre's heretofore ambiguous homosexuality moves from subtext to text. When the day comes in which an iconic (male) figure of hegemonic *legality*–say a Wong Fei-hong or a Dirty Harry–is openly gay, things will be quite different.

Johnnie To's *A Hero Never Dies* apparently lacks the self-congratulatory deconstructionist irony of *The Longest Night* and *Too Many Ways to Be #1* (1998/1997),[5] two films that were also produced by his Milkway Image company which seek to decode (and recode) triad-film formulae. But this is deceptive; whereas those films were, say, post-Godardian in their self-conscious subversion of formal narrative, the codes *Hero* is concerned with are not narrative ones in and of themselves, but the sex/gender coding necessarily built into that linear narrative design. If accepted at face value, the second half of *A Hero*'s narrative is a pointlessly predictable exercise from a director better known for his non-ironic sentimentality. As a tragedy, the film doesn't work as do To's other melodramas[6] because its tragic arc is manufactured, not organic; only if accepted as meta-narrative is the film successful, and meaningful.

A Hero Never Dies, superficially in the vein of the post-John Woo gunplay subgenre, preoccupies itself with the ambiguity of its character relationships to redefine the genre not in terms of traditional plot schemata but in terms of homosexuality. The plot is divided into two halves, the first original and the second a string of cliches; so recognizable and pre-ordained are these cliches that we must use the originality of first half to understand the meaning of the otherwise pointless second. It soon becomes obvious, however, that the predictability of the second half is an intentionality that lays bare the obviousness of generic homosexual codes. The obviousness of the laws of action-genre plotting and the obviousness of the feared sexual transgression of the heroes are linked inextricably in the genre's demands, and the realization of this link is the hinge of the film's meaning.

Two professional killers, Jack and Martin, work for feuding gang bosses but nevertheless share a private relationship of sexual taunting, both friendly and fatalistic. A series of sexual symbols suggests the repressed homosexuality of their game-playing:[7] the laser sight of Martin's rifle playing lovingly over Jack's prone head, or the ramming of the fronts of their cars into each other (neither car is willing to be taken "from the rear"). Martin is even dressed in a cowboy hat, as if to explicate the film's connection with the famously homosocial (or, as in *Red River*, homosexual) action-world of the American Western. They meet to share each other's wine, seeing whose is better–that the red wine symbolizes the "sharing" of their blood is made blatant when their wounded bartender later bleeds over the glasses. Not sanctioned by their respective (heterosexist) gangs, these meetings exist in a limbo of undefined sexuality, an illegal space within the underworld. Their loyal girlfriends bring the wine to their meetings, as if they were keepers of the mens' blood–yet the men are clearly more interested in each other. The legal heterosexuality of the straw-women becomes the familiar transitive device of illegal homosexuality between the real-men. Thus reality (the mens' desire) and legality (the rules the generic plot must follow) are polarized.

The climax of their meta-illegal gamesmanship is "legalized" in the film's middle, an elaborate shootout in which Jack and Martin are double crossed by their bosses, mostly because they have been secretly seeing each other without their bosses' knowledge. Although justifiably unsanctioned because their

meetings interfere with the bosses' attempted peace negotiations, subtextually they are punished because the illegality of their secret (sexual) space
threatens the avowed heterosexism of the triad lifestyle. Their games become
legalized when they–and their sexual tension–are moved from their erotically
private space to the sanctioned manliness of open violence; yet it is only
within this violently legalized space that the mortality–and thus the full
reality–of their desire can surface. During this gun battle, they spy each other
through either side of a wall's small hole. The wall is the barrier preventing
their homosexual union, and the hole an anus offering up a consummation; as
men of overdetermined masculine strength (i.e., violence), however, they will
reconcile their unresolved homoerotic tension with bullets. They shoot
though the wall, their phallic bullets opening up the wall's anal entrance
larger and larger until they can see each other more clearly (their vision of
homosexuality is actualized), and continue riddling each other with lead.
Because the genre demands they masochistically express their interest in
each other with strong violence and not weak love, they are trapped in a
(straight) world dooming them from the start. After the shootout, both are left
mortally wounded.

Thus begins the second, intentionally cliched half of the film. Jack and
Martin conveniently recuperate at a hospital; the narrative disjunction between the fade-out which saw them left for dead and the hospital they now
magically appear in clearly demarcates the film's two halves. Jack's girlfriend manages to rescue him from his ex-boss's assassins, but in the process
endures a horribly and melodramatically disfiguring fire. Meanwhile, Martin
has had both legs amputated–a castration–and his girlfriend must care for
him. Jack cares for his burned girlfriend and Martin's girlfriend cares for him;
the disabilities are according to heterosexist axes of power, i.e., removal of
masculine power (independence, potency) and female power (beautiful skin).
At this point, sexual desire is coded through dominance and submission–one
of each heterosexual pair is disabled, and soon enough both women will die
so that Martin can substitute for Jack's girlfriend. Thus, the device of transitive homosexuality progresses to the next level of symbolism. Maleness
being defined by potency and action, not biology, Martin the amputee is
effectively feminized. Later, when he attempts to assassinate his boss, he will
continually fail because he is now a "woman" in a man's world. More so,
trapped in his wheelchair he will become lifeless, statue-like, not merely
impotent but an emasculated corpse.

The plot continues: Martin's woman is shot dead by his ex-boss. She
attempts to be heroically masculine as she stands up for Martin against his
ex-boss, but as a (heterosexual) woman, she has no chance. Jack's girlfriend,
meanwhile, begs to be put to death to end her suffering. Yet the women's
roles–and especially that of Jack's girlfriend, who has only two significant

scenes after she is burnt–are apparently disposable, characters constructed only to obfuscate the central section of the film before they can conveniently be disposed of. The death of the women is the cue for the two men to unite in order to destroy their ex-bosses in the customary final act. The overdetermination of the second half forces the audience to bide its time until the underdeveloped women are disposed of, such that the "real" (i.e., male) action can begin. The hyperbole of Jack's girlfriend's suffering, in fact, is only to pathetically compensate an underdeveloped character who would not otherwise warrant pathos.

In Woo's seminal *The Killer* (1989),[8] the sexual relationship between cop and killer is predicated on morality: the admiration Danny Lee's cop has for Chow Yun-fat's killer threatens to disrupt the former's chaste heterosexuality, delivering him over to the side of a homoerotic criminality. In the lawless, amoral world of *Hero*, the only hope for the characters' survival is their interdependent bond in an otherwise nihilistic universe. Contrary to Woo, *A Hero*'s gunplay, though stylized, is antiromantic, first signalled when the heroes dryly (and complimentarily) shoot a wizened, wicked fortune-teller in either of his feet. The homosocial bond of loyal male honor, *yi*,[9] exists as a natural condition in Woo, as in most HK gangster films. In *Hero*, however, there is no real *yi*, only self-interest, for Jack and Martin only reunite when all other options, including those that involve their women, have failed them. Jack and Martin's final bond, through which they will indeed kill the villains, is both desperate and perfunctory, qualities which only parody the idea of *yi*. After Martin loses his legs and his woman, he attempts to assassinate the villain on his own; but, emasculated, he must fail, and spends the rest of his time longing for Jack's wine bottle he sees through the window of his old bar. *Yi* is an ideal of brotherly symbiosis; Martin's passivity and submission, however, haven't the agency necessary to either give or receive *yi*. When Jack and Martin reunite to climactically eliminate the villains responsible for the death of their women, their reunion does not represent a consummation of their original homosexual desire, but only a channelling and homogenization of that desire through a normative action climax. In this climactic shootout, Jack and Martin are blank-faced, unblinking zombies who demonstrate none of the erotic interest in each other we had seen in the film's first half. The scene having the same mechanical, formulaic feel as the rest of the film's second half, they are there to simply finish off the bad guys, and have mysteriously forgotten about their sexual tension. The genre has thus "lobotomized" them, safely transmuting their homosexual desire into the regressively outward violence that action genres use to solve all their problems.

Martin, being pushed in his wheelchair, continues being the "passive" (i.e., female) partner and, seemingly already dead, does not bleed when shot in the finale. With eyes hidden and motionless behind sunglasses, he is unable to meet the gaze of other men on their own terms. The end of the final shootout sees Jack pull Martin's impotent phallic trigger-finger for him so he can finish off his ex-triad boss–the only allowed consummation of their homosexuality is both displaced towards an "other" and contextualized as murder (violence equals strength). The murderous consummation is an act of negation against the criminal legality that has predetermined their plight. The criminal world's intra-legality is immoral and its meta-illegality (i.e., its transgression) is moral. Jack and Martin are thus the heroes by default, simply because they are better than anyone else in the film's diegesis. Having no discernable qualities beyond their shooting skill, the film's satire is its suggestion that they must be the heroes even though they only ape the codes of *yi* without legitimately engaging them–as indeed do most of us who are not heroes in real life. In the end, Jack and Martin, mortally wounded, die along with the villains.

In the film's brief coda, patrons of their old bar tell legends about the pair's tragic-heroic exploits. What becomes legendary is not the fatalism of their romance's unrequitedness, but a heterosexual whitewashing of their legend; the genre must itself fictionalize the romance it will not allow, rationalizing homosexual relations by rewriting them as nontransgressive. Thus, the film's subversive homosexuality is itself comically subverted–Jack and Martin's homosexuality is re-mythologized second-hand into a heterosexuality by barflies who presumably wouldn't know the real details of their relationship ("And that's the way the genre wants it!" director To seems to suggests). They die not because they are criminals, but because they are not heterosexuals, or have no women left to go home to. Because the anti-homosocial (and totally asocial) possibility of the men forgoing each other is not an option, the genre offers them only fatalistic nihilism. In *Scarface* (either Hawks's or de Palma's 1983 remake) the genre will punish the hero not for his extreme violence–which fits right in with the genre's demands–but for his tragic love for his sister, his Achilles' heel. Thus, the gangster genre can moralize to its audience and counteract accusations of nihilism by saying that it does indeed have *some* rules (in its conservative formula, deviant violence is better than deviant sex).

Homosexuality, like incest, is a taboo fearsome enough to be illegalized by both social and antisocial (criminal) laws. *A Hero*, however, satirizes the tragic death of the protagonists–instead of moralizing them as *Scarface* moralizes the death of its hero–because the taboo it exploits is the homosexuality that everyone knows is latent in triad films *anyway*. We know that this taboo, *unlike* incest, always underlies the life of a *yi*-abiding (Hong Kong) gangster hero, and we know what punishments the genre would distribute should he ever try to push his subtextual desire into text. (Comparatively, because incest is totally alien to the gangster lifestyle, there is at least some rationale for denying it.[10]) The heroes' repressed homosexuality is sort of the film's unconscious; *A Hero*, in its schizophrenia, detects this homosexual anarchy and punishes its heroes (with death) on the generic *pretext* that their martyrdoms will make them "better" heroes. By trying to avoid charges of nihilism or anarchy, the genre becomes instead a sadist, if this is how it must treat its "children" when they "misbehave." How can we take this film, poker-faced as it is, at face value if it tries to ridiculously justify its simultaneous punishing and mythicizing of it heroes by suggesting they can only be mythicized *if* they are punished? It is this genre paradox that *A Hero* internally mocks. A non-heterosexual hero will not die (according to the film's title) only because the genre might sustain his legend with its own fictions, which in this case is actually represented diegetically via the bar storytellers. But the barflies' fictions stand in for generic (and social/legal) hegemony–the legends spun will be of a *yi* between Jack and Martin that never existed, and not of the unrequited homosexuality that did exist between them. The film's satire is its revelation of the genre as a ridiculously neurotic and sadistic God: it offers the homosexual heroes an "acceptable" heterosexual conversion in the presence of their women, only to first kill off the women to maintain its homosexual universe and then paradoxically kill off the men because they weren't heterosexual enough.

The film's disruption of narrative lies in its reversal of the codes of generic homosexual expectation. In Woo's films, or even in Western male bonding films–for example Donner's *Lethal Weapon* (1987)–the expectation is of an initial homosexual fear that climactically and "naturally" evolves into asexual homosocial love, the irrational fear of erotic love (more than mere sodomy) being replaced with a hegemonically Platonic sentiment (or, in the West, a quasi-Platonic sentiment, as in a *Lethal Weapon*). In *A Hero*, the expectation is reversed: right at the beginning, Jack and Martin's adolescent games of sexual denial define an *a priori* homosexual relationship that is not a climax but simply a *given*. Then, after a homosexual first and second act, we get heterosexuality in the third and fourth acts, as the women's fates come into play. The fifth act–the mens' reconciliation and union–is merely the fatalistic end the audience had predicted an hour before. But since we have already been made privy to the homosexual subtext in the first half, the second half's overconventional lip service to heterosexuality is disingenuous. But although the film's narrative shifts between homo-and heterosexuality, the characters do not shift, and behave independently of the film's displacements, such that the genre is forced to "lobotomize" them when it realizes their same-sex desire will not dissipate on its own. This independence is of course ironic, since it is also the overdetermination of the homosexual climax which the heterosexuality of the film's second half has intentionally, yet only temporarily, derailed. But the *transparency* of this displacement is the joke, a satirical inversion of the traditional linear structure in which an asexual homosociality is the rationalization of initial homosexual fear. Here, the initial homosexuality, though coded of course, is not at all feared but embraced and toyed with all too blatantly (guns, cars, wine). The introduction of tragic heterosexuality is *intentionally* unconvincing, and the built-in tragedies of the genre are exposed as expectation-driven myths to reinforce a hypocritical hegemony which pretends to prize homosociality while punishing its heroes with martyrdom when they go too far. The heroes of Hollywood male-bonding films–such as *Lethal Weapon* or *Die Hard*–usually represent legality, not transgression, and thus the presence of the nuclear family looms in their backgrounds to diffuse any illegal sexual deviance. In *A Hero*, where there is no marital or biological family (only a male triad "family"), the homosexual criminals have little choice but to become martyrs, as prescribed by the genre's own hegemonic rationalizations. The male characters' desires operate independently of the genre's desires, while their characters' actions follow genre expectations. The incongruity between individual desire and social expectation equals death, politely rationalized as "martyrdom." But martyrs need a cause, and theirs is the perpetuation of generic homophobia.

This "mechanical" outline of *Hero,* the meaning of whose predestined conclusion seems predicated on the sexual symbolism we see at the beginning, may reduce the entire film to a game, a *reductio ad absurdum* of closeted male action films. Writer-producer Wong Jing and director Clarence Fok's (a/k/a Clarence Ford) entirely sincere film *Cheap Killers*, on the other hand, may indeed mark some kind of belated landmark not only in HK cinema but in the international waters of gender-coded action films. Here is *A Hero*–or any other male action film–without homophobic codes and without a demand for its repressedly homosexual heroes to be martyrs. What replaces homophobic codes, however, are misogynist ones–as opposed to *A Hero's* "merely" sexist codes. Feminist critic Joan Mellen, in *The Waves at Genji's Door,* compares the "healthy" misogyny of the samurai hero to "the latently homosexual hero of the American Western."[11] (117) But is her criticism of his misogyny predicated on the supposition that he is simply homosexual, or that he is a *latent* homosexual? *Cheap Killers*, regressively, actually suggests the former. No longer content with the cultural euphemisms of subtext and asexual homosociality, *Cheap* may be the first mainstream violent action film by a commercially viable producer and director to posit openly gay male heroes as its protagonists.[12]

Director Clarence Fok (a/k/a Clarence Ford) has a history of films with homosexual themes.[13] His early *On Trial* (1980) presents Leslie Cheung as Wing, an impoverished young "teddy boy" at a Catholic boys school who is in a sexually ambiguous friendship with his wealthy and slightly effeminate (he is a cellist!) classmate Pao. Ashamed when Pao discovers he is a lowly washroom attendant (a la Murnau's *The Last Laugh* (1924), no less?), Wing flees from Pao's sympathy: "I won't let you see me again until I become rich." Wing, on a balcony above, takes off his shirt and throws it down to Pao, an act of both defiance and sexual confusion; Pao picks up the shirt and keeps it as a memento. Although there is no explication of homosexuality, the curiosity of the shirt-stripping scene and the relative eroticization of Cheung's body (he is later shown partly nude, masturbating in an erotically lit scene), testify that the traces of Fok's gay subtext begin to emerge here. In the end, Wing will become a drug addict and will then be killed by his dealers, while spoiled Pao will triumph above his own capitalist father's expectations as a musician. Wing's homosexuality will lead him to criminality, and thus tragedy; Pao will be able to successfully and aristocratically sublimate his desire through his music. Here, the unbroachable axes of homosexuality hinge on classism–in fact, the film is also known as "Job Hunter" and its Chinese title can literally translate as "Unemployed Life." (Money can always buy acceptability, gay or otherwise.) Pao lives because he is rich, yet emptily so, because his sublimations are asocial and do not fully acknowledge Wing's tragedy. The film's final freeze frame on Pao's victorious face at a music recital is in fact director Fok's sarcastic indictment of the oppressive class system to which he has surrendered. We know Pao has not forgotten Wing, but it must remain a secret from his adoring audience–i.e., heterosexist legal society.

Fok's 1984 film *Before Dawn*, a garish piece of urban nihilism that perhaps out-does Patrick Tam's *Nomad* (1982), uses violence as a sublimation of the protagonist's latent homosexuality. A high-school student is taunted by a male prostitute (who is, of course, eventually murdered); despite their ostensible antagonism, the student develops an unadmitted attraction to him. The only moment of bodily contact between them is, importantly, when the student bloodily slashes the prostitute with a knife in denial of his attraction. The substitution of one bodily fluid for another–blood for semen–has since become more blatantly sexualized in action films by John Woo (and his countless imitators), whose archetypal images of the male hero in sensuous slow-motion closeup, drenched by sweat and blood, are now familiar. Fok, in a previous collaboration with Wong Jing six years before *Cheap Killers*, had already treated lesbianism as a form of male heterosexual entertainment in his "category 3" (HK's NC-17 rating) *Naked Killer* (1992), whose story of rival lesbian assassins meshed exploitive female sexuality with Fok's signature hyperedited violence to elicit a predictable cult following.[14] More interesting is a sequence from his action-comedy *The Black Panther Warriors* (1993), in which an infantile adult male character, in paroxysms of anxiety, calms himself by sucking on the nipples of the macho male leads (including iconic HK heartthrob Tony Leung Kar-fai, no less) when his pacifier is no longer available! That the scene is played for absurd burlesque does not diminish its representation of the differences between sexual "acceptability" in mainstream HK and Western cultures.

With *Cheap Killers* (1998), Fok makes his first unapologetically gay male film. It may be a valid criticism of *Cheap* that it indirectly uses its ambition to be a "serious" (i.e., non-camp or non-"category 3") action film to avoid the unprecedented risk of exploiting a more graphic male erotica for a gay audience in the way that *Naked Killer*'s female sexuality catered to a heterosexual audience.[15] Indeed, the film has no explicit sex, yet the groundwork for the film's interpretation is transparently signalled in unmistakable detail in nearly every scene, such that there can be no doubt that Wong, HK's most commercially-oriented producer, intended to explicate to the public the genre's homosexual implications, about which only academics had previously enjoyed speculating.[16] The gay love story of *Cheap*, whose presence is inarguable and requires no critical defense, is nevertheless one of initial coded repression–yet one that does surface into actuality–and where one might have wanted it to go further, it sadly pulls back its punches. Furthermore, the blue print of male homosexuality the film provides is one largely staked on misogyny,[17] yet Wong's regressive, archetypally-motivated script is given power by Fok's stylish, sincere direction.

Sam and Yat-tiu are two assassins, the former a repressed homosexual with an autistic child, the latter an ostentatious womanizer; whereas assassins Jack and Martin of *A Hero* dressed in repressive blacks, they dress in dazzling pure white, a prefiguration of an openness to come. An early dialogue establishes their initial sexual polarity: "Except women, what interests you?" Yat-tiu responds jokingly, "Lots of things–dating, screwing . . ." Yat-tiu, breaking the homosocial (yet effectively homophobic) law of triad loyalty, falls in love with Ting, the gold-digging yet abused young wife of their cruel boss, Ma. Her goals of freedom and empowerment are symbolized by her dream of owning a champion racehorse, just as she is now owned as property by the cruel Ma. The double image is yet ironic, for her own desire to possess is merely an inversion of the male power she struggles against. When she does finally come to own a horse in the film's second half, she will be under the control of yet another villain, "Doctrine King" (whose very name signifies hegemony), and will not have broken free by using the weapons of the enemy (power/ownership). She will change allegiances, but, hardly a feminist, she will not challenge formal patriarchy. A malevolent version of the triad women of *A Hero Never Dies*, Ting's ambition is limited *a priori* by the generic conditions of her "life" as a woman.

Ma assigns the two to assassinate a racehorse owner, whom they chop in half. As with the leg amputation in *Hero*, a series of symbolic castrations will be displaced to other bodily locales throughout the film. They blind the horse owner's gay Anglo henchmen ("Blonde") in one eye, but leave him alive as a gruesome testament to their handiwork. Negating the desirous eye, his potency as a desirer is challenged, the male-male gaze at this point manifesting itself in aggressive violence. During the film's early action scenes, the Sam and Yat-tiu's eyes are cinematographically masked with a shaft of light, a technique which owes more to comic books than to the silent era's "masking" of frames. Drawing extra attention to the murderous gaze, this sadistic scopophilia can be a subversively homosexual version of Laura Mulvey's traditionally heterosexist and objectifying "male gaze." The weapon effectively becomes the eye itself, its sadistic gaze doling out violence through its command of the total body, an active subjectivity with which the audience is invited to sympathize. This is sort of the opposite of Bunuel's severed eye in *Un Chien Andalou* (1928), an act of sado-masochism which represents an "assault" on the eyes of the seeing audience, a subversion of the social body that is the film's ostensible *raison d'etre*. Their homosexuality not yet fully active, Sam and Yat-tiu's highlighted gazes become the lethally encoded loci of sublimated homosexual desire; in the second half of the film, once the two killers become lovers, their gazes will never be highlighted again, for such sublimation/coding obviously becomes superfluous in light of their "outing."

Sam, though gay, has an autistic son and a wife whose absence is conspicuously unaccounted for; in a conservative formulation the film probably invites, his homosexuality may be equated with familial dissolution or inappropriateness, its biological product being deformed. A young would-be cop, Sunny, clad in a more youthful version of the wedding-day white that is Sam and Yat-tiu's standard attire, cares for the son, providing the legalized heterosexual fathering (or "policing") Sam cannot. Meanwhile, adulterous Yat-tiu and Ting rendezvous in a music-video style scene replete with billowing purple draperies and the unambiguously symbolic flowage of a waterhose over their bodies; the actual sex act is not shown, with only conventional music cues filling in the "evidence" of their romantic details. But Yat-tiu is unsure of his future. Warning Ting of his lowly triad class status, he says, "Yat-tiu: in Chinese, that means 10 bucks." This is an ironic foreshadowing of the fact that he is not gambling with money but with the devious heterosexuality Ting personifies–for she will later double-cross him. The "cheapness" of the title is not only the value placed on them as killers but will become their value as homosexuals within an antisocial law (criminal society) whose deviance from social law does not happen to coincide with a deviance from social law's sexual hegemony. The criminal society must be even more homophobic than the hegemonies it rebels against; it must guard extra carefully its criminals' anarchy to make sure it is the right kind of anarchy.

Discovered by a vengeful Ma, Ting and Yat-tiu kill him with gardening shears, an instrument of castration, and hide the news of his death from Sam. Although she convinces Yat-tiu to buy two rings "to bind [their] hearts together," the opportunistic Ting nevertheless soon gravitates towards the villainously powerful "Doctrine King"–heterosexuality is unfaithful, and only Sam and Yat-tiu's homosexual bond will stand the final test of monogamy. Sam notices Yat-tiu's ring: "I don't want you to be ruined by a woman." Yat-tiu responds, "Sam, you'll become gay sooner or later," a line whose foreshadowing is ironized by the predestination of the genre's inherently homosexual becomings. When Sam and Yat-tiu later become criminals *to* the other criminals, the free play of the two-variable formula of meta-transgression will allow their homosexuality to become actualized.

Doctrine uses Yat-tiu and Sam's sparing of Blonde's life as a pretext to kill them in another eye-masked shootout; masking occurs at the moment of the death blow, equating sadistic violence with male orgasm ("the little death," as they say in French). Escaping, they swear half-jokingly yet prophetically, "Whoever isn't righteous will become impotent." Blonde, now allied with Doctrine, soon traps Sam and Yat-tiu. Blonde chops off three of Yat-tiu's fingers–fingers that hold both his (male/phallic) gun and his heterosexually binding ring. Blonde, seeking revenge for his blinding, emasculates Yat-tiu by robbing him of his sadistically-inclined fingers, and is subsequently raped by him and his 14 henchmen ("14 Brothers, let's fuck this pig!"). Interestingly, Blonde does *not* gouge out Yat-tiu's sadistic eye, as was done to him–for at this point, Yat-tiu's gaze had been (mis)directed towards Ting, and his sadism is redirected and funnelled through his trigger finger, which is conflated with the heterosexual symbolism of the ring it now bears. (Sam's purely homosexual gaze is never in question.) Although Blonde is (by the film's own indeces) gay, he is non-transgressively gay because his role epitomizes normative masculine violence. A mere rapist with no partner, his non-romantic homosexuality is little more than a tame perversity. It is Sam and Yat-tiu's *love* which is the threat to genre.

Meanwhile, Ting betrays Yat-tiu for Doctrine, justifying her jealousy: "Why is there room only for Sam in your life?" Sam, left for dead, rises and sees Yat-tiu's severed finger with the ring still intact. He appropriates the ring, wearing it in his stead–he has become Yat-tiu's husband, and his wearing of the now differently symbolic ring is an anal penetration. After Sam's mother and son are assassinated–the destruction of his heterosexual ties are finalized–Sam and Yat-tiu go underground and become the stuff of street legend. As a group of triad boys says, "What should we learn from [their] story?–Don't love women, just cheat them." In *A Hero*, the myth-telling scene of the coda–the fictionalization of the diegesis of a film already a fiction–is where the story ends; Jack and Martin's homosexual bond becomes the stuff of narrative legend and thus the bread-and-butter (and circuity) of the genre itself. *Cheap* goes one *big* step further: their legends are spun while they are still alive (though hidden, both physically and sexually), and they will live to both negate the mistaken legends of others and to create their own. In the end, they will not die or become martyrs, and by doing so assert their sanity and (sexual) independence against the oppressive and neurotic fictions of the genre they inhabit.

After his gang rape, Yat-tiu becomes an impotent drug addict, his "unrighteousness" having fulfilled its promise–his single devotion to Ting, which challenged his boss's patriarchy, is in this context deviant behavior, in addition to thrusting a wedge into the professional code of *yi*'s homosociality. So begins the film's second, openly homosexual half. This structure–which this film will ultimately and unconventionally carry beyond the usual limitations of the genre–is what To's *A Hero* satirizes. Here, the homosocial first half turns into a homosexual second half; in *A Hero*, a textual homosexual first half is confused by a textual heterosexual second half only to finally collapse at the possibility of that initial homosexuality's return. In *Cheap*, however, the linear plot progression, in addition to having no legal or heterosexual environment, is in the hands of director (Fok) willing to subvert the genre and unwilling to turn his gay heroes into masochistic martyrs.

"It doesn't move; everyday I try to wake it, but it seems to be asleep," the impotent Yat-tiu says. Sam's being forced to care for invalid Yat-tiu recements their bonds, and they finally become lovers. As in *A Hero*, a formula of initial heterosexuality followed by a "castration" is the necessary prelude to the epiphanic actualization of homosexual love. In *A Hero*, the dominant/submissive axes instigated by Martin's dismemberment were permanent. In *Cheap*, not only will Yat-tiu regain activeness through sheer will, but when he does so he will also be activated as a homosexual, one equal and *not* submissive to Sam. Sam was already gay; Yat-tiu will "become" gay by realizing the one who has always loved him most was Sam. Of course, he is only able to do this after being ostracized from conventional triad laws, entering into the freedom of being a total outlaw from both legal and illegal societies. The severing of Yat-tiu's finger may have emasculated him for the moment, but it is also the prelude to his homosexual (re-)humanization. As with the romantic interlude between Yat-tiu and Ting, in which a waterhose substituted for bodily fluids, the romance between the two men is evasive yet slightly less coy: they wash each other (in slow-motion close-up) and bathe together (in long-shot) and there is a close-up of Yat-tiu uncontrollably urinating in his underwear (again, displacement of bodily fluids/impulses). Most tellingly, precisely the same romantic music cue that played for Ting and Yat-tiu now plays for Sam and Yat-tiu. But instead of the music-video gloss of the Ting scene, festooned with flowingly deceptive veils, their scene occurs within the nakedly Bressonian sincerity of a spare apartment, whose love requires no smoke-and-mirrors stylistics.

Ting, now a powerful female boss who would rather sell her younger sister to Doctrine than have her courted by newly-ordained policeman Sunny, uses her femininity to ascertain power but has no power to challenge male hegemony. She learns of Sam and Yat-tiu's survival and sends killers to finish them off. In a hotel room fight,[18] Yat-tiu rediscovers his masculinity in an orgy of phallic impalings, the results of one splashing semen-like blood across his face. Previously, Sam and Yat-tiu's eyes had been masked with an unnatural shaft of light at the moment of their killings, the illegality of their unactualized homosexuality transformed into an "acceptable," sadistic gaze in keeping with their masculine roles as killers. Now that their gazes have lovingly turned towards each other, this sadism is no longer required; although a shaft of light, the "masking" technique was actually a veil disguising and displacing their gazes' true desire. The veil is henceforth dropped, and director Fok drops the cinematic technique of masking with it. They continue to kill, but only out of survival, not displaced sexuality, for their (homo)sexuality is now correctly "placed." When blood splashes across Yat-tiu's eyes in the hotel fight, or across Sam's eyes when he finally kills Doctrine, the imposed eye-mask is removed with a cathartic realization of flesh-and-blood life. Unlike Martin in *A Hero*, who remains emasculated, Yat-tiu recovers his manhood and no longer assumes a submissive (feminine) position. Arms wrapped around each other, Sam and Yat-tiu, bleeding profusely, continue to chop their way through a small army, each dismemberment of a villain a symbolic appropriation which re-members themselves. Sam and Yat-tiu are both activated equally as masculine killers and as homosexuals; whereas in their initial killings they were puppets of criminal hegemony, their anarchic killings here subvert the status quo by successfully exploiting its contents (violence/strength) within the transgressive form of their homosexual love.

Conveniently rescued by Sunny from the few remaining killers, a mortally wounded Yat-tiu says to Sam, "Take care of yourself," and selflessly asks for Sam to return the ring he had appropriated from the former's severed fingers. Of course, Sam refuses, and they both survive, setting the stage for a final showdown. Sam goads Ting by stealing her prize horse (a symbolic rape), the animal alternately symbolizing her own sexual dominion (over a male) and the unspoiled purity of Sunny, whom Doctrine will soon kidnap to exchange with the horse. First, Sam confronts Ling. She, jealous of their homosexual love, says "You never courted me." Sam insults her, "I never use public toilets," only for Ling to return the favor: "Public toilets? Oh, I have almost forgotten–Sam doesn't like women." In the finale, Doctrine, Blonde, and Ting hold Sunny hostage; Sam and Yat-tiu surprise the villains by decapitating the horse. By castrating Ting's "child," they destroy her femininity (as mother to the horse) while castrating her attempts at masculinity (as a figure of rising triad power). Sunny, now substituting for Sam's dead son, becomes a symbol of successful legal male heterosexuality as opposed to Sam's autistic natural son. Ting's cross-gendered persona is pitted against a broader (nonerotic) homosexuality, now that (straight) Sunny is included in their equation.

The climax continuing, Blonde and Yat-tiu–the former who had led a gang-rape of the latter–now interlock the barrels of their shotguns not as a phallic penetration but as two phalluses butting heads, a position analogous to Jack and Martin butting the heads of their cars in the first half of *A Hero*. Their shotguns are blown apart (a phallic stalemate), but Yat-tiu slashes Blonde's throat. Again, no "masking" is used during the death blow because firstly its coding would be gratuitous now that Yat-tiu is openly gay; and secondly, the masking's sadism is unnecessary because the homosexual repression the sadism was based upon has been dispelled.

Sam blows apart Doctrine, who has mortally wounded Sunny; Doctrine's blood and flesh spray into Sam's eyes, the finality of their conflict being the further negation of scopophilic sadism along with the negation (death) of the other, the "gazee." But a cackling Ting wounds both Sam and Yat-tiu with a shotgun; as she turns away to board her helicopter, we are granted a rare yet invaluable and affecting moment of insight. As she turns towards the camera, her face transforms from that of a smilingly caricature to the tearful visage of a jolted lover, and but for a moment the film's misogynist formula is rebutted. The tears force us to rethink all that had transpired, and we realize the camera's gaze has privileged the heroes' male homosexuality at the expense of vilifying female heterosexuality. Without the "tears scene," a moment the audience sees what Sam and Yat-tiu cannot, the film might merely be a politicized or heterophobic inversion of the generic cinematic homophobia represented by, say, Simon Yam's gay villain longing for iconically heterosexual Chow Yun-fat in Ringo Lam's *Full Contact* (1992).

Nevertheless, with gasping breath, Yat-tiu pulls the trigger of his gun with his wedding ring, now placed in his necklace, the bond of heterosexuality transformed into a vengeful anus. He shoots down the helicopter's rope ladder, from which Ting dangles. She falls to her death. The films's final shot is of Sam and Yat-tiu, in slow-motion approaching the camera, as "pioneering" homosexual outcasts in a criminal society (and film genre) whose homosexual meaning has not yet been fully admitted to. The film's inclusion of Sunny threatens to derail the film's own ostensible thesis, as it sides his heterosexual legality (literally–he is a cop) with the killers' homosexual illegality into a single moral union. But Sunny's legality, though righteous, proves ineffectual in the conclusion. He is only there to further the plot, to be kidnapped and shot, and his boyish legality proves no match for the major villains. Although he will survive the finale, his character is given no climactic privilege by either the plot or the camera–this is reserved entirely for Sam and Yat-tiu's slow-motion shot. Their final pose is one of defiant survival, and they will need no barflies to write their legends for them (as in *A Hero*). Against genre expectation, they have effectively destroyed the heterosexist opposition, perhaps a first in commercial/mainstream action film history.

Cheap Killers is an exercise in un-coding the coded genre roles that *A Hero* satirizes (what is underneath the codes turns out to be, of course, displaced misogyny). The post-Woo gunplay subgenre from which they draw inspiration is a modernization/urbanization of the *yi* of the swordplay films popularized by director Chang Cheh (Woo's mentor) and the Shaw Brothers in the 1960s and 70s. Although it is probable that North American "queer" interpretations of Hong Kong action films may be only but for the lack of any other (non-romantic) homosocial tradition in the West, it is also worthwhile to note the progression of the homosexuality inherent in Chang's own films.[19] For example, Chang's early film *The Assassin* (1967) presents a classical world whose plot hinges on filial piety and Confucian patriarchal hegemony; by the time of his *Five Deadly Venoms* (1978) or outrageous *Five Element Ninja* (aka "Super Ninjas") (1982), any lip service to Confucianism is abandoned in favor of worlds of bare-chested homosocial contact and violent interpersonal penetrations oozing bodily fluids. *Five Element* is an orgy of hyperbolically masculine bloodletting in which men are literally ripped limb from limb to the accompaniment of orgasmic blood geysers which leave the breathless heroes soaked head to toe. It is indeed true, however, that the fineries of his artistic ambitions had slowly declined over the years, such that *The Assassin*, one of his richest works, seems more conventionally "mature" than the joyously simplistic heroism of *Five Element*, at which time he was single mindedly indulging his homosocial fantasies at the expense of the niceties of film production. But it would be this inherently homosocial tradition by which the HK triad films are most directly inspired. But although this tradition is old in film, its explication is largely new, and its outright *politicization*–as in *Cheap Killers*–still in its infancy.

In contrast to these two male films, director Yip Wai-man's *Portland Street Blues* (1998) presents a protagonist (Sandra Ng Kwun-yu, in her best role) who is an openly lesbian triad gang leader. The film was conceived as a spin-off of director Andrew Lau and writer-producer Manfred Wong's young male triad series *Young and Dangerous* (1996-8; 6 parts so far), itself based on a comic book, and in which Ng's character "Sister 13" occasionally played a subsidiary role.[20] Although the male bonding of the *Y&D* films may share some generically "Eastern" (Chinese) similarity with the generic modes of *A Hero* and *Cheap*, the archetypally butch/femme characterizations of *Portland*'s female characters posit this film somewhere between traditional martial genres and Eurocentric performative theory/constructions. The *Y&D* series revitalized the then-unfashionable triad film genre, yet not as feast of romanticized action, as it had been in the new wave of the mid-1980s-early 90s, but as a gritty serial melodrama patterned on clockwork formulae of male bonding and betrayal. Although *yi* is at the heart of the series, it is adamantly heterosexual without a hint of the closeted homoeroticism of its generic ancestors; presumably male homosexuality would be too horrifying for its target audience of contemporary, Westernized teenage boys.[21] Indeed, the only openly and heroically homosexual character is the butch lesbian Sister 13; on the other hand, because action heroines do not have the automatically "latent" homosexuality of their male counterparts, as Mellen suggests above, the visibility of her homosexuality is that much more crucial. The "legality" of Sister 13's character within antisocial triad law is, however, rationalized in terms of masculine role-playing, as indeed she wears only unflattering and/or male attire. And because its protagonist is an avowed lesbian accepted by the criminal world, many of the traditional *male* (il)legalities of the gangster genre must be modified such that this "lesbian contingency" can adapt to masculinist hegemonies without challenging them. Still, the character of Sister 13, now given a spotlight in her own vehicle, sets the stage for a richer and more rewarding film than any of the *Y&D* dramas.

We are introduced to Sister 13, one of the twelve district bosses of the Hung Hing (triad) society, as she demonstrates confident leadership when punishing her traitorous, buxom lover, who is ritualistically pummeled in the breasts (female castration). In a shot remarkably similar to Ting's "tear scene" in *Cheap Killers*, Sister 13 turns away from the characters and towards the camera to shed a private tear in defiance of her procrustean duties, a secretly effeminate display belying her social role. The camera as objective truth-teller allows psychological insight other characters are not privileged to. Yet *this* tear scene occurs right at the beginning of the story of Sister 13 the butch protagonist, where the tear is reserved for the end of Ting the (femme) antagonist. For the homosexual female heroine, duty is emotion's facade, but for the heterosexual female villain, there is only the emotion of vengeful desperation itself. A lone woman in a male world, Ting has no social duty, only an individual will to survive. Keeping emotion and duty separate is the stuff of heroism–yet if Sister 13 were a man, a tear shedding scene would be both unnecessary and inappropriate, since we "like" our cinematic men to be unfeeling sadists. This invites comparison to the traditional *giri/ninjo* (duty/ human sentiment) dichotomy in the Japanese *yakuza* film. As Mellen suggests,[22] the fact that the yakuza hero is predestined towards patriarchal subservience to his prescribed *giri* reveals the genre's inherently sexist conservatism. He will always choose his male lord over the female love interest, the moral aesthetics of the *giri/ninjo* binary presenting a quandary only the aesthetics of the genre that produces such quandaries can solve. Or, since genre laws are themselves as neurotic as those of the real legal society they reflect, it takes a neurosis to cure a neurosis, as Freud said. The social duty/personal sentiment duality is merely an academic one since we know the hero has no real choice in the end anyway (or, he always makes the same choice). Analogously, that Sister 13 is predestined towards duty–that there is no effective choice between external duty and internal personality because the two are inextricable in her constructed universe–may make her a man whether she is homosexual or heterosexual.

Sister 13's father once said, "It would be great if you were a boy." She responded, "[Thus,] I always considered myself a man . . . Do you know why?" As if to answer visually, we then witness her ascension to masculinized triad power in flashbacks. Before she was Sister 13, she was the small-chested "Teenie" (in a characteristically male world, small breasts invertedly substitute for a big penis), an overall-clad tomboy whose father (a typically pathetic Ng Man-tat) is a grovelling underling in the Hung Hing gang world and whose best friend is "Yun," an archetypally feminine (long hair) student. They share a mutual attraction to "Coke," (Alex Fong Chung-sun, the actor who incidentally played Sam in *Cheap Killers*) a handsome boxer who belongs to Hung Hing's rival gang Tung Sing. Our *a priori* knowledge of Teenie's lesbianism (even if one has not seem the *Y&D* films, this film's opening breast-pummelling scene is more explicit about her homosexuality than anything in Andrew Lau's *Y&D* "sibling" films) necessarily shades the credibility of her attraction to Coke.[23] Although we must speculate about such distinctions, and although the film refuses to distinguish between homosexuality and bisexuality, there is enough textual evidence to suggest that this is the story of a bisexual girl who "becomes" a lesbian woman. Arguably, it is her indoctrination into the triads which fully homosexualizes her; in their world, a lesbian–to them, a fake man–is more acceptable as a boss than a "real" woman.

In the first of two warmly lit "bed scenes," Teenie and Yun lie next to each other (clothed), gazing lovingly at a photo of Coke with each of them at his either side. He becomes the rationalized heterosexual mediation (or buffer) for their latent homosexual attraction, sort of the distaff equivalent of the heterosexual mediation provided by Martin and Jack's girlfriends in *A Hero Never Dies*. The obvious homoeroticism of these scenes clearly suggests at this point Teenie is a (confused) bisexual, not an adamant heterosexual. Yun, her head on Teenie's shoulder, giggles, "If you don't move out, I'll stay with you . . . I love you . . . let me kiss you!" The joking teenaged denial of what will later be exposed as tragic sincerity is for the moment a briefly missed opportunity, later to be veiled in nostalgic unfulfillment.

Plot mechanics spin when "S.O.B.," a cruel triad boss, steals Teenie's father's winning lottery ticket. Replaying a trick they had successfully enacted on a doltish male teacher, Teenie and Yun attempt to cheat S.O.B. out of his money by feigning prostitution services. For them, who have no real boyfriends, heterosexuality is just a game. The plan backfiring, the father is wounded in a rare but failed bit at heroic redemption[24]–but the girls escape. The family's masculine agency (potency) is displaced from biology (the father) to sociology (butch Teenie, more "male" than her father), foreshadowing Teenie's future as "Sister 13, the Man." The girls separated, Teenie is taken in by a pretty female drug addict (played by heterosexual starlet Shu Qi) who, as we see in meta-flashback, was abused by her corrupt cop boyfriend James, who aborted their child in impromptu fashion by kicking her in the stomach. The film's only representative of the law, James (unsubtly) represents the immorality of the corrupt legal heterosexual society that the triads romantically rebel against. In *Cheap Killers*, the sterling young cop Sunny showed that in that film's subversively (male) homosexual world, male heterosexuality was pure but *weak*, ineffectual. The greatest transgression of *Cheap* is that reverses the genre's strong/weak binaries, such that heterosexuality is the weak one; furthermore, male homosexuality is both strong (violent) *and* loving, subverting the genre's traditional binary opposition, which pits strength against love. *A Hero*, having no onscreen character representing legality and having no *textual* desire to subvert convention, has nowhere to displace its sexual legalisms save directing them at itself. Thus, that film ends with an apparent sort of suicide, and we must read into the film's subtext to find the reasons (or the "suicide note," so to speak).

Portland's plot still operating in flashback, Coke kills S.O.B. and out of gratitude Teenie swears devotion to him–yet their courtship is tamely represented by a barely sexualized sunset motorcycle jaunt. Although Teenie has a crush on Coke, her allegiance to him is predicated on triad loyalty after his killing of S.O.B.–her ties to him are channelled through the masculinist hegemony of the criminal society that will later, ironically, fully lesbianize her. So Teenie's emotionalisms are properly reserved for the homosexual reunion of herself and Yun, whose embrace prompts swollen chords of incidental musical emotion that dwarf any of the film's heterosexual interludes. They lie down again in the film's second "bed scene," lit again with intimate reds and oranges (blood-colors, as in *A Hero*'s red wine). Their actions–mutual girlish fondlings–misdirect longing in a triangulation with Coke, whose photo is again positioned between them as buffer. Unable to express themselves, their homosexual longing is activated only when cloaked as heterosexuality. Yet it is not only Coke as an individual that stands between them, but the heteronormative relationship he represents, and their allegiance or rebellion against it in the future. Noticing Coke and his fellow male triads worshipping the maleness of General Kwan[25] (a symbol of *yi*), she realizes the difference between male and female; later, as Sister 13, she will dress as a man to embody her role, her sexual object choice equating her with the male gender. She will and must become a man, a brother, so she too can participate in *yi*. She cannot successfully love Coke, so she will, in effect, *become* him.

After humiliating Teenie in a drunken outburst at dinner ("Show Coke your picture!"), Teenie responds, "You know very well that I like him . . . why do you flirt with him?" Teenie feels betrayed not because Yun loves Coke per se, but because she is choosing a man over herself; at no time does Teenie's butch character convince us that an erotic bond even exists between her and Coke. The argument separates them for a second time, and Teenie rips Coke's picture to shreds–ironic because it is the picture's deferred homo-sexuality that binds the girls' hearts. The picture representing both illusory heterosexuality and sublimated homosexuality, its destruction is also the destruction of Teenie's ambiguous bisexuality. It is from this point on that she will be reconstructed by the criminal world as a lesbian; she will not construct herself as a lesbian, because as a criminal she has no true self. In voice-over, the older Sister 13 tells us, "Later, I discovered that I love women more than men, but I don't quite understand women's hearts." The bisexuality inherent in this statement, however, is largely ignored by Sister 13's (not Teenie's) own subsequent definition as a "lesbian."

Shu Qi's druggie pops back in to provide a homosocial substitute for Yun's absence, wearing a mask so as not to be recognized by the mad James–yet it is no less a mask than the male drag Sister 13 will wear to hide her tears. Teenie becomes determined to join Hung Hing, and plans to murder police-man James to court the gang's favor. Here, organized criminality in a sense coincides for with homosexuality, but it is within this same transformative moment that Teenie will effectively cease being a woman. In the traditional male gangster worlds, homosexuality is always taboo; a woman's lesbianism, however, within male gangster hegemony will turn that woman into a straight man by dint of her sexual object choice. For a female heroine, some sympa-thy may exist for butch lesbians because their butchness is prized apart from femaleness, as a rare achievement exceeding their biological predicament (i.e., the fact they happen to be female). A male does not earn sympathy for butchness because he doesn't need to be constructed that way, he is supposed to be that way naturally. At the same time, it is Sister 13's choice to be a criminal, yet we are unsure if it is her choice to be exclusively homosexual, as her butch lesbian persona is a caricatured patriarchal construction of Teenie's identity as Sister 13 and not as Teenie *per se*. Sandra Ng's character is known only through socially constructed names (nicknames), not essentialist (famil-ial) ones. Thus her "real" sexuality is unnamed, nonexistent. But gender performativity within masculinist institutionalism is hardly "post-structuralist" in its fluidity; although drawing upon Westernized archetypes, its construction within already sexist hegemony negates the possibility of transgression and mobility. Sister 13's masculinized performance is not for *herself*, but in accordance with rules exterior to her sexual freedom. Her lesbianism does *not* represent her sterling personal moral code which rises above legal homophobia and thus wins the hearts of audiences—if she does win their hearts, it is not because she is a sexualized lesbian but because she can perform as strongly as any man. Her compensatory personal morality, that necessary characteristic of non-martyred gangster hero(ines), seems to stem from the fact that she appreciates the love that representatives of heterosexual immorality, in both the social world (James) and the antisocial world (S.O.B., her other rivals), take for granted. She appreciates it more than they do because she cannot have it. Coke, meanwhile, although straight, is not seen as immoral by the audience because he will be excommunicated from triad hegemony—his overly anarchic killings of triad bosses later in the film will ultimately make him an outlaw within criminal society.

In a possibly militant statement against normative heterosexuality, Teenie and Shu Qi's character murder James on his wedding day. Teenie shoots him wearing Shu Qi's trademark mask. By killing James, a corrupt cop (legal society is even more immoral than illegal society), the now criminal mask she wears invalidates her standing in legal culture—which is corrupt and undeserving of allegiance anyway—and standardizes the homosexuality of her persona within a deviant society by making her predictably homosexual instead of disruptively bisexual. Her transformation from civilian bisexual to illegal homosexual demands her destruction of a representative member of the corrupt legal society as a foreshadowing of her later antisocial rebellion; after this act, she is no longer a civilian. Shu Qi's character lies on top of James, delivering the death blow: "I love you . . . but I hate you more." Shu Qi's femme character, now a real criminal, will not be heard from again, as her femme criminality has no place within organized crime. So, too, do her words of bitter love have no place within anti-society—thus the secrecy of Sister 13's "tear scene."

We return to the present, with the now-powerful Sister 13 trading in her ambiguously tomboyish overalls for the full drag of a man's black suit. She accidentally meets again with Yun, who, now a few years later, is an actress playing the role of ancient beauty in the romantic Taiwanese television serial "My Cousin Yuen Kwan." But Sister 13 has not lost Teenie's jealousy and insecurity: "Did you sleep with him [Coke]?" She answers, "Teenie, you are so stupid . . . Do you pretend not to know it? The one I love is you." Up until this point, our subjectivity has been privileged to Teenie/Sister 13, and we have assumed that the "beautiful" Yun was heterosexual. In fact, the femme but lesbian[26] Yun was merely performing heterosexuality, as she now literally performs a classically heterosexual role on her TV show. The "Yuen" in the name of her TV character can be roughly translated as "femininely frail," an idea consistent with the passivity of Yun's own behavior. Furthermore, a romance with one's "cousin" would be perhaps the least transgressive form of eros in traditional China, further signalling her retreat into normative role-playing. For Yun, civilian life offers only mandatory heterosexuality, her femme appearance ironically being the reason she was chosen to portray a heterosexual on TV. For Sister 13, the antisocial world of crime at least offers butch lesbianism, if *only* butch lesbianism. Like the tear scene, this dialogue offers an inverted glimpse into a character beyond subjective privilege. Yun says: " . . . I failed to make you realize it [my love for you]." As a civilian, Yun had been repressed by the corrupt legal world, which allows for no display of homosexuality, butch *or* femme. Homosexual play for Sister 13 is biologically female but performed male, i.e., in terms of violent strength. Yun, a civilian and not a criminal, is allowed to be a feministically beautiful lesbian because she is not part of the intra-legal gangster hierarchy; however, as a civilian, she must remain wholly closeted. Teenie, a civilian bisexual, sublimated her gay desire to Coke, not being able to cope with homosexuality on normative civilian terms; Sister 13, however, understands all too well, but as a butch figure must choose masculinized strength over love. The film too, as part of the conservative triad genre, sets up Sister 13 for failure–her true love remains unrequited, and the only sexual relationship she is allowed as an "out" lesbian turns out to be a betrayal, the buxom girl whose breasts were pummeled in the beginning. Feminine beauty is either a ruse or a danger. It is a catch-22: Sister 13 can be "out" only as a criminal, but her love only exists in the unbridgeable legal world.

The plot comes to a manufactured head as Sister 13–one last time–meets Coke, now on the run for injuring "Prince," another boss. For the first time she actually embraces Coke, and her face registers confusion. Do we, for but a fleeting moment, no longer see lesbian Sister 13 but bisexual Teenie, or is the confusion a disgusted reaction against her old bisexuality? The film refuses to answer the question, but that *something* is rekindled within her upon this meeting suggests her "natural" bisexuality is surfacing against the butch lesbian role she plays in accordance with her "male" role, which retroactively negates the free play of the bisexuality she once enjoyed, if never really acted upon.

After the exposition of the extended flashback sequence, the plot must overcompensate for its lack of forward thrust with a plot-heavy final 30 minutes. Soon, Coke will be killed by Sister 13's enemies–the buxom lover from the opening and the rival triad boss to whom she is now heterosexually attached. Coke must die to conveniently remove the subversive possibility of Sister 13 "reverting" to her unstable bisexuality, just as Jack and Martin's girlfriends must die in *A Hero* to ensure that their sexuality (or lack thereof) is fully determined by the insecure and neurotically controlling God of genre.

The buxom lover whom Sister 13 had excommunicated in the beginning now meets with Sister 13 for a final showdown. During the showdown, she scoffs to 13, "Doesn't he know you're a lesbian?", speaking of a male business partner who has expressed heterosexual interest in her with the gift of a ring. Like Ting with her "public toilet" line in *Cheap Killers*, female heterosexuality appears to be homosexuality's antagonist. This, of course, is the genre's smokescreen, since both of these women, though ambitious, are themselves but pawns within a male world. The insult to Sister 13's lesbianism comes from the buxom lover, and not the buxom lover's new male boss/lover, just as the insult to Sam's gayness in *Cheap* comes from Ting, and *not* Doctrine–yet it is the hegemony that males like Doctrine represent that is the true evil. This, of course, is consistent with the genre's misogyny, which not only exploits women but scapegoats them as well by having them mouth the genre's own masculinist prejudices.

Comparing Sister 13 to the traitorous, buxom lover, we might say the latter is in fact *traitorously* buxom, for her femme persona in combination with the new knowledge that she is a bisexual in the underworld now marks her as transgressively unstable to both Sister 13 and the genre which is controlling her. Her femme bisexuality–first a lover of Sister 13 and then betraying her with a male enemy–transgresses the film's internal laws of gender performance in a way that Sister 13 could not. Teenie the repressed bisexual was not indoctrinated into the triad's antisocial order (although she must know *about* it, since her father is an emasculated triad), and as a civilian her sexual instability could only pose a threat to civilian (social) law, as would civilian Yun's homosexuality. As Sister 13 the lesbian criminal, her outlaw butchness is her legality within outlaw structure. The only moment she transgressed law as a civilian was the very moment that made her both no longer a civilian and a "total" lesbian (killing James). And as a civilian, she only played with heterosexuality–in the early scenes in which she fooled her doltish teacher. Society's legal homophobia became Teenie's internalized personality, regulating/repressing her homosexuality, rationalized as asexual friendship with Yun and displaced towards Coke (in the bed/picture scenes).

The film barely characterizes the buxom lover–a shame, since much of its meaning hinges on her part. She is traitorous both as a femme homosexual and a femme heterosexual; whereas taboos within the criminal world are generally built into the "weakness" of a character's sexual status, her intra-illegality is that she has no avowed status at all, in any world. In the final confrontation, she claims she is straight, only having pretended to be Sister 13's lover at the beginning–but her screams and tears in the film's beginning render that denial hollow. She is punished in the beginning because she is not butch enough (she is tricky, sneaky, and therefore womanly, in addition to her femme demeanor); at the end, she is punished because her second betrayal is a betrayal of the genre itself. One should pick a side and stick with it–whether that "side" is a particular triad gang or a particular form of pigeonholed sexuality. Although all three of the film's major female characters are to varying degrees bisexual, Sister 13 and Yun are let off the hook, so to speak, because their performances are unidirectional in their object choice. (Yun performs as a heterosexual even though she is not; Sister 13 performs as a lesbian even though she is/was bisexual.) However, the untrustworthiness of the buxom lover's criminal/gang allegiances is equated with the "untrust-worthiness" of her sexuality. "Buxom" has taken advantage of the two-vari-able system of meta-illegality to exploit its instability for her own individual-istically sexualized gain. In this criminal world, female bisexuality is by its nature (or, if you prefer, lack of "nature") evil and punishable, its necessarily "double" ("bi") nature meaning one can never *love* single-mindedly. To be trustworthy, one must be a man–even if one is a woman, like Sister 13, who prizes love even though she cannot have it.

In a sense, the buxom lover's meta-illegal transgression is analogous to that of Sam and Yat-tiu in *Cheap*: both transgress sexual hegemony for their own survival against the genre's self-perpetuating demands. But in *Portland*, generic misogyny now arises, albeit discreetly, in a film created by men who probably (and mistakenly) also thought their lesbian heroine Sister 13 was a feminist (alas, lesbianism and feminism can be mutually exclusive!). Sam and Yat-tiu can be victorious in their transgression because they are men, playing with and in a long history of homosexual space the genre had already laid before them, and through their especial heroism extending it to an un-precedented (and transgressive) degree. As a woman, the buxom lover has no heroic feminine tradition to draw upon, and is objectified as the villain, whereas the male variant of Sam and Yat-tiu, obviously, are subjectified as heroes. Because the buxom lover is undercharacterized and has little screen time, we might assume she has valid offscreen reasons for what she is doing; because she is an untrustworthily bisexual woman, those reasons don't matter and she is vilified.

Sister 13, remember, is effectively a man, not a woman, and is thus exempt from this misogyny; a woman like the buxom lover would simply not be allowed to be the protagonist in a mainstream genre film today (as of this writing, at least). It is not lesbianism *per se* that is transgressive, because the conservatism through which it is construed can refashion it to its own liking. The analogously nontransgressive gay male variant would be Blonde in *Cheap Killers*, who is both a villain and a non-threat because the violence of his masculinity is normative. Blonde would be theoretically redeemed if he were capable of loving a man even as a (masculine) man, in the way that

Yat-tiu's intra-illegal transgressions (with Ting) can be redeemed. In *Portland*, both heterosexual and lesbian love is coded as heterosexuality, because Sister 13 is a "man" and thus her early relationship with "Buxom" was performatively heterosexual. Paradoxically, for Sister 13 to fall in love with a man would make her a gay male, and thus weakly effeminate. Thus, *Portland* reveals itself to be a conventionally masculine genre film by its rationalization of female homosexuality in terms of male performance; *Cheap*, on the other hand, is willing to allow its gay male heroes to be gay *and* strong. Simply, for *Portland* to be more transgressive/liberal, an untransformed Yun and not a butch Teenie would have to grow up to be a triad boss.

The character of "Buxom" is actually a much more complex issue than that of Ting in *Cheap*, whose heterosexuality was equated with both capitalism (upward mobility from Yat-tiu to Doctrine) and homophobia. As a bisexual, "Buxom" is caught between capitalism and homophobia, her predicament unwilling to let her combine the two: she performs as a bisexual to further her own goals, but as an illegal/immoral bisexual the genre will not allow her to fulfill them. Because the film in general denies the morality of legal heterosexual love as well–James, representing the law, murders the unborn product of his heterosexual union–the only choice in *Portland* is the reinforced and monitored codes of the slightly freer criminal world. Yun's civilian femme lesbianism is most tragic of all: it is a filmic world in which butch lesbianism–i.e., being a man–is the best a woman can do.

In the confusion that accounts for the climax, Sister 13 kills her new male rival (who is barely characterized), and "Buxom," with whom he had conspired, is captured and punished. Interestingly, "Buxom" is not killed, as if she were not a *real* villain but only a puppet, as if the film (and genre) *acknowledges* her ill-fated predicament and spares her the full punishment she would receive if she were a man (and thus responsible for her actions). But we conclude that "the best a woman can do is to be a man" because of Sister 13's final pose. She shoots the villain not alone, but only after her entire gang and the gangs from the other *Young and Dangerous* films have miraculously appeared to witness[27] the male villain being trapped and rendered helpless. It is the gang's witnessing of the event that makes it real in the criminal world, and of course Sister 13 must perform as a male–i.e., violently–by shooting the villain in view of her onlooking peers. Originally she is reluctant to do so, but when the plot makes the villain sneakily (effeminately?) pull out a gun, the film forces her to shoulder her violent male duty. Her righteousness can only exist as a public performance, and, her performance being male, only as a man in keeping with generic moral hegemonies. The criminal world's own laws must be spectacularly publicized to overcome criminality's inherent potential for individualized anarchy. Furthermore, that the cast members from the other films appear as *physical* signifiers of the genre itself means she is both validated by and positioned within generic morality.

A Hero and *Cheap* are more directly derived from HK martial genres, while *Portland* embodies Western notions of gender performance, although still in the formal service of those genres. Let us conclude by comparing the endings of the three films. We have already said that *A Hero* ends with Jack and Martin's deaths, followed by a coda in which their homosocial and repressedly homosexual legacy becomes the stuff of bar (and genre) legend. The heroes live only in the fiction of the genre which controls both them and their sexualities. In *Cheap*, Sam and Yat-tiu are transgressively allowed to be openly gay, defeating heterosexist hegemony, though at the expense of increasing the action genre's misogyny, as if to suggest the absolute amount of the genre's neurosis were unchangeable and must increase somewhere if it decreases elsewhere. In *A Hero*, the genre's misogyny is that it must kill its women, and its homophobia that it must kill its men, amusingly, because they live in a misogynistically *homosexual* genre; this amusement is the key to *A Hero*'s interpretation as satire. The "triumph" of *Cheap*, though arguably heterophobic and inarguably misogynistic, is that Sam and Yat-tiu love each other without being feminine–it is at least a tiny triumph over convention. This is true of seemingly all male film conventions; as Gregory Barrett in *Archetypes of Japanese Film* states, describing the Japanese archetype he calls "weak passive male" (which includes the conventional/legal samurai): "Man is not feminized because he is homosexual but because he is in love."[28] (118) Here, man *is* homosexual, in love, and, for once, *not* feminized. Sam and Yat-tiu are now total outcasts who will inscribe their own legends beyond the genre's traditional limitations–an inscription that is a further act of male power.

In the final shot of *A Hero*, the heroes are invisible, only a story. In *Cheap*, the final shot is of the two heroes alone, visible and individuated against all societies, storming the camera in slow motion. It is as if they will now storm the audience's own hegemonic prejudices: having destroyed the signifier, they will now destroy the referent. The final shot of *Portland*, however, is a version of the final shot of *Cheap*, only neutered and resocialized to hegemonic gangster solidarity–the "solidarity march," in fact, is the standard final shot for a *Young and Dangerous* film. After Sister 13 kills the villain, she is joined by her own gang and the gang members made popular by the original *Y&D* films, whose characters the audience immediately recognizes as iconic of their genre. In the final shot, Sister 13 walks down the street leading a collective gang–with her at the center–defiantly towards the camera. But her visibility as an individual lesbian is surrendered to the (only) mass identity which will accept her. Furthermore, as the collectivity of her group legitimizes her, we as the collectivity of a film audience are also asked to legitimize her morality of presumable "butch righteousness." The genre itself–symbolized by the well-known male cast members[29] from *Portland*'s sibling films–recognizes Sister 13's power (as a man), and the film is apparently proud of her for it. But what is Sister 13 defying in her pose for the camera, and can she even be defiant if she cannot be individuated from her hegemonic group? Sam and Yat-tiu's defiance is their outcasted homosexual love, and they defy anyone to take it from them. Sister 13 may be defying anyone to take away her power (or "manhood"), but we are not entirely convinced she really wants it. Perhaps like "Buxom," she has little choice– but unlike buxom, she happens to be the story's heroine. The phalanx of admirers that joins her for her final walk towards the camera may convince us she has found a "home" in the triad society, but we are not convinced she is really "herself" in the first place–so how can she be home if she doesn't even exist as herself? The sexual confusion that registers on her face when she sees Coke for the last time suggests she is capable of asserting her independently confused will against controlling and necessarily un-confused genre–but the over-simplicity of the final shot conflates the idea of Sister 13 sweeping such transgressions under the rug herself and the idea of the genre doing that sweeping for her. Thus, whatever heroism she may have is the genre's, and not *hers*. We believe Sam and Tat-tiu are transgressively heroic because they have homosexually individuated their wills against the repressive genre from which they were borne. Sister 13's heroism, on the other hand, is strictly conventional: she is a heroic lesbian but she is not heroic *as* a lesbian. In order to transgress genre, she would need a romantic partner, but *only* as a nongeneric lesbian–obviously a paradox. As a generic lesbian, she must yearn for love as do generic women but remain alone as do generic men–and join the asexual homosocial company of men as a man. The conventions of real-life social law coupled with the conventions, or legalisms, of film conspire to create static representations that mirror and perpetuate the status quo of legal society. When it comes to sexuality, genre–like puritanical social law–must be transgressed, which is what *Portland* will not do. In fact, the textual visibility of *A Hero, Cheap,* and *Portland*'s homosexuality is in inverse proportion to their liberality and progressiveness. *Portland* is the most openly gay of the three but its gender constructions are the most conventional. *Cheap* is the only one to, in fact, transgress the genre's homophobic closure (even while its male leads never even kiss), but only to reinforce its misogyny. *A Hero*, on the other hand, indulges in all the genre's cliches with disarming style only to satirically wash its hands of the entire affair, a spoof of the overdetermined fatalism that we as genre fanatics are supposed to take seriously. But *A Hero*'s homosexuality is indeed still subtextual, and can get away with this seemingly apolitical (or nihilistic) mischief.[30]

But no genre film is really apolitical. Because genre by its nature caters to the prefabricated, conservative expectations of its audience, its fictions always reinforce models of moral hegemony, like any mythical system. The laws of genre are an accepted boundary separating the legal social reality of the spectators from the unrealizable models of gendered behavior law played out on the screen. But in a closeted society (and moreso in Hong Kong/China), this "unrealizability" acquires an extra meaning for *homosexual* spectators–homosexuality, too, is as unrealizeable on screen as it is in life, if not moreso. The atheistic (or antitheistic) *A Hero Never Dies*, which seeks to undermine myth itself and which identifies genre as a sadistic "God," attempts to explain genre's sadistic insecurity in terms of homophobia. We might ask, "Why must genre be sadistic?" but we might as well ask "Why does *Cheap Killers have* to be misogynistic?" We might assume films mirror the audience and the audience its films, *ad infinitum*. But the audience does not control the origin of its arbitrary myths and cannot know what possibilities even exist if that formal myth-making presents only the same single option endlessly. Conventions create people more than people create conventions–"personal responsibility" is just as much a hegemonic illusion as is homophobia. The single option presented, of course, becomes law–the law of heterosexism or whatever the case may be.

In *Portland*, the mythic, worshipped "God" is merely the collective group to which Sister 13 has surrendered her bisexual identity; by "allowing" her to be a lesbian, it actually limits her freedom. In *Cheap*, the heroes become Gods themselves when they assert their autonomy above the hellish genre they inhabit and must somehow escape. It will be the test of time which will determine if these three films will stand as acts of subversive will (to varying degrees), or if their transgressions, if not forgotten altogether, will be newly homogenized into a more conservative mythology; perhaps the latter is indeed the inescapable power of making genre films in the first place. If *Cheap Killers'* Sam and Yat-tiu, apart from the misogyny of the film they inhabit, do indeed win genre audience's hearts despite their unapologetic gayness, there is hope that audiences can overcome the generic hegemonies that they have accepted as their own, recognizing and then criticizing the infantile homophobia that informs most action films. Or if, as Freud said, it takes a neurosis to cure a neurosis, perhaps we might resist the neurotic excitements of the action genre as it stands now and look for a more progressive neurosis to cure our societal ills. Or we can look for a less neurotic God.

NOTES

1. Unlike the standard Hollywood action film, Hong Kong action films have also allowed for female protagonists of martial ability equal to their male counterparts. However, the swordswomen of, say, post-King Hu Hong Kong films become asexualized in their impersonation of male martial roles. In the contemporary "female"

Hong Kong action films following Corey Yuen Kwai's *Yes, Madam* (1985), the young heroines may have personal victories over male (and female) villains, but in no way challenge the hierarchical political structure that employs them and in which they struggle. In fact, many HK police films go out of their way to show a portrait of Queen Elizabeth II hanging on the police captain's wall. The equation of female martiality with asexuality is standard in HK police films (*Tiger Cage* (1988), *Royal Warriors* (1986), *Righting Wrongs* (1987), etc.)–the embodiment of legality in a woman must be asexualized, because lawfulness itself must be oppose sexual unconventionality. An exception, such as Godfrey Ho's 1990 *Lethal Panther,* a distaff version of Woo's *The Killer,* sees to it that the anti-legal female antihero is cold and passionless, whereas Chow Yun-fat's hero in Woo's film is allowed to be romantically male. The gender of the martial content action is democratized but its formal impetus is male (and, by extension, action films' audiences are of course predominantly male). Also witness the importation of *Yes, Madam*'s Michelle Yeoh for the James Bond film *Tomorrow Never Dies* (1997). Her formal deputation as "Bond Girl" sexualizes the content of the very martial skill she was imported for, thus automatically making her second fiddle to the male hero. She can be lethally sexy *and* legal, but despite her skill we are not convinced she is Bond's equal: because of her sexualization, her martial competence is only a "surprising" overcoming of her female biology.

2. It is interesting to note that among indigenously produced HK films of 1998, *Cheap Killers* was #32 and *Portland Street Blues* was #33 in box office gross, as if their homosexual agendas were entirely transparent to a shared core audience.

3. For our purposes here, the gangster film is defined as a film whose moral order is constructed by and within a hegemonically and hierarchically *organized* criminal world. This definition, of course, excludes tangential genres such as *film noir* or the detective film, which may include gangster characters but not as moral (anti-)heroes.

4. It is noteworthy that in *Bonnie and Clyde*, Clyde's historical bisexuality is changed to the more acceptable aberration of impotence.

5. *The Longest Nite* (1998) was directed by To's disciple, Patrick Yau. In an interview at Toronto's 1999 Fantasia Film Festival, To expressed disappointment with the immaturity he perceives in Yau, who had since been remanded to television duties. Although To's definition of "maturity" is unclear, the discrepancy may be predicated on the ability to naively accept *A Hero Never Dies* as straight-faced sentimentality, whereas Yau's films are aggressively satirical assaults on the necessary antirealism of genre film-making. It is disingenuous of To to criticize Yau's films for their immaturity, and to pass off *A Hero* as a film with no ironic subtext. But perhaps Yau's *textual* transgressions went too far into what To calls "immaturity."

6. Any possible sentimental interpretation of *A Hero* would be mechanical and overdetermined compared to To's more ingenuously naive *Barefooted Kid* (1993) and *Loving You* (1995). To's *All About Ah-Long* (1989) is a genuine tragedy and his *A Moment of Romance 3* (1996), though not ultimately tragic, is plotted like one save for a last-minute happy ending. Given the saccharine sentiment of these precedents, and the lack of sweetness in *A Hero*, I must conclude it is meant to be ironic by To's own standards.

7. To's recent film *Running Out of Time* (1999) is in fact one long, running "game" between a clever cop and the dying thief who continually outsmarts him. In the final scene, the thief disguises himself in female drag and pretends to be the cop's girlfriend to fool their mutual enemy. To make the relationship believable, the cop kisses him on the cheek, a "winking" gesture at the audience acknowledging the homosexual subtext that has been operating all along.

8. Woo has reluctantly admitted to both Eastern and Western critics that there indeed may have been some (unintentional) gay subtext in *The Killer*. In Stanley Kwan Kam-pang's *Yang and Yin: Gender in Chinese Cinema* (1996) and elsewhere, he has admitted that had the film been made in Hollywood the sexual connotations would probably have been disallowed. Indeed, Woo's most successful U.S. film, *Face Off* (1997), whose story of fleshly male identity-exchange has homoerotic potential on an almost metaphysical level, subverts Woo's usual homosocial universe by centering the reunion of the nuclear family in its denouement, an "inserted" Hollywood theme absent from Woo's post-*A Better Tomorrow* (1986) films. This bastardization of non-Eurocentric meaning may be the flip-side of the 1997 issue: in choosing between Western freedom and communist rule, ostensible capitalist "freedom" may prove to be equally oppressive.

The Killer decenters the ostensible heterosexual relationship between killer Chow Yun-fat and Sally Yeh, the singer he accidentally blinds with his bullet. Yeh's sexual status in the film degenerates from heroic focus to the mere distraction of a bikini girl in a boxing ring once Danny Lee's cop arrives, providing Chow with the mirror-image of his (legalized) soul; Yeh devolves into a heterosexual buffer for their homosexual tournament, reassuring the audience that what they are witnessing is anything but a heterosexual antagonism culminating in her capture. Yeh's blindness ("I only see shadows") is also her blindness to the Chow-Lee relation, which blurs the line between (homosexual) criminality and (heterosexual) legality. Chow and Lee never know each other's real names–what they themselves experience is "unnameable" (a la Oscar Wilde?). Appropriately, Chow is climactically blinded himself, and now each potential heterosexual partner is incapable of consummating the heterosexual vision; only the union of Chow of Lee has been "visualized."

9. For a discussion of *yi*, see Stephen Teo's *Hong Kong Cinema: The Extra Dimensions*, Chapter 11. For a slick spoof of *yi*, see Blackie Ko Sau-Leung's film *Days of Being Dumb* (1992), in which the two bumbling triad heroes continue to sleep together despite the romantic introduction of a woman into their bed.

10. Although it may also be argued that homosexuality among triad brothers is a form of "fraternal incest," I am primarily interested here in homosexuality of the actual, and not the metaphorical, variety.

11. Mellen, Joan. *The Waves at Genji's Door*. New York: Pantheon Books, 1976.

12. It is admittedly arguable if there have been other mainstream commercial action films with gay heroes (not supporting players) before *Cheap Killers*, although I am hard pressed to think of one whose very *raison d'etre* was the systemic explication of previously latent gay coding. Perhaps Takashi Ishii's overrated *Gonin* (1995) comes close, its only outstanding sequences in its story of five thieves being those two which involve homosexuality. In the first, Kitano Takeshi's *yakuza* character rapes his underling; Kitano, as another yakuza, would also rape an underling in his

own *Boiling Point* (1990), and in both cases the rapes are blackly comic. Here, homosexuality is also relegated to criminality, but is presented as decadent and ridiculous. *Gonin's* second scene of interest features two mortally wounded thieves sharing a forbidden kiss before one of them dies, an obvious subversion of the traditional dying-hero's embrace, also a staple of the American Western. The two heroic thieves, unlike Kitano's anti-heroic yakuza character, seem sincere in their homosexuality. Thus, their operating as "good" criminals purifies their kiss within the 2-variable system of homosexuality/criminality. The film's attempt to criticize Japanese capitalism–the five thieves are "forced" into crime via economic hardship, and one of them, a former corporate wage-slave, enters criminality to rescue his masculine potency–is subsumed by its homosexual thesis. It should be noted that at a 1998 screening of *Gonin* at Toronto's Fantasia Film Festival, the kissing scene drew "boos" from the audience and then reactionary applause in equal measure, revealing both the scene's blatant calculation and the depressing (frightening?) ease of that calculation's success. The five protagonists of Ishii's in-name-only sequel *Gonin 2* (1996) are this time all female, and there are no homosexual acts, as if the presence of female homosociality implies a "necessarily" titillating homosexuality that male homosociality does not.

13. Recently, in fact, Fok plays a gay martial arts master in producer Wong Jing's execrable, homophobic *Body Weapon* (1999), in which a gay rapist inexplicably rapes women (?) because the macho hero rebukes his advances. It is admittedly baffling why Fok would play the effeminate, witless stereotype that he does here, for although Fok's images of homosexuality as a director are often perverse or antisocial, they are not "colorful" stereotypes.

14. As Fok's only film to receive a legitimate (albeit very limited) US theatrical release, *Naked Killer's* fantastic and slickly produced Asian lesbianism further appeals to the politico-sexual paternalism of "hip" Eurocentric audiences. Obviously, the male homosexual variant that is *Cheap Killers*, although devoid of explicit sex, would be a harder sell.

15. The possible erotic exploitation of male homosexuality–which *Cheap Killers* unfortunately does not do–would not delegitimize its "seriousness"; rather, as a generic film its revolutionary political statement would be stronger (think of Jarman's subversion of the Biblical film in *Sebastiane* (1976), for example).

16. Wong Jing's treatment of homosexuality has been uneven, to say the least, although suffice it to say that Wong treats most subjects as a *farceur*. In his comedy *Boys are Easy* (1993), a typically cross-dressed Lin Ching-hsia courts a cooing, wildly effeminate Tony Leung Kar-fai; though hardly progressive, it does typify an almost normative procedure of casual gender play and fluidity in HK's recent "mo-lei-tau"-inspired surreal comic universe.

17. The misogynistic variety of homosexuality is particular neither to the East nor the West. Obviously indefensible, it does have a long history–*Cheap Killers* may be of the same mold as Saikaku's accounts of the Japanese *onna-girai* ("woman-haters," as opposed to bisexuals) in *The Great Mirror of Male Love*, for example.

18. Clarence Fok often steals scenes from other films (see, for example, his *Iceman Cometh* [1989], or his unfortunate *Chungking Express* rip-off *Passion 1995*). The hotel fight has an obvious resemblance in both action and theme to the hotel

shootout in John Woo's *A Better Tomorrow 2* (1987). In that film, Dean Shek plays a man driven to insane impotence by the murder of his young daughter; when killers are sent to finish him off, he regains his righteous sanity in a burst of cathartic heroism. In Woo's film, the tragedy is the challenge to family lineage and Shek's heroism redefines his heterosexual ability to shoot, kill, and by extension possibly have more children. In Fok's *Cheap Killers*, the unification of the two males asserts the "sanity" of homosexuality in contradistinction to the family–particularly since Sam has demonstrated far more concern about Yat-tiu than for the recent death of his own family.

19. Interviewed by Stanley Kwan in his 1996 documentary *Yang and Yin: Gender in Chinese Cinema*, an aged Chang freely (and with good humor) admits to a Freudian interpretation of the various phallic symbols and violent bodily penetrations that characterize his work.

20. *Portland Street Blues* was also written and produced by Manfred Wong, suggesting it is perhaps he more than director Yip Wai-Man who is responsible for the film's success.

21. In *Sexy and Dangerous* (1996), the female triad girls usually treated as window dressing are allowed the center stage, as both heroines and villains. The English title itself, however, frames the film as a particularly heterosexual adventure, and whatever empowerment they may seem to acquire in the film is mitigated by their initial categorization as "Sexy." Produced by Wong Jing and directed by Billy Tang Hin-sing, it is a capitalization on the success of *Y&D*.

22. Ibid. See Chapter 9.

23. It is interesting to note the English plot synopsis for *Portland Street Blues* on the packaging for the film's video and DVD release. It reads: "In the male-dominated triad society, a young woman named Sister Thirteen struggles to the top (not without compromise) and makes her mark on Portland Street. Only one man can bring her down–the man she loves." Not only is this synopsis wrong–the man who can bring her down is not Coke, the one she loves–but any mention of her homosexuality is scrupulously avoided. Unless, of course, her sexual identity is one of the synopsis's ambiguous "compromises." Notably, the Chinese-language plot synopsis *does* mention she is a lesbian.

24. Ng Man Tat has often played a loser who makes a heroic bid for redemption; see *A Moment of Romance* (1990), *Best of the Best* (1992), *Love on Delivery* (1993), etc.

25. It is worth noting that the altar to General Kwan, famously depicted in the classic novel *Romance of Three Kingdoms*, is also a fixture in Chinese police stations, suggesting the ideal of brotherhood he represents overarches both legal and illegal societies. The legality of the *yi* of police groups, of course, resists the homosexuality the illegality of the gangster's *yi* invites.

26. Because the film in general refuses such distinctions while simultaneously begging them, it is not clear whether Yun is supposed to be a lesbian or a bisexual; however, because she is a civilian and not a triad, both would be equally transgressive in her legal world.

27. This is a common conclusion for the whole of the *Young and Dangerous* series. After the hero has been framed for a crime, he proves his innocence and righteousness in front of gang members who act as the triad world's impromptu *demos* of

impartial judges. Their impartiality as antisociety's objective legality always sees through the villain's ruses and acquits the wronged hero.

28. Barrett, Gregory. *Archetypes in Japanese Film*. Selinsgrove: Susquehana University Press, 1989.

29. The "well-known" cast members are led by Cheng Yee-kin, now famous for the *Y&D* series and whose character is equated with normative heroic male potency.

30. It is also true that Clarence Fok has indeed a history of gay films and Sandra Ng has a history of masculinized roles (including mannish cop roles such as in Jeff Lau's *Thundercops 2* [1989])–whereas no one associated with *A Hero* has any similar career investment in making a case for sex/gender transgression.

Remembered Branches:
Towards a Future
of Korean Homosexual Film

Jooran Lee

SUMMARY. Korean cinema has long labored under an imported Confucian homophobia which, through its effects if not its causes, seems to mirror the Western conception of the closet. Recent cinematic developments in Korea, including a queer film festival in Seoul, are slowly but surely beginning to change that. Using as primary texts the recent Korean gay film *Broken Branches* and the long-forgotten lesbian film *Ascetic: Woman and Woman,* my essay hopes to serve as a set of introductory remarks on a queer Korean cinema culture whose surface has only just been broached. *[Article copies available for a fee from The Haworth Document Delivery Service: 1-800-342-9678. E-mail address: <getinfo@haworthpressinc. com> Website: <http://www.HaworthPress.com>]*

Discussing Korean gay and lesbian films is like drifting in space without sunlight or oxygen. One searches, blindly, gaspingly–and mostly in vain–simply trying to discover the existence of such films. Since the first Korean film *Fight for Justice* (1919), actually an "interlude" motion picture to be shown between the acts of a stage play, and the historical drama *Arirang*[1] (1926), a film often considered to have raised Korean film to the

Jooran Lee is a freelance writer for *Buddy*, Korea's only gay magazine, as well as for various journals, magazines, and webzines. She studied French and English Literature at Sookmyung Women's University. She completed her MA with "A Study on Christopher Isherwood's 'Down There on a Visit,'" the first study of Isherwood written in Korean.

Address correspondence to the author at: 435-1 (4-F) Changan 3-dong, Dongdaemoon-Gu, Seoul 130-103, Republic of Korea (E-mail: oasisuk@chollian.net).

[Haworth co-indexing entry note]: "Remembered Branches: Towards a Future of Korean Homosexual Film." Lee, Jooran. Co-published simultaneously in *Journal of Homosexuality* (The Haworth Press, Inc.) Vol. 39, No. 3/4, 2000, pp. 273-281; and: *Queer Asian Cinema: Shadows in the Shade* (ed: Andrew Grossman) Harrington Park Press, an imprint of The Haworth Press, Inc., 2000, pp. 273-281. Single or multiple copies of this article are available for a fee from The Haworth Document Delivery Service [1-800-342-9678, 9:00 a.m. - 5:00 p.m. (EST). E-mail address: getinfo@haworthpressinc.com].

level of art, realism had been the foundation and mainstay of Korean cinema. Rebelling against Japanese colonialism, and then coping with the aftermath of the Korean War, it was through realism that Korean society expressed its sociopolitical ideas. After the war, Korean literature, fine arts, music, and films were so preoccupied with redressing the country's political problems realistically that little room was left for discourses on sexuality. Throughout the eighty years of Korean film history, no Korean film has been explicitly and publicly categorized or promoted as "homosexual" cinema, as are gay and lesbian films in the West. While religion–usually Christianity–has been the major obstacle prohibiting homosexuality in Western films, it is the imported Chinese Confucian family system that is mainly responsible for restraining homosexuality in Korean films.

Traditionally, homosexuality had not been too objectionable, or detestable, in Korean society. A king of the Shilla Dynasty, Hyegong (758-780) used to wear female dresses and was known to fancy men. A king of the Koryo Dynasty, Gongmin (1330-1373), had, in addition to his royal guards, his own special guards, formed with handsome young boys with whom he had sexual relations.[2] But contemporary Korean film audiences generally expect to see only heterosexuality in films that rarely go beyond the realism, or the hegemonies, of their daily lives. Only more sensitive audiences can perceive a vaguely homosexual or bisexual atmosphere concealed in a few Korean films whose producers and directors dare not speak aloud their gay or lesbian subtexts. In this limited film world, however, there are two Korean films in particular which we can now designate, respectively, as lesbian and gay: *Ascetic: Woman and Woman,* and *Broken Branches*.

Ascetic: Woman and Woman has only recently been rediscovered and acclaimed as the first Korean lesbian film. When first released in 1976, it was largely dismissed by audiences, although it is director Kim Su-hyeong's favorite work among his own numerous films and was awarded best film of the year by the Korean press. Kim Su-hyeong (1945-present), a prolific director, concentrated on comedies in the 1970's before turning his interests, in the 1980s and 90s, towards erotic films. Kim's most popular film, the hetero-erotic *The Wild Strawberry*, was popular enough in adult cinematheques and the rental video market to warrant six sequels, all directed by himself.

Ascetic, however, is far from Kim's usual work, which generally focuses on heterosexual sensuality. The film's heroine, Young-hee, is a fashion model who suffers from the horrifying experience of being raped by three men when she was nineteen. Intending to comfort her, a female artist named Noh Mi-ae asks the psychically tormented Young-hee to be her model. Having been abused and beaten herself at the hands of her husband, Noh Mi-ae sympathizes with Young-hee, who gains self-confidence by virtue of Noh Mi-ae's support, both emotional and financial. Jun, a fashion designer[3] who studied abroad, approaches Young-hee and gives her an opportunity to appear as the top model of his catwalk show. Young-hee falls in love Jun and leaves Noh Mi-ae, who begs her not to leave for this heterosexual option. When Young-hee then discovers Jun has betrayed her for another woman, she returns to Noh Mi-ae. But alas, the grief-stricken Noh Mi-ae has already committed suicide.

Director Kim Su-hyeong frames many scenes of *Ascetic* with artistic resonance. Scenes of Noh Mi-ae with Young-hee at her atelier, or a yellow-clad Young-hee wandering about in the woods, are staged and framed to evoke the impressionist oils of Monet. Yellows and reds conspire to summon an atmosphere of feminine sensuality. Birds and insects, emblems of nature, symbolically surround Noh Mi-ae and Young-hee, as if to suggest their homosexual relation were in keeping with nurturing, natural orders. This framing is not akin to the synthetic or manufactured art of the fashion-world for which Young-hee foolishly leaves Noh Mi-ae. Rather, this presentation of "natural art" reflects the naturalness of Noh Mi-ae's love for Young-hee, an art destroyed when Young-hee leaves her for Jun, whose heterosexual artistry is seen as unnatural (as well as exploitive). Jun's masculinist exploitation is only a trap which Young-hee ironically sees instead as an escape, a vindication of a previously abusive heterosexuality. But Jun's masculinity is in fact part of the very same hegemonic system responsible for Young-hee's rape and Noh Mi-ae's marital abuse.

As *Ascetic*'s two heroines transform their patronal relationship into real and symbiotic lesbianism, they construct a barrier between themselves and the violent male world that has abused them. Scenes such as Noh Mi-ae painting on Young-hee's naked body as if it were a canvas and massaging her with honey were so shocking at the time of the film's release that audiences who perceived the film's implied homosexuality wondered how the director managed to get away with such frank scenes in a hostile Korean climate. In an interview with the Korean gay magazine *Buddy*, director Kim Su-hyeong said that his intention was to make a feminist film, rather than a lesbian one: "I found women in our androcentric society to be birds in a cage. So in this film I tried to express my faith in the idea that women should free themselves from the cage in which men captured them."[4]

In the seventies, when the director made *Ascetic*, gay and lesbian theory was not widespread in Korean society. Instead, progressives and liberals in Korea discovered the feminism that was then flourishing in the West, and feminism was appropriated as a new trend among Korean artists (as any new "ism" had always been trendily adopted in Korea). Thus, there was nothing apart from Western feminism which Kim Su-hyeong could employ to approach issues of homosocial femininity in his film. The use of feminism was not a contrivedly "safe" pretext for *Ascetic*'s homosociality, designed to placate conservatives and keep them at bay. Rather, the director simply did not duly recognize lesbianism in itself, for the very concept of lesbianism was not allowed to ripen in the political atmosphere of the 70s. Therefore, Kim Su-hyeong–like many other artists of the time–clung to a feminism which may seem outmoded by the standards of current theory. *Ascetic* should not be misunderstood in the way literary critic Bonnie Zimmerman has character-ized lesbian feminism;[5] nor can it be denounced as Indian-Canadian director Deepa Mehta's *Fire* (1996) was by some in the gay community, who accused it of concealing and encoding its lesbianism within a mask of more socially acceptable (and excusable) feminism. But as time passed and lesbian move-ments arose in Korea, Kim Su-hyeong admitted he did not mind if *Ascetic* was accepted as either feminist or lesbian.[6]

It may be said that *Ascetic* has too little criticism against male-dominated society to be regarded as feminist and too little sexual interplay between Young-hee and Noh Mi-ae to be described as lesbian. Han Chae-yoon, a chief editor of *Buddy* and a leader of Korea's lesbian community, however, affirms that *Ascetic* is the first lesbian film in Korea, despite the fact that the explica-tion of its homosexuality is compromised. But the female bonding of Noh Mi-ae and Young-hee is more meaningful than it seems. When Young-hee asks her why she is unwilling to let her leave for Jun, Noh Mi-ae significantly responds, "Because I gave you my whole life." These words will revolution-arily define the sympathetic solidarity lesbians should stand for–whereas heterosexual Jun would never give Young-hee his life, Noh Mi-ae is willing to place not only her sexuality but her entire being in Young-hee's hands. Thus, when Young-hee leaves Noh Mi-ae, she takes the life Noh Mi-ae sacrificed for Young-hee with her; in a sense, Noh Mi-ae needn't commit suicide because she is already dead. This female homosocial imperative responded to the needs of women in the 1970s, fostering a homoerotic and homo-emotional bond that would embolden the female voice to resist mascu-linist hegemony. Though critically acclaimed, and historically significant, it is a pity that *Ascetic* is not seen or appreciated more widely.

The second markedly homosexual Korean film is *Broken Branches* (1995). In 1995, Vancouver International Film Festival programmer and East Asian film specialist Tony Rayns visited Korea and happened upon the commotion surrounding Park Jae-ho's second film. Park Jae-ho (1958-pres-ent) is a promising new director who in 1985 graduated from the Korean Film Academy, many of whose alumni now lead Korea's major film world. His debut feature *Madame Liberal 1990* (1990), a remake of the same-titled heterosexual melodrama produced in 1956, was selected as one of the year's best by the Korea Film Commission.

After seeing *Branches*, Rayns called it "the most interesting new Korean film I have seen so far this year," and proceeded to christen it with a new English title (and equip it with English subtitles) to introduce it at the Dragons and Tigers section of the 14th Vancouver International Film Festival. The original Korean title is *Neilro Hurunun Kang*–"The River Through Tomorrow." Understanding that in Korea branches symbolize the offspring of the parental tree, Rayns's English title proposes to express the film's story of the rise and fall of a family whose generations have been broken, scattered, alienated.

Contrary to the aesthetic colors of *Ascetic* two decades earlier, which coupled a divergent lesbianism with a non-realistic style also diverging from Korea's norm, new-generation director Park Jae-ho keeps *Broken Branches* within the bounds of realism. However, *Branches* is unwilling to turn its characters into homosexual martyrs in the manner of *Ascetic*, its liberal optimism hoping to instead escape such suffocating traditions. Spanning the years of the 1950s through the 1990s, the film is divided into three chronological chapters: "Father," "Hope," and "Family." Jung-min, the film's narrator, is born in 1959 into the extended family of a tyrannical Confucian patriarch named Park Han-seop, whom Jung-min's mother had married as his third wife with two children from a previous marriage. A land-owner, Park Han-seop is obsessed with ancestor worship and has strict ideas about male (patriarchal) morality and female subservience.

The first chapter, "Father," deals with the clashes between the young and old generations in and outside the Park household during the post-Korean War days. The narrator's brother and sister rebel against the old orthodoxies on which their step-father Park Han-seop insists. The brief second chapter, "Hope," is about the deaths of fathers–both the patriarch Park Han-seop and the similarly dictatorial Korean president Park Chung-hee (1917-1979). Although both deaths must signify the vanishing of the old generation and the advent of the new, this does not mean the old systems must be destroyed in order to make way for social progress. Director Park Jae-ho does not scheme to subvert the old. Rather, he hopes the deaths of heterosexist fathers will diminish only the more conservative aspects of the old generation. Thus we will be prepared for a liberal environment that will embrace various sexual identities–for in the final chapter, the narrator will offer the possibility of a reconciliation between the old and new.

The final chapter "Family," reveals that Jung-min is gay. A fledgling film director in his 30s, Jung-min meets an older man, Seung-gul, at a gay bar, and they quickly develop a relationship. But as a married man with children, Seung-gul is compelled to remain closeted, while Jung-min wants to spend more time with him and solidify their relationship. Not understanding their relationship and thinking Jung-min is only a friend of her husband, Seung-gul's wife tries in vain to be Jung-min's heterosexual matchmaker. Jung-min is soon invited to the 70th birthday party of his stepmother, Park Han-seop's second wife. Jung-min arrives at the party with older lover Seung-gul, and they bow before the 70-year old woman like husband and wife. Jung-min then introduces Seung-gul, in front of all family members present (most married with children), as his lover. This union represents, he says, the younger generation's attempt to reconcile its differences with the older. Only though "outing" and liberating the sexuality of a Confucian hegemony which seeks to repress the variations in its own identity will the scattered "branches" be able to rejoin their tree, and only by this will the tree re-accept them. Because the gap between the generations is great, it will take an equally great transgression (i.e., homosexuality) to undergird the bridge between old and new. A reconciliation by and though queerness will thus be one of the greatest possible, since it redresses the homophobia underlying Confucian patriarchy (and indeed most hegemonies), a fear which is too often the impetus for oppression.

In *Broken Branches*, director Park Jae-ho does not simply challenge conventional (Confucian) family values, or seek to destroy them through a gay protagonist. Rather, the gesture of Jung-min introducing Seung-gul to his family proposes a new alternative to family values, reconstructing them in terms more benevolent than standard heterosexism. This liberalization of Confucianism is not a one-sided youthfulness, however, since Seung-gul's older-generation identity also reveals the gayness hidden within the old regimes. Alternating between the narrator's childhood and the present, the film moves from static hostility towards reconciliation and reform. In a 1990's Korea where gay liberation is only still taking shape, *Broken Branches* is regarded as a unique and exceptionally brave film for gay men jockeying for their rightful position within the family system.

Although *Ascetic* and *Broken* are the most notable examples of Korean homosexual film, there are others. Director Ha Kil-jong's *The Pollen of Flowers* (1972) is well-known as an implicitly homosexual film, one which displays his common theme: the lust from which all human beings are doomed to suffer. Based on Lee Hyo-suk's novel of the same name, the film is reminiscent of Pier Paolo Pasolini's *Teorema* (1968) on account of its plot: a handsome young man charms and seduces all the members of a well-to-do family and destroys their lives in the process. But unlike the Marxist subtext of Pasolini's film, *Pollen* avoids schematic political meaning. The novel on which the film is based was written in 1939, and author Lee Hyo-suk had been influenced by the nineteenth-century European Decadents, who were characterized by world-weariness, self-consciousness, and contempt of morality and religion, and who sought new stimulations through artistic refinement and "degenerate" behavior. Consistent with the Decadents' indifference to the practical politics of their day, *Pollen* focuses instead on human relationships. The handsome young man, Dan-joo, and the master of a beautiful blue house, Hyun-ma, have an especially tense and obsessive bond. Dan-joo explains his relationship with lover/patron Hyun-ma to Mi-ran, a little sister of Hyun-ma's mistress, who also has a crush on him: "Our relationship is fateful. Hyun-ma and I fight, cry, and hug each other like children." Although this line may implicitly excuse homosexuality as an infantile indulgence, there can be no question that when Hyun-ma bites Dan-joo's ear in a storm of jealousy, it is an inarguably sexual moment implying a gay rape.

Is There a U.S. Moon in Itaewon? (1991) is a cliched, regressive look at the life of transvestites and transsexuals.[7] *Is There a Moon* is the story of a transsexual striptease performer who is willing to do anything for amounts of money miserable enough to reinforce a capitalist/bourgeois audience's stereotypical view of transgender "immorality" and cheapness. Although transgendered personae were present and accepted in old Korean culture (for example, as tribal shamanic figures), *Is There a Moon* reflects the public opinion of transsexuals in present Korean society, the criticism of the film by Korean gay and lesbian activists which ensued notwithstanding. Despite its perpetuation of negativity, the films caused a sensation in Korea, as audiences were shocked that a real-life transsexual, and not a professional actor, played the lead role. This male-to-female transsexual became a notable guest on some television shows after the film's release, and although the film he starred in did him little justice, his mere appearance in public was enough to encourage Korean would-be transsexuals to come out of the closet.

The development of the gay movement in Korea reached a crossroads in the late 1990s. As soon as Hong Kong cinema hero Wong Kar-wai received a Best Director award for *Happy Together* (*Chen gwong tsa sit*) at the 1997 Cannes Film Festival, a film importer supported by a large Korean corporation imported the film and applied for a ratings certificate before its release in Korea. Fearing that Wong–who indeed has many young Korean fans–would through his film encourage homosexuality and thus endanger public morals, the Korean Performing Arts Ethics Commission banned the release of *Happy Together*. A whirlwind of argument, both for and against the ban, erupted both in the press and the public. Public opinion showed that the Ethics Commission's decision went too far and that their criteria on which their censorships are based should be liberalized. To everyone's surprise, the dispute over *Happy Together* actually resulted in the dismissal of the Korean Performing Arts Ethics Committee–and the establishment of the Korean Council for Performing Arts Promotion, whose regulations were more relaxed than those of its predecessor. Consequently, censorship rules gradually began to relax: The Korean Council enacted sanctions against only two lewd films, while the Ethics Commission had forbade all homosexual films, even if only suggestive. At last *Happy* was released in Korea in 1998 with the Korean Council's permission, and of course became a long-running hit.

The other turning point occurred when a gay and lesbian film festival in Seoul ran into censorship in 1997. The festival was supposed to be held at the Alumni hall of a private university–but on the first night of the festival, the electricity was turned off by university authorities. The police stated that they could not sanction a gay and lesbian film festival. As the festival was cancelled "on account of sexual prejudice," a small number of gays from homosexual equal-rights groups formed an arrangement committee to lawfully host the gay and lesbian fest in Seoul. At first the committee announced the official name of the festival as the "Seoul Queer Film and Video Festival," defined it as a biennial event, and submitted a written application for permission to the government. By virtue of the arrangement committee's efforts and by favor of the government authorities the first "Seoul Queer Film and Video Festival" was held at Art Sonje Center in November, 1998–and was favorably noticed by the press.

The moderate attitude towards the ratings certificates of gay films by the Korean Council for Performing Arts Promotion[8] and the success of the 1998 Seoul Festival, both hopefully ushering in a brighter future for Korean gays and lesbians, were partially supported by Korean president Kim Dae-jung's policy on homosexuality. When Kim Dae-jung was elected at the end of 1997, he gave an interview to a progressive newspaper: "Although I do not advocate same-sex love, I think we should not categorically prohibit such. One needs to approach activities of lesbians and gays as a part of security of human rights. It is necessary to embrace them as members of society instead of confining them to taboo." Now saying that censorship of films has to be based on review by civil experts and not the government, President Kim Dae-jung's political party expressed regret for the cancellation of the 1997 queer film festival–which had happened just before he won the election.

Recently, a new direction in Korean cinema has arisen. Independent filmmaking, less reluctant to deal with homosexual subjects because it doesn't depend on the economics of nationwide or worldwide popularity, has drawn young Korean directors with tendencies towards GLBT themes. Korean independent films had emerged in the middle of the 1980s. As low-budget enterprises, independent films could free themselves from the fetters of government sponsorship; accordingly, Korean independent films in their early days were anti-government and anti-capitalist. In the 1990s, they have broadened their themes and delved deeply into personal affairs, shedding the political baggage of their 80s predecessors. Whereas short films were once the mode of choice for young Korean independents to express political dissatisfaction, now they have come to embody the implicit politics of gay or lesbian relationships. Some, such as director Lee Hee-il's *Everyday Is Like Sunday*

(1997, 20 mins.) and Choi So-won's *J* (1998, 10 mins.), captured the attention of audiences. *Everyday*, about the meeting and separation of a gay couple, was shot in the pseudodocumentary style commonly employed by many independent directors–a style which is possibly the modern version of Korea's old penchant for realism. The plot of *J* concerns the violent jealousy one girl harbors for another. Director Choi So-won is well-known among young Koreans as a programmer of the "One Hundred Thousand Won Video Film Festival," a very small competition for short independent video films whose production budget should not exceed 100,000 Korean *won* (no more than about 80 U.S. dollars) according the festival's unique rule. She is now planning her next work, appealingly entitled *Lesbian Horror Video*.

Although still rarely dealing with issues of homosexual equality, and not yet approaching the level of gay and lesbian political visibility common in Western cinema, Korean cinema is now moving to tolerate gay, lesbian, bisexual, and transsexual/transgender movements as it moves towards the new millennium. Hopefully, Korean cinema will carry out a great duty for the sake of all of us: to let Korean society recognize homosexuality not as taboo, by means of films that will inform and move the old and new generations towards a sexual reconciliation–indeed the very harmony *Broken Branches* optimistically imagines.

NOTES

1. Director Na Woon-kyu (1902-1937) was the most outstanding and influential cine-artist during Korean film's early days. He also took the leading role in *Arirang*, in addition to writing its screenplay.

2. Unfortunately, Gongmin was murdered by his favorite guard, who had been bought off by the opposing political party.

3. Ha Yong-soo, the actor who played Jun, in fact became a menswear designer whose suits are popular among male entertainers; he also works managing new Korean actors.

4. "An Interview with Kim Su-hyeong." *Buddy*, No. 4. 1998. 35-36.

5. See *Feminist Studies*. 7, 3, pp. 451-76.

6. *Buddy*, ibid.

7. Also see the Korean transsexual film *Mascara* (1994).

8. As of June 1999, the new organization "Korean Board of Film Classification" took over the role held by the Korean Council for Performing Arts Promotion.

Queering Bollywood:
Alternative Sexualities
in Popular Indian Cinema

Gayatri Gopinath

University of California, Davis

SUMMARY. In this essay, I demonstrate through numerous examples taken from four identifiable Hindi film subgenres queer themes which, though nontransgressive in their native Indian context, acquire subversive value and serve as queer points of identification when viewed from a non-nationalist bias. Watching particular films with this "queer diasporic viewing practive," sex/gender play which is normative (yet still coded) in the land of the films' production can be reclaimed as queer through the differently subjective lens of transnational spectatorship, a lens removed from patriarchy, sexism, and homophobia. This particularly becomes apparent in the Bollywood dance sequence–the frequent site of Hindi sex/gender play–whose coded queer desires are much easier to de-code (or re-code) when in the diaspora. *[Article copies available for a fee from The Haworth Document Delivery Service: 1-800-342-9678. E-mail address: <getinfo@haworthpressinc.com> Website: <http://www.HaworthPress. com>]*

India is the largest film-producing country in the world, and films made in India, especially in the huge film factories of Bollywood (as the Bombay film

Gayatri Gopinath received her PhD in English from Columbia University, and is currently Assistant Professor of Women and Gender Studies at the University of California, Davis. Her work on sexuality, migration, and South Asian diasporic cultures has appeared in the journals *Diaspora*, *Positions* and *GLQ*, as well as in the anthologies *Asian American Sexualities* (ed. Russell Leong, 1995) and *Burning Down the House: Recycling Domesticity* (ed. Rosemary George, 1998) (E-mail: ggopinath@ucdavis.edu).

[Haworth co-indexing entry note]: "Queering Bollywood: Alternative Sexualities in Popular Indian Cinema." Gopinath, Gayatri. Co-published simultaneously in *Journal of Homosexuality* (The Haworth Press, Inc.) Vol. 39, No. 3/4, 2000, pp. 283-297; and: *Queer Asian Cinema: Shadows in the Shade* (ed: Andrew Grossman) Harrington Park Press, an imprint of The Haworth Press, Inc., 2000, pp. 283-297. Single or multiple copies of this article are available for a fee from The Haworth Document Delivery Service [1-800-342-9678, 9:00 a.m. - 5:00 p.m. (EST). E-mail address: getinfo@haworthpressinc.com].

industry is known), are circulated throughout an ever-expanding network of South Asian diasporic communities throughout South Asia, North America, the Caribbean, the Middle East, East Africa, and elsewhere.[1] Given the vastness of its reach, surprisingly little critical work has been done on the reception, consumption, and distribution of popular Indian cinema within these different diasporic locations. While Vijay Mishra argues that the introduction of Bollywood films in the diaspora in the 1930s was "a crucial factor in the continuation of culture and in the construction of the imaginary homeland as a homogenous identity,"[2] I would argue that Bollywood cinema circulates in the diaspora in less predictable ways; indeed this paper suggests that Bollywood provides "queer diasporic" audiences with the means by which to reimagine and reterritorialize the "homeland" by making it the locus of queer desire and pleasure. My interest in tracing the possibilities of "interpretive interventions and appropriations"[3] by diasporic audiences allies my project with that of feminist film theorists such as Judith Mayne, Valerie Traub, and others who theorize female spectatorship.[4] In her analysis of the mainstream Hollywood film *Black Widow*, Traub argues that the appropriations and readings of "lesbian" spectators exceed the film's strategies of containing lesbian pleasure within a heterosexual matrix: "Insofar as the film cannot be read separately from the transaction taking place as it unrolls before an audience, *Black Widow* becomes an event of cultural production, a moment in which "lesbian" subjectivities are constructed."[5] Similarly, this essay begins to trace the influence of popular film in constituting a particular "queer diasporic subjectivity," one that confounds dominant Euro-American constructions of "gay" and "lesbian" identity and that negotiates between the spaces of multiple homes, communities, and nations.

I employ what I call a "queer diasporic viewing practice" in order to "see" the various articulations of same-sex desire in particular examples of popular Indian cinema. This viewing practice conceptualizes a viewing public as located within multiple diasporic sites, and the text itself as accruing multiple, sometimes contradictory meanings within these various locations. In other words, I place these films with a "queer diasporic framework" which allows us to conceive of both the text and the viewer in motion. Cinematic images which in their "originary" locations simply reiterate conventional nationalist and gender ideologies may, in a South Asian diasporic context, be refashioned to become the very foundation of a queer transnational culture. Furthermore, queer diasporic readings within such a framework allow us to read non-heteronormative arrangements within rigidly heterosexual structures as well as the ways in which queer articulations of desire and pleasure both draw on and infiltrate popular culture. While queer reading practices alone cannot prevent the violences of heteronormativity, they do intervene in formulations of "home" and diaspora that–in their elision and disavowal of the particularities of queer subjectivities–inevitably reproduce the heteronormative family as central to national identity.

While I focus on a range of popular Indian cinema from 1960 to 1996, I also discuss examples of what is known as "middle cinema," that is, the spate of "socially conscious" films made in the 1970s and early 1980s that attempted to chart a middle course between "art" films and the song-and-dance formulae of popular Hindi film.[6] In including different genres within my discussion, I hope to examine the ways in which each genre both allows for and forecloses the possibilities of representing non-heteronormative desires and subjectivities on screen. Interestingly, many of the scenes I discuss are of song-and-dance sequences; the fact that forty percent of an average popular Indian film is made up of song-and-dance or fighting sequences suggests that these scenes may need to be taken just as seriously as the film's main plot or narrative. Indeed, these sequences often act as a place of fantasy that cannot be contained or accounted for in the rest of the narrative; not surprisingly, it is often in these moments of fantasy that queer desire emerges.

In an attempt to provide some coherence to a vast range of material, my analysis is organized into four sections: "Sexing the Sisterhood," Budd(y)ing Boyfriends," "Macho Mems, Sissy Sahibs," and "Hijras and Homos." Clearly, these sections are somewhat arbitrary and hardly offer an exhaustive treatment of popular Indian cinema. Instead, I hope to begin an examination of the various ways in which popular cinema encodes alternative sexualities and desires, and makes certain spaces available for their representation. A project such as this is interested not so much in looking for "lesbians" in Bollywood, but rather in looking for those moments emerging at the fissures of rigidly heterosexual structures that can be transformed into queer imaginings.[7]

SEXING THE SISTERHOOD: FEMALE HOMOSOCIALITY/FEMALE HOMOEROTICISM

This first section considers a series of films made between 1960 and 1994 that depict archetypal spaces of female homosociality such as brothels, women's prisons, girl's schools, the middle class home, and the zenana. Popular Indian film is saturated with rich images of the intense love between women in the context of these women-only spaces. Not surprisingly, these spaces allow numerous possibilities for intense female friendship to slip into queer desire; I am thus interested in pointing out some of the visual codes used in popular films to depict that slippage between female homosociality and female homoeroticism that a text like Chughtai's "The Quilt" so brilliantly exploits.

The first two scenes under discussion depict moments of female bonding and female homosocial desire in films where the relationships between women are secondary to a familiar plot of heterosexual love and romance. These scenes are interesting because they act as brief instance in otherwise utterly conventional films that momentarily interrupt the dominant heterosexuality of the narratives. For instance, *Gehri Chaal*, a 1973 vehicle for Bollywood icon Hema Malini, opens with a shot of the heroine cavorting on a tennis court with numerous female companions, while cooing to them, "let go of my hand, what if somebody sees us, what if we both get caught." Yet the rest of the film never refers back to this opening scene of explicit female-female desire, and the heroine predictably ends up in the arms of a handsome male hero. Similarly, the immensely popular 1994 movie *Hum Aapke hain Koun* offers a moment of explicit female-female desire as comic relief in an otherwise staunchly conservative narrative extolling middle-class, Hindu, patriarchal family values. The sequence takes place during a women-only celebration of an upcoming marriage, around which the film's entire plot revolves. Into this space of female homosociality enters a woman cross-dressed as the film's male hero, in an identical white suit, who proceeds to dance suggestively with the heroine (played by Madhuri Dixit) and with various other women in the room. What follows is an elaborate dance sequence where the cross-dressed woman and Dixit engage in a teasing, sexualized exchange that parodies the trappings of conventional middle-class Hindi family arrangements (that is, heterosexuality, domesticity, and motherhood). Halfway through the song, however, order is apparently restored when the cross-dressed interloper is chased out of the room by the "real" hero (Salman Khan). The cross-dressed woman disappears from both the scene and indeed the entire film, and Salman Khan proceeds to claim his rightful place opposite Dixit.

What meanings, then, can we ascribe to these brief instances in both *Gehri Chaal* and *Hum Aapke* of explicit erotic interplay between women? Clearly, neither scene is purely transgressive of conventional gender and sexual hierarchies; in *Gehri Chaal*, the erotic interplay between the women is literally a prelude to the primary narrative of heterosexual courtship and domesticity, while in *Hum Aapke* the cross-dressed woman seems to merely hold the place of the "real" hero until he can make his entrance, and indeed hold in place the hierarchical gendered relations in the scene. *Hum Aapke's* brief interlude of gender reversal and implied female homoeroticism seems to locate the film within Chris Straayer's definition of the "temporary transvestite film," those which "offer spectators a momentary, vicarious trespassing of society's accepted boundaries for gender and sexual behavior. Yet one can relax confidently in the orderly [heterosexual] demarcations reconstituted by the film's endings."[8] Indeed, both these films can afford such transparent renderings of female homoerotic desire precisely because they remain so thoroughly convinced of the hegemonic power of their own heterosexuality. However, the fact that gender reversal in *Hum Aapke* occurs within a space of female homosociality renders the implied homoeroticism of the scene explicit to both the characters and the film's audience, and as such makes it eminently available for a queer diasporic viewership. For a "queer South Asian viewing subject," then, the scene foregrounds the ways in which South Asian popular culture acts as a repository of queer desiring relations; it also marks the simultaneous illegibility of those relations to a heterosexual viewing public and their legibility in a queer South Asian diasporic context.

It is critical to note that upon *Hum Aapke's* release, the popular press attributed its tremendous and sustained popularity to its return to "family values," a phrase that apparently referred to the film's rejection of the sex and violence formulae of other popular Hindi movies. However, this phrase speaks more to the ways in which the film works within Hindu nationalist discourses of India by articulating a desire for a nostalgic "return" to an impossible ideal, that of the supposedly "traditional" Hindu family and kinship arrangements that are staunchly middle-class and heterosexual. The incursion of female homoerotic desire into this ultra-conventional Hindu marriage plot–both suggested and contained by the scene between Dixit and her cross-dressed partner–threatens the presumed seamlessness of both familial and nationalist narratives by calling into question the functionality and imperviousness of heterosexual bonds.

Two other films that depict the slippage between female homosociality and female homoeroticism are the 1984 *Ustav* (dir. Girish Karnad) and the 1981 *Subhah* (dir. Jabbar Patel); in both, female homoerotic desire plays a more active role in the narrative rather than simply serving to briefly interrupt heterosexual relationships. *Ustav* takes place primarily in and around a brothel and *Subhah* in a women's reformatory, and both hint at the alternative forms of sexuality that exist outside the middle-class home as represented in the previous two films. *Ustav* belongs to the genre of courtesan films that plays on the nostalgia for an ancient erotic Indian past (the latest example of which is Mira Nair's 1997 film *Kama Sutra*).[9] In *Ustav*, the film star Rehka plays Vasantsena, a fourth century prostitute who falls in love with a young Brahmin merchant named Charudutt. Halfway through the film, Charudutt is temporarily shunted out of the narrative by a growing friendship between Vasantsena and his wife Aditi. In a telling scene, Vasantsena and Aditi sing to each other after exchanging clothes and jewelry. This act of making oneself desirable, of dressing and undressing, donning and discarding saris and jewelry in particular, is a sexually loaded trope in popular Indian cinema, having connotations of wedding nights and signifying a prelude to sex. The film reworks the typical love triangle of popular film where two women compete for the man's attention; here, it is Charudutt who is sidelined while the two women play erotically together. Interestingly, feminist analyses of the film have critiqued this scene as merely "playing out the ultimate male fantasy," whereby female bonding between the wife and the courtesan enable the man to "move without guilt between a nurturing wife and a glamorous mistress."[10] Clearly such an interpretation misses the more nuanced eroticism between the two women that a queer diasporic reading makes apparent.

Ustav's reversal of the standard heterosexual triangle is also evident in the 1981 middle cinema film *Subhah*, starring Smita Patil. Upon its release, *Subhah* was heralded a feminist fable, in that it followed the struggles of a middle class housewife named Savitri to leave the confines of middle class domesticity and become the warden of a women's reformatory. Savitri's process of individuation is figured in terms of movement, with her leaving behind the gendered, hierarchical family arrangements of the middle class household and entering instead the confines of the all-women's reformatory. The film ends with a familiar image in "middle cinema" women's films, with Savitri on a train, embarking alone on an unspecified journey after having left both her family and the reformatory behind.

What distinguishes *Subhah* from the other so-called women's films of the era is that it explicitly references female same-sex eroticism, by naming the relationship between two of the inmates in the reformatory as "lesbian" (the English word is used). Predictably, the "lesbianism" of the inmates is held apart from the burgeoning feminist consciousness of the film's heroine: Savitri labels the two inmates as pathological even as she tries to defend them to her superior. The physical and psychic movement of the feminist subject, then, is opposed to the fixity of the "lesbian" characters who remain firmly situated within a narrative of sickness and pathology. Indeed on a narrative level, the film is unable to articulate female desire and sexuality–let alone female same-sex desire–in terms other than pathologization; Savitri herself is shown repeatedly refusing sex with her husband but never actively desiring.

Yet one instance in the film exceeds its own narrative trajectory and hints at alternative narrativization of female same-sex desire. Significantly, the scene is one of the few song-and-dance sequences in the movie: the women are seen here celebrating a festival, and the camera cuts repeatedly from the face and body of one the "lesbian" characters to that of the other, who gazes at her adoringly. The scene reworks the familiar triangulation between characters in song-and-dance sequences in popular Indian film, where two women dance for the male character whose appraising gaze orchestrates the scene. In *Subhah*, however, a triangulated relation forms between the two lesbian characters and Savitri, who is drawn into the circuit of exchange of looks between the two, and both returns and receives their admiring and curious glances. The scene is interesting in that, however briefly, it articulates female desire outside the realm of pathology in a way that the rest of the narrative is unable to do. Instead, the scene hints at the particular forms and organizations of female same-sex desire that are produced within the homo-social spaces of the middle class home; and these forms exist, surprisingly, even when those spaces are thoroughly saturated by the state's patriarchal authority.

As this scene in *Subhah* suggests, narratives that explicitly name female same-sex desire as "lesbian" may be less interesting than those moments within the narrative that represent female homosociality in the absence of "lesbians." Such a moment is particularly apparent in the 1983 Bollywood epic *Razia Sultan* (dir. Kamal Amrohi), where Hema Malini plays a Mughal princess pining for her male lover while being comforted by her maidservant (Parveen Babi). The scene takes place in a small boat, as Parveen Babi ostensibly sings to Hema Malini about her lover while caressing and eventually kissing her from behind a white feather. This sequence is a brilliant reworking of the visual conventions of the Bollywood historical epic in that it explicitly references the famous scene in the classic 1961 film *Mughal-e-Azam* (dir. K. Asif), where the hero Dilip Kumar kisses the heroine Madhubala while passing a white feather in front of their faces. While *Razia Sultan's* use of this masking device has a lot to do with the censorship exigencies of Indian film, it also speaks to the ways in which female homoeroticism is visually encoded within popular cinema; female homoerotic desire and pleasure are often mediated by and routed through heterosexuality as well as class difference.[11]

I do not mean to suggest that implicit encodings of alternative sexuality are necessarily superior to explicit representations; however, I would argue that scenes such as the ones I have discussed above suggest alternative formulations of female homoeroticism that cannot necessarily be produced in popular film under the sign of "lesbian." These scenes become eminently available for a queer diasporic viewership because they encode female homoeroticism outside the logic of homophobia. Instead, they gesture to a model of what we can term a queer South Asian femininity, where gender conformity and indeed hyper-femininity do not necessarily imply heterosexuality. In much of popular Indian film, as I will discuss in the following sections, explicit gender transgression in women is definitively (and sometimes violently) resolved into heterosexuality. It may therefore be more useful for queer purposes to draw on those moments where hyper-gender conformity encodes female homoeroticism, and as such allows queer sexuality to erupt at the interstices of heterosexuality.

BUDD(Y)ING BOYFRIENDS: MALE HOMOSOCIALITY/MALE HOMOEROTICISM

The depiction of male friendships has a long tradition in Indian cinema. From the 1960 film *Chaudvin Ka Chand* (dir. M. Sadiq), to the buddy movies of Amitabh Bachchan and Dharmendra in the 1970s, to the current buddy duo of Akshay Kumar and Saif Ali Khan, men in popular Indian film are often depicted within an erotic triangle involving a woman and another male friend: very often, both men forfeit the heroine and opt for the friendship of the other man instead. In this section, I focus primarily on the buddy movies of the seventies and early eighties, as it is during this time that the buddy movie in Bollywood seems to come into its own. As in Hollywood film, male bonding and barely disguised same-sex desire that accompanies it often comes at a price; predictably, women and effeminate men, for instance, have no place in this macho brotherhood.

The prototypical hero of the buddy movies of Hindi cinema is the mega-star and some-time politician Amitabh Bachchan, who for at least twenty years has successfully depicted a series of tough men with strong morals. In an early Amitabh movie, the 1973 vigilante film *Zanjeer* (dir. Prakash Mehra), which was the first in a long line of Amitabh's films that cast the hero as outlaw, Amitabh plays a cop-turned-vigilante who befriends a Pathan gambler (Pran). In *Zanjeer*, as in most of Amitabh's movies, male friendship is articulated in the same hyper-romantic terms used for heterosexual relationships; in one scene, for instance, Pran dances joyfully for Amitabh and effusively proclaims how love has changed his life, and eventually envelops Amitabh in an embrace. As is typical of many films of the buddy movie genre, Amitabh's female love interest in *Zanjeer* is distinctly secondary to his friendship with Pran. The generic elements evident in *Zanjeer* are repeated in the quintessential male buddy movie of the seventies, the 1975 masala western *Sholay* (dir. Ramesh Sippy) also starring Amitabh. The romance of male friendship is clear in a scene from *Sholay* which has Amitabh and his male friend (Dharmendra) singing a duet about their undying loyalty and love for each other. Diasporic gay men have been quick to seize upon the barely veiled desire between the two, and have used the song as a queer anthem at Gay Pride parades in New York and San Francisco. Although throughout the film male friendship keeps heterosexual love interests at bay, *Sholay's* ending conveniently restores the primacy of heterosexuality by having Amitabh die heroically by saving Dharmendra's life.

A somewhat later Amitabh buddy movie, the 1980 film *Dostana* (Dir. Raj Khosla), attempts to replicate the formula of *Sholay* but makes no such attempt to resolve male friendship with heterosexuality. In fact, *Dostana* makes blatantly apparent the ways in which male bonding codifies male same-sex desire. The film also shows how this romantic male bonding and desire often relies on sexism and misogyny. *Dostana* is structured through the typical male buddy triangle of two men ostensibly competing for the attentions of the same woman (Zeenat Aman). It quickly becomes apparent that Zeenat's role is simply to act as the object of exchange between the two men;

as a bonding device that serves to cement male friendship, she gets passed around from one to the other at various points in the film. The homosocial triangulation that structures *Dostana* is most apparent in a scene in where Amitabh and his buddy have a fight, ostensibly over Zeenat, and in the language of a lover's quarrel Amitabh sings to his friend about his grief over the loss of their friendship.[12] The camera very obviously traces the triangulated desire among Amitabh, his male partner, and Zeenat; what is striking in this scene is that while both men appear somewhat animated and active in different ways, Zeenat remains curiously inert, and simply stares blankly into the camera. Zeenat is useful in this scene, and indeed in the entire film, only insofar as she acts as a conduit between the two men; indeed, by the film's end Zeenat has disappeared entirely. The movie closes with a shot of the two men embracing and walking hand in hand into the sunset, as the words "This friendship will live forever!" flash on the screen.

However, it is not only women who are violated by romantic male bonding. In the 1983 film *Holi* (dir. Ketan Mehta), male bonding takes a more sinister turn as the homophobia that underlies desire between straight men is made remarkably explicit. *Holi* takes place in that quintessential arena of male bonding, male desire, and homophobia: the boys' school. In a wrenching scene, an effeminate boy who has had "relations" with other boys in the dorm is harassed and pushed around by them; his harassers insult him by calling him a "girl" and saying that "he's worse than a woman," implying that he's too weak to fight back. The scene graphically depicts the ways in which, in a heterosexual context, male same-sex desire can tip into violence both homophobic and misogynist.

Thus the buddy movie and its depiction of male bonding is one of the ways in which desire between men is referenced in popular film. These depictions, however, may simultaneously rely on sexist ideologies, as well as the rejection of effeminacy or any other version of non-heteronormative masculinity. Whereas "Sexing the Sisterhood" detailed the privatized spaces of female homosociality which allow for certain forms of homoeroticism to flourish, this section demonstrates the remarkable latitude within public spaces for male friendships that can easily tip into homoeroticism. While the gendered distinction between public and private is predictable given the legacies of colonial and nationalist constructions of "home" and family, these distinctions are complicated within the films I have discussed here: both male and female erotic friendships are fostered within the strictly patrolled public institutional spaces of schools and prisons. In my next section, I turn from same-sex eroticisms within single-sex institutions to a series of cross-gender identifications in a variety of Bollywood films which seem to register some awareness of alternative sexualities and genders.

MACHO MEMS, SISSY SAHIBS:
CROSS-GENDER IDENTIFICATION

Even a cursory glance at popular Indian film offers up numerous representations of men and women who defy gender stereotypes. Men in dresses or
with feminine mannerisms, and women with short hair, trousers, and a tough
demeanor, have figured quite prominently on the Bollywood screen. In particular, cross-dressing of both men and women has been a standard comedic
and plot device in popular Indian film for decades. These representations are
useful for queer purposes in that they hint at other possibilities of gender and
sexuality that fall outside the confines of traditional heterosexuality; however, the films I discuss here also tend to shut down these possibilities almost as
quickly as they raise them.

Bollywood seems to have responded to the growing visibility of a lesbian
and gay movement in South Asia with a marked increase in recent years in
representations of characters that are explicitly cross-gender identified. In the
1996 film *Raja Hindustani*, for instance, the heroine's main sidekicks are an
effeminate man and a masculine woman who predictably provide much of
the comic entertainment in the film, mostly through the confusion they generate among other characters as to the "true" nature of their sex. In *Raja
Hindustani*, as in much of popular film, feminine men are given a limited,
ritualized role as either comic figures or as hijras.[13] Masculine women, however, do not have even these limited options for representation, and are more
often than not made to disappear from the film entirely, as they do in both
Raja Hindustani and in *Hum Aapke Hain Koun*, the film discussed in the first
section of this essay.

Scenes of cross-dressing are often followed by dramatic moments of revelation that re-establish proper gender roles and identification. In the 1995
Baazi, for instance, the hero Amir Khan cross-dresses in order to entrap the
villain, who is under the impression that he is about to have sex with an
attractive woman. Instead, Amir Khan strips off his drag and, in a display of
macho virility, beats him up. This excessive revelation scene anxiously confirms the hero's heterosexuality by violently disowning and punishing any
queer desire or pleasure opened up by the act of cross-dressing. A similar
moment of revelation and a return to one's "true" gender occurs in the 1970
film *Mera Naam Joker* (dir. Raj Kapoor), which stars the actress Padmini
cross-dressing as a feisty and independent vagabond and circus performer
who wields a knife and is called Minoo Master. Minoo Master's butch tough-
ness, however, prefigures the inevitable revelation scene, where Minoo is
exposed as Mina, a curvaceous beauty who dons a sari, grows her hair, and
eventually becomes a wife. Minoo Master's domestication as Mina points to
the ways in which masculine women in film are not allowed to exist more

than momentarily, and are inevitably feminized in order to be drawn back into heterosexuality.[14]

This is not to say, however, that popular Indian cinema lacks images of strong, independent women. On the contrary, from the early stunt films of Australian-born Hindi film star Fearless Nadia in the 1930s and 1940s to the latest action films of the tremendously popular current South Indian action film star Vijaya Shanti, popular film has reveled in images of tough women on screen. Nadia's persona as "the lady with the whip," as she was known in the thirties, acted as a precursor for Amitabh's action films of the seventies, and particularly for the films of Vijaya Shanti. Vijaya Shanti's films, with names like *Police Lockup* and *Lady Boss*, are tremendously popular among women at least in part because she offers an image of a tough yet glamorous woman who defends both herself and other women from predatory men. However, both Nadia and Vijaya Shanti are able to enact their tough woman personae because they remain quite clearly recognizable as attractive, heterosexual women. Nadia played upon the stereotype of the sexually liberated foreign woman, while Vijaya Shanti, despite her short hair, big gun, and police outfits, still retains the big-eyed, fair-skinned aesthetic of the prototypical Indian female film star.

The 1996 Madhuri Dixit film *Anjaam* makes clear both the possibilities and limits representing non-traditional gender roles in popular film. Madhuri plays an innocent widow who has been thrown into jail due to the machinations of various villainous men. She arrives in prison only to be thrown at the mercy of a cruel and semi-masculine female warden, who calls her a whore, tells her to strip, and proceeds to beat her up brutally when she resists. The prison warden is, of course, a stock character familiar from B-movie prison films in the U.S., where women's prisons are imagined as notorious sites of lesbian sexual predation and sexual violence. *Anjaam's* prison warden seems to follow in this tradition but is shown in the following scene in bed with her male superior; she is thus quickly and firmly re-established as properly feminine, heterosexual, and sexually available, as are most other masculine women on the Indian screen. The ultra-feminine heroine, meanwhile, transforms into a Devi figure, a wrathful feminine goddess wreaking revenge on all those men who have wronged her. However, the most drawn-out and gory scene of violent revenge is reserved for the female warden, whom she beats up and eventually hangs in a scene so violent that it is hard to watch (and one wonders here at the voyeurism that the film both evokes and plays upon in watching women kill each other). The depiction of Madhuri as an incarnation of Devi denotes the traditional space available for women within popular culture to be strong, aggressive, and even violent–and still be seen as properly female, feminine women.[15] If Madhuri-as-Devi embodies an acceptable representation of female strength, the prison warden–with her vaguely masculine demeanor–comes to symbolize an unacceptable version of female power, and is brutally punished as a result. The film thus pits a feminist-coded character against a queer-coded one, and the latter loses out on all counts. Feminist accounts of self-realization, in other worlds, are achieved within Bollywood cinema at the expense of the queer or masculine female character. Certainly a queer reading practice can uncover moments of visual pleasure in the image of a tough or masculine woman on screen, but the pleasures of either desire or identification are brutally foreclosed by the swift and unusually violent punishments that always await such characters. This points to the limits of accounts of queer spectatorship which prematurely celebrate the abundance of queer-coded characters in mainstream Indian cinema. In short, popular Indian film does have a place, up to a point, for representations of those men who do not embody a virile, heterosexual mas-culinity, and those women who reject a weak, passive form of femininity. However, as I am arguing, we quickly reach the limits of these unconventional gender representations: effeminate men are comic relief or are shunted into the category of "hijra," while strong women are acceptable only as long as they can still be contained with heterosexuality and properly feminine behavior.

HIJRAS AND HOMOS: "PERVERSE" SEXUALITIES ON SCREEN

If the possibilities of representing gender transgression in popular film are necessarily limited, as discussed in the last section, the possibilities of repre-senting sexual transgression are all the more so. In this section, I explore the ways in which popular film explicitly marks certain characters as somehow sexually aberrant. Hijra characters remain the most obvious and common manifestation of sexual and gender transgression in popular film. Hijras, who may be cross-dressed biological men, eunuchs, or hermaphrodites, form communities that have a ritualized, historically rooted role in Indian society. For a queer South Asian viewership, the relative visibility of hijras on screen on the one hand makes apparent other forms of sexual and gender subjectivi-ties than those available within heterosexuality. On the other hand, as pre-viously mentioned, "hijra" becomes a generalized category for all forms of gender or sexual transgression, and thereby closes down the possibilities of representations of other forms of non-heteronormative genders or sexualities.

Representations of hijras locate and limit the possibilities of gender trans-gression by creating a category of people who supposedly embody the full extent of both sexual deviance and gender cross-identification. Thus in the 1974 film *Kunwara Baap*, a group of hijras is depicted singing a song that comes to represent hijra identification; this song is replayed in later films like *Raja Hindustani* to mark all non-normatively gendered characters (such as effeminate men) as hijra. While *Kunwara Baap* did usefully allow for the visibility of hijras within mainstream cinema, it also denied hijras complex subjectivities by fixing the hijra as a symbol of gender and sexual deviance. In later films such as *Anjaam*, hijras have been represented as comic characters or as villains who nevertheless manage to articulate oblique critiques of the ways in which they are maltreated, ridiculed, and marginalized in mainstream society.

Despite the prevalence of the hijra character as the primary marker of sexual otherness, there are other characterizations of explicit sexual deviance in popular film. One such characterization becomes apparent in the 1991 film *Mast Kalandar*, starring Anupam Kher as an effeminate homosexual named Pinkoo. Pinkoo's flamboyant effeminacy is meant to provide comic relief, while his pink Mohawk and penchant for speaking English mark him as respectively foreign and upper-class. This characterization of male homosexuality as now not simply a hijra identification but as foreign and alien clearly resonates with conventional framings of sexuality within nationalist discourses. In a sense, the Pinkoo character makes clear the ways in which male same-sex desire, when it is consolidated into an identity in popular film, can exist only on the level of stereotype. I do not mean this as a call for "positive images" of gay men in popular Indian cinema; rather, I am suggesting that within popular cinema, the most interesting representations of non-heteronormative desire may exist in the absence of "gays" and "lesbians." The limitations of representing explicitly marked "homosexual" characters in popular cinema is particularly apparent in *Holi* and *Subhah,* two films previously discussed that fall under the rubric of social realism. *Holi*'s gay male character is the object of virulent homophobia and violence, and is subject to a brutal bashing from which he escapes only to commit suicide. Similarly, in *Subhah*, the film marks the two characters as "lesbian" only in order for them to be pathologized and singled out for punishment. Ultimately, both films subsume sexuality and a critique of homophobia under seemingly more important issues such as class and gender oppression. Thus non-heteronormative sexual subjects exist in popular cinema as "lesbians" and "gay men" only if they provide comic relief or are punished and killed in predictable ways.

CONCLUSION

This necessarily schematic survey has attempted to locate the potentialities and the limits of representing non-heteronormative genders and desires in popular Indian cinema. While the codes and conventions of popular cinema do open up the possibility for the emergence of same-sex eroticism, it is often achieved at the expense of the effeminate male or masculine female character. Given the limits of popular Indian cinema in enabling queer pleasure, desire, and fantasy, it is no surprise that queer South Asian diasporic film and videomakers in the 1990s have both drawn on and decontextualized the conventions of popular Indian cinema in their work. For instance, Pratibha Parmar's 1991 *Khush*, which documents an emerging diasporic South Asian queer movement, intercuts talking heads interviews with fantasy sequences of two women, clad in Bollywood-inspired finery, watching old Hindi movie extravaganzas while stroking each other's hair. Similarly, a 1996 documentary on a South Asian transgender activist shows her as in the persona of a Bollywood starlet named Nina Chiffon, complete with jewelry, silk sari, and high heels, waiting for the train on a New York City subway platform.[16] We next see her in the subway car, flirtatiously swinging from pole to pole and lip-synching to a Hindi film song. I would indeed like to close with the image of Nina Chiffon's performance of the hyperbolic femininity of Bollywood screen goddesses, as it captures the ways in which queer diasporic subjects both appropriate and remake the representations available to them in popular culture in order to reterritorialize even the most unlikely of public spaces.

NOTES

1. This article based on a video-clip show and lecture presentation entitled "Desi Dykes and Divas: Alternative Sexualities in Popular Indian Cinema," co-created with Javid Syed and commissioned by the 1997 New York Lesbian and Gay Film Festival.

2. Vijay Mishra, "The Diasporic Imaginary: Theorizing the Indian Diaspora," *Textual Practice* 10:3 (1996), 446.

3. Valerie Traub, "The Ambiguities of 'Lesbian' Viewing Pleasure: The (Dis) Articulations of *Black Widow*," in *Body Guards: The Cultural Politics of Gender Ambiguity*, eds. Julia Epstein and Kristina Straub (New York: Routledge, 1991), 309.

4. Mary Anne Doane, "Film and the Masquerade: Theorizing the Female Spectator," *Screen* v. 23 n. 3-4 (Fall 1982): 74-87; Judith Mayne, *Cinema and Spectatorship* (New York: Routledge, 1993); Valerie Traub, "The Ambiguities of 'Lesbian' Viewing Pleasure," in Epstein and Straub. 309-328.

5. Traub, 322.

6. Most of the films I focus on here are Hindi; while I want to avoid replicating dominant nationalist discourse that frames "India" as both North Indian and Hindi-speaking, my access to non-Hindi films was limited. I suspect that a very different set of categories and conclusions would be arrived at if one were to focus this project on particular regional cinemas (such as Tamil or Malayali) as each has very different cinematic traditions, and may reflect different formulations of sexuality and gender.

7. Attesting to the ways in which these films circulate in the diaspora, many of the films I was working with in this essay were pirated copies and did not always identify the film's director. I have included information on the director and year of release wherever possible.

8. Chris Straayer, *Deviant Eyes, Deviant Bodies: Sexual Reorientations in Film and Video* (New York: Columbia UP, 1996), 44.

9. For a feminist analysis of the courtesan film genre, see Sumita Chakravarty, *National Identity and Indian Popular Cinema, 1947-1987.* (Austin: U. of Texas P, 1993), 269-305.

10. Chakravarty, 284.

11. The intertextuality of *Razia Sultan* and *Mughal-e-Azam* is underscored by the fact that the director of *Razia Sultan,* Kamal Amrohi, wrote the screenplay for *Mughal-e-Azam* some twenty-five years earlier. See Ashish Rajadhyaksha and Paul Willemen, *Encyclopaedia of Indian Cinema* (London: British Film Institute, 1994), 42.

12. Obviously my formulation of the erotic triangle in this section draws upon Eve K. Sedgwick's generative model of homosocial desire in *Between Men: English Literature and Male Homosocial Desire* (New York: Columbia UP, 1985).

13. Hijras occupy a "third gender" or transgender category in India; representations of hijras will be further discussed in the following section.

14. For a discussion of the representation of the fate of masculine women in Hollywood and queer independent film, see Judith Halberstam, "Looking Butch: A Rough History of Butches in Film," in *Female Masculinity* (Durham, NC: Duke UP, 1998).

15. For an excellent discussion of women protagonists in rape-revenge films, see Lalitha Gopalan, "Avenging Women in Indian Cinema," *Screen* 38:1 (1997): 42-59.

16. *Julpari* (dirs. Swati Khurana and Leith Murgai, 1996).

Memories Pierce the Heart:
Homoeroticism, Bollywood-Style

R. Raj Rao

University of Pune

SUMMARY. In this essay, I enjoy using Amitabh Bachchan, perennial idol of the Bollywood screen, as a point of departure for ruminations on the construction of male friendship and male love within both Indian cinema and its primarily male audience (which, in a sense, represents in turn Hindi culture at large). Using translations of songs from Amitabh's films interlaced with my own personal experiences, we see how homosexuality thrives in covert yet recognized places in Indian culture, and how subtler forms of homosexuality are actually engendered under the auspices of normative patriarchal culture. Songs were translated by the author in collaboration with Jia Das. *[Article copies available for a fee from The Haworth Document Delivery Service: 1-800-342-9678. E-mail address: <getinfo@haworthpressinc.com> Website: <http://www.HaworthPress.com>]*

Amitabh Bachchan is *the* ex-superstar of Bollywood, Bombay's Hollywood. He was recently voted the greatest star of the millennium in a poll

---

R. Raj Rao received his PhD in English Literature from the University of Bombay, and did post-doctoral studies from the University of Warwick. He is the author of *Slide Show* (poems), *One Day I Locked My Flat in Soul City* (short stories), *The Wisest Fool on Earth and Other Plays*, and *Nissim Ezekiel: The Authorized Biography*. He has also published much criticism in scholarly journals in India and abroad. He has been a visiting writer at the International Writing Program, University of Iowa in 1996. Rao is currently working on a novel, and on his second book of poems, *BomGay*, already made into an award-winning short film of the same title by Wadia Movietone (Bombay). He is a professor in the department of English, University of Pune, founder of Queer Studies Circle, a gay-lesbian student group, and in his own words, a radical utopian.

[Haworth co-indexing entry note]: "Memories Pierce the Heart: Homoeroticism, Bollywood-Style." Rao, R. Raj. Co-published simultaneously in *Journal of Homosexuality* (The Haworth Press, Inc.) Vol. 39, No. 3/4, 2000, pp. 299-306; and: *Queer Asian Cinema: Shadows in the Shade* (ed: Andrew Grossman) Harrington Park Press, an imprint of The Haworth Press, Inc., 2000, pp. 299-306. Single or multiple copies of this article are available for a fee from The Haworth Document Delivery Service [1-800-342-9678, 9:00 a.m. - 5:00 p.m. (EST). E-mail address: getinfo@haworthpressinc.com].

conducted by BBC News on the internet, in which Cary Grant stood third, Marilyn Monroe seventh, and Sir Lawrence Olivier tenth. Amitabh Bachchan typifies one of the greatest paradoxes of our times. In the 60s, before he came on the scene, Hindi (Indian) movies were romantic. Heroes and heroines ran around trees as they sang love songs to each other. These heroes, ranging from Dilip Kumar in *Gunga Jumna* to Shammi Kapoor in *Junglee* to Rajendra Kumar in *Arzoo* to Rajesh Khanna in *Aradhana*, came across as soft, even effeminate. They were hypersensitive men who loved and pined away for their lovers with an intensity usually seen only in women. In 1973, when Amitabh appeared in his first successful film *Zanjeer* (directed by Prakash Mehra), he changed all that. Here was a police inspector, a six-footer, who was setting out to avenge the murder of his parents that he had witnessed as a child. There was no time for romance. The need of the hour was to be as tough and macho as possible; only then would he accomplish his objective. The heroine in *Zanjeer*, played by Jaya Bhaduri, whom Amitabh in real life would marry, wasn't indispensable. She was incidental. The conventional heroine was replaced by a male "best friend," played in this case by the actor Pran, without whose active support Amitabh would have never been able to get his parents' killers. As a result, Amitabh and Pran get very close in the film, becoming emotionally dependent on one another. Their love, which (in the Greek sense) is amative love to start with, gradually becomes adhesive, although neither of them is fully alive to its implications. The evidence for this is present everywhere–in the characterization, the dialogues, and especially in the songs the two men sing. And this is where the paradox lies: two men who believe they represent the masculinity principle to the utmost degree find they cannot live without each other; they are happy only when they are together.

The song that Pran sings to Amitabh in *Zanjeer* is as follows:

Yaari is my religion,
My yaar is my life.

I won't regret
Dying for the sake of yaari,
I'd sooner die than see my friend morose.
The fairground of happiness
Is where we are together.

Why does the flower of my garden look so sad?
Is he the victim of ill-will?
Have no qualms, friend, let me into your heart.
Let me know
The price of your smile.

Shall I bring you the moon and the stars?
Shall I bring you sights that gratify the senses?
I'm grateful you are my friend,
Your smile is my greatest treasure.

When my yaar smiles,
My youthfulness returns.

I shall elaborate on the meaning of the words "yaar" and "yaari" a little later. Suffice it to say that here they mean "friend" and "friendship" respectively. *Zanjeer* set the pace for a host of similar films where Amitabh Bachchan was the sulking anti-hero with a mission (usually revenge), for which he needed to team up with a male partner, often with more heroic characteristics than he himself possessed. Invariably, the two men sang songs which betrayed how much they were in each other's hearts. We attempt below English renderings of three such songs from films that were box-office hits; there is a good deal of intertextuality among the lyrics. This first song is from Ramesh Sippy's *Sholay* (1975), where Amitabh sings with Dharmendra (the he-man of the Bombay movie industry) as they ride a 350cc motorbike, itself a phallic symbol:

We won't end this friendship,
We shall be together even in death.

Listen, my friend,
Your victory is mine
My loss is yours
Your sorrow is my sorrow
My life is your life.

For you I will risk this life
For you I will play with fire,
Make enemies of the whole world.

People see us as two,
But actually we are one
O God, bless us
So we never separate,
Never wound one another.

We shall eat and drink together,
Live and die together
Till life lasts.

In Hrishikesh Mukherjee's *Namak Haram* (1973), Rajesh Khanna, that romantic "phenomenon" of the 1970s (referred to earlier), sings the following love song to Amitabh as the latter films him with a video camera:

> Lamps burn, flowers blossom,
> Yet finding a friend in this world
> Is no child's play.
>
> When a man is separated from his yaar
> His heart is in bad shape.
> Memories pierce the heart.
>
> Look, don't be vain about your youthfulness.
> If a yaar asks for your life
> Give it to him by all means.
> Youth is transient,
> The warmth of friendship
> Is eternal.
>
> Health and wealth all disappear in time.
> The whole world becomes an enemy.
> Only a friend offers
> Lifelong companionship.

Finally, there's director Raj Khosla's *Dostana* (1980), in which Amitabh and Shatrughan Sinha, Bollywood's villain turned hero, sing to one another:

> Even if the whole world turns an enemy
> Let our friendship prosper.
> We swear by this friendship
> Not even death can separate us.
>
> If anyone asks us where we live
> We tell them
> We live in each other's hearts,
> That is the only address we have.
>
> May our friendship prosper.

Numerous other examples can be given, for Amitabh Bachchan reigned supreme in Bollywood for almost two decades in the 70s and 80s. It's not as if he didn't do the odd romantic movie, say a *Kasme Vaade* (Ramesh Bahel, 1978) or a *Silsila* (Yash Chopra, 1981), where he had to sing and dance with his heroine in the rain, or run around trees. But he was awkward in such films, and they did not gain widespread acceptance with the audience.

The audience for an Amitabh movie was predominantly male, young men in their twenties and thirties. His films were perceived as "action films," not quite meant for women. In the 50s and 60s (the romantic age), women in India frequented the movie theaters, either with their menfolk or with other women, more often than they did in the 70s and 80s. The love stories of the time were supposed to appeal to the emotional side of our natures, and women were principally regarded as emotional rather than rational beings. Their husbands and fathers thus gave them permission, as it were, to step out of the house and go to the cinema. With the onset of the action era, women's visits to the cinema decreased. They were convinced that films that abounded in fight sequences (*dishoom-dishoom* movies as we call them in India) were stunt films lacking in emotional content. This also coincided with the advent of video. If women wanted to see *Sholay* or *Zanjeer* (and indeed Amitabh Bachchan was the heart-throb of many of them), all they had to do was borrow a video cassette of the film from the neighborhood video library and see it in the privacy of their own homes, far away from the lecherous cat-calls of men in the cinema-hall.

The bond that Amitabh Bachchan formed with other male actors on the screen, complemented by the presence of an all-male audience that had gathered to watch him, engendered a sort of homoeroticism in the dark of the movie hall. Anyone who has been in a cinema theater in India knows the conditions that prevail. The seats are narrow and cramped, worse than economy class seats in a Boeing 747, so that a maximum number of persons can be accommodated. Air conditioning, more often than not, is nonexistent; even if the theater is air-conditioned, the air-conditioners often don't work on account of power cuts or drives in the city to save electricity. There are few fans in the auditorium. As a result, body odors permeate through the theater and add to the sleazy atmosphere. Take a look at the audience as the movie is showing (as I have frequently done), and you are likely to find young men all over each other, clasping hands, putting arms around shoulders and waists, even a leg on a leg. Few of these men might be consciously gay. Nor would they dare to exhibit such behavior if it were their wives or girlfriends that were sitting next to them: that would be too black-and-white. Here, on the other hand, is an ambivalent greyness that provides enough of a buffer should anyone suspect what is going on. After all, same sex closeness exists in every walk of Indian life, especially among the lower-middle classes: in bedrooms and public transport, on the street. India is like that only. What conspires to give this a sexual coloration is that social mores in India do not permit men and women to be demonstrative until marriage, and even then never in public places. Sex is only for procreation, not entertainment. Also, sex has nothing to do with love. Every Indian thus grows up with a certain degree of sexual repression. Even if one is not born gay, it is so easy to become gay in India. But, coming back to our audience within the context of the movies they are watching, their "deviant" behavior, even if some part of their mind is prompted to call it that, is sort of validated by the actions of the matinee idol. If Amitabh Bachchan can express undying love for other men on the screen, all in the name of *yaari,* why can't they too indulge in a little mischief?

In the late 70s and 80s, I was still in my twenties, studying and later teaching at the University and University-affiliated colleges in Bombay. I had, by this time, discovered that I was gay. I often bought a ticket and went to an Amitabh Bachchan movie (yes, in those days he was my favorite actor too, and I even tried to imitate him!), not just to see him, but also in search of sexual adventure. Though the degree and intensity of my experiences varied, I rarely came back disappointed. At times I went to the movie with a guy I had picked up at a park or public loo, and throughout the movie we merely held hands. At other times I found myself seated next to someone I fancied. As the lights went off, the action began, so to speak, both on the screen and off it. Frequently, my "victims" readily yielded to my advances. For the next three hours or so, we had a good time, oblivious to the people around us, who thought we were only *yaars,* for we took care not to unbutton our trousers. Sometimes, if the seats of the back row were full, we discreetly moved to the middle or front of the theater, where the half-empty seats offered us a measure of privacy. But it's not as if it was always I who initiated the action. I distinctly remember the time when, half-way through a movie, as I happened to glance at the guy sitting to my left, I found he was aroused, had gotten his dick out of his trousers for an airing, and was waiting expectantly for me to fondle him. I did, not the type who is accustomed to looking a gift horse in the mouth. Although I personally never went that far, this chap later gave me lurid accounts of men who wanked and sucked each other off in movie halls, all while the film was on!

Of course, I'll be exaggerating if I suggest that I was always successful in finding a partner whenever I went to the movies. I got my usual share of rebuffs and dirty looks from homophobic strangers (about whose homophobia I did not know), and a couple of times I was all but bashed up. However, I like to see a glass of water as half-full rather than half-empty.

As the songs we have translated indicate, Amitabh Bachchan was a *yaar* of his co-heroes in the films cited above, and their relationship was based on *yaari.* What exactly do the words *yaar* and *yaari* mean? I've already stated that they would loosely correspond to the words "friend" and "friendship." But a *yaar* is much more than a friend, and *yaari* goes far beyond the Western notion of Platonic friendship, which, above all, is non-sexual. In his essay "Yaari," Raj Ayyar explains: "A yaar is an individual with whom one feels a deep, almost intangible connection. Definitions of this term have varied through time, sometimes denoting a lover, at other times a friend. For me a yaar embodies elements of both a friend and a lover, and I yearn for just such a connection with a man in my life" (Ratti, 167).

Ayyar is not alone in his yearnings. The character portrayals of Amitabh Bachchan and his co-heroes, reinforced, no doubt, by the songs they sing, prove that they too have precisely the same expectations. Sex might not be openly projected on the screen, but on the basis of internal evidence, we have every right to conclude that the two characters are involved in a sort of sexual relationship off the screen, and what is more, don't find it necessary to go out of their way to conceal it. When *Namak Haram* was released in 1973, I remember reading a review of the film in Bombay's popular movie magazine *Filmfare*, in which the reviewer spoke about the "touch of homo" in the two central characters. I didn't quite understand then what she meant, or perhaps understood only intuitively. But I do know now. "Yaar" is a suitably ambivalent term. As Ayyar says, it means both friend and lover, accounting for that buffer, that grey area that I refer to above. A man may call his male friend a *yaar*, but a husband will also use the same word to describe his wife's lover. The word "bewaffa" ("unfaithful"), which occurs in another song in *Dostana*, has similar resonances. The lines are:

> My friend, what's wrong!
> I hear you've turned unfaithful.

Amitabh Bachchan sings these lines to Shatrughan Sinha in a tear-filled voice. A husband who catches his wife in bed with her lover will also think of her as unfaithful, a *bewaffa*. Because the word "yaar" here can be interpreted any which way (that is, as friend and lover), it provides a convenient alibi in India, both for the external world and for the practitioners of *yaari*. The chaps with whom I was having it off in the theaters would, like the people seated all around us, deal with their own built-in homophobia and/or fear of being found out, by thinking of me as their *yaar* for the three hours during which the movie was on. It's a cultural thing, restricted to the subcontinent and unknown in the contemporary West where all touch is construed as purely sexual. Writer Naseem, without using the words "yaar" or "saheli" (the female equivalent of "yaar"), says in her article "Reflections Of An Indian Lesbian": "It is not difficult to be a lesbian or a gay male in India. The social segregation of men and women provides enough space for friendships between people of the same sex, which may lead to sexual relations" (Sukthankar, 332).

Amitabh Bachchan is now past his prime, but refuses to retire from Hindi films. I have not seen any of his recent releases,[1] but from what I have heard about them, he is still made to team up with other, younger men like Govinda, and Daler Mahendi. I on my own part have stopped going to movies, preferring to bring my lovers to the privacy of my own flat instead (which I did not possess in the 70s). But *yaari* continues in the movie halls of Indian cities, literally with gay abandon. The next generation of Bollywood heroes is faithfully following in the footsteps of Amitabh. One of them, Saif Ali Khan, reportedly beat up Bombay-based activist Ashok Row Kavi when he suggested in an article that the song Saif sang with co-hero Akshay Kumar in the film *Main Khiladi Tu Anari* ("We two, we are different") revealed that they were more than just acting.

And, needless to say, *yaari* goes on among audiences with the same ferocity. It is a legacy that we, as a nation, ought to be extremely grateful for. For it's an umbrella concept that ensures that no Indian shall be left to die alone.

NOTE

1. Indeed, a middle-aged Amitabh Bachchan has re-emerged in Verinder Raj Anand's *Major Saab* (1998) and K. C. Bokadia's *Lal Baadshah* (1999), among others. In both, Amitabh's portrayals self-consciously exploit the legacy of his macho screen persona, and reflexively construct the heroism of his characters from the real-life hero worship of the actor. *Lal Baadshah,* in fact, is a sort of (self-) parody of the "quintessential" Amitabh Bachchan persona, most conspicuously in a scene in which superheroic Amitabh does not deign to speak to the murderously enraged villain because he is too busy having a leisurely cup of tea. (Ed.)

WORKS CITED

Rakesh Ratti (Ed.) *Lotus of Another Color: An Unfolding of the South-Asian Gay and Lesbian Experience*. Boston: Alison Publication Inc., 1993.
Ashwini Sukhtankar (Ed.) *Facing the Mirror: Lesbian Writing from India*. New Delhi: Penguin Books India, 1999.

The Changing Image of the Hero
in Hindi Films

Ashok Row Kavi

SUMMARY. Beneath the surface of the Bollywood cinema is a perco-
lating gay culture trying to break free, waiting for the moment to
emerge from subtext into text. For now, in what we might now call a
period of transition, the Bollywood hero has been (particularly in the
past three decades) the focus of increased homoeroticization, with his
body becoming a spectacle at every turn. Unfortunately, what has facilitated this is a veiled (and sometimes not-so-veiled) form of misogyny,
in which the heroine's role is minimized such that, rather than another
filmic character falling in love with the hero, the audience itself is invited to see the macho (and perhaps narcissistic) hero as unattached and
therefore available for homoerotic desire. *[Article copies available for a fee
from The Haworth Document Delivery Service: 1-800-342-9678. E-mail address:
<getinfo@haworthpressinc.com> Website: <http://www.HaworthPress. com>]*

One has just to see two Hindi motion pictures separated by nearly five
decades. One is *Achyut Kanya*–"The Untouchable Girl"–produced by the
now-defunct Bombay Talkies in the 1940s; the other is *Judwaa*–"Twins"–

Ashok Row Kavi is editor in chief of *Bombay Dost*, India's oldest registered gay
news magazine and chairperson of the Humsafar Trust, an NGO which focusses on
male sexual health with special emphasis on teaching safer practices to gay men and
men-having-sex-with-men (MSM). Ashok is a graduate in Science and lives in
Mumbai where he and his friends gravitate between AIDS prevention programs and
Bollywood fantasia (E-mail: arkavi@bol.net.in or humsafar@vsnl.com). The Humsafar Trust runs India's only gay drop-in center provided by a local city government.

[Haworth co-indexing entry note]: "The Changing Image of the Hero in Hindi Films." Kavi, Ashok
Row. Co-published simultaneously in *Journal of Homosexuality* (The Haworth Press, Inc.) Vol. 39, No. 3/4,
2000, pp. 307-312; and: *Queer Asian Cinema: Shadows in the Shade* (ed: Andrew Grossman) Harrington
Park Press, an imprint of The Haworth Press, Inc., 2000, pp. 307-312. Single or multiple copies of this article
are available for a fee from The Haworth Document Delivery Service [1-800-342-9678, 9:00 a.m. - 5:00 p.m.
(EST). E-mail address: getinfo@haworthpressinc.com].

307

produced in the 1990s in Mumbai's Bollywood movie machine. The former has the evergreen hero Ashok Kumar playing a man trying to break the insurmountable caste barriers suggested by its title, while the latter is more concerned with the fabulous bodies of its pair of heroic twins, both played by the boisterous brat Salman Khan. Not only is the contrast startling by way of story-lines, the characterization of the social milieu, and the value systems of the hero, but it is the very hero himself who has changed. In *Achyut Kanya*, Ashok Kumar is always covered and clothed in *dhoti-kurmas*, while the new avatar that is *Judwaa*'s hero seems to be baring his body at every opportunity afforded onscreen.

The image of the hero has been the most mobile of mutants within movie-dom. The eroticization of the male body is a theme which has progressed dramatically in the highly image-conscious medium of film, which has virtually replaced all the traditional performing arts in India. This progression has occurred though subtle but subversively, and irreversibly, directed movements starting in the late 1950s. The momentous arrival on the scene of the chocolate hero Dev Anand into Bollywood was the beginning of this eroticization of the male. A Lahori graduate who would become a bird of fortune in Bombay, Dev Anand brought with him a highly stylized form of acting through which he created and focused his sexualized screen persona. There was something not just haunting about him–he possessed a strange effeminacy that bordered on the childlike. This was, of course, a sedulous method of removing the male from the dangerous sphere of being the patriarchal monster, the sphere in which the Indian matrix had placed him.

Dev Anand had an innocuous sensuality about him that conspired to make his heroine into an Oedipal figure. It was not for nothing that Dev Anand became a quaint counterpoise to that powerful heroine Waheeda Rehman, who virtually "killed" the producer-director Guru Dutt, who committed suicide in a heart-broken love affair with her. But the behind-the-scenes gossip pointed more to the ambiguities of Rehman's own sexual orientation, which horrified the romantically-inclined. Regardless, she was a cold-hearted woman whose affection was difficult to procure through normal romancing. Dev Anand did manage to procure it through a loving relationship that seemed, however, to preclude sex; instead, the focus of attention was drawn back to him, to the potential sexuality offered by himself to any male who cared to see him as, indeed, somebody not attached to a woman.

The songs in Dev Anand's *Kala Bazar* (1960), for example, such as *Apni To Har Aaah Ek Toofan Hai*–"Each Sigh of Mine Is Like a Typhoon"–are mostly highly male-eroticized songs. They appear to be directed towards unattached males (in the audience) who will understand the hero's lonely existence, as the following line makes clear: "Opperwala jana kar unjaan hai"–"The guy above knows everything but pretends he doesn't." This self-centered male eroticism, of unattached-ness and solitude, reached its zenith in Vijay Anand's *Guide* (1965), where the heroine just disappears in a puff of ambiguity while the hero becomes a martyr to the rain-gods! "Parama Yagna" (human sacrifice) personified.

The first significant step in the full eroticization of the male was in the rise of the elastic hero Shammi Kapoor, from the "RK" clan.[1] Shammi Kapoor achieved this eroticization through a highly personalized form of high camp behavior and acting which made himself the focus of attention. The heroine in all of his movies was a silent, still, and slightly startled persona who drew attention away from herself through a very low-profile performance. Meanwhile, dancing and prancing around her in a mixture of plastic and erratic movements would be the hero, as he redirects the audience's attention to his highly vibrant, sexualized performance. But even Shammi did not strip, show his bare waxed chest, or flaunt the pelvic movements with which the hero of the eighties and nineties frontally assaults the spectator.

Shammi not only brought freshness to his roles, but he externalized the character of the hero himself. The hero now was no more the repository of the traditional value system, which had shaped the Indian Renaissance and the struggle for India's freedom; he was instead a fragile, faithful symbol of the younger Indian, born post-Independence. This post-Freedom persona of the hero lays more stress on the physicality of the young man himself. The heroine was not only no longer the vehicle wherein desire was addressed, but she also slowly shifted erotic values away from herself and back to the male by sometimes sexually teasing and touching the hero on his chest and back. Shammi Kapoor's heroines were usually all new-comers, such as Asha Parikh, Amita, and Vidya Sinha. Voluptuous and vapid, these three would move into Hindi filmdom like so many zombie-like dolls. Unlike older heroines such as Nargis or Madhubala, they did not, or simply could not, support storylines in their own right. They were merely appendages to this high drama of the eroticization of the male, and did not represent a legitimate heterosexual partner for the hero to engage. In the 1960s, the subtle homosexual themes in director Raj Kapoor's *Sangam* (1964) and Satyen Bose's *Dosti* (1964) had already heralded the marginalization of the heroine. It is thus ironic that the lascivious Vyjayantimala, who had previously risen to high erotic eminence in such films as Bimal Roy's *Madhumati* (1958), later saw her status as sex-symbol marginalized in *Sangam*. One of her clones, Padmini, tried to demonstrate the very limits of female erotica in Radhu Karmakar's *Jis Desh Mein Ganga Behti Hai* (1960). But, in only one of her earlier films, the Indian censor board could not handle Padmini's wet body writhing under a waterfall, a scandalous scene which prompted debates galore in the Indian press.

Later on, the high-camp gay subtext of the film *Pakeezah* (1971, directed by Kamal Amroshi) took India's subterranean gay world by storm, a film in which the heroine's stature as the film's erotic focus was effectively destroyed. There is an incredible exchange of dialogue in the film, in which the heroine Meena Kumari actually tells a *tongawalla* to "take her to the graveyard" when she is asked about her destination–it marks the death of her female eroticization as well. Meena Kumari was on her last legs in real life, and there was indeed poignant behind-the-scenes news of how her husband was counting her financial assets while she lay on her deathbed.

However, a new trend started with a completely new generation: the ubiquitous Amitabh Bachchan. Amitabh's popular yet subtle anti-hero image started with Prakesh Mehra's *Zanjeer* (1973), but, with his career still in its chrysalis stage, he had already come into his own with the role of a life-time in *Anand* (1971), in which he evoked a silent, quiet, brooding sexuality. The plot is about a dying cancer patient who is looked after by a wonderfully humane doctor (Amitabh). The doctor, a paragon of virtue, makes his presence felt through a tacit yet strongly homoerotic bond with the dying patient. The patient, played by the then-superhero Rajesh Khanna, effectively killed the last of the chocolate heroes. Rajkesh Khanna and Amitabh Bachchan also did a terrific job in Hrishikesh Muhkerjee's *Namak Haram* (1973), where the homoerotic male bond between the two principals is delineated with disarming clarity. In a revealing scene in the same year's *Zanjeer*, Amitabh is made the focus of "yaari" (male bond) in a highly sensual male dance performed by the evergreen Pran as a pathan. The pathan tribes, from the north-west frontier province, have indeed always been open in their displays of homoeroticism.

This sophisticated, concerted effort at shifting the erotic focus onto the hero and gently pushing the heroine into the background had been effectively represented in *Zanjeer*, a watershed in Hindi filmdom. It inaugurated the slow but steady climb of the homoerotic themes that continued with the Amitabh-Dharmendra combination in *Sholay* (1975), where an equally homoerotic song was enacted openly for audiences. The song–*Yeh Dosti, Hum Nahi Toden Ge* ("We Shall Never Break This Bond of Friendship")–features lyrics plainly homosexual in content. One verse, openly sexual, says: "I will take anything from you"–"Tere Liye Lelenge." "Lelenge" is Hindi street slang for the phrase "getting fucked." Amitabh, only apparently the most heterosexual of Hindi film heroes, may have initiated his career with a strong silent-type image, but he also went on to play with gender. In Prakash Mehra's *Laawaris* (1981), Amitabh plays a cross-dresser, in full drag singing "Mere Angane Mein Tera Khya kaam Hai" ("What Business Do You Have in My Backyard?"). Amitabh's insistence on downright homosexual themes could verge on misogyny, signalling movies to completely focus on men to the utter exclusion of women.

Though there would be women-centered films, in which actresses such as Dimple Kapadia, Rehka, and others tried to reverse the trend, Amitabh's towering personality defeated them at the box office. Even Rehka's *Umrao Jaan* (1981) was just a cult period movie in the mold of the gay-campy *Pakeezah*; its popularity was further debilitated by Muzaffar Ali's Muslim-centric direction. Even the *mujra* (dancing girl song) in *Umrao Jaan,* "Dil Cheeze Khya Hai," became a gay theme song played out–and acted upon–by gay men.

It was in the film *Silsila* (1981, directed by Yash Chopra) that our homosexual theme was so casually, and yet so openly, brought up that it escaped even most gay men. The film was said to reflect a so-called real life scandal–between Amitabh Bachchan and Rekha, the then top pair in filmdom. Never mind the parallel gossip about an alleged lesbian affair between Rehka and her private secretary Farhah. The film monthly *Cine Blitz* was sued for Rs.six crores (Rs. 60 million) by Rehka for printing pictures of Rekha and a rather butch Farhah together; it got mysteriously sorted out with a simple apology. Nevertheless, in *Silsila*, the male duo, Amitabh Bachchan and Shashi Kapoor, are showering together when the soap drops to the floor. When each anticipates the other bending down, suddenly both start laughing uproariously and Shashi Kapoor says, "I'm not going to bend down. I know what happened last time." This is the clearest reference to the "penetrating" image of Amitabh Bachchan.

The gay construct in *Silsila* is of gay men as we recognize gay constructions in the West. There is no playing around with gender; it is a straightforward, clearcut sexual bonding held above the usual male bonding revealed in Hindi cinema through the decades. However, this construction has required a slow and steady evolution through numerous years of groping in the jungles of male-bonding themes. When Shashi Kapoor dies in *Silsila*, Amitabh smashes a TV set in grief, becomes unstably emotional, and otherwise suffers a breakdown. His secondary consolation prize is the film's perfunctory heroine, Rekha, who cuddles and comforts him, saying, "Well, you'll have to be happy with me." This is a telling commentary on the state of the Hindi film heroine.

There have been openly male bonding-themes in Hindi films, as in Mahesh Bhatt's 1991 *Saathi* (whose title means "Friend," anyway), and even *Veeru Dada*. Mahesh Bhatt, who has been mostly open about his own bisexual nature, has even tried to demonize and criminalize the *hijra* sexual minority in *Sadak* (1991), in which the veteran Sadashiv Amrapurkar plays a hijra who is involved with criminal rackets. Mahesh Bhatt's pictures, seemingly not a part of mainstream Hindi cinema, wound up bombing at the box office. The brilliant woman director Kalpana Lajmi did try to make a film, *Darmiyan*, addressing alternative sexuality, but even she, too, ended up criminalizing *hijras*, a sexual minority under great stress in India's modernizing economy. This film was also a box office failure, largely because gay men were furious about how depressing alternative sexuality was portrayed to be. It was the first time that many gay men had started getting angry about the presentation of gay lifestyles.

Nevertheless, the point stands that the gay construct itself is now firmly entrenched in Indian society. The mass-circulated Hindi gossip magazines openly mention the gay lifestyle of many of the top stars in Hindi cinema. The Hindi magazine "Mayapuri" even runs features where the heads of Hindi heroes (Akshay Kumar is my favorite) are superimposed on female torsos. The magazine, a top-seller at half a million copies, is evidence that there is obviously a market out there that likes to see its heroes gender-bending. There are gay scripts floating around in Bollywood. Gay themes have already been attempted in a series of TV programs, and homosexuality and lesbianism have become central themes on talk shows. Still, a *real* mainstream gay theme film will be an unforgettable landmark in Hindi cinema.

NOTE

1. Shammi Kapoor is the son of early film actor Prithviraj Kapoor. He is also the brother of actor-director Raj Kapoor, and brother of actor Shashi Kapoor. (Ed.)

Long Life of a Short Film

Riyad Vinci Wadia

SUMMARY. What follows is an account of my personal experiences as an independent Indian film director who had the fortune to make the country's first openly gay film, the short *BOMgAY.* That said, I would like this essay to be accepted as, rather than a critical appraisal of Indian cinema, a humbly autobiographical account of one individual caught in the hectic throes of political (and cinematic) visibility. *[Article copies available for a fee from The Haworth Document Delivery Service: 1-800-342-9678. E-mail address: <getinfo@haworthpressinc.com> Website: <http://www.HaworthPress.com>]*

I wish to share with you the story of why and how I came to produce *BOMgAY,* a short film that had the dubious distinction of becoming India's first "gay" film. As I sit to write this I realize now that the "why" is more important than the "how." For in that "why" lies the real beauty of this endeavor. The "how," which was so important to discuss at the time of its release, has paled in significance with the passage of time.

In the summer of 1996 I was in my prime. A newspaper profile had dubbed me "the Young Turk" of Bombay's independent cinema industry and I half believed it. My reputation had been built on the fact that at 27 years of age I had already produced and directed a feature length film that had had international acclaim, and that I was a scion of an illustrious family that had a sixty-year history in film production. My grandfather, JBH Wadia, was a pioneer producer-director who had founded the erstwhile Wadia Movietone

Riyad Vinci Wadia is an internationally recognized independent film-maker. He is also a writer, curator, and guest lecturer on cinema and cinema history. He is 32 and resides between New York and Bombay.

Address correspondence to the author at: 326 West 14th Street, NY, NY 10014 (E-mail: cinema@mindspring.com).

[Haworth co-indexing entry note]: "Long Life of a Short Film." Wadia, Riyad Vinci. Co-published simultaneously in *Journal of Homosexuality* (The Haworth Press, Inc.) Vol. 39, No. 3/4, 2000, pp. 313-323; and: *Queer Asian Cinema: Shadows in the Shade* (ed: Andrew Grossman) Harrington Park Press, an imprint of The Haworth Press, Inc., 2000, pp. 313-323. Single or multiple copies of this article are available for a fee from The Haworth Document Delivery Service [1-800-342-9678, 9:00 a.m. - 5:00 p.m. (EST). E-mail address: getinfo@haworthpressinc.com].

Studios in 1933. As I carried the mantle of my family's reputation I was well aware of the charade that I was perpetuating by appearing as a dynamic film-maker all set to steer the course of my inheritance well into the next century. When asked, I would talk with great flourish about the several projects I was working on and the great stories I wanted to tell. The reality was that I felt I was in the creative doldrums. An impasse had set in two years earlier after the initial success of my debut feature, *Fearless–The Hunterwali Story* (1993).

What I didn't realize then was that this doldrums was a necessary phase and that actually I was drifting with a purpose. Not that the drift was on calm waters–in fact quite the opposite. You see, in the aftermath of the release of *Fearless* at the London Film Festival in 1993, my personal life underwent a sea change. Having achieved in one shot all my life's ambitions–monetary success, fame, respect of my peers, etc., what was left was just one issue I had to deal with. My gay identity locked deep in the proverbial closet.

This was driven home to me in that winter of '93, in London. I was staying for the duration of the festival with an old family friend who was gay. He and his boyfriend of ten years lived together in central London and led a picture-book, openly gay life that I had read about but till then never witnessed. While I was deeply closeted I was very comfortable with my gay identity on a personal level. It was the act of expressing my gay identity and all that it would entail for my family and my social environment that made it difficult to make the no-turning-back decision to open that closet door. Temperamentally, too, I was loath to do things in half measures, which meant that if I were to ever discuss my gay identity I would first and foremost have to reveal it to the persons closest to my being, my parents. Once they knew, I believed I would be comfortable with the concept of letting anyone and everyone know. For then it would not matter to me what people thought.

My observation of my London hosts' bliss and my need to finally find that bliss for myself was sharply put into discussion when a letter arrived at the London Film Festival desk with my name on it. It was from (the late) Mark Finch, director of the San Francisco Lesbian & Gay Film Festival, inviting my film and me to attend the 1994 edition of that festival, all expenses paid. The lure of 10 days in that fabled city, my film mainlining at the fabulous Castro cinema with me at the center of attention in the gayest spot on the planet, was too much for me to resist, and I accepted instantly. It was only a few days later that my bravado started to crumble. How was I to explain to my family (with whom I lived in Bombay) and my friends (not to mention the Indian press that seemed to be hanging on my every word) that I was going to show a film at an exclusively lesbian and gay event? In a deeply closeted society such as exists in India, where even issues surrounding heterosexual sexuality are seldom discussed in the open, this was surely asking too much.

On my return to Bombay I hid the news of my acceptance to this festival for a few days. Then a fax arrived from Mark Finch discussing travel arrangements and other such technical details and I knew the time had come to take a deep breath and face the consequences. I gingerly mentioned the news to my parents, speaking a little too fast and a little too disinterestedly. They took in the news without too much ado–apart from a query about why a gay film festival would want to show a film on the life of my grand aunt, Fearless Nadia, who was not gay. I had anticipated this and casually showed them a review that had appeared in "Variety," which praised the film and mentioned that its camp subject and feministic heroine would be of interest to gay and lesbian audiences worldwide. I also threw in the fact that now that the film was made I needed to recover money and every potential market should be explored. Thus using capitalism and media manipulation, I thought I had managed to evade turning the handle on the closet door. But I felt angry at myself for having cheated the issue. In the festival entry form I had marked off one of the boxes alongside the questions "is the director of the film gay?"

A few days later, the 26th of December 1993 to be precise, as I was alone with my mother driving home in her car, we came across a beggar woman carrying a beautiful child in her arms. My mother wistfully looked at the child and wondered aloud as to when she would become a grandmother and have a baby to play with and love. I can't say what came over me. Perhaps it was the weeks of tension and debating whether I should say I was gay, or if this was actually the occasion I was seeking to finally rid myself of the shackles of needless duplicity, but I blurted out that she shouldn't look to me for that to happen. Without missing a beat she turned to me and bluntly asked, "Why? Are you otherwise inclined?"

My coming out was rapid. One day my mother, the next week my close friends, the following fortnight my brother, a few days later my father, and within two months my general social circle. Over the next eight months I was travelling the world from festival to festival, from San Francisco and Los Angeles to Cannes and Toronto to Hong Kong and Tokyo. Alive, free, exhilarated and gay, gay, gay! The pink champagne bottle had been popped and the bubbles were overflowing. I found and lost love, became a fixture at gay bars and discovered Lycra. I started to read and become aware of gay issues and re-evaluate my life and its direction. I quickly became aware about the silent yet powerful gay mafia that ran the international film world and started to bask in being the new boy on the block. It was during this time that the seed was planted in my head to make a gay film based in India. Both Mark Finch and later David Overby (a programmer with the Toronto film festival) encouraged me, spending some precious hours giving me insights as to how the gay distribution network worked. The more I traveled internationally, the more I came out to straight friends in India, and the more I realized that I had a story that needed to be told cinematically. It was a subject that needed to be addressed publicly, now that I had addressed it personally.

By the summer of 1995 I had written and discarded some fifty ideas for gay stories. As I discovered for myself the gay world that lived and thrived in the shadows of the gullies of India's urban underbelly, I kept changing my mind on the exact angle I wanted to tell the story from. A collaborative attempt to work on a television project with filmmaker Kaizad Gustad introduced me to the work of R. Raj Rao, a writer and poet who had just released his book of short stories "One Day I Locked My Flat in Soul City." A slim volume, which I read in a matter of hours, this book was the first work I had read from an Indian author that was able to capture the essence of being a homosexual in India. It told its stories primarily from a middle class point of view, a point of view that I found interesting to read and document. I didn't waste time. I traced Raj to a University in Pune (a town a couple of hour's drive from Bombay) and a few weeks later had acquired the rights to adapt his book for the silver screen. We decided to write the screenplay collabora- tively, meeting on weekends.

As we went about this venture, we found that it wasn't as easy as we had hoped. Struggling to write and make a living proved to be difficult for both of us. One weekend Raj would have commitments; the next weekend I would have to be elsewhere. All this meant that our writing process became way too extended and we lost the thread. I became disenchanted when, after the initial rush of creativity had worn off, I found that raising the money for making a gay film from India was not going to be as easy as I had envisaged. My friends in the international festival gay mafia, who had seemed so close and easily accessible when I was on the festival circuit, suddenly seemed very far away now that I was once again stuck in Bombay.

By the time the summer of 1996 had rolled around the gay feature project had almost stalled. Prompted both by some friends and a pressing need to keep busy, I started to occupy myself with other projects. One such project centered on transgender issues in a patriarchal society. Titled *A Mermaid Called Aida*, it was a documentary on Aida Banaji, a notorious transsexual from Bombay. Intended for television release, the making of this feature length film was a bumpy and long-drawn journey. It gave me an opportunity to focus on gender politics and sexual identity and very soon the buzz in Bombay's film industry was that I was a director working on bold new films.

Then one afternoon Raj called me and asked if he could come around to show me some poems he had recently written. He was invited to attend the writing program and workshop at Iowa State University and was keen that I film him with a video camera reading some of his poems. He wanted to have some visual material to take with him, as the other writers who were invited to the program would also have cinematic representation of their work.

That evening, as I read the three typed pages of poems, a shiver went down my spine. Raj's poems were so explosive, so in-your-face gay, and so incisive of the urban gay milieu that he and I had been trying to capture in our screenplay. What wasn't working in our prose came alive with vitriol in his poetry. I was determined to make something of this work. My decision was further bolstered by the fact that I had just completed some banal ad film assignments that had brought in some money–money that I could use to fund a short film project. I called Raj the next day and said I was keen to make something of this material, but not just have him read his poems against a backdrop. I was keen to explore the poems with my own vision and bring to screen the power and passion of the poems as I had encountered them. Raj was agreeable. His only request was that I have the film ready in time for his departure to the U.S., only eighteen days later!

There are some moments in one's artistic career where the mind, the soul and the medium all mesh together to create a work that comes from the heart. For me, the making of *BOMgAY* was that moment. The confluence of twenty-seven years of being in the closet, two years of being hedonistically out, and the confidence of regaining pride and self-worth all came together to shape a film that, while twelve minutes short in length, is very long in its evolution.

Because of Raj's deadline, things moved at such a speed that even today I am amazed that we were able to create what we did in such a quick span. Perhaps it was this very speed that allowed the film to come from the subconscious and not from some calculated or thought-out plan. After putting the phone down on Raj, I called up my friend Jangu Sethna. Jangu was one of the few gay men in Bombay who had been out since his childhood in the early 70s. He had worked in film production in various capacities over the years and had a keen sense of the urban gay culture of Bombay. He had switched careers in the early 90s and had become a respected landscape artist. I was keen to collaborate with Jangu and asked him to come on board this project as my associate director. A few hours later we were sipping coffee and he and I started to furiously ideate on our interpretation of Raj's poems.

The next morning we had our storyboards down on paper. We felt good. We had let our stream of consciousness flow wild and true and we had come up with images and story lines that came from our collective experiences. I was clear about one thing when we started the ideating process: we were not going to fall shy or act coy just to please some societal norms. We were going to make a short film as we saw it. The only restriction would be the budget. I had earmarked a total budget of two hundred thousand rupees (then equivalent to approximately U.S. $5000). We were determined to shoot on Beta as film would have been prohibitive and a far lengthier process, difficult to achieve in our timeframe. There is an inherent difficulty in translating the subjectivity of poetry to the objectivity of film. A poem offers unlimited variations to interpretation to a single reader each time that reader goes through it. In visualizing the film, Jangu and I were freezing once and for all a visualization of the poems as we saw them on the day we drew the storyboards.

Now came the tough part. Putting together a team of professionals to work on a film that was bound to gain some notoriety is not easy. In India making a film that will shake mountains or threaten the peace is not considered avant-garde. It's seen as being childish. "Five thousand years of cultural evolution" is a phrase often thrown at any attempt to contest the status quo. I was keen to involve as many people from the gay community in Bombay as I could, but found after a few initial phone calls that most fought shy of coming on camera or working behind the scenes for fear of being clearly identified. It was the old syndrome: if you work on a gay film then you must be gay. Just as "if you had a friend who identified himself as gay then, ergo, you were gay." This prompted me to call in some of my friends who were clearly not gay. I brought in Neha Parikh, a senior production manager, and got her to make the initial phone calls. This worked wonders. She got Tejal Patni, a heterosexual, who was the "hot" new videographer in Bombay. He was then producing a popular fashion show on Channel [V]. We contracted Ashutosh Phaatak, also a heterosexual, to do the music score. Ashutosh, now a major music director in India, was then starting out and had just the musical sensibilities I felt this film needed. Plus he had really cute hands.

Casting was proving to be tricky. I decided to tackle casting myself. When I was very young my grandfather had shared with me a trade secret. He told me that he always went for the most difficult aspects of a job first and then finished up with the easier tasks. In our case, we knew getting an actor to perform in the nude, with some frontal nudity, was going to be the make-or-break aspect of our film. If we could convince two actors to do this for the sequence we had set in the public library then we were assured that our worries were over. I called my friend Rahul Bose. He was an actor of some repute in India, having performed in the legitimate theater and having done one feature film. That film was Dev Benegal's independent masterpiece *English August* (1994), where Rahul had played the central role. There were some sequences in the film that were clearly homoerotic, and Rahul had done some nudity in that film too. I decided to play reverse psychology on Rahul and told him I was casting for an experimental art film and wondered if he had met any actors that he could recommend to me for the principal roles. I told him about the library sequence and said it would require a really talented and fearless actor. Rahul immediately suggested himself but I told him to reconsider it, as he had a high profile and it may not be wise of him to take on a role that could have adverse effect on his career. It is to his merit as an actor that he saw through my bluff and told me to fuck-off feeding him that crap line. That same afternoon he was at my office and we went over the script. He loved it and was all ideas as to how he would do it. I offered him both choices: to play the "sodomiser" or the "sodomisee" (sic). Sensing that the latter was the more challenging, he opted for it.

Once we had an actor of Rahul's standing in the film the rest of the roles filled in easily. My pitch to others went "well, we have Rahul in . . . now do you want to do it?" And they did. There were some that accepted to do the film in the name of the "cause" as well. Within 48 hours of starting the venture we had shaped the film as an "important" work of "socio-politics" that "needed" to be made. My own coming out in Bombay society and the fact that I was making the film under the venerated banner of my family's company, Wadia Movietone, also added legitimacy. For the narration of Raj's poetry we requested the National Award-Winning actor Rajit Kapur to lend his voice. Rajit is one of the leading actors in India's art and independent film scene and that year had made a splash in Shyam Benegal's *The Making of the Mahatma*,[1] playing the role of a dashing Mahatma Gandhi. When Rajit agreed to participate in our venture I was overjoyed. It showed that the film we were making was being taken for all the seriousness that we had intended.

Getting permissions to locations was especially benefited by the fact that we were a recognized film unit and not some new kids on the block out to have fun or disturb the peace. Within six days of starting we were on a roll. There were a few glitches—some actors dropped out at the *nth* hour and some locations (especially the underground bathrooms and shooting on the train) had to be used "guerrilla" style. The most stressful shoot was the library sequence, where the librarian supervising the location had to be distracted and led away while our actors got nude and simulated sex. The librarian kept trying to hang around the set and the actors (Rahul Bose and Kushal Punjabi) became adept at slipping in and out of clothes every time he would reappear without notice. At one point the librarian caught on to what was going on and started to scream, saying "You are making a perverted porno." Jangu Sethna expertly handled the situation by reasoning with the librarian: "How can Wadia Movietone, the maker of great Indian cinema films for over 60 years, be involved in something so base!" The librarian then accepted our lie that we were making a social service film about ragging on college campuses! I had to sign a letter stating the same and only then did the librarian agree to let us proceed.

While such incidences in retrospect seem funny, the real threat of being caught by the law while making this film was felt by all of us at the time. It was a fear based on the fact that we were, indeed, breaking the law. To start with, we were making a film about homosexuality and quite openly depicting acts of homosexuality—crimes punishable with life imprisonment in India under the Indian Penal Code. We could also have been booked under several other laws for making what could easily be termed "lewd," "lascivious," and/or "perverted" films. Our actors could have been hauled to jail as could the crew and our suppliers. This threat was not taken lightly by us and we went through the entire shoot constantly keeping an eye out for any potential trouble. Section 337, which states that carnal intercourse against the course of nature is punishable by life incarceration, is a law that has seldom come to the courts, but is used repeatedly by the police and the state to threaten, coerce bribes from, and otherwise subjugate the public. A relic inherited from the English colonial period, this law has seldom been discussed because to discuss it would invite a description of sexual behavior, something that most Indians shy away from.

When the shoot was completed we rushed right into post-production, and because of the sensitive nature of our material I decided to edit the film on an AVID system myself. What initially emerged were six short films ranging in length from 30 seconds to two minutes. All together they made for nine minutes of running time. Jangu and I were very excited with our work. We knew we had done justice to our vision. Our next concern was how we planned to present it. We showed the six vignettes to friends, both straight and gay, and listened to what they had to say. Most felt that we would need to put these films into some sort of context. I too felt that if I were to screen these films for a more general public then I would have to find a way to deflect the film's strong images (and Raj's very strong poetry) by some sort of covert gimmick. I decided to set the six films in a sequence, using inter-titles between each to construct around them a quasi-socio-political frame. While the language of the inter-titles was academic, the thoughts expressed in them by me were heartfelt. They helped give our film a veneer of respectability, a film that otherwise would have been seen as simply provocative. Our final film was now twelve minutes long.

Now came the all-important decision: to get the film sent for censorship or not. We debated this for a long while and came to the conclusion that it would be an exercise in futility. The film not only contained images that would be seen as profane but also had language that was unacceptable to current censor laws. We knew that all we would achieve would be to create controversy and that was not our intention. Instead I devised a plan that I felt would be much more effective. The plan rose out of my understanding of advertising and marketing, trades I had experience with as an ad film-maker.

There is a hierarchy in the media and arts. Film is at the top of the hierarchy, followed by literature, then by journalism, and then by visual arts like painting and sculpture. Film is atop this exalted pedestal because it has the potential to reach the widest audience and cuts across social and educational barriers. It is also seen as a medium that is the most expensive and collaborative to work with; hence any idea that can be made into a film must have passed through much discussion and consideration before making it to its final form. While this is not entirely true, especially in the Mickey Mouse world of video production, it is a reputation that the film medium generates. And it is this reputation that allows film to be used for propaganda in the most effective way. And it was with a propagandistic stance that I went about marketing and screening *BOMgAY.*

In December of 1996 I had finished work on *A Mermaid Called Aida* as well, and I requested a friend at the prestigious National Center for the Performing Arts (NCPA) to let us use that venue to premiere both of my recent works. Like New York's Metropolitan Museum complex or Berlin's Volksbuhne, the NCPA provided me with a platform that allowed my work to be seen as art, and serious art at that. For the screening we invited a select band of journalists, film critics and television crews, as well as some friends and crew members. I was rather nervous. Two years of living a life as an openly gay man and my reputation as a film-maker were finally going to come together at this screening. It was a decision I had taken without too much preparation, rather letting it evolve in fits and starts. The screening went splendidly and both films were well received. There were several questions asked and the session went on till late, ending up in the gardens outside the theater complex.

One of the debates that surrounded the film was my claim that the film was "India's first gay film." Many came forward and said this was not true. They cited a film called *Adhura* (incomplete) which was made a few years earlier by one Ashish Balram Nagpal. I investigated this claim and found that this film was actually a pilot for a television series that never got screened. Furthermore, it was a story that revolved around a bisexual man and had a brief and rather derisive homosexual subplot. I stuck to my claim. That is not to say I was in any real way proud of my achievement. I wish gay films had been made many years before I came to make *BOMgAY,* and then, too, in abundance. That would have gone a long way in helping me and so many, many others in not having to struggle as hard as we still have to in the contexts of our identity and cultural and social acceptance.

Over the next several months the film received reams of newsprint. It opened up an extensive discussion on homosexuality in India and it brought the "g" word into people's homes. I was invited to guest on talk shows and lifestyle programs, where lengthy excerpts of *BOMgAY* were screened. Within a few short weeks I started receiving letters from small towns and far away cities–from gay men–wanting to know how they could get hold of a copy of the film. I was approached everywhere I went by men who would come up to me and tell me of some gay guy they knew, or some friend they wanted to give the movie to. It seemed to me that before my very eyes a whole new gay world was coming alive.

Strangely in all the press that the film received there was not one reaction that was negative or derogatory. It surprised me that no one seemed to find the film objectionable or worth raising any ire over. In fact, the most severe reprimand the film received was from gay activist Ashok Row Kavi, who reviewed both films in the *Times of India*. He wrote that *BOMgAY* painted a portrait of south Bombay (read: Westernized Indian) gay life and was far removed from the realities faced by most gay men in the rest of India, especially men who lived in underprivileged socio-economic classes. I agreed whole-heartedly with Ashok on this. My film was never intended to be a realistic portrait of an Indian gay community because, as I saw it, there is no such thing as the Indian gay community (or to stretch the discussion, there is no such reality called India!). An Indian in my opinion is a person who dwells in a geo-political entity called India. That's where the similarity between one Indian and another ends. At its lowest common denominator India is an amalgam of several universes and time zones, a geo-political entity in which the 14th century and the 23rd century coexist, and whose citizens are not from any cohesive culture. *BOMgAY* tries to portray the emergence of a small gay community that dwells in Bombay and who choose to interpret the word 'gay' as practiced and loosely defined by the cultural, social and ideological expressions as seen in the western hemisphere. Of course this interpretation becomes mutated with the ground realities of living within the other cultures that exist with and alongside Bombay.

With *BOMgAY* and the resultant media frenzy, the press was hungry for more gay related stories. It legitimized the efforts of social activist and once and for all declared that India had a gay community that had a voice in the arts. Whereas once gay issues were seldom heard about, now there is some reportage of them almost every day. More and more guys have come out of the closet in recent times and have started demanding some semblance of rights. While the road to acquiring these rights is a long one, the thought of a revolution is no longer fantastical. Following soon after in the steps of *BOMgAY* were a slew of gay theme films. Some of these films were directly the result of the hype that surrounded *BOMgAY*. Deepa Mehta's *Fire* (1996) brought lesbianism into focus (inciting riots and becoming a political weapon in the hands of right wing fundamentalists) and Kaizad Gustad's *Bombay Boys* (1998) had a confused gay protagonist too. Wheelchair-bound Bombay born writer, Firdaus Kanga, starred as himself in Warris Hussain's *Sixth Happiness* (1997), with scenes of his homosexual awakening being playfully portrayed. Even Bollywood has nodded to the emergence of an urban gay identity with Subhas Ghai's *Taal* (1999), which features a very camp queen choreographer (played by real life gay choreographer Mahesh "Pankola" Mahboobani) prancing around the leading lady. The most recent film to bring gay and bisexual issues to its central story line is Dev Benegal's *Split Wide*

Open (1999), which has just been completed and will premiere in the spring of 2000. Rahul Bose stars in this as well, and plays a street hustler who is educated by a gay Roman Catholic priest. Further gay images are to be found in recent television serials and music videos and short films, most produced in Bombay.

The most startling gay Indian film since *BOMgAY* is a stunning documentary by 22-year-old Nish Saran of New Delhi. This young filmmaker is representative of the new generation, having grown up in a world where being gay is no longer revolutionary, yet a world that still does not accept homosexuality. In his film, Nish confesses to his mother on-camera about his being gay and tackles issues of HIV/AIDS and fear of ostracization. The film recently had private screenings in India and has regenerated media frenzy on gay issues, this time bringing into sharp focus the need to discuss sexuality in a time of medical catastrophe.

My own quest continues. I am still working on bringing the screenplay (now completed by scriptwriter Shuchi Kothari) of R. Raj Rao's short stories to the screen. It's tentatively–and perhaps subliminally–entitled *Second Chances*.

NOTE

1. Also known as *Apprenticeship of a Mahatma*. (Ed.)

Transvestites and Transgressions:
Panggagaya in Philippine Gay Cinema

Rolando B. Tolentino
University of the Philippines

SUMMARY. Philippine cinema has long afforded spectators constructions of queerness not only deviating from Western queer theory but also from other continentally Asian homosexual traditions. Using as my primary text Lino Brocka's 1978 film *My Father, My Mother,* I examine how indigenous ideas of transsexuality and transgender are not only constructed by alternatively sexual images manufactured and appropriated by the Marcos regime, but how those sexual images construct and perpetuate class divisions as criteria of an ongoing Philippine sexual economy. *[Article copies available for a fee from The Haworth Document Delivery Service: 1-800-342-9678. E-mail address: <getinfo@haworthpressinc. com> Website: <http://www.HaworthPress.com>]*

This essay on transvesticism uses the cinema during the Marcos regime to discuss an aspect of gay discourse, *panggagaya* (mimicry). In this regard, I read *panggagaya* as performed in transvesticism as an alternative to the pedagogical or historical construction of bodies and sexualities during the Marcos era. On the one hand, transvesticism deconstructs the Marcos-era national culture; on the other hand, by the very characteristics that so define

Rolando B. Tolentino earned his PhD in Film, Literature and Culture at the University of Southern California on a Fulbright grant. He has published works on Philippine post-coloniality, identity, and cultural politics. He teaches in the Film Department at the University of the Philippines.

Address correspondence to the author at: University of the Philippines, Film Department, Mass Communication, Diliman, Quezon City 1101, Philippines (E-mail: roland@ netwarp.com.ph).

[Haworth co-indexing entry note]: "Transvestites and Transgressions: *Panggagaya* in Philippine Gay Cinema." Tolentino, Rolando B. Co-published simultaneously in *Journal of Homosexuality* (The Haworth Press, Inc.) Vol. 39, No. 3/4, 2000, pp. 325-337; and: *Queer Asian Cinema: Shadows in the Shade* (ed: Andrew Grossman) Harrington Park Press, an imprint of The Haworth Press, Inc., 2000, pp. 325-337. Single or multiple copies of this article are available for a fee from The Haworth Document Delivery Service [1-800-342-9678, 9:00 a.m. - 5:00 p.m. (EST). E-mail address: getinfo@haworthpressinc.com].

panggagaya, its limits are exposed. Transvesticism, like other identities poised outside of hegemonic subjectivities, is constructed always as "work in progress," never thoroughly complete, always in the process of becoming.

Transvestism's reworking of spectacle through performance calls attention to bodily, gender and sexual constructs. Characterized by its portability, transportability, performance and transgression, the transvestite's spectacle provides a self-reflexive operation in which ideal excess is projected for the material lack. The Marcoses, through some thirty years of conjugal dictatorship, disseminated images of their virile bodies embodying beauty and power where they become, in their minds, the "be all and end all" of power. Through national rituals that mark the spectacularization of their presidential bodies, the Marcoses have enforced a cultural grid to differentiate and hegemonize their bodily claim to power. Transvestism's spectacle operates by recoding the signifiers of the presidential bodies in its own gender, sexual and class based terms. This means that the transvestite's recoding of national codes also resignifies his desire to move beyond categories which impede, in actual material bases, the very limits of such transgression.

"There can be no culture without the transvestite," so goes Marjorie Garber's daring claim.[1] In this essay, I use Lino Brocka's *Ang Tatay Kong Nanay (My Father, My Mother*, 1978) to draw connections between transvestism, politics, desire, and the possibilities and limits of transgression. I begin with a sketch of the gay male character in cinema whose deviant body is consumed by the film's intense desire to contain it. The transvestite's body is doubly deviant and therefore doubly needing containment. His body is ambivalently marked. On the one level, he lays claim to martyrdom for the purer forms of devotion and suffering, analogous to the image of the mother-nation. On the other level, his excessive bodily transformations mark a desire for signifiers of upper class, analogous to the image of the presidential bodies, and female sexuality. For all the *gay* display of lifestyles and life choices, pain and suffering become the interior core of gay being. Thus the codes he transgresses are also reconstituted by the impossibility of the demands staked. I advance the discussion further by differentiating what appears as a ventriloquist act in the transvestism's "gaya" from mimicry, a breakdown of codes in which significations of power become arbitrary and culturally decipherable. Similar to what Butler has already foregrounded with regards to drag in *Paris Is Burning*, transvestism is posed as "neither an efficacious insurrection nor a painful subordination, but an unstable coexistence of both."[2]

TRANSVESTITE IN CULTURE AND CINEMA

Homosexuality and transvestism have always been on display through the conscious bodies of both the performer and the one attached to the performing body. Similar to artists and intellectuals in the service of national power, Imelda Marcos had a coterie of gay hairstylists, make-up artists, fashion and interior designers that trailed her in social events. This group of gay fashion artists legitimized Imelda's appearance, being and use of beauty, validating the apotheoses of the conjugal dictatorship.[3] While gayness is accepted and even displayed in the corridors of national power, the transvestite is marginalized for its position affixed to working class culture. The consignment to, yet prevalence in, "low" culture is a marker of the transvestite subculture that involves a process of peripheralization and survival tactics in the margins. Homosexuality is a modality to analyze this working class gay subculture, but it is also limiting–it negates class, among others, as a factor in transvestism. Class is reintroduced in the analysis of power negotiations in cinema and culture. For this essay, transvestite is defined as working class gay crossdressing or gay transgendering to designate the subcultural sphere where power is imbibed in gender and class terms. I use this term instead of transgender because of the overt impediment of female sexuality in the present transvestite's discourse.

Ang Tatay Kong Nanay (1978) explores a transvestite's life as a parent. Coring Derecho (portrayed by Dolphy, the most-known comedy star) owns a beauty parlor and is involuntarily placed in charge to care for a former companion's child. Dionisio Hamon, the platonic companion, returns to Coring with a child after disappearing for a year; he disappears again to join the U.S. Navy. Coring baptizes the child as Marlon Brando Hamon, after the idol whose pictures together with Dionisio's are plastered around the bedroom dresser and beauty shop mirrors. As the infant grows, Coring isolates his gay friends by acting straight, and making them act similarly in the child's presence. In time Dionisio returns for a visit, and is comforted by Coring's good rearing of Marlon. When he rejoins the navy, the child's mother–a former hostess turned rich widow–convinces Coring of the necessity of a mother and child bond. He begs for time, weaning the child on his unjustified outbursts and scoldings. The child is not happy either, being with his rich mother who does not have the time and patience for him. He escapes, goes back to Coring's apartment. The final scene presents their reunion, Coring returning late in the morning from a gay beauty contest where the sleeping Marlon awaits him.

Coring's efforts to police his gay sexuality are analogous to the ways gay sexuality have been contained in cinema. Excess is allowed to be displayed only to be contained in the inability to fully compensate for the "essential" lack. The transvestite embodies high fashion and female sexuality. Crossdressing is the performance marker of transvestism. By excessively wearing what is perceived as high (formal/evening) fashion, the transvestite exteriorizes the pleasure of temporal movement to "high" society. Tied to the elite's display of their own wealth, the transvestite of the working class displays his own version or translation of the perceived pleasure of wealth. He however does more than recoding wealth; he too recodes female sexuality.

The dominant strain so far in Filipino gayness is the homosexual's desire to be in the place of woman. With or without cross-dressing, the underlying premise of Philippine homosexuality is female sexuality–though in more recent years, this dominant paradigm is being challenged by an in-progress indigenized version of the western politicized gay subject, mostly introduced by gays in the academy and middle class. Transgender queerness is being replaced by latent gay politics. This paradigm, however, remains emplaced during the Marcos era even when "revolutionary" ideals were being pursued by the legal and underground mass movements that marked the absence, if not repression, of gay issues. The dominant paradigm hinges on the biological essentialism of female sexuality; the desire to be a "complete" woman, therefore, underscores gay angst and a social double standard. "Gay" becomes the source of both social fascination and outcasting. Male heterosexuals accept gay encounters and relations in periods of their lives. Gay-heterosexual relations are common, and are sexually and economically motivated. The working class gay supports the needs of the often more economically marginal partner, who in turn, willfully exchanges sexual favors. On another level, gay relations actually support the macho culture of having women and gays fall for its sexual prowess. Like Imelda's gay entourage, the gay figure becomes a display that validates machismo culture. A gay to gay (*kauri*; of the same mold) relationship is considered *lesbiana* (lesbian) and incestuous, and therefore a taboo in the gay subculture. Thus the gay's relationship with male heterosexuals is always temporal, premised on the male partner's eventual return to the family narrative of marriage and having children. Marriage, however, does not preclude gay relationships; sometimes, gay support for the partner's household continues in the barter of sexual favors for economic goods. The gay's constant slippage of relationships hinges on the essential non-attainment of female sexuality. Though beyond the reach of most working class gays, transsexualism remains a fantasy option for this gay politics. Female sexuality becomes the impossible standard in which gayness is made to approximate. Gay pleasure is temporally constructed, in the in-between spaces of angst and pleasure in the performance of being a "complete" woman.

These possibilities and limits of transvestism are foregrounded in *Ang Tatay Kong Nanay*. As a Filipino critic has stated, Philippine cinema views homosexuality as an excess and the homosexual is seen as a transgressor, a non-conformist who must be repressed. Hence, "narratives are structured around the idea of discovery and persecution."[4] Excess is put on display by Coring's cross-dressing in the public spheres of *baile* (dance), beauty contests, and fashion shows in the plaza. In these staged events, a translation of high fashion is indelibly represented by tall wigs, thick make-up, sequined long gowns, and feathery drapes. Coring's beauty parlor becomes a public sphere where transvestism is likewise performed in the everyday, where agency is attributed to the way he manages the shop. Excess is also performed through speech and gesture, pointing to the bodily registers of Marcos' presidential body. In the scene inside a taxi, Coring's transvestite group loudly engages in gay talk, particularly tackling love with a heterosexual and being a gay person. When a friend throws Dionisio's picture outside the cab, Coring assaults the fellow transvestite. The driver almost loses grip of the steering wheel, and throws the group out of his cab. Walking the streets alone at dawn, Coring is cajoled by the garbage collectors but nevertheless treks straight home.

"Gayness" is implicated through the performance of feminized bodily parts. Though *malantik* (curvilinear, as in the curves of eyelashes and fingers) and *malambot* (soft, refined), pedagogically characterized gay gestures and speech, these parts are parodied in everyday performance. Coring's friends are loud and vulgar in their private everyday selves; in the staged public spheres, however, these characteristics are retranslated to soft and refined. While Coring's translation of transvestism in the everyday represents a more refined and softer version than his friends, he remains patriarchal in the way the shop and household are managed. He shouts at and assaults his worker friends, and scolds his aunt and child for failing to conform to his ways.

Thus the possibilities are made limited even in the performance of staged and everyday transvestisms. Multinational fashion and masculinity are transposed as the markers of desire for social mobility and female sexuality. Coring dresses as Miss Spain in a beauty contest, and wears an iconic long gown in an intertextual reference to Hollywood and local films. His mirrors are plastered with pictures of Brando and Dionisio; the desire for multinational masculinity is integrated in the naming of Hamon's son. Coring's performances as a "real" beauty, shop manager, household head, and platonic lover on the one hand, and as fantasized beauty contestant, fashion model, and socialite on the other underscore female sexuality as a source of another layer of sexual pleasure and pain.

What then results from this unstable relationship between excess and lack is a "commerce of tears," a hysteria analogous to the female lead's suffering in family melodrama. Pleasure and pain are mostly experienced in heightened modes, with one always dialectically attuned to the other. But unlike the containment of the female lead in the domestic melodrama, the transvestite does not temporally self-destruct in the single performance of and containment from the subversive act. Transvestism is manufactured in the daily performance of a *working* class and sexuality. Coring's forced assumption of the parental role and his continuous devotion to Dionisio bear the cross of martyrdom, another idiom of affinity between the transvestite and woman in melodrama. Martyrdom is founded on religious and nationalist ideals of giving up the self for the larger social purpose. In nationalist discourse, martyrdom has historically privileged the role of elite figures, culminating in the national hero's transmutation of death by execution into a folk belief that only martyrs are *"binabaril sa Luneta"* ("shot in Luneta," site of Rizal's execution). Ironically Luneta, the most prominent city park, also serves as a site for gay encounters with men. As such, police surveillance hovers in the space of gay promiscuity and nationalist martyrdom. While continuously being reminded and forewarned of this belief, the transvestite nonetheless forgoes his own self-interest for what is deemed to be a larger ideal, whether this be love and support for a man, helping out (even beyond his own reach) friends and relatives, or assuming the responsibilities of others. The assumption of meta-personal matters adds to the anguish and torment of transvestite pleasure, believing that self-sacrifice can conquer all.

This self-sacrifice is also analogous to religious or nationalist discourse of nation-building. The homosexual-heterosexual relationship, after all, is one based on sexual and economic charity. This value system necessitates a geopolitical space where class and sexual boundary crossings always remain a fantastic possibility and a material impossibility. While liaisons with male heterosexuals are possible and more often than not tolerated by the family and community, gays also suffer from their own limited definition of possible relationships. While they are able to embody staged signifiers of high society and female sexuality, the materiality of returning to everyday working bodies similarly limits that which they seemingly wish to transgress. Working bodies are differentiable from performing bodies; while there is a performative quality to working bodies, work is a pedagogical requisite for transvestism. In other words, a transvestite will not have the economic advantage if he does not engage in work; its "cultural capital" is tied to sexual imperatives, performing the active sexual role as the tacit component of macho culture.

There is a dual libinidal movement going on in this peripheralization of the subcultural sphere of transvestites. On the one hand, in the realm of fantasy, the transvestite activates what he perceives are the privileged signifiers of social and sexual mobility. The material component to this dimension is that the transvestite works to earn money for the purchase of multinational fashion and support for a heterosexual partner. On the other hand, in the realm of "the real," the transvestite also activates another form of economic-sexual relationship among his fellow marginalized individuals. The fantasy component to this aspect is that the transvestite is positioned as economically empowered, bearing the possibility, nonetheless limited, of assisting another body from below. While the staged performance of transvestism integrates the body within the ideal, the everyday performance provides the undercurrent for the material exchange of peripheral bodies. The staged body performs the ideal, the everyday body operates within the material condition. While speaking of a double standard, a politics of "counter-materiality" should also attempt to qualify the emphasis on tolerance and acceptance for gays, especially within the already marginalized sphere. Deviance, in order to realize a political project, as Stuart Hall states, must contain some manifest political aim or goal, as well as perhaps a latent content of socially deviant attitudes and life-style. Their activities tend to fall outside the consensual norms which regulate political conflict, and they are willing to employ means, commonly defined as "illegitimate," to further or secure their ends. In life-style, attitude, and relationships they are socially unorthodox, permissive, even subversive."[5]

The gay in cinema of the Marcos era has not always realized the potential of a counter-materiality through solidarity of or alliance among the margins. What cinema has represented is a gay politics that shifts from a class emphasis to self-empowerment imperatives. *Tubog Sa Ginto* ("Dipped in Gold," 1971) deals with the double life of a closeted married man. Though he is blackmailed by a conniving (and allegedly straight) hustler, the rich man nevertheless chooses to indulge in this blackmail play in exchange for more sexual favors. Homosexually deprived, he shoots his lover caught raping his wife. She then witnesses her husband shooting himself after giving a tender kiss to the lips of the dead lover. While the film strongly identifies the problem of repression, it has also weakened the closeted position by representing the individual as lacking the "superego" integral to the homosexual drive. Blackmail in the moneyed economy has replaced the charity aspect of working class transvestite subculture. This is echoed in Brocka's social drama film *Manila Sa Kuko ng Liwanag* (1975), depicting the rich homosexual as a paying client in a casa, with a Pekinese dog to boot. The homosexuals of the working class are either on the streets acting out a beauty pageant or on the park, cruising for willing male partners. The rich homosexual's penchant for his pet dog foregrounds the recurring dog metaphor in the film–a dog continuously beaten eventually fights back. In this case, the body of his pampered dog is juxtaposed to the male lead's paid body, constructed similarly to connote the subordinated experience of patronage existence. Like the rich homosexual in *Tubog,* the homosexual in *Manila* performs the active sexual role, at the same time they pay for the services of their partners. The emphasis on gay capital and his sexual function privilege the active position to those who have forms of accumulated wealth. Similar to the male patronage of female sex workers, the paying body is given the privilege to activate the sexual play.

In *High School Circa 65* (Maryo de los Reyes, 1979), Roderick Paulate's character invoked a hilarious yet sympathetic portrayal of a teenaged gay in a nostalgic film of the parochial 1960s era. Dolphy's pre-*Ang Tatay Kong Nanay* films with a gay male lead character reconstitute the loud, comic-relief stereotype of gays. Paulate's post-*High School Circa 65* would lay claim to these subgenres of comedy films, becoming heir apparent to Dolphy's gay film throne. What was heightened in this stereotypical portrayal of gayness is its various placements in comedic function. Even in the small-town films, for example, the loud gay beautician is part of the micropolitical landscape that also comprises the powerful mayor and businessmen, prostitute or other woman, town's fool, and overly religious spinster, among others. This emplacement would be interrogated by *Ang Tatay Kong Nanay* and *Manila By Night* (Bernal, 1979), both involving the dramatic portrayal of gays as lead characters. Bernardo essayed a role of a couturier in *Manila*, whose business base is located in his own residence. Such proximity of business and home underscores the intimate relationship a gay individual ascribes to work and domestic spheres. While helping maintain the lover's household, with the live-in woman's approval, the gay character also engages in one-night encounters with men met in bars and discos. What these two films actualize is the "humanization" of the gay figure–a move out of the debilitating effects of stereotypical depictions of gays–providing a counter-materiality in the deviant lives and politics of gays and transvestites.

A similar materialization is posited by the gay lover in *Midnight Dancers* (Mel Chionglo, 1995), who provides support to the family of his married partner, even helping out the wife to process her papers to work in Japan. Complicity with the underground sexual economy is also accounted for in the gay figure. In Brocka's *Macho Dancer*, all the *mama san* (club managers) are middle-aged gays. These figures are differentiated by their maternal management from the overtly exploitative registers of the police and syndicate.

Nick Deocampo's two independent documentaries posit politics which diverge from commercial cinema. The films neither "humanize" nor dehumanize the gay subject; these are polemic pieces that foreground the politics of gay and gay film-making in the Philippines. On the one hand, *Oliver* (1983) and *Revolutions Happen Like Refrains in A Song* (1988) attempt to draw connections among homosexuality, poverty, and the dictatorship. On the other level, these films privilege the independent film and video movement, and more specifically gay independent film-making and the independent film-maker, as the stimuli to a "revolutionary cinema" in the Philippines. Drawing from the "Third" cinema texts, Deocampo writes, "As a reaction initially triggered by the dictatorial machinations of the Marcos government, a new generation of film-makers sought release from the established system of iconographic representations and thought perpetuated during the twenty-year regime and entrenched within a cinema, and a media, which had become subservient to the dominant ideology of the dictatorship."[6]

In the aftermath of the "February 1986 Revolution," Deocampo deciphers his own subjectivity as a Filipino gay film-maker in *Revolutions Happen Like Refrains in a Song*. He situates the context of his film in the broader discourse of gay independent film-making in the Philippines as doubly repressed–and therefore having the potential for double subversion. The film provides the culmination of a journey that begins with repression and ends with a coming to terms with individual subjectivity where sexuality provides a dominant role in its shaping. However, Deocampo implicates his awakening via the "1986 Revolution" to a people's awakening of their own identity, one that also has been repressed in the years of dictatorial oppression.

Deocampo's rhetoric eventually translates (homo)sexuality as a perversion of poverty so naturalized in Philippine society. This is furthered in constructing Oliver (the subject of his first documentary of a trilogy on sexuality, poverty and prostitution) as his alter-ego. Oliver is both subject and object of Deocampo's film and identity. As object, Oliver is positioned as the product of poverty, the literal subject of Deocampo's film. The film-maker thus poses, "Is Oliver free if every night he has to degrade himself for others?" Deocampo recycles in this film an earlier footage of Oliver inserting a stick of strings in his anus and Oliver's spider web performance in a gay bar. As subject, he is positioned as a representative of homosexuality, with whose masquerade and absent father/strong mother figures Deocampo's own personal enunciation identifies. Deocampo's own question implicates his own identity as a Third World gay film-maker: "How do people like Oliver live yet affirm life and creativity?" Oliver then becomes an object that defines Deocampo's own subjectivity.

A teleological model seems to be at work in the recent historical positioning of gays in film. In this model, the dominant paradigm of gay subculture is affirmed and disputed. The beginnings marked the stereotypical depictions of gays and transvestite along tragi-comic lines. A divergent stream within commercial cinema sought to prop up the gay figure as integrally different in society. In independent cinema, gay politics was inadvertently positioned as the quintessential subversive force in cinema in general. While mainstream cinema made absent the gay director, Deocampo's independent film-making catapulted the gay film-maker as primal trope in signifying individual subjectivity and national identity. What these nodes show are the maneuvers toward a gay film practice and aesthetic. What is being obstructed consequently is the already queer subject in film. This trajectory is being supported by the coming out of gays in the academy and middle class. Philippine cinema, I would contend, is already ambivalently marked in sexual and gender terms. Brocka's lead male character is constructed out of excessive masculinity, only to be contained in subsequent feminization. His films' lead female characters invariably are endowed with a level of agency, whether rightfully of wrongly, to change their fates. His gay figures provide both critiques of, and complicity with, the hegemonic culture.

With the exception of the transvestite figure in *Ang Tatay Kong Nanay*, what is being left out in the historical positioning is transvestism as an idiom of queer politics in film. This obfuscation is possible because of the difficulty of positioning transvestism in the larger cultural exchange. Transvestism's transgendering is marked by signifiers of social mobility and female sexuality; however, even these identificatory nodes are also ambivalently positioned. The working class transvestite's embodying of female sexuality transpires in a bifurcated manner. On the one hand, the excessive performance of multinational fashion and desire is tied to an identification with the figure of the "new woman": having wealth and disposition, access to travel and men, a high-profiled personality, and so on. On the other hand, the performance also jives with the figure of the marginalized sex worker: on the streets, promiscuous, gutsy, loud, en massely profiled in police raids and media coverages, etc. The transvestite's sexual role is effected through divergent gender registers: though in female guise, he actively assumes a role in the sex act at the same time that he also assumes a maternal position as confessor, friend and motivator to the heterosexual partner. The transvestite functions both maternally and sexually to his partner.

The transvestite's body is in the liminal space of the presidential and metropolitan bodies. Like other metropolitan bodies, he too shares in their economic emaciation. Like the presidential body, he spectacularizes his body, calling attention to the possibilities and limits of class and gender ideals. Unlike the presidential body, his is limited by the criteria he sets to transgress. His body displays a promise of social mobility, attracting voluntary attention among less economically deprived people. Though emaciated himself, he temporally assists an equally or less economically deprived individual, whether it be a gay like himself to be trained in the same job, a distant relative seeking accommodations in his place of residence, or a heterosexual lover's family in need of economic support. His body is also sexually deployed. Unlike the bodies of women in multinational work, his is traditionally affixed to beauty occupations, as hairstylist, manicurist and pedicurist, make-up artist, and so on in which, more often than not, he is pivotal to the enterprise. Unlike the metropolitan bodies, he remains visible even in the peripheralization of the margins. A fixture in the rural communities and slums, he is an agent of sexuality to young men, and of aesthetics to women.

"GAYA" IN IMPERIAL AND NATIONALIST DISCOURSE

The concept of *gaya* (imitate, mimic) foregrounds the transvestite's operation of mediating and transforming high and low. Gaya comes from the word *gagad*, meaning *uliran* (model). The concept points to a copy as gauged through the model; and as mentioned above, the model usually is western or American-based. It pokes fun at the lack of indigenous originality, or at a colonial mentality (*kaisipang makaalipin*, literally meaning "enslaved consciousness"). The pun "*gaya-gaya puto maya*" ("those who copy are as dense as a powdery rice sweet"), used to tease imitating children, provides a nationalist critique of the nature of reproducing colonial and imperial imperatives.

Homi Bhabha cites the concept of mimicry in colonial discourse as the moment of the breakdown of signifiers, where codes of colonizer and colonized implicate each other. This analysis of the mimic act implies and implicates the other, privileging liminality and promoting the breaking down of hierarchies. Bhabha's mimicry, however, fails to mention the counter-hierarchization, if not equivalence, of epistemes. This analysis homogenizes the signifying field, erasing the literal and epistemic violence in the enforcement and translation of colonial and imperial histories. While not discounting the angle that indeed everyone that enunciates is also enunciated in colonial discourse, the margin's claims are dehistoricized and deligitimized in that moment of breakdown. Furthermore, the margin's agency and actual historical strides are constructed as absent in the discourse.

Emmanuel Reyes' framing of Philippine cinema provides an analogue to this discourse. He cites that the aim of his project is "to examine Philippine cinema for what it is rather than what it has failed to be."[7] Subject to the (western) standards of good cinema, Philippine cinema is already premised on its failure to comply with these notions. The sweeping generalization neglects both the enforcement of imperial history in the national space, and deprives the national if not the local spheres of any agency. It also denies the historical gains of Brocka, Ishmael Bernal, Marilou Diaz Abaya, and Mike De Leon, among others, to interrogate, retextualize and internationalize national cinema. Reyes' remark also obscures the various internal dynamics of the national cinema, a nostalgia for a purely art cinema.

On the other hand, Deocampo's writings on gay independent cinema simplify the assignment of agency and history to this stream of national cinema. In his project of inserting a history of independent cinema and gay film-making, he equally obscures the relational positioning of the various forces that comprise national cinema. Agency and history are bestowed unilaterally on this cinema, privileged in its capacity to articulate a periodization of Philippine cinema based on revolutionary ruptures and their ensuing changes. This teleological periodization foregrounds his project of gay cinematic politics: cinema is introduced with the 1896 Revolution, and culminates in the "February 1986 Revolution," with the counter-maneuver of independent cinema articulating the true nation. Furthermore, gay film-making is privileged within this cinema. What is produced in this teleological framing is an overestimation of agency and history on the privileging of a margin in cinema, a reversal of Reyes' proposition.

Gaya provides an idiom to articulate and historicize the liminality of transvestism in national culture. It provides for modes of imperial critiques from a post-colonial perspective. The transvestite in *Tatay Kong Nanay* points to the characteristics of the subculture–performative, portable and transportable, transgressive attempts at identity formation. Gaya works through an attempt to compensate for the lack: that which is copied is that which is missing. The paradox however lies in the presence of a model on which the copies are based. Though copies approximate the model, these can never be the model itself. Copies do not have a metonymic function; even in its accumulation, it can never signify the model. These can only have a metaphoric function, naming the place of the other. Yet the dialectics of model and copy already preclude the possibility of the copies becoming the model.

Where then do we locate sites of subcultural resistance? Butler calls upon "the critical task [as] to locate strategies of subversive repetition enabled by . . . constructions, to affirm the local possibilities of intervention through participating in precisely those practices of repetition that constitute identity and, therefore, present the immanent possibility of contesting them."[8] What is left then in the dialectics is the metaphoric application of gaya as subsidiary. This means that the transvestite's differential use of class and gender markers are to be constituted through a sustained reiteration of counter-materialization. The subculture is represented as a subsidiary of national culture, a vital subcultural mediating liminality that has a capacity to transform the national. Within the various subcultures that comprise the national, the sustained support for the reiteration of counter-materialization is based on the acknowledgement of difference. What then is desired within the various cultures is the familiarity with the differences that exist within the national. The multiplicity of difference, not its enforced integration, becomes the political and cultural vernacular of articulating the nation. Such allowance for difference eventually paves the way for constructing alliance politics among the margins.

NOTES

1. Marjorie Garber, *Vested Interests: Cross-Dressing and Cultural Anxiety* (New York: Routledge, 1992).

2. Judith Butler, *Bodies that Matter: On the Discursive Limits of "Sex"* (New York: Routledge, 1993),137.

3. Frederick L. Whitam differentiates between Philippine and U.S. leadership's tackling of gays and national power. Both President and Mrs. Marcos appeared publicly at organizations of fashion designers and hairdressers to present awards for the

bayot's [gay] contributions to the Philippine economy. This sharply contrasts with the attitudes of President and Mrs. Kennedy, who reportedly chose Oleg Cassini as the first lady's dress designer because he was a "known" heterosexual, thus avoiding the possibility of scandal in the White House." "Bayot and Callboy: Homosexual-Heterosexual Relations in the Philippines," *Oceanic Homosexualities*, ed. Stephen O. Murray, (New York: Garland, 1992), 236).

4. Emmanuel Reyes, *Notes on Philippine Cinema* (Manila: De La Salle U P, 1989), 54.

5. Stuart Hall, "Deviance, Politics, and the Media," *The Lesbian and Gay Studies Reader*, ed. Henry Abelove et al. (New York: Routledge, 1993), 67.

6. Nick Deocampo, "Homosexuality as Dissent/Cinema as Subversion: Articulating Gay Consciousness in the Philippines," *Queer Looks Perspectives on Lesbian and Gay Film and Video*, ed. Martha Gever et al. (New York: Routledge, 1993), 398. Also see his "From Revolution to Revolution The Documentary Movement in the Philippines," *Documentary Box* #5 (Oct. 15, 1994), 15-18.

7. Reyes, 1.

8. Butler, *Gender Trouble: Feminism and the Subversion of Identity* (New York: Routledge, 1990), 147.

Index

Psychopathology and Psychotherapy in Homosexuality, edited by Michael W. Ross, PhD (Vol. 15, No. 1/2, 1988). *"One of the more objective, scientific collections of articles concerning the mental health of gays and lesbians. . . . Extraordinarily thoughtful. . . . New thoughts about treatments. Vital viewpoints." (The Book Reader)*

Psychotherapy with Homosexual Men and Women: Integrated Identity Approaches for Clinical Practice, edited by Eli Coleman, PhD (Vol. 14, No. 1/2, 1987). *"An invaluable tool. . . . This is an extremely useful book for the clinician seeking better ways to understand gay and lesbian patients." (Hospital and Community Psychiatry)*

Interdisciplinary Research on Homosexuality in The Netherlands, edited by A. X. van Naerssen, PhD (Vol. 13, No. 2/3, 1987). *"Valuable not just for its insightful analysis of the evolution of gay rights in The Netherlands, but also for the lessons that can be extracted by our own society from the Dutch tradition of tolerance for homosexuals." (The San Francisco Chronicle)*

Historical, Literary, and Erotic Aspects of Lesbianism, edited by Monica Kehoe, PhD (Vol. 12, No. 3/4, 1986). *"Fascinating . . . Even though this entire volume is serious scholarship penned by degreed writers, most of it is vital, accessible, and thoroughly readable even to the casual student of lesbian history." (Lambda Rising)*

Anthropology and Homosexual Behavior, edited by Evelyn Blackwood, PhD (cand.) (Vol. 11, No. 3/4, 1986). *"A fascinating account of homosexuality during various historical periods and in non-Western cultures." (SIECUS Report)*

Bisexualities: Theory and Research, edited by Fritz Klein, MD, and Timothy J. Wolf, PhD (Vol. 11, No. 1/2, 1985). *"The editors have brought together a formidable array of new data challenging old stereotypes about a very important human phenomenon . . . A milestone in furthering our knowledge about sexual orientation." (David P. McWhirter, Co-author, The Male Couple)*

Homophobia: An Overview, edited by John P. De Cecco, PhD (Vol. 10, No. 1/2, 1984). *"Breaks ground in helping to make the study of homophobia a science." (Contemporary Psychiatry)*

Bisexual and Homosexual Identities: Critical Clinical Issues, edited by John P. De Cecco, PhD (Vol. 9, No. 4, 1985). *Leading experts provide valuable insights into sexual identity within a clinical context–broadly defined to include depth psychology, diagnostic classification, therapy, and psychomedical research on the hormonal basis of homosexuality.*

Bisexual and Homosexual Identities: Critical Theoretical Issues, edited by John P. De Cecco, PhD, and Michael G. Shively, MA (Vol. 9, No. 2/3, 1984). *"A valuable book . . . The careful scholarship, analytic rigor, and lucid exposition of virtually all of these essays make them thought-provoking and worth more than one reading." (Sex Roles, A Journal of Research)*

Homosexuality and Social Sex Roles, edited by Michael W. Ross, PhD (Vol. 9, No. 1, 1983). *"For a comprehensive review of the literature in this domain, exposure to some interesting methodological models, and a glance at 'older' theories undergoing contemporary scrutiny, I recommend this book." (Journal of Sex Education & Therapy)*

Literary Visions of Homosexuality, edited by Stuart Kellogg, PhD (Vol. 8, No. 3/4, 1985). *"An important book. Gay sensibility has never been given such a boost." (The Advocate)*

Alcoholism and Homosexuality, edited by Thomas O. Ziebold, PhD, and John E. Mongeon (Vol. 7, No. 4, 1985). *"A landmark in the fields of both alcoholism and homosexuality . . . a very lush work of high caliber." (The Journal of Sex Research)*

Homosexuality and Psychotherapy: A Practitioner's Handbook of Affirmative Models, edited by John C. Gonsiorek, PhD (Vol. 7, No. 2/3, 1985). *"A book that seeks to create affirmative psychotherapeutic models. . . . To say this book is needed by all doing therapy with gay or lesbian clients is an understatement. " (The Advocate)*

Nature and Causes of Hoosexuality: A Philosophic and Scientific Inquiry, edited by Noretta Koertge, PhD (Vol. 6, No. 4, 1982). *"An interesting, thought-provoking book, well worth reading as a corrective to much of the research literature on homosexuality." (Australian Journal of Sex, Marriage & Family)*

Historical Perspectives on Homosexuality, edited by Salvatore J. Licata, PhD, and Robert P. Petersen, PhD (cand.) (Vol. 6, No. 1/2, 1986). *"Scholarly and excellent. Its authority is impeccable, and its treatment of this neglected area exemplary." (Choice)*

Homosexuality and the Law, edited by Donald C. Knutson, PhD (Vol. 5, No. 1/2, 1979). *A comprehensive analysis of current legal issues and court decisions relevant to male and female homosexuality.*

ABOUT THE COVER PHOTOS

When shooting a model, international fashion photographer Shimomura Kazuyoshi imagines himself as a movie director seizing "a moment in drama." Normally the creator of glossy, luscious images, he finds his inspiration in the films of Suzuki Seijun and Japan's classic Nikkatsu cinema as well as in the homoerotic work of Mishima Yukio. Shimomura's uncharacteristically stoic cover photos here were conceived and commissioned in 1998 by Kawaguchi Takao and Kawakubo Aki of the Tokyo International Lesbian & Gay Film & Video Festival, and feature Tanaka Mayumi, a dancer with the Kyoto-based mixed-media performance troupe dumb type. Tanaka is also known for her drag performance in the Japanese club scene. Thanks to Jonathan M. Hall for arranging the appearance of Shimomura's photos in this volume.